A WORLD HISTORY OF YIDDISH THEATER

VAGABOND STARS

A WORLD HISTORY OF YIDDISH THEATER

VAGABOND STARS

NAHMA SANDROW

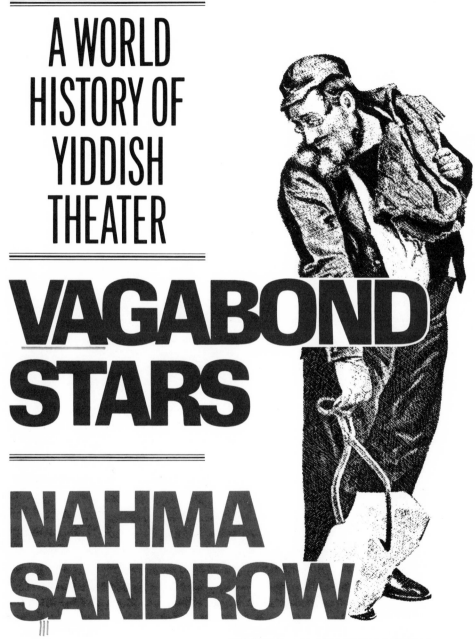

HARPER & ROW, PUBLISHERS
New York, Hagerstown, San Francisco, London

This book is dedicated to my father,
Rabbi Edward T. Sandrow,
and to the Yiddish actors and audiences,
murdered in Europe and Russia,
whose memory he honored.

Permission for illustrations is gratefully acknowledged:

American Jewish Historical Society. Pages 100 (left), 110, 117, 121, 130, 137, 153, 171, 188, 265, 269, 273, 277, 293, 398, 404, 406.

Collection of Joseph Haberman, Los Angeles. Page 100 (right).

Museum of the City of New York. Pages 35, 50, 76, 83, 95, 103, 144, 148, 173, 176, 182, 194, 218, 252, 255, 274, 275, 281, 287, 290, 292, 295, 297, 332, 363, 389, 397.

Photographic Archive, Jewish Theological Seminary of America. Page 7.

YIVO Institute for Jewish Research. Pages 9, 17, 42, 58, 61, 81, 86, 177, 184, 196, 211, 213, 215, 220, 228, 233, 237, 245, 307, 310, 319, 325, 327, 334, 353, 355, 357, 367, 368.

FIRST EDITION

Designed by Luba Litwak

Library of Congress Cataloging in Publication Data

Sandrow, Nahma.
  Vagabond stars.
  Bibliography: p.
  Includes index.
  1. Theater—Jews—History. 2. Gordin, Jacob,
1853–1909. I. Title.
PN3035.S25   792'.09   75–25065
ISBN 0–06–013756–8

77 78 79 80 81 10 9 8 7 6 5 4 3 2 1

CONTENTS

ACKNOWLEDGMENTS

MANY PEOPLE HELPED ME to write this book.

Numerous theater people in the United States and Israel were most generous with their time and recollections. This list of names includes actors, directors, and producers: Celia Adler, Morris Adler, Eva Adler, Jacob Ben-Ami, Mina Bern, Ben Bonus, Joseph Buloff, Pesach Burstein, Charlotte Goldstein Chalfin, the late Charles Cohen and his wife Rose Pivar (secretary of the Hebrew Actors Union), Moyshe Dluzhnovsky, Shimen Dzigan, David Ellin, Zilia Elman, Natan Gilboa, Josef Glikson, Sam Goldberg, Eliezer Greenburg, Michel Greenstein, the Iditron Company and their adviser Avraham Yudovitch, Jacob Jacobs, Jacob Kalich, Ida Kaminska, Yosef Levinson, David Licht, Lillian Lux, Bella Maisell, Meir (Marion) Melman, Molly Picon, Jack Rechtzeit, Hanna Ribber, David Rogow, Hershel Rosen, Josef Shakrub, Leon Schachter, Zvee Scooler, Dan Shemer, Mary Soriano, Ruth Vool, Herman Yablokoff (president of the Hebrew Actors Union), Sheftel Zak. Joseph Green allowed me to hear, and quote from, Wolf Younin's taped interview with him.

From the Yiddish State Theater of Rumania: Franz Auerbach, director; Israel Bercovici, dramaturge; Seidy Glück-Rippel, and Mano Rippel.

From South Africa, Mr. Max Angorn was kind enough to write me a long letter; D. Diamond, executive director of the South African Jewish Board of Deputies, also wrote to me. From Australia, P. Ringelblum sent me a great deal of information; Lily Solvey, organizing secretary of the United Jewish Education Board, and Eve Symon, editor of the *Australian Jewish Times*, were helpful too.

I am grateful to the librarians and archivists who assisted me in finding sources, facts, and illustrations. At the YIVO Institute for Jewish Research:

Dina Abramsowicz, chief librarian; Bella Weinberg, assistant librarian; Marek Web, archivist; Janet Blatter, assistant archivist and curator; and Zosa Szajkowsky. At the Theatre and Music Collections of the Museum of the City of New York: Theodore H. Fetter, curator; Dr. Mary C. Henderson, assistant curator; Grenville Cuyler, former assistant curator; Dorothea Hecht; and especially Esther Enzer, consultant, Yiddish Division. At the American Jewish Historical Society: Dr. Mordechai Waxman and Dr. Nathan M. Kaganoff. The staff of the Research Library of the Library and Museum of the Performing Arts at Lincoln Center, division of the New York Public Library. In Jerusalem, Israel Goor, curator of the Museum and Library of the Performing Arts, was most gracious.

For information, good advice, and a wide variety of good turns, I want to thank Mikhl Vaynapl Ben-Avram and Nahkman Rapp of Shidurey Yisroel (Israeli radio); my uncle Dr. Abraham Duker, of Brooklyn College; Shifra Epstein; Gershon Friedlin; Yankl Gutkowicz; Kenneth Harvey; Milton E. Krents and Will Sandy of the William E. Wiener Oral History Library of the American Jewish Committee; Jill Lesko; Professor Tom Lewy of Tel Aviv University; Miriam Sandrow; Professor Mordke Schaechter of Columbia University; Professor Khone Shmeruk of the Hebrew University; Dr. Mark Slobin of Wesleyan University; Dr. Bernard Witlieb of Bronx Community College; Richard Zuckerman; and most especially, for his comments, Joseph Mlotek, educational director of the Workmen's Circle.

The poets Wolf Younin and Sylvia Younin gave me serious, extremely painstaking criticism and encouragement. Dr. Barbara Kirshenblatt-Gimblett of the University of Pennsylvania and YIVO and Dr. David G. Roskies of the Jewish Theological Seminary of America have always been wonderfully generous with me, as my teachers, colleagues, and friends. Stanley Kauffmann helped me, as always, with his valuable criticism and advice.

I thank my agent, Gloria Miller, and my editor, Nach Waxman. I thank Susan Schnur, my editor and my pal.

I am grateful to the National Endowment for the Humanities and to the Research Foundation of the State University of New York, whose grants helped me to write this book.

I appreciate above all my dear husband, William M. Meyers, for all his help and all his encouragement, and for this poem:

> These bones must play: scattered like the remnants
> of fallen stars, they cast themselves at night
> into companies and rehearse again
> in Yiddish, a language the bones know best.

These bones must play because life's dramatic
and they get closest to life by playing;
beyond the footlights, unruly bone piles
will live again by seeing themselves portrayed.

The curtain goes up and Shulamis waits;
Shmendrik can still get a laugh by falling;
what plot can outrage sensibilities
for whom life is a comic reversal?

They play Haman with a toothbrush mustache;
the bony audience clatters applause,
then carries the actors to their star train,
carries them on their shoulders triumphantly.

January 23, 1975

NOTE ON TRANSLITERATION

IN THE COURSE OF WRITING this book I discovered that it is impossible to transliterate Yiddish words, especially proper names, in a fully satisfactory manner.

The difficulties of transliteration reflect the cultural and linguistic complications that are the background of my subject. For example, regional accents in Yiddish differ widely; a word in Yiddish characters may look the same but be pronounced very differently by two readers. Also, actors sometimes changed the pronunciation or even the spelling of their names, giving themselves Rumanian or Polish or Spanish accents as they toured. Officials at Ellis Island gave some immigrants new names which barely approximated the originals.

Furthermore, systems of spelling Yiddish have varied drastically over the years. In the nineteenth century, for example, Germanic spelling and pronunciation seemed classier than plain Yiddish, and many writers adapted accordingly. This chaos, especially in the nineteenth and twentieth centuries, when there were widespread attempts to stabilize Yiddish as a written language, led to such cases as this: posters that advertise an actor variously as Sigmund Feinman, Sygmund Faynmann, and Zigmunt Faynman. (Analogous inconsistencies occurred in English during the Renaissance, when the English language was undergoing somewhat comparable processes; witness the various spellings of Shakespeare's name.)

Readers of English are accustomed to combinations like *ei* and *ch* to render Yiddish phonetics. However, those are Germanic rather than direct transferrals from Yiddish to English, and they are often used inconsistently, even haphazardly. Clearly, a serious study of any aspect of Yiddish culture demands a consistent system, and a system created specifically to make words in Yiddish accessible to English-speaking readers. The fact that most books in English appear without such a system reflects a widespread disrespect for Yiddish culture, even on the part of Yiddish speakers—an assumption that a study of the Yiddish language does not require the same refined machinery as studies of other foreign languages. It is exactly this attitude that Yiddishists and reformers of Yiddish theater pitted themselves against. I felt that if I had allowed this book to slide along in the same sloppy fashion, I would have been betraying my subject.

The YIVO Institute for Jewish Research has devised a clear, simple system for transliterating Yiddish phonetically into Roman characters:

ey	=	as in the English h*ey*
ay	=	as in the English sk*y*
i	=	as in the English sk*i*
e	=	as in the English h*e*n
tsh	=	as in the English ma*tch*
kh	=	guttural *h*, more often rendered in English as *ch*, as in "Sholom Alei*ch*em" or "Le*ch*aim"

The system renders all other sounds just as in English. There are *no* silent letters in this system, so that the name Tsine, for example, has two syllables and the name Mirele three.

I followed the YIVO system for all quotations, terms, and titles. When it came to proper names, however, I had more decisions to make.

It is common, for example, to give the first name Jacob (English) or Yaakov (Hebrew) instead of the Yiddish Yankev; the name Abraham (English) or Avraham (Hebrew) instead of the Yiddish Avrom; and so on. Thus I gave the author Peretz the first name Isaac instead of the Yiddish Yitskhok. But I changed my mind when Dr. David Miller of Queens College confronted me with professorial firmness: "Would you call Johann Sebastian Bach 'John' Bach? Or Antonio Vivaldi 'Anthony'? Would you call Henrik Ibsen 'Henry'? Obviously not. Then why take such liberties with Yiddish names?"

He is right. For that reason I have tried to stick to the Yiddish forms of first names, transliterated by the YIVO system, even though I am aware that the persons themselves may occasionally have signed the English or Hebrew or some other forms, according to their mood or where they happened to be at the time.

I tried at first to be scrupulously consistent with family names too, accord-

ing to the YIVO system. One of my sources of encouragement was Dan
Miron's excellent *A Traveler Disguised*—a book, written in English, that
proceeds from the assumption that literary criticism dealing with Yiddish
literature can be as sophisticated as criticism of any other literature, and whose
commitment to consistent transliteration follows from that position.

However, I eventually concluded that such stringent consistency is not
really satisfactory either. The writer Peretz, for example, is so familiar as Peretz
that the YIVO spelling Perets, which Miron adopts, seems ultimately to
obstruct rather than to help the reader. Therefore I have written the name
as Peretz (with the full name Yitskhok Leyb, or Leybush, Peretz rather than
the rather more common Isaac Leib Peretz). For the same reason, I have
retained the familiar Sholom Aleichem instead of the consistent Sholem
Aleykhem, H. Leivick instead of the consistent H. Leyvik, and so on. Unfortunately, names are sometimes familiar in more than one spelling; Avrom Goldfadn, for example, often appears as Avraham Goldfaden. In such cases, I tried
to choose the most familiar form. In any case, the way a person chooses to
sign his own name when writing in Roman characters must surely be the
definitive version.

A related stipulation is that a person who is Polish or Rumanian already
has a spelling of his name in Roman letters. To transliterate his name by the
YIVO system directly from the Yiddish is a distortion. Thus the Polish
Zygmund Turkow must remain Zygmund Turkow, even though his name
transliterated from Yiddish would be Zigmund Turkov.

I have found it harder to be consistent than Miron, perhaps, because
whereas most of his subjects are no longer living, many of mine still are, and
naturally they would be offended to find their names in print in a form other
than the one they themselves are accustomed to use.

In other words, I have, as stated before, used the YIVO system for all
quotations, terms, and titles. After much consideration, I have used it, too,
for first names except when I was positive that the person had deliberately
identified himself with another spelling. For family names, I have used whatever spelling is most familiar in each individual case, or whatever spelling the
person seems to have preferred, turning to the YIVO system when the name
has not been widely seen in Roman characters in any version.

To follow up any reference, in Yiddish or English, in a card catalogue,
encyclopedia, or index, my reader will have to be ready to try a variety of
spellings. In the process, he will experience firsthand a controversial, emotional, and symbolic area of Yiddish scholarship.

The Pale of Settlement at the End of the 19th Century.

1 PURIM PLAYS

LEADING OFF THE FESTIVE PARADE come the clowns. All sorts of clowns. First the *marshelik,* grand marshal of the revels, riding a horse through the Prague ghetto, wearing the elaborate baroque gentleman's costume of his day—the 1740s—and showing the way with his staff. Following him is a *nar,* or fool, a red veil like a woman's over his head, a spangly blue mantle covering him and his horse together. The mantle is hung with pastries. As he rides, he nibbles away at his costume and imitates bugle noises without a horn.

Next comes the clown-hero of the day, and of the parade, and of the play that is to follow. He rides enthroned on a wine cask pulled along by a crowd of schoolboys, students at the local *yeshive* (Talmudical academy). He is the crazy Purim King, a Bacchus, fat as a frog, waving an enormous wineglass and smiling, smiling.

Then come more clowns, each one master of his own absurdity. One hung with kitchen utensils, wearing an upside-down pot for a hat and jigging up and down. Another dressed as a servant girl, who leads an old *nar* behind "her" by a string. A clown who keeps rushing out among the crowd of spectators to kiss the old ladies. A harlequin in the green costume associated with the figure called Pickleherring. A clown doing tricks on the back of a wooden horse. The Half-Fool, who is dressed like a harlequin on one side and a sensible man on the other. (He may be the one to speak the prologue when the play starts.)

And then, after the clowns, Biblical figures. Moses carrying the Ten Commandments. Aaron in his priestly robes. Then wagons and floats with trade guilds in state: the shoemakers marching with an enormous metal boot to the music of their own band. The schoolteacher with silver books. A doctor

1

preceded by his son carrying his medical license on an embroidered cushion.

Musicians! Musicians in all sorts of costumes. One group dressed like Turks with turbans and beards. Yisroel the dwarf playing his fiddle on top of the flagpole, sixteen ells up, though there's too much noise to catch even a single note down below.

Crowds of masqueraders dancing through the ghetto streets. And all the procession winding toward—the Purim play.

The first expression of Yiddish theater—indeed, the only one until the nineteenth century—was the *Purimshpil*, or Purim play, which celebrated the holiday of Purim in early spring.

The Purim holiday commemorates a post-Biblical episode of Jewish history, and Purim plays reenact that episode, as recorded in the Old Testament Book of Esther, known as the *megile*. Haman, prime minister to Ahashuerus, King of Persia, plots to kill off all the Jews in the kingdom. The heroes of the story are the Jewish sage Mordecai and his young cousin Esther. Providentially the beautiful Esther wins the king's heart and becomes Queen of Persia, replacing Queen Vashti, who has fallen from favor and is hanged. Mordecai and Queen Esther foil Haman's plot, and the king has Haman hanged on the very gallows that had been prepared by Haman for Mordecai.

On Purim (as on only one other Jewish holiday, Simkhas Tora) Jews are supposed to be frivolous. On Purim a Jew is actually supposed to get so drunk that his head spins and he curses the virtuous Mordecai instead of the murderer Haman.

Inside the synagogue to this very day, on the holiday of Purim, the reader chants the *megile* to a congregation of enthusiastic adults and children who stamp and whistle at every mention of the wicked Haman. They whir *gragers* (noisemakers), drowning out Haman's name with grinding, popping sounds, and interrupt the reader repeatedly while he performs such verbal tricks as reciting the names of Haman's ten sons all in one breath.

As early as the fifth century, in the region near Antioch, it was the custom for Jews to gather in the synagogue courtyard in a happy, untidy procession. Sometimes they went outside the city gates, carrying a dummy representing Haman, whom they hanged in effigy and burned in a bonfire. Around the fire they sang, told jokes, and traded insults.

In 408 Emperor Theodosius II ordered the Haman bonfires stopped and accused the Jews of using the Haman story to camouflage a reenactment of the crucifixion. But apparently the Jews could not bring themselves to give up their holiday, for in 415 word spread in the area that they were using Christian children instead of effigies. A pogrom followed, which wiped out a large

Copper engravings of early Purim celebrations. *(Top)* Purim procession, Prague, 1741. *(Bottom)* Masked Purim players, Central Europe, 1657.

proportion of the local Jewish population, and their bonfires along with them.

In medieval Europe, *yeshive* students danced in the streets for the glory of the Purim King. Sometimes they wore headdresses with goatlike horns. (Already in ancient Greece a connection had been established between the season, theater, and a goatlike divinity.) The Purim King and the goat horns were in no way part of Jewish ceremonial law, but custom had attached them to the Purim season, just as it had to the Christian Shrovetide or Mardi gras season. Exchanging *shalekh-mones,* gifts of sweet cakes and wine, became traditional on Purim, as did games, riddles, and noisy pranks. A "Purim Rabbi" and his disciples parodied prayers and commentary the way the medieval Christian King of Fools parodied the Mass. (Even the eighteenth-century *hasidic* rabbi of Volozhin, known throughout Poland for his gravity, sat at table among his students with his coat turned back to front.)

When Purim plays appeared, evidently by the sixteenth century, they shared many qualities with the Christian mystery plays of the late Middle Ages. Since European cultural currents flowed eastward, however, and most Jews lived in the area that now comprises Germany, Czechoslovakia, and Poland (and were themselves gradually migrating eastward), Purim plays reached their high point in the seventeenth and eighteenth centuries, a hundred years and more after their counterparts had gone out of fashion in England and France. Purim plays bore a special resemblance to the German Nuremberg Shrovetide plays, or *Fastnachtspiele;* this connection was reinforced by the circumstance that the Yiddish language originated in the Rhineland and is closely linked to German, so that Yiddish culture can be said to have developed within the German cultural orbit.

(There were almost no Russian Jews at all until 1772, when the partitions of Poland began. Even then almost all Russian Jews were forced to live in Russia's southwestern section, closest to Poland. That ghetto area, called the Pale of Settlement, became increasingly overcrowded but remained rigidly within its bounds until it was abolished during the Russian Revolution of 1917.)

The oldest published *Purimshpil* text, printed in Frankfurt am Main, dates from 1708, and its title page promises:

> A beautiful new Ahashuerus play, composed with all possible art. Never in all its lifetime will another be made so well, with such pretty and beautiful lamentations in rhyme. We know that whoever will buy it will not regret his purchase, because God He commanded us to be merry on Purim. Therefore have we made this Ahashuerus play enjoyable and beautiful. Therefore you householders and boys had better come quickly and buy this play from me. You will not regret the cost.

On Purim day, or in the days just preceding and following, after parading
and wandering in bands through the streets, *Purimshpilers* burst in at neighbors' houses—sometimes by invitation and sometimes by surprise—and performed their play. (Christian mummers and carolers did the same, and so did
German *Fastnachtspielers*.) A group might be three or four *shpilers* or, in big
cities, as many as thirty, including musicians.

Usually they played at the homes of the richer members of the community.
Though all ghetto houses were crowded and overcrowded, the dining rooms
of the comparatively wealthy were likely to be bigger than other people's, so
there was more room for the show. Into that dining room crowded the host;
his wife, beaming in her special beaded silk-ribbon headdress; their dinner
guests; their servants at the kitchen door; their neighbors; and, peeping in
through the windows and hanging off the window sills, everyone else who
could not squeeze in, and lots of children. Many of the children were stuffing
themselves with raisins and *homontashn* (triangular poppy-seed cakes named,
by popular etymology, for Haman's hat). The musicians found themselves a
corner too, big enough to set up a bass fiddle and with elbow room to bow
it.

When the actors finished and bowed, their goodbye verses always hinted
in a pretty straightforward way for the *groschen* (pennies), the brandy, and
the honey cakes their host had to offer them.

> Honored host,
> What's in the house?
> Hey, get a move on.
> Bring out the brandy.
> Open your cupboard.
> Don't forget honey cake.
> Hey, time for treats!

> Honored hostess,
> What have you got?
> What's in your cupboard?
> Let's have some cheese.
> Don't you be stingy.
> Bring out your butter.
> Hey, time for treats!

Or, more simply:

> Today is Purim,
> Tomorrow—no more.
> Give us a *groschen*
> And show us the door.

Christmas mummers always ended with this sort of *quête;* their descendants, Christmas carolers, still do.

Purim plays, like Christian mystery plays, were usually based on Bible stories. It was usually the Esther story from the *megile,* but sometimes they used other tales: the Old Testament story about Joseph's brothers selling him into slavery and years later meeting him again at the court of Egypt; Jonah and the whale; David and Goliath; the sacrifice of Isaac; the wise decisions of King Solomon; Sodom and Gomorrah; Moses confronting Pharaoh; Hannah, who wanted a baby and finally gave birth to Samuel. There were also non-Biblical legends of the devil Ashmoday and the prophet Elijah.

Purim plays also drew occasionally from secular stories. *Deaf Yeklayn,* for example, is a knockabout medieval farce about a deaf, stupid, henpecked man and his misadventures with a cow. As early as 1588 there was one called *The Scholar and the Devil,* which seems to have been the Faust story. Scenes of "the gypsy wedding" or "the gypsy and the bear," with a man prancing in a fur coat worn backward, were popular, and remained so through the nineteenth century. Secular plays sometimes took the place of Biblical ones entirely, but more often they were only interludes. This interweaving of secular entertainment with the sacred was also typical of the mainstream of European folk theater.

The plays' episodes go along with quaint forthrightness. Characters announce who they are and what they want. Goliath says:

> I am Goliath, the mighty and strong.
> The whole world shakes when I come along.
> I am the one.
> Beyond me are none.
> I will break all your limbs, every bone . . .

. . . and then he fights. Abraham dutifully takes Isaac to the mountaintop, but right on cue God provides a ram for the sacrifice. There is no psychology and no philosophy.

The words, too, sound quaint to modern ears, like the English *Second Shepherds Play.* Most often they are rough rhymes, in a jingly, brisk, and swinging meter with patterns and repetitions like folk songs. Here, for example, are two scenes from a version of the story of Joseph. First, an angel appears to Joseph to warn him of his brothers' plot.

ANGEL   Joseph! Joseph! What are you doing here?

JOSEPH   Friend! Friend! My brothers I seek.
Friend! Friend! This heat has made me weak.
I will not find my brothers soon, I fear.

Purim players entertain a well-to-do German Jewish family in *Purim at Home*, a painting by Moritz Oppenheim, Frankfurt-am-Main, nineteenth century.

ANGEL　Joseph! Joseph! Your brothers have gone elsewhere.
　　　　Of brotherhood they will make you despair.

JOSEPH　Friend! Friend! Though they pierce my heart,
　　　　For my father I will do my part.

In the next act, when Joseph is a slave in Egypt, he is approached by his master's wife.

ZELIKHE　Ah, Joseph, my child!
　　　　I'm feeling very sick.
　　　　I'm sick not from my sickness
　　　　But only from your beauty!
　　　　I'm a dear little woman in her prime,
　　　　I have a man who's old.
　　　　My dear little skin is like snow, so white—
　　　　If you were only bold!
　　　　He lies in bed all night and sweats.
　　　　He says he's cold. He frets.
　　　　No heat can his weak body hold
　　　　Because he is already old.

　　　　Ah, Joseph, my child!
　　　　Give me your dear little hand.
　　　　I am so sick
　　　　Because of your beauty.

*(*JOSEPH *rejects her.)*

> Husband Potiphar,
> Come in here!
> God will make you weep!

*(*POTIPHAR *enters.)*

> The Jewish slave,
> He wants with me to sleep!

(They take JOSEPH *away.)*

This is the sort of doggerel amateur actors might learn by heart and pass along by oral tradition, year after year, generation after generation. In fact, in the last few years several elderly people have recited *Purimshpiln* into tape recorders. They came from villages in different parts of Eastern Europe, and they had not heard the plays for half a century, but what they remembered was very similar, and in places the dialogue they chanted was word for word the same.

Some of the more than fifty fragments and variants of plays that have been preserved in writing rise to a more sophisticated sort of poetry. Here, for example, is a verse from a *megile* play. It is a farewell by Queen Vashti (Queen Esther herself rarely appears in these plays). The farewell song was a convention for both Vashti and Haman, and was often quite touching, even for the villain.

> Fields and woods and you high hills,
> Dark, dark woods and deep, deep dew,
> Wild woods, beasts, and river waves,
> Flying birds and deep-finned fish,
> Help me weep my woes aloud.
> Echo on my moans, my pains.
> Help me, fields, and help me, stones.
> Help me, every feeling soul.
> Help me, help me, help me, every feeling soul.

Purim plays usually began with a formal prologue (as did mummers' plays). Typically the Prologue figure, often called a Herald or a Runner, burst in from the street, bowed elaborately to the merrymakers inside the house, and started off something like this:

> My noble sirs, a play you'll see
> If you'll look and listen patiently.
> If you'll look and listen patiently,
> We'll show you what happened in a Persian cit-tee.

Meanwhile the actors' parade had reached the house, and the Prologue, who was usually the director and chorus leader too, called them in one by one from the street as they were needed. There was a formula for this too:

Herayn, herayn, herayn,
Reb Mordecai du mayn.

(Come in, come in, come in,
Mordecai [or whoever] of mine.)

Whereupon the actor bounded into the house, bowed directly to the audience, and introduced himself. As his role ended, he said a formal goodbye, sometimes a lengthy one, like Vashti's, more often as terse as this speech of Haman's:

Now this world I must be leaving.
Gentlemen and sirs, to you all a good evening.

Then the actor sat down comfortably in the audience to watch till it was time to join in the grand finale of song and dance and refreshments.

In time, songs and dramatic interludes, both sacred and secular, were interpolated between scenes. By the mid-eighteenth century an elaborate show might have included a Bible story in several short acts, interspersed with

(Top) The *marshelik* entertains a festive wedding banquet with an intricate speech based on religious and Talmudic material. *(Bottom)* The *badkhen*, or wedding bard, accompanied by the musicians, addresses his rhymed sermon to the bride; These picture postcards were printed in New York in the early twentieth century.

as many as ten separate songs, plus extra comic interludes and acrobatic flipflops—maybe fifteen or twenty episodes in all.

Every Purim play included silly slapstick fights. Somebody gets knocked down. Sometimes he dies. And sometimes he then bounces back to life, as happens occasionally to Haman. (This echoes the magic pattern of resurrection which pagans playacted to help the spring drive away the winter. Mummers showed St. George slaying a Turk, whereupon a comical doctor came in and brought him to life. Passion plays showed Jesus Christ's crucifixion and resurrection.)

And every Purim play included clowns and fool figures, grafted from the clowns that had been familiar to Jews and non-Jews alike since ancient times. In fact, the earliest, and for a long time the only, professional Yiddish theatrical performers were the Yiddish clowns.

Throughout the Middle Ages, troupes of clowns, mimes, and acrobats roamed Europe telling jokes, acting skits, singing, and walking tight ropes in village marketplaces. They were even hired by the pious to liven up mystery plays. There were also court jesters. Among the marketplace clowns and the courtly clowns there were always some Jews.

Within the Jewish world, professional clowns were hired for the more elaborate Purim plays. They appeared, too, at ghetto social events; at fashionable wedding parties as many as fifteen or twenty clowns of various styles might be employed. In fact, in the mid-fourteenth century a magistrate of Cracow found it necessary to limit the number by law to eight. (As late as the nineteenth century, *hasidic* rabbis who lived surrounded by disciples employed their own court jesters.)

There were as many different sorts of Yiddish clowns as there are styles of Jewish comedians today: Lenny Bruce, the Marx Brothers, Woody Allen, Danny Kaye, Mort Sahl, Myron Cohen, George Burns, Zero Mostel, Jerry Lewis, and so on. The distinctions depended somewhat on specialty and somewhat on historical circumstances of time and place. But the *lets, nar, marshelik, badkhen,* and *payats* are all brothers.

The *lets* (an ancient word which appears in the Talmud) and the *nar* (German for "fool") are the simple silly gross clowns, descendants of the Roman comics in pointy caps who hit each other over the head with bladders and took pratfalls. In the middle of a Purim play they might spew out strings of nonsense interspersed with rhymes: "I went to the Leipzig fair prayer hair mare, and there I was cold as a bear and I ate dairy meat and meat-milk-butter soup." (The food is blatant nonsense in light of Jewish prohibitions against eating dairy and meat foods together.)

The *marshelik* is the master of ceremonies. He appears as an entertainer at festivities, but he does not always make fun. He is graver in style than the others and delights in intricate Talmudic wordplay and disputation. He carries a marshal's baton and dresses with dignity.

The *badkhen* is not only quick-witted at making jokes, but also nimble at turning a phrase and spotting a Talmudic allusion. His specialty is weddings, where he chants a long rhymed sermon to the bride and the women guests, the first line of which is traditionally "Weep, bride, weep." He then describes the responsibilities of married life; if the women cry, he's a success. Afterward he amuses the party with a stream of comments about the event, also in rhyme and mostly improvised on the spot. One Russian *badkhen* in the late nineteenth century was known for an extra little gimmick of his own: he played the fiddle behind his back—with gloves on!

The *payats*, who derived his name from the Austrian and Polish *pajac*, is often the Prologue to the Purim play and tells the actors when to enter and when to exit. If the audience's attention seems to be waning, he may stand on his head, or he may spin out puns based on Hebrew and Yiddish words that sound alike but mean different things. Another of his tricks is to alternate lines of a prayer in Hebrew with lines in Yiddish. The Hebrew and Yiddish words at the ends of the lines rhyme, but the Yiddish words either mock the preceding Hebrew line or else have nothing at all to do with it. This is the effect:

> "Blessed art thou . . ."[Hebrew]
> I'd like a pretty woman now . . .[Yiddish]
> "Who has kept his people holy."[Hebrew]
> For a bit of roly-poly.[Yiddish]

Besides clowns, and closely related to them, were the stock characters who infiltrated Purim plays. These were descended from the ancient Roman "masks" and the Italian commedia dell'arte figures: The old man trying to maintain authority over a young son or young wife (Pantalone). The phony learned man, charlatan, or quack, forever spouting Latin tags and pig Latin (Dottore). The sly servant playing tricks on his betters and outwitting them all (Harlequin); his dumb sidekick seconds him as best he can but practically trips over his own feet. The bragging soldier, who's really a coward and a bore behind his fierce mustaches (Capitano). And the toothless witchy old woman, played by a man.

From the Renaissance on, some of the stock figures kept the same name no matter who played them and what went on in the plot. Others split off into strings of first cousins, as it were, so the English watched the Harlequin-like

Jack Sausage or Jack Pudding, the Germans and Austrians flocked to see Hans
Wurst play his tricks, and the Dutch and Czechs loved Pickleherring.

Jews saw these performers in towns all over Germany and Poland, as well
as at the big fairs of Leipzig, Danzig, and so on. One of the better-known
seventeenth-century Hans Wurst players, Jacob Riz, was actually Jewish.
Harlequin, Hans Wurst, and Pickleherring soon became familiar figures in
ghetto entertainments. As Italian commedia dell'arte troupes, as well as several
English troupes that improvised with Italian gusto and style, toured Middle
Europe, crotchety Pantalone, windy Dottore, and bragging Capitano became
equally familiar friends in Yiddish.

Sometimes these characters simply popped into the action of the Purim
play, disrupting the story—as when Pickleherring, dressed in his familiar
green, appears as Potiphar's servant, or when, as a devil in the form of a dog,
he trades quips with Abraham before the sacrifice of Isaac.

Sometimes, on the other hand, a Purim play character took on the "mask"
of a stock character and merged with it. For example, Goliath became the
boasting soldier Capitano, all silly strut till he's defeated:

Little Jacob Riz of Prague. The
rhyme in German below this
seventeenth-century copper en-
graving calls him the "Jewish
Hans Wurst, the aristocrats' entertainer" and adds that neither
his courtly dress nor his small
stature diminish his manhood;
his wife has six children to prove
it.

> I am Goliath, the mighty and strong.
> The whole world shakes when I come along.

It takes a lot of food to satisfy such a big hero.

> Thirty-forty loaves of bread
> Are just a sup.
> Thirty-forty barrels wine
> Are just a cup.
> Thirty-forty pairs of oxen,
> Just a bowl of noodle soup.

King Ahashuerus became in some versions an old man worried that young Queen Esther was cuckolding him—Pantalone, of course.

Mordecai's change is startling. The popular demand for a clown evidently became too much for the dignified sage of the Bible story. As years went by, he sometimes turned up as Prince Mondrino or Mondrish the Court Fool (*mondry* is Polish for "clever"). In one version he arrives at the Persian palace in rags and is described by another character as a beggar who goes to every family's celebrations with his knife and fork at the ready. More often he combines his foolery with the charlatan's bluster or Harlequin's mischief, as when he functions as matchmaker between his cousin Esther and King Aha-shuerus. After explaining blithely that Esther is the daughter of a whore and a thief, her complexion is yellowish-green, and her stockings are grubby, he continues in typical twisty style:

> Other girls have red cheeks and black eyes, but she has red eyes and black cheeks. Other girls make the bed and heat the oven, but she makes the oven and warms the bed. What other girls have on the bottom she has on top, and what they have on top she has on the bottom. So . . . do me a favor and kiss her bottom. Your majesty, if you pay my fee for matchmaking, I'll give you a sermon. Why don't you ask what about, you old fool?
> Listen and you'll hear:
> "Be sick as a dog all year."
> Late and early, early and late,
> Haman should fall and break his pate.

A similar cheerful distortion of the Bible story for the sake of comedy occurs when Haman justifies his plan to wipe out the Jews by accusing them of letting their women go to ritual baths. He calls that an unnatural act. To his audience, who know that it is humdrum and harmless, he becomes not threatening, but absurd.

Many Purim plays include a routine that was a specialty of the stock character the charlatan Dottore, in which the entertainer pretends to deliver a lofty address, but lets it come out garbled and perverted. We have seen that

Yiddish clowns such as the *lets, nar,* and *payats* performed this sort of trick too, and not only in the course of plays but on other occasions as well. It was a special favorite in Yiddish, possibly because of the reverence in which Jewish tradition holds words and the high social position of learned men.

In addition to the pleasures of clowns and stock characters, acrobats and dancers, Purim plays always had musicians. Yiddish communities loved music. Their folk songs were rich, varied, and delightful. Music was part of every celebration. By the mid-sixteenth century Jewish musicians had organized professional guilds, and even non-Jewish wedding parties were among their customers. All but the smallest and most amateur groups of Purim players brought along instruments—a fiddle, at the least. Often professional or semi-professional musicians joined up with Purim players for the holiday season.

Cantors and choirboys often participated in Purim plays. Sometimes they scandalized the pious by using the same melodies both for rowdy Purim songs and for prayers. Often these were Italian opera tunes, which were the craze in Central Europe in the seventeenth century. As evidence of their popularity, in 1718 a printer who wanted to sell his playbook advertised it as "a new kind of Ahashuerus play, just like an opera."

Music was not only a treat for intermissions, but was also woven into the plays. Joseph's brothers sing a drinking song before selling him into slavery. And early in the story of David and Goliath, the Herald commands:

> Open the gates, the doors, and all.
> Players, play a march. Here comes King Saul.

The staging of Purim plays was presentational, as are many folk theaters, from medieval mystery plays to Japanese Kabuki. The stories were told through conventional symbols rather than by trying to create an illusion of life. The stage was often a platform, or only a space, in somebody's dining room or in a *yeshive,* and nobody pretended that he was anywhere else. Characters recited lines in a sort of sing song chant, instead of trying to sound emotional. For scenery and costumes most Purim plays used simple symbolic indications. King Ahashuerus wore a gold paper crown. Angels wore white paper wings. Bible characters wore nightshirts for robes and carried wooden swords. Soldiers wore Cossack boots, whether they were generals or Haman's palace guards.

Similarly, distances and actions were primarily symbolic. When Abraham takes Isaac up on a mountain to sacrifice him, the actors indicate their journey by walking twice around the bare space and then saying that they have arrived. Haman dies when soldiers cross swords over his head. Vashti dies when they put a "long hat" on her which covers her face; then they tap her with a sword and she falls down. When Joseph passes Mother Rachel's grave on his way to slavery in Egypt, another actor may simply place a sign saying MOTHER RACHEL'S GRAVE on an overturned bench and creep behind the contraption to speak Rachel's lines; it doesn't matter if the audience sees him do it.

Some exceptional Purim productions did try for a degree of illusion. A painted backdrop was not so unusual after the start of the eighteenth century. Purim plays sometimes rose to the ingenious mechanical stage devices associated with mystery plays in Western Europe. At a 1711 production of *The Selling of Joseph* in Frankfurt, for example, audiences thrilled to razzle-dazzle effects including "fire, heavens, and thunder claps," as well as Pickleherring in a multicolor costume. The show drew such crowds that two sentries had to climb a nearby water tower and watch that nobody got out of hand. (The mayor canceled the show before its two weeks were up, either because such crowds were dangerous or because too many Christians were among them.) Plays were performed not only in private homes and *yeshives,* but also in public halls, and after the eighteenth century we hear of buildings erected especially to provide a place for big Purim play productions; however, these were relatively rare.

Despite all the similarities between Jewish and Christian folk plays, Purim plays continued in their original form much longer than their counterparts. Mystery plays were pretty well gone from England by Shakespeare's day. The Oberammergau passion play is preserved in Bavaria like a museum exhibit. Anthropologists study mummers' plays in Newfoundland and a few other cultural outposts. In modern Russia, pageants and playlets celebrate a new faith, secular rather than divine. All these cultures have acquired professional theaters, in which professional actors perform sophisticated dramas nourished from popular sources, while the impulse toward popular theater has largely found other outlets.

Purim plays, on the other hand, have remained Purim plays. True, their number diminished drastically in the late nineteenth century, and then under Hitler and Stalin in the twentieth. A large proportion are now presented in simpler form, and not in Yiddish but in English, Hebrew, or whatever language the community speaks. They have kept their identity, however, and to this day, children dress up as King Ahashuerus or Queen Esther, Russian Cossacks or cowboys or hippies. They organize plays and carnivals at Hebrew schools. In Trenton, New Jersey, and elsewhere, Jews still exchange *shalekh-mones,* and neighborhood youngsters drive from home to home in crowded cars to present playlets, sing, and play recorders. At *hasidic* Purim parties, the punning repartee burlesquing scripture is scholarly, intricate, and hilarious. Young men crowd into *yeshive* study halls to watch comic skits that are a cheerful mixture of traditional story and topical joke—in 1974 in Brooklyn's Williamsburg section, one student draped a white burnoose over his head and sat stiffly on a makeshift throne to represent the oil-proud king of Saudi Arabia —enriched by songs and rhymed dialogue which have passed down through student generations. The *marshelik* who led a procession through the Prague ghetto in 1741 still has brothers in Purim parades through Orthodox neighborhoods of Brooklyn and along the broad boulevards of Tel Aviv.

One force for the preservation of Yiddish folk theater in its original form and function, as part of the Purim holiday celebration, was the traditional rabbinical antagonism toward other types of theater.

As long ago as Roman-ruled Palestine, the rabbis recorded in the Talmud their strong antipathy to theater, which they called *moshav letsim*—literally the "seat of scoffers." We know of Jewish actors, such as Elitiros who was a favorite at Nero's court, and fragments remain from a tragedy about the exodus from Egypt written in Greek by a Jew named Ezekielus. But most Jews respected the rabbis' strictures. The rabbis objected that the only theater there was was pagan, and they were right. Drama was officially connected with the worship of ancient gods, gods figured in many of the plots, and sacrifices actually preceded many performances. The rabbis also said theater was barbaric, and often they were right in this too. In Rome, many shows included slaves, sometimes Jewish, being massacred by wild animals or by each other. The rabbis also said that the comedy was vulgar, stupid, lewd, gross, childish, loose-minded. They said that in the audience there were always wanton women and other sorts of corrupting influences. And in general one should be studying Torah or thinking serious thoughts instead of idling time away watching idiotic antics. (The Puritans whose regime, from 1649 to 1660, shut down all the theaters in London used many of the same arguments.) The majority of pious Jews in the Middle Ages and, to a much lesser degree, well into the twentieth century agreed.

The relationship between religion and theater was problematic for Christians too. The Synod of Constantinople in 692 denounced playacting. Later the church fostered mystery plays, but when their influence became too strong and seemed too dangerous, they were kicked out from the nave to the doorway, to the church steps, and finally into the secular world, where they became professional theater. In 1673 Molière was nearly denied a Catholic burial because he was an actor. However, the situation within the contemporaneous Jewish community of Central and Eastern Europe was stricter still, for there simply could be no official life as a Jew outside the religious jurisdiction.

Among the most austerely Orthodox, even Purim plays were considered sinful. Thus we read typically that when the plague or a fire broke out among

Purim players of a later day, decked out in false beards and makeshift military uniforms, celebrate the holiday in Szydlowiec, Poland, in 1937.

the Jews of some city, the community understood at once that it was God's punishment for having indulged in too much theater over the last few Purim seasons. They repented with tears and resolved never to have any more theater at all. Then, ten years later—another Purim play. In 1737 the *kehile* (Jewish community authorities) went so far as to denounce a group of Jews to the mayor of Warsaw, who intervened to prevent a play performance.

Jewish tradition included a variety of specific prohibitions that severely inhibited the development of Yiddish drama beyond the Purim play to a professional theater. Orthodox Jews disapprove of a woman's voice heard singing. No decent Jewish woman would perform onstage. True, occasionally a woman clown, acrobat, singer, or dancer did appear; Ruza, Feygele, and the other women whose names we know worked in professional troupes with their fathers and husbands. But women did not act in plays. The prohibition was enough in itself to severely restrict the development of professional Yiddish theater, since Jewish law forbids men to dress up as women, except on Purim.

The Jewish ban on making images may well have been a subtle factor in the containment of theater within the religious holiday. Jewish law has always prohibited making images such as portraits and sculptures, even masks. And since drama is an imitation of life, it is possible that on some level Jewish culture was inimical to it. Besides, fiction in drama, as in the novel, leads to exploration and glorification of the individual rather than the group, which is counter to the traditional Jewish ideal. Purim plays reinforced community values rather than emphasizing individual heroes like Joseph and Mordecai.

Jewish law limited Purim plays to one short season, the season associated in all European cultures with springtime and resurrection, parades and theater. It is the season of the Greek Dionysian festival, of the Roman saturnalia, and of the medieval Feast of Fools, when students and young priests careened drunk and singing through the streets. At this season still, Mardi gras brings gorgeous processions and a riotous release from normal behavior to Trinidad and New Orleans. However, even when Purim plays extended for a week or two before and after Purim day, one season a year obviously could not support professional performers. Purim players remained *yeshive* boys or tailors' apprentices who earned their few coins once a year, or otherwise dignified citizens who were raising money for poor girls' dowries or some other favorite charity. Clearly, the Yiddish community could not develop a cadre of serious professional actors.

Purim plays were also limited in their dramatic material. Whereas Christian plays had as sources both the Old and New Testaments plus the lives of the saints, so that they proliferated into great cycles lasting days, Purim plays used only about twenty Biblical episodes and legends. They went over and over the same ground, elaborating it and interpolating local and secular matter as tropes, rather than using wholly new stories. The process echoes the Talmudic method of scholarship: interpretation and reinterpretation. Almost all the scholarly activity in the Yiddish communities was like this; the point was to fill the space energetically and creatively, rather than to expand.

The Purim play was spatially constricted. Born in the ghetto and *shtetl* (townlet), where synagogues were often limited with precision by the local gentile authorities and no additions or repairs allowed, it developed in cramped dining rooms, twisty streets, and narrow courtyards (as contrasted with the mystery play's echoing cathedral, wide cathedral steps, and market square). Significantly, ghetto artists produced lavish gold-embroidered velvet covers for the Torah scroll, paper cutouts as delicate as lace, colored banners—everything intricate, bright, and full of life. Rarely anything monumental.

The small performance space is a metaphor for a further kind of limitation. The holiday was bounded by the threat of disapproval and the general hostility of the outside world. A local governor could punish the Jews if the performance seemed to him to be offensive. He could arbitrarily ban performances, just as he limited where Jews could live, what work they could do, what clothes and how much jewelry they could wear, and when they could marry. For the Jews to flaunt a victory over their enemies as indiscreetly as they do on Purim was rare, and to do it on a large scale was out of the question.

An important impediment to the development of Yiddish theater beyond Purim plays was the lack of a social base. To become a high, conscious art, practiced by professionals, theater needs a community that officially values it. It also demands a community that is stable and prosperous enough to support it, at least minimally. This most ghettos and *shtetlekh* could not provide.

A final reason why Purim plays remained Purim plays was the *mame-loshn* (mother tongue)—the Yiddish language. Yiddish was considered a mere *jargón*, unfit for literary use. Until the mid-nineteenth century, a Jewish intellectual in Middle or Eastern Europe used German, Polish, or some other tongue for his literary efforts. Thus if he wrote a play, it would be a German or Polish play, not part of the culture of the Yiddish community. Hebrew was too sacred a language for secular plays or even most other secular uses, and anyway, only the more learned spectators would have understood it. The result was that until the nineteenth century there could be no Yiddish playwrights and no serious Yiddish drama.

So for all these reasons, until the nineteenth century virtually the only theater forms that existed in the Yiddish language were popular forms that had not been created by individual artists but had evolved through generations and been handed down as tradition. "Popular" theater, literally theater "of the people," generally appeals to the lower and less educated classes, to local rather than cosmopolitan interests, to the values of the community rather than of the individual. It stresses performance and spectacle over verbal subtlety, show over literature, feelings over ideas, the actor over the audience. It also assumes a unity between performers and audience.

As we have seen, the principal form of Yiddish popular theater was the Purim play, presented from the sixteenth century to the twentieth by the Yiddish-speaking Ashkenazic Jews of Central and Eastern Europe. (Eventually such plays were brought to other parts of the world, from South Africa to Argentina, by Ashkenazic Jews or their descendants who had left home, taking with them their language and culture.)

Although some Yiddish communities presented folk plays at the winter holiday Hanukka, and some enjoyed plays at rich families' weddings, such plays were so similar to Purim plays in style, content, and feeling that they, too, can be considered to belong to the genre "Purim play." The other forms of Yiddish popular theater—jesters and clowns, singers and acrobats—were also at home within the Purim play context, and enriched the play by their presence.

The Yiddish community preserved these popular theater forms intact into the twentieth century. Instead of expanding out of them, the community compressed them, containing their energy and warmth. Thus popular theater reflected the intimacy of the individual Yiddish *shtetl*, which directed its vitality inward under the rule of its own *kehile*. This compression of all the community's potential zest for theater into so short a season added extra intensity to the pleasure.

Purim plays derived a special warmth from their continued closeness to the source of cultural expression. First of all, the use of *mame-loshn*, rather than a scholarly or upper-class language, kept the experience psychologically close to the hearer. Direct and unsophisticated, the plays were accessible to everyone, just as the *megile* was read aloud regularly in synagogue and studied as part of the body of religious writings. Even if you weren't rich, learned, or related to a rabbi, you were comfortable knowing what to expect. And when comic liberties were taken with the story, they were always the same kinds of liberties, so they themselves came to be part of tradition and thus familiar.

The theater occasion itself was intimate, for since Purim plays were generally performed in people's homes, the players were, in a way, guests. Performers and spectators were part of the same small group. Under his cotton-wool beard, King Ahashuerus might be the local water carrier, and everybody would recognize him. He'd know them too, and when he made a crack about some local rich man, everybody got the joke. (Social satire was always a volatile element in Yiddish popular theater.)

The plays' characters were everyone's common ancestors, only a few generations back. Abraham, Isaac, Jacob, and Joseph are everybody's great-grandfathers; everybody knows their stories. In fact, the history is more than shared; it merges into the very moment when the happy group is watching the play. The Jewish conception of history as a continuum makes no distinction between Pharaoh and the Czar, between Mordecai, who stood up for the Jews in ancient Persia, and Theodor Herzl, who stood up for them in Europe thousands of years later. So when Haman strode about in Cossack boots in Russian Purim plays during the period of pogroms, it was not a gesture of bringing the play up to date; rather, it was natural, appropriate costuming. In the same tradition, in a Purim play in France in 1944, Haman wore a little black Hitler mustache.

Purim plays are still around, and *badkhonim* still jest in rhyme at traditional weddings. But in the nineteenth century, the energy and warmth of Yiddish folk theater, its compressed vitality and intimate intensity, were released to animate a new, real Yiddish theater.

2 DRAMAS OF THE ENLIGHTENMENT

AROUND 1830, A POLISH-JEWISH DOCTOR named Shloyme Etinger wrote a play in Yiddish. He called the play *Serkele*, after its strong-willed villainess. Etinger's intellectual friends passed the handwritten manuscript of *Serkele* along to friends in other cities. In middle-class Jewish parlors in Eastern Europe, reading plays aloud was a newly fashionable way to spend the evening. As another Yiddish amateur playwright of the period explained in a rhymed prologue: plays "seemed right/ For friends to read together on a pleasant winter night." Decanters of wine and a samovar for strong tea stood on the sideboard, as the lively circle savored the novelty of a sophisticated literary work composed in Yiddish.

Probably everyone in the cozy parlor lamplight had seen many Purim plays in his youth. Probably most of them still continued to give a coin for brandy, and an indulgent smile, to any Purim players they happened to see. In the 1830s Purim plays were still flourishing. Folk theater kept its vitality—among the folk.

But Etinger and his friends were not exactly "the folk." They were much more educated and worldly than the Jewish masses. They knew about plays because they could read and see them in Russian, Polish, German, French—languages the Jewish masses of Eastern Europe did not understand. Formal, sophisticated dramas had not yet been written in Yiddish. Etinger and a few other amateurs were the first Yiddish playwrights, who consciously constructed works of art for the pleasure of a cultivated audience.

In developing beyond folk plays, Yiddish theater followed a general pattern that had occurred in Western Europe in the Renaissance but reached Eastern Europe centuries later. In every case, the "high" drama of an intellectual elite merged gradually with the "low" folk theater to produce a modern national theater; in every case, this happened as the community acquired both a sense of national identity, including a modern vernacular, and an urban middle class. But whereas in other cultures the entire process extended over centuries, in Yiddish it was telescoped into one generation, so that Etinger's friends would live to see a lively professional Yiddish theater serving a growing public.

The medieval playwrights in Yiddish had been a small group. *Yeshive* students, like their non-Jewish counterparts at universities and at court, wrote academic dramas for their peers in the form of mock debates. One such writer, Menakhem Aldendorf, contrived dialogues between the Countryman and the Townsman, between Winter and Summer, between Wine and Water, between Virtue and Vice, between Hanukka and the other holidays. For centuries this represented the limit of academic playwriting within the Yiddish community. Such few worldly and aristocratic Jews as there were in Central and Eastern Europe cultivated their taste for drama at the local prince's court, and not in Yiddish. There were, of course, no Jewish princes.

The element of Yiddish society which eventually produced the dabblers like Etinger and his audience was distinct from "the folk." The position of the Yiddish social class that initiated deliberate playwriting was not exactly analogous to that of its European counterparts, however. These were not the richest people in the Yiddish community, nor the most powerful. They were not necessarily well-born, nor married into prestigious families, though almost invariably they were middle class. They were the enlightened intellectuals.

Historians call the mid-eighteenth century in Europe the Age of Enlightenment, in accord with the conviction among intellectuals of the period that the human being was emerging at last from the dark ages of ignorant superstition. In the category of superstition they included all established religions, though the flavor of the era was Protestant. It seemed that man, especially dignified middle-class man, was coming out into an era of humanism, rationality, secularism, science, and progress toward light. Enlightened people recognized that everyone was equal—potentially, at least—under the natural laws of right and reason. They believed that people ought to be liberated from oppressions based on superficial cultural differences—including anti-Semitism.

Most Ashkenazic—Yiddish-speaking—Jews were outside the mainstream of European culture in the eighteenth century. Indeed, no country accepted them as full citizens. However, some members of Yiddish communities now began to participate in the Age of Enlightenment. The Jewish Enlightenment began in eighteenth-century Germany under the leadership of the gentle genius Moses Mendelssohn. By the nineteenth century, as the larger current of European culture seeped eastward into Poland and Russia, changing its tone to suit its new environments, so did the Jewish Enlightenment.

To enlightened Jewish eyes, Jewish ritual seemed reactionary and superstitious. It seemed to keep Jews isolated from modern Western life. Jewish members of the Enlightenment set themselves to try to elevate Jews from what they considered the depths of prehistory and make them modern, rational people. They urged Jews to learn non-Yiddish culture, beginning with ancient paganism and necessarily exploring much that was specifically Christian. They aimed to shift emphases within the Jewish community from traditional observances to philosophy and ethics, and from community to individual relationships between man and God, man and state, man and man.

In Germany, the ultimate result was often almost total abandonment of Judaism: assimilation. But farther east, the Enlightenment turned its reforming energy toward creating a modern humanistic Jew, and greatly enriched, modernized, and transformed Jewish life.

"Enlightenment" in Hebrew is *haskala*—in Yiddish, *haskole*. The Jewish intellectuals most alive to *haskole*, especially in Eastern Europe, and active in its service, were called "enlightened ones": *maskilim*. Etinger was a *maskil*. He discovered forbidden secular learning early; perhaps he sat on a *yeshive* bench, like many of his contemporaries, hiding a science book or even a novel behind his Talmud. The congenial parlor guests reading Etinger's play *Serkele* were all *maskilim*. Indeed, all the nineteenth-century Jewish playwrights up to the birth of the professional Yiddish theater were *maskilim*.

It is only logical that these earliest playwrights and audiences would be *maskilim*. After all, as we have seen, the traditional values of the community were strongly against theater of any kind except Purim plays—and even these had been questioned. Moreover, tradition often (though not always) resisted all secular knowledge; this resistance, as well as the hostility from outside, kept members of the community ignorant of intellectual currents and pastimes outside the ghetto.

The Yiddish Language

The effect of *haskole* on the Yiddish language was extremely significant for the development of Yiddish theater. In many European cultures the emergence of a rich national theater was associated with the development of the national vernacular into a suitable literary vehicle, replacing the "high" language, usually Latin, the language of academic dramas and other intellectual pursuits. Almost the same is true of Yiddish.

The literary language—the Latin, as it were—of educated Jews was Hebrew. However, unlike Latinists, Jews reserved their high language for sacred or at least philosophical purposes. They did not write on most secular matters in Hebrew. They did not chat, or quarrel, or sing love songs in Hebrew. All that was done in the vernacular, Yiddish.

Yiddish was the language of the Ashkenazic Jews of Central and Eastern Europe. (It was never the language of the Sephardic Jews of Spain, Arabia, and Africa.) In the late Middle Ages, when the Rhineland was a major center of Jewish population, Yiddish developed out of Old High German plus a great deal of Hebrew, Romance, and other linguistic elements. As the Jewish population emigrated eastward in the next few centuries, Slavic elements entered the language. English, too, developed largely from German sources, which is one reason why Yiddish and English have words in common. Like English, Yiddish developed into a distinct language with its own syntax and flavor.

On the popular level, Yiddish was a literary vehicle from the first. A series of epic poems in Yiddish survives from 1382. Books were printed in Yiddish beginning in the sixteenth century. There were holy legends, parables, sermons, and interpretations of prayers. There were also poems and even romances of medieval chivalry. Yiddish chivalric romances included tales of King Arthur and his Round Table. The most famous romance was a long cycle, adapted from the Italian by Elia Levita in 1507, about the adventures of a gallant knight named Sir Bovo d'Antona. It was so enormously popular over the centuries that Sir Bovo himself entered the language. Because his name coincidentally sounds like the Yiddish word for "grandmother" *(bobe)*, the title *Bovo Mayse (Bovo Story)* gradually became confused with the expression *bobe mayse* (grandmother story), and it remains a popular idiom meaning an old wives' tale.

"Grandmother story," "mother tongue"—such idioms are symptomatic of a cultural attitude toward the language which existed even before *haskole*. Yiddish was for profane, workaday use, as opposed to Hebrew for Sabbath use. Most Yiddish literature was directed to unlearned people. Women, who were rarely educated, read Yiddish stories and sermons or Yiddish translations of Hebrew prayers and Bible stories. Uneducated men indulged in such stuff too, but they were a little embarrassed about it. Yiddish literature was for the ignorant laboring masses, as opposed to the aristocracy of Hebrew scholars. Yiddish was for folk-song lyrics and Purim plays.

With the profound changes that *haskole* brought to European Jewry came changes in attitudes toward Yiddish. In Germany, where *haskole* began, and where government policy allowed Jews more freedom than they received farther east, the language disappeared along with the sense of distinct cultural identity. Perhaps the similarity of Yiddish to German accelerated the process.

The same was largely true of the rest of the formerly Yiddish-speaking communities in Western and Central Europe: France, Czechoslovakia, Yugoslavia, Hungary. In these countries, the history of Yiddish theater virtually ends with *Purimshpiln*. (Besides, the base of the Yiddish population was still shifting eastward.)

For a while even *maskilim* in the east were uncomfortable about Yiddish. Indeed, they didn't even call Yiddish a language, although they normally spoke it and even thought in it; they called it *jargón*. Most of them were from the educated middle classes, and Yiddish seemed to them not only workaday but low. Furthermore, though they themselves generally knew Polish or Russian, they felt that, as a parochial language, Yiddish cut Jews off from the larger culture of the countries where they lived and from European culture as a whole.

Even more painful, Yiddish felt to them like a travesty of the German language, which they revered for its association with Moses Mendelssohn and his disciples. Because of the prestige that Westernness and specifically Germanness held for them, calling someone a "German" or a "Berliner" came to mean not where he was born, but that he was a *maskil*. This attitude led some *maskilim* to speak either German or a Germanized Yiddish, which emphasized the Germanic component in Yiddish and added new German words and syntactical constructions. In time this *Daytshmerish* came to be a sort of bastard dialect, neither German nor Yiddish. *Daytshmerish* hung on into the twentieth century, at last becoming a linguistic affectation, especially on the stage. But by then most writers had long since repudiated it in favor of pure Yiddish.

Many *maskilim* started to write a modernized Hebrew. It was *haskole*'s bold innovation to use the sacred tongue for secular essays, poems, even novels. This was part of the general *haskole* drive toward secularization and its insistence on the value of secular writing. It was the *maskilim* who first translated the literature of the world, including ancient and modern plays, into Hebrew.

And now German joined Hebrew as another learned "Latin," opposed to the Yiddish vernacular. (Similarly, in the Polish and Russian societies which surrounded the Jews, the upper classes had their elite languages for theater, literature, and salon conversation: German, English, and especially French.) This double legacy—from the traditionalists, for whom Yiddish was profane, and from the *maskilim*, for whom it was vulgar—has continued from that day to this. It has colored Jews' unconscious attitudes toward the language, as well as toward the literature, including drama, for which Yiddish is the vehicle. Many modern Jews who cannot actually speak Yiddish irrationally consider the very sound of the language as comical, especially when it is being put to what seems an incongruously serious use. (In *Languages in Contact* Uriel Weinreich points out that among immigrant communities in America, when a language seems to be obsolescent, the reaction is similar.)

Ironically, however, the *haskole* mission to enlighten the masses soon led the *maskilim* straight back to Yiddish. For "to demolish a building," the fabulously popular nineteenth-century Eastern European Yiddish novelist Meyer Dik explained rather patronizingly, "you use a pickax, not a golden needle"; to enlighten a Jew, they had to speak to him in his own language— Yiddish.

Early Yiddish Dramas of the Enlightenment

Etinger and the other playwrights of around 1830 shared a definition of themselves as teachers. This was in keeping with the traditional Jewish view, which demanded some justification for an indulgence in theater. It was also in keeping with the idea articulated two thousand years earlier by the Roman poet Horace: drama should be "delightful and instructive," a sort of sugar-coated pill for moral lessons. As it happened, this medicinal concept was especially pervasive in Europe just before Etinger's day, as embodied in a genre called, broadly, bourgeois drama.

Etinger joined the mainstream of Western theater at a period when it was still dominated by bourgeois drama (also variously called sentimental drama, sentimental comedy, tearful comedy, and domestic comedy). It began in England in 1731 with a cautionary tale called *The London Merchant; or, The History of George Barnwell,* which showed that virtuous young apprentices had better keep away from wicked women, and is represented at its best in English by Sheridan's *The School for Scandal* (written in 1777) and in German by Lessing's *Emilia Galotti* (1772). By Etinger's day, romantic tragedies and melodramas had superseded these moral tales in Western Europe; but the bourgeois drama was still very popular in Poland and Russia, where the form was geared to a fiercer social satire.

European bourgeois plays, like the novels which developed at the same time, concerned themselves with the individual secular human being, his conscience and his social relationships. The characters were most often middle-class people, rather than the peasant of popular low comedy or the kings and queens of high tragedy. The plays aimed to teach sensible social behavior. The plots moved irresistibly toward a moral conclusion. Despite the extremely improbable twists this obligatory conclusion necessitated, the high-flown sentimental language, and the impossibly noble heroes, the plays were essentially realistic. They showed familiar types of people behaving in recognizable ways, and tried to mix comic and pathetic elements together in a natural fashion. These devices were supposed to make the lesson strike more deeply home.

This bourgeois genre was especially appropriate for the first Yiddish dramas, because the middle class it spoke to was only just then appearing in Eastern Europe. The Enlightenment, including *haskole,* was primarily a middle-class movement.

Furthermore, studies of social behavior, oriented toward realistic observation, seemed particularly suitable to Yiddish values, which focused on social behavior rather than on an individual hero's spiritual crisis. The aspect of humanism which both Yiddish tradition and Eastern *haskole* stressed was the position of human beings in this world rather than at the center of the cosmos. The *haskole* context was a rational world, which could be comprehended, rather than a mysterious universe. Yiddish dramas of ideas concerned the establishment of ethical order, not the heights and abysses of tragedy.

The first two Yiddish amateur plays that we know of were written by two *maskilim* in Germany: *Reb Hennoch; or, What to Do About It* by Yitskhok Euchel (1793) and *Frivolity and Religiosity* by Aaron Wolfsohn (1796). Both

Ida Kaminska in the title role of *Serkele,* by Shloyme Etinger, presented by the Yiddish State Theater of Poland in 1963.

riducule *shtetl* superstition. In dramaturgy and tone they are crude—somewhat reminiscent of *Gammer Gurton's Needle*, probably written in the 1550s, which was one of the first university plays in English.

Etinger was one of three amateur playwrights writing some thirty years later in Eastern Europe. His *Serkele* and, to a lesser degree, his contemporaries' plays are bourgeois not only in moral tone but also in form.

Serkele is a standard tearful comedy. David Goodheart goes away on a trip west from Lemberg, leaving his business and his young daughter in the care of his sister Serkele. Six years later he returns to find that Serkele has declared him dead and made a false will declaring herself his heir. Worse, she has treated his daughter like a servant and most recently has allowed her and her sweetheart to be falsely accused and arrested for theft. His return sets all to rights. He makes Serkele repent and sends her factotum in crime to jail. He arranges a suitable match for Serkele's own daughter, who was to marry the factotum. He arranges several matches more, and provides dowries for them all. At the last he forgives Serkele, but encourages his brother-in-law to control her more firmly. David Goodheart, a benevolent man, wise, sermonizing, and rich, who suddenly appeared at the end of a play to reward the virtuous and punish the guilty, was a familiar figure in bourgeois drama. The scenes move along smoothly. The minor characters are deftly drawn.

The following passage is the opening of the last act of *Serkele*. David Goodheart comes home to Lemberg. Before he reveals his true identity, the author calls him Stranger. I have tried to convey the Germanized Yiddish of David Goodheart by rendering it in very fancy English, as if an American were imitating the diction of a British aristocrat in the movies. It sounds stiff and affected now, but it was impressive then. The innkeeper's Yiddish is colloquial and realistic. He mixes in some local Polish, indicated by italics. A Litvak, he has a regional accent that the other characters consider ridiculous, which Etinger indicates by reversing his *s* and his *sh*.

STRANGER   *(Sits in front of the door of the inn, on the bench, dressed for traveling in German-style clothes.)* I am extraordinarily weary. This has indeed been a journey! By day and by night, upon land as upon water, with nowhere the right to rest myself—until at last, to the praise of God the Almighty be it said, I am now once more, after six years' passage, in my own native homeland. How all here seems to be altered and improved, I might even say beautified. To my eyes, the streets—how clean, the houses—how charming and pretty. God! But does the internal correspond with these externals? Strange! Verily, it is strange enough that after so many martyred years, after these extraordinary pangs of longing and yearning for the darling of my heart, I have been unable to discover any tidings of her. *(He remains a moment silent in thought.)* Dear child! How have you prospered here during the time of my absence from home? Has your health kept step with my fortune? Pure little daughter! How do you look now? Has the delicate bud grown to be the hoped-for little tree? Have you, in fulfilment of the wish of your father, who loves you above all else, have you grown to resemble his holy, his never-to-be-forgotten wife, Rachel? Or . . . *(He remains sitting, sad and thoughtful. Then he pulls himself together.)* No, no, away with these hellish thoughts. Ah, all-powerful creator, thou who hast so oft supported me in my trials, heavenly father of all creatures! Take from me all your blessings, my health, my life, take all, all, but this beloved, this beautiful child, take her not! *(He remains silent awhile.)*

SHMELKE   *(Comes from the street, a stick in his hand, and is about to enter his inn. Stops short when he sees* STRANGER.*)* Oh, oh! Good. God in heaven hash shent me a cushtomer. *(Takes off his hat and bows deeply in front of the* STRANGER. *Speaks this line in Polish.)* We humbly greet the gentleman. What ish the lord'sh wiss?

STRANGER   *(Does not notice* REB SHMELKE. *Continues talking to himself.)* What indeed would be my happiness, my life, without this child?

SHMELKE   *(To himself.)* Aha! A German!

STRANGER   *(Notices* REB SHMELKE.*)* Might you perhaps be the host of this establishment?

SHMELKE   *(Goes up closer to the* STRANGER *and bows deeply as before. Remains standing there and speaks very rapidly.)* Yesh, good shir! You are altogether entirely welcome, your honor. What will your highnesh be pleashed to command? A lovely, fine, painted, brightly lit room, a magnifishent shtable, fress hay, a wonderful meal and drink, anything your honor can wiss for, a nishe old mead, a delightful glash of wine, everything noble—only made jusht eshpeshally for your highnesh! Right away thish moment they'll be running to bring your lordship a tea, a coffee, a shtrong glash of punch, a liqueur, a Shwish cheeshe, a marinated herring, a Hungarian roasht, a shmoked fiss—all, all, your honor can get it all from fat Shmelke Troynks, and for pennies, made jusht for your highnesh! Jusht to pleash your highnesh!

STRANGER   *(To himself.)* I am extremely gratified that this man has not recognized me. *(Aloud to* SHMELKE.*)* You have made an error, my dear Reb Shmelke. I am a Jew.

SHMELKE   *(Puts on his hat at once.)* A Jew! *(To himself.)* My nightmares from my head into his, if I wouldn't have sworn he was a Polish nobleman! *(Sits down next to the* STRANGER *and shakes his hand.)* Sholom aleichem! Where are you coming from? Where are you going?

Etinger uses language like a dramatist. It is an old convention to have higher and lower characters speak differently; Shakespeare's Macbeth speaks blank verse, while the Porter speaks everyday prose.

In these Yiddish plays, the "good" characters speak a very Germanized Yiddish. This is justified because the "good" characters are inevitably *mas-*

kilim, so they know German. Furthermore, in Etinger's *Serkele,* David Goodheart has just been traveling in Central Europe and his daughter's sweetheart, a fine young student, was born in Prague. Later on, Serkele's stupid daughter tries to show off by speaking in the same elevated manner, but it comes out as so garbled a *Daytshmerish* that it is practically gibberish. The other characters laugh at her, and David Goodheart himself has to ask for a translation into Yiddish.

Etinger wrote a great deal besides plays, though the Russian censors, who were even harsher on Yiddish authors than on the rest, kept most of his works out of print. He translated many literary works, including Schiller's play *Die Räuber.* He was one of the first to try to make Yiddish modern and literary, and is remembered as a real reformer. In *Serkele,* the language serves for lively dialogue, with suitable distinctions in diction for character and for regional accents. It also serves, perhaps for the first time, for detailed stage directions, including new words for "act" and "scene." Censorship prevented *Serkele* from being published until 1861, but it was an influential play nevertheless. For although it seems never to have been done professionally in the nineteenth century, we do know of at least one amateur performance at a *yeshive* in Zhitomir in the 1860s—a performance about which we will hear more later. *Serkele* was revived with considerable publicity in Warsaw in 1922.

The First Jewish Recruit in Russia, written by Israel Aksenfeld in the same period as *Serkele,* also has a distinct *haskole* moral. It, too, uses language to make its points. In 1827 Czar Nicholas I had ordered soldiers to be drafted into the army, including an especially high proportion of Jews, who were often kidnapped as boys. Under the new edict, Jewish cantonist soldiers served for twenty-five years, and many never came home. Aksenfeld wanted to show that Jews should appreciate this chance to serve equally as loyal citizens with their neighbors. He also wanted to expose the heartlessness of the more powerful toward the lower classes within the Jewish community. In his play, the people of a small Jewish village are scrambling to avoid the draft, although their village is so small that only one man is to be taken. A number of the community leaders get together and trick a happy-go-lucky scamp into volunteering, convincing him that his sweetheart wants him to do so to prove his love.

The play ends sadly. As soon as poor Nakhmen marches proudly off to sign up, the sweetheart dies of shock and a broken heart, and her mother goes mad from grief. Nakhmen's blind old mother is left to accuse the conspirators, who have felt very smug and clever all along but now are suddenly eaten up with remorse.

The play has a lot of strong moments, including the melodramatic final curtain. A vivid range of character types speak realistic colloquial prose appropriate to their various temperaments and social classes. The seething atmosphere in town provides a situation for energetic humor, as in this exchange from the fifth scene.

(Early morning in the study of REB AHARON, *the ox merchant, the richest and most learned Jew in the town. He is reading and writing at his desk as his clever and pretty wife,* PERELE, *enters, wrapped in a shawl.)*

PERELE   *(Laughing so hard that* AHARON *is startled and upsets his books, papers, and ink.)* Aharon, you must hear who it was that came to see me so early, while the whole town was asleep. Can you guess? *(Laughs so hard that she cannot speak.)*

AHARON   If you laugh so, I never will hear. . . . I beg you, Perele, stop your laughing at last.

PERELE   If I want to make myself stop laughing, I must remind myself that the ukase was passed to take Jews away as soldiers; it's the only way I can quiet my laughter. Do you know who came running to me? None other than Hirsh-Leyb the Fool. Nu, well, and can you guess why? You'll never guess till I tell you. Do you remember, my dear Aharon, when Fat David married off his daughter Tsivele, that pretty girl, in such a hurry to Hirsh-Leyb the Fool, and nobody could believe that such a successful businessman, and a shopkeeper, would give his one and only daughter, and such a pretty girl too, to the idiot of the town —and hold the wedding right away, the very next Sunday? Well, you know what everyone in town was saying, don't you remember?

AHARON   Yes, I remember. But I didn't pay attention, for I am convinced it's a lie. Nu, tell me, then, I beg you.

PERELE   I must not forget that they're coming to take Jews away as soldiers, otherwise I won't be able to tell the rest. *(Heaves a breath.)* Hirsh-Leyb makes straight for me and asks me—I really have to imitate the way he said it. "Perele, Perele, you are so clever, tell me, how many months does it take a Jewish woman to have a baby?" I answer him as if I am amazed at the question. "That depends on the father; sometimes the father is an unlucky *shlimazel,* and the wife can go ten years after the wedding without a baby. The wife of a handy fellow makes a *bris* [circumcision or naming ceremony] at the end of a year, and a really handy fellow's wife—at the end of nine months. A very clever rascal—maybe seven months." He asks: "How about four months?" To which I answer: "Aha, that one must be both clever and handy. He is one in a million." Whereupon my Hirsh-Leyb stands still, his mouth open, full of joy, and with the middle finger of his right hand he gestures again and again toward his own heart. I pretend I don't understand what he means. So at last this Hirsh-Leyb of mine closes his mouth enough to say: "That's me, the handy fellow, the clever one, the one that is one in a million. How long since my wedding? Only just four months, and my Tsivele is already having a baby. The old woman is with her already. I went to call her myself." Ha-ha-ha. *(*PERELE *laughs.)*

Aksenfeld wrote dozens of plays and novels, though—largely because of censorship—only one play besides *The First Jewish Recruit in Russia* was published in his lifetime. *Man and Wife, Brother and Sister* is about sweethearts who discover at the altar that they are long-lost brother and sister. The plot illustrates Aksenfeld's lesson that Jews should be sure to register all their births and other census records with the proper Russian officials. Aksenfeld lived in Odessa on the Black Sea, a gay cosmopolitan city known as a hotbed of *haskole*, where his own home was a sort of salon. When the Odessa pogrom broke out in 1871, the manuscripts of his other plays were lost.

During a cholera epidemic, Etinger, who practiced medicine without a license, was called to the bedside of a *maskil* named Avrom-Ber Gotlober. The two men had already heard of each other; Gotlober did not quite have Etinger's stature, but he was known for his writings and especially for his poems and songs. Etinger entered the sickroom, glanced once at Gotlober, and said cheerily and briskly, "What do you need cholera for? You'd be better off hearing my *Serkele*." He read the manuscript to the patient—maybe he carried it around in his black bag—and instead of catching cholera, Gotlober caught the desire to write a play in Yiddish.

Like *Serkele* and *The First Jewish Recruit in Russia*, Gotlober's comedy *The Bridal Canopy; or, Two Weddings in One Night* circulated so widely in handwritten manuscripts that by the time it was printed, in 1876, there was no author's name on the title page. Indeed, the publisher probably had no idea at all who wrote it.

In *The Bridal Canopy*, a young couple are about to be separated because their parents have matched them up to others for the sake of prestigious family connections. He is to marry an ugly, half-blind, old-maid rabbi's daughter, and she is to marry a scholar's son with a squashed-in nose so ugly that he is to wear a bridal veil over his face until after the wedding ceremony, so as not to upset her. The young couple have never even met their spouses-to-be, who are arriving that very day from other towns for the two wedding ceremonies. Yosele, the young hero, outwits them all. By elaborate trickery he himself, a veil over his face, contrives to marry his own sweetheart. Then, by another twist, he gets the two well-born undesirables together under the wedding canopy. The lively atmosphere, sympathetic pranksters, gay dialogue, and rather improbable intrigue is similar to Oliver Goldsmith's bourgeois comedy *She Stoops to Conquer; or, The Mistakes of a Night*. But the atmosphere, character types, language, and attitudes are distinctively Yiddish.

Hasidism and Haskole

Thus *haskole* contributed to Yiddish culture literate playwrights who had a newly flexible vernacular and a respect for secular arts. Meanwhile, simultaneously with *haskole*, another major movement swept Eastern European Jewry. This was *hasidism;* and its contributions were to stimulate and to legitimize the culture of the masses, including their humble *mame-loshn.*

The literature *hasidism* produced reflected the movement's approach to Judaism. Like *haskole, hasidism* stressed the value of the individual man and of his personal thoughts and beliefs. Like *haskole, hasidism* wanted to free Jews from the rigid religious establishment. But *hasidism* valued the common man's mystical experience above the scholar's Talmudic learning, or the *maskil's* cultivation. *Hasidism* encouraged the popular arts. It glorified spontaneous song and dance as expressions of joy in the divine. It encouraged the creation of simple lyrics in the vocabulary of the masses. Rabbi Nakhmen Braslover, great-grandson of the Baal Shem Tov (Master of the Good Name), who founded *hasidism*, improvised long narratives which his disciples transcribed in 1815; they can still be read, in the original and in Martin Buber's adaptations, either as enchanting folk tales about princesses in towers, talking birds, and dragon-slayers, or as philosophical allegories. *Hasidism* increased literacy among the masses and even accelerated the growth of the Yiddish publishing industry, because pious disciples longed to read and reread their rabbis' wise sayings.

Haskole and *hasidism* were produced in the same era, with the decline of the traditional *kehile;* Moses Mendelssohn and the Baal Shem Tov were contemporaries, in fact. But the two movements took opposite routes, and *maskilim* and *hasidim* hated each other as much as traditional Orthodox believers hated them both. Literature of the time, including drama, reflected the contemporaneousness of the two movements less than it did the chasm between them.

Within one generation, *hasidism's* emphasis on heart rather than mind began to be expressed, from the *maskil's* point of view, as a rigid anti-intellectualism. *Maskilim* denounced it as medieval and battled to liberate the masses from its influence; Joel Linetski's novel *The Polish Lad,* based on his own miserable youth among the *hasidim*, savagely ridiculed the wonder-working rabbis who enforced ignorance and isolation. *Maskilim* made *hasidim* the villains and clowns of their plays. For example, Gotlober's primary message in *The Bridal Canopy* is the mindless brutality of *hasidic* family life.

Like Linetski, Gotlober broke away from a *hasidic* family. He had been married off at fifteen and then two years later forced to leave his young wife and baby on charges that he was infecting them with modern ideas. In his play, the young couple defy a whole menagerie of grotesque *hasidic* caricatures. He even inserted the following song, which refers to many *hasidic* disciples' practice of living together at their rabbi's court most of the year and, while there, of praying through the night:

> He bows, while praying, to the earth
> And at the word "heaven" up he springs.
> He sleeps till midnight on the bare earth
> But after midnight never sleeps.
>
> He doesn't come home till Sabbath eve,
> But this year two circumcision parties gave,
> For he's faithful to God's order: "Give
> A son even to your female slave."

This sort of song, and the figure of the *hasid* as hypocritical, promiscuous, gross, stupid, remained a motif in Yiddish plays and entertainments, although a century later the representation of the *hasid* was rendered with much more sympathy or even humor. The image of the *hasid* then became filtered and subdued, acquiring an endearing Old World charm, as in Marc Chagall's nostalgic evocations. In later portrayals his singing and dancing and his beatific piety became his predominant traits.

The *hasidim,* for their part, considered the worldly *maskilim* sinners in every way and denounced all their doings. Pressure by *hasidim* may actually have intimidated Jewish printers into refusing to print some manuscripts of Aksenfeld's which the censors had passed. *Hasidim* never wrote plays themselves, for theater was anathema to them. Nevertheless, *hasidism*'s influence on Yiddish language and culture helped create the popular Yiddish theater and its public.

By the 1860s, propelled by the influences of *haskole* and *hasidism,* many writers who had long been using Hebrew switched to Yiddish. By the very process of writing and translating widely into Yiddish, they slowly refined the language into a modern literary medium. The appearance of Yiddish-Russian and Yiddish-German dictionaries acknowledged that Yiddish had acquired the dignity of a language, rather than a *jargón. Kol Mevaser,* the first substantial widely circulated Yiddish newspaper, began publication in Russia in 1862.

Aside from theatrical writings, a whole rich secular literature was taking shape: novels, stories, essays, poetry. The storybook tradition in Yiddish—

This photograph, reprinted in a Yiddish newspaper, was entitled "The Oldest Picture of Yiddish Theater." It shows a scene from Shomer-Shaikevitch's play *Der Diskantist (The Collection Agent),* performed in Odessa 1876. The actors, from the left: Sigmund Mogulesko in female role, Aba Shengold, and Edward Margules.

דאָס עלטסטע בילד פֿון אידישען טעאַטער

medieval romances and later moralizing parables full of adventures in exotic places, of princesses and castles, magic spells and shipwrecks—enriched by *hasidic* myths and allegories, now was channeled into *haskole* fiction. *Haskole* novels ranged from grim social satire to serialized sensational romances by Meyer Dik and, later, the even more popular Schomer-Shaikevitch. All over Eastern Europe entire households got together to buy a single flimsy-paper volume. Or they rented a one-chapter installment every Friday from the horse-and-wagon book peddler and read it aloud with the neighbors on Sabbath afternoon. Dik published over three hundred novels, and though tens of thousands of copies were printed of each, many of his novels have disappeared. They were read until they fell apart.

In the next twenty years the three classical Yiddish authors established themselves. The first was the pseudonymous Mendele Moykher Sforim (1836–1917), "Little Mendel the Book Peddler," who came to be known all over the Yiddish-speaking world as the grandfather of Yiddish literature. He fused the varieties of Yiddish that were spoken in several different regions and created a universal sophisticated literary medium. Coincidentally, he and Gotlober taught at the same school. The other two classical authors were Yitskhok Leyb (or Leybush) Peretz (1852–1915) and Sholom Aleichem (1859–1916)—the latter a pseudonym meaning "Greetings," or "Peace Be with You." All three began by writing Hebrew. Indeed, Mendele Moykher Sforim and Sholom Aleichem used pseudonyms because, at the start, they'd have jeopardized their intellectual reputations by writing seriously in Yiddish—the *jargón*. Yet by the time they died, they were part of an energetic literary scene, including a vigorous professional Yiddish theater.

The Broder Singers

Besides the development in the mid-nineteenth century of Yiddish drama and fiction, and of *maskilim* and *hasidim,* another institution evolved quite independently in the Yiddish world, as an outgrowth of genuine folk art. This was *Di Broder zinger.*

The Broder singers were bards or troubadours like the earlier German meistersingers—colorful, flamboyant figures who performed songs and mono-logues, which they often composed themselves. They were the first profes-sional actors and producers in modern Yiddish culture.

The Broder singers were essentially secular *badkhonim,* who appeared at the lively wine gardens and inns which were proliferating in Eastern Europe, instead of only in respectable Jewish households. And instead of being essen-tially pious, they were usually *maskilim* and freethinkers, though many of them continued to preach as they entertained.

(By the late nineteenth century the *badkhonim,* or wedding bards, were the only Yiddish ceremonial clowns left in any numbers. Their jest-ing had adjusted to modern times. *Badkhonim* commented not only on the bride's family and traditional morals, but also on politics; one of the most famous of them all, Eliakum Zunser, set out for New York just hours before the czarist police came to search his house for subversive writings. The only other comparable figure still active in Yiddish com-munities in the late nineteenth century was the *magid,* or itenerant preacher, with his vivid flow of Yiddish parable.)

The Broder singers got their name because the first well-known entertainer of this type came from the Galician (eastern Polish) city of Brod or Brody. Brod happened to be a center of *haskole* activity, and as part of the Austro-Hungarian empire, it was relatively free for Jews. The widening influence of *haskole* brought to cafés growing numbers of Jewish patrons, ready to ignore rabbinic disapproval. Brod's material prosperity also contributed to the devel-opment of café entertainment. Brod, like other major towns, was on the expanding trade routes to Western Europe. The industrial revolution, moving eastward, was building up an Eastern European middle class, and railroads brought audiences to cities. Merchants, including Jews, traveled, saw shows, and demanded more.

The first Broder singer was named Ber Margoles, but he called himself Berl Broder, which means simply "Little Ber from Brod." He began his career as a boy working in a shop making boar bristle brushes. While his hands kept moving, he entertained the other boys with a flow of songs and quips. When he got a job as a buyer for an export firm, he traveled farther and farther from home. He stayed at inns, where he developed a reputation for the songs and monologues he improvised in good fellowship over glasses of wine. In a few years, the name Berl Broder became as generic as "Tex" for a singer of cowboy songs. By the 1860s many "Berl Broders" were singing and acting in Poland, Russia, and especially Rumania, where the wine was most plentiful.

Another early Broder singer, Yakovka Dubinsky, started as a baker's apprentice. He saw cabarets for the first time when he was doing his army service in Vienna. He was delighted that such nice things existed in the world and reasoned that Jews should have this too. Still other Broder singers began as professional entertainers in languages other than Yiddish. Probably, though, most originated as *badkhonim,* and many continued to go back and forth between the two professions.

Although some of the Broder singers' songs were simply lyrical tunes, most were more elaborate: extended, emotional, dramatic poems set to music. Broder singers generally based their routines on recognizable character types (possibly comic figures from a Purim play), and then amplified these types into rudimentary playlets. They often began, "I am a poor shepherd" or "poor water-carrier" or "poor woodcutter," and then told the life story and feelings of such a prototypical laborer, using appropriate actions and gestures.

Yakovka specialized in children's roles. As quite an old man, he was still playing a schoolboy, stuttering badly as he explains to his rabbi why he played hooky. Most Broder singers' numbers were more serious, however, as "Night Watchman" by the original Berl Broder:

> I'm a poor night watchman.
> I lie awake and think all night
> That my lot is harder than any other man's.
> For me there is no night.
> Every other creature God created
> Rests with his kind in their nest.
> But I lie on the cold ground, ill-fated,
> For God sends me no rest. . . .
>
> I carry loads all day, for I'm a porter.
> All night I watch in the streets.

I carry heavy bricks. I carry mortar.
Whose body aches as mine does, and whose feet?
I would thank my God and bless Him
If I could only rest and ease my weary bones,
But whenever someone comes, before I pass him,
I must not fail to call out, "Halt, who goes?"

Sleep, sweet Sleep, you dearest brother,
You strengthen people with your art.
If I could rest my limbs like any other,
I'd have fresh energy to start
Another night of wakefulness and cold.
You'd give me life. But I must go again
To watch the streets. For bread my life is sold.
Again you've flown away, Sleep, from my pain.

Not only were the Broder singers' roots in the popular art of the jester; their sympathies, too, were with the people. Sometimes they satirized rich Jews who exploited poor Jews, or ignorant *hasidic* rabbis who exploited superstitious believers. Most often the subjects of their monologues were poor laborers, as in "Night Watchman," or the porter who speaks in this song-recitation by Velvl Zbarzher, a particularly gifted poet whose personal life echoed François Villon's. As the song begins, a poor porter laments that he must carry a heavy load, though he is sick and weak and, moreover, bound hand and foot. . . .

But everyone who sees him answers, "Hey,
You must be crazy, or your senses are astray.
You aren't bound, I see no ropes or chain,
And where's the heavy load, as you complain?"

"Listen then," he says, "I'll make it clear.
On my poor back I carry sixty years.
I carry loneliness and want upon my head,
And my great worry—how to make my bread.

"In my poor heart I carry child and wife.
I also bear a sad old wound of love.
I am old, but love still pains my life.
What more, my friends, can one poor man complain of?

"In my throat I carry heavy laws,
The laws of kings—ah! they are heavy too.
A heavy lock upon my mouth weighs down my jaws.
I hear but dare not speak; no word bursts through."

Then at last a merciful passer-by comforts him:

"Come with me and you'll forget your woes.
You'll rest with me, my friend, for I am Death."

Some Broder singers stood at a lectern in a frock coat, a carafe of wine ready to hand, and sang, but others acted out their compositions, wearing rudimentary costumes, wigs, and make-up. Thus Yakovka, as one of the pioneers of the form, wore a goatskin and smeared his face with soot. At the other extreme, later performers collected small troupes to join in choruses and sing individual roles. One popular number, for example, was called "The Thief." It began with a *hasid* hiding some money in his room, going to bed—which called for real stage action—and falling asleep. In comes a thief and steals the money. There's a big fracas and the thief gets caught. Someone asks him why he did it, how he became a thief, and in answer he sings a long song about his life.

Thus the Broder singers arrived at drama. At the same time, with the encouragement of the circumstances of Eastern European Jewish life, they were establishing the secular performer as a professional in the Yiddish community. They were training themselves as performers, and also training a wide audience, who were ready for more elaborate theater when it appeared in 1876.

In the preceding half century, the Yiddish community had experienced a sort of renaissance. The culture had added to its Purim plays a group of academic plays by amateur playwrights of a relatively high social class. It had developed its vernacular as a modern literary language. It had developed a sense of itself as a nation, stable and economically solid enough to support theater. It had developed a group of professional Broder singers: proto-actors, performing in proto-theaters, creating a knowledgeable audience.

By coincidence, Etinger's patient Gotlober, who read *Serkele* on his doctor's prescription, taught music to the boy who would in 1876 write, direct, and produce the first professional Yiddish play. By another coincidence, while this young Avrom Goldfadn was a student of Gotlober's, he was also getting his first taste of theater—playing the title role in a student production of *Serkele*. Within a decade of 1876, Gotlober could write proudly to a friend: "Little Avrom Goldfadn . . . studied with me in my house privately as well as in school. He paid special attention to the way I wrote in Yiddish; that was his passion. Now I don't have to tell you, you know yourself who he is and what he has written since then."

3 AVROM GOLDFADN

AVROM (OR ABRAHAM) GOLDFADN (OR GOLDENFUDIM) was the father of Yiddish theater. He took that title himself, and no one has ever disputed it. Beginning in 1876, it was he who wrote the first professional plays, music and all, and he who produced them. It was under his guidance, in his own troupes, that the Yiddish theater began to take shape. When he was old and out of style, when Yiddish theater was developing along lines he could not approve, when the actors he'd trained wouldn't give him a job, Goldfadn wrote that his child had grown away from the loyalties of its youth and become a stranger, a *goy* (gentile). But that wasn't altogether true. Yiddish theater maintained permanently very many of the characteristics of its youth. It also kept a close resemblance to its father, the man himself, Avrom Goldfadn.

Goldfadn combined in his own personality and career many of the elements that had come together to produce Yiddish theater. He was a folk singer and folk poet, product of the popular Yiddish cultural tradition of the *shtetlekh* (townlets) of the Eastern European countryside. He was a Russian *maskil*, heir to modern European secular enlightenment. Furthermore, by nature he was a trouper, an artist, a dreamer, an intellectual, a hustler, a scrapper, a con man, a romantic, a dandy, an optimist, and a one-man band—and his child was a chip off the old block.

Goldfadn circled his destiny for years before 1876, when he finally committed himself to Yiddish theater. By then he'd developed a reputation as poet and songwriter; before he was out of school, in fact, he had published two volumes of lyrics, and his compositions were in the repertories of many of the Broder singers. In one of his volumes of lyrics, called *Di Yidene (The Jewess)*, there were even two little plays or skits that probably were performed by one of the wandering companies of cabaret bards. But all these activities did not seem to him to be the real business of his life.

At the "real business of life" he seemed to be a flop. He tried teaching school for a while, but couldn't earn enough to eat. He opened a ladies' hat business in Odessa, but went bankrupt and had to leave Russia to escape his debts. In Vienna he tried medical school, without success. Then he edited several Yiddish journals, including a humorous one in partnership with Joel Linetski, the *haskole* writer, by then well known, who had been a schoolmate of Goldfadn's. Though he enjoyed the work, the newspapers always collapsed. In 1876, at the age of thirty-six, Goldfadn went to Jassy, Rumania, because a friend had advised him to try to start a local Yiddish newspaper there.

Like Brod, Jassy had been profiting from trade routes to the west. In 1876 there was a particularly large number of successful traders there because in anticipation of the Russo-Turkish War, a major Russian army supply head-quarters was located in the area, offering a chance to get rich quick on military contracts. So it seemed to Goldfadn that here was a likely public for a Yiddish newspaper. It had not occurred to him, because it had not occurred to anybody anywhere yet, that here was a likely public for a Yiddish theater.

The story of how Goldfadn actually came to found a Yiddish theater in Jassy in 1876 has several versions. In fact, from this step on, every incident in the history of Yiddish theater has several versions, all told in later memoirs and reminiscences by eyewitnesses or participants, and all contradicting one another violently. Some stories report small-time professional Yiddish theater companies putting on plays in cafés just before Goldfadn began, and Cesar (or Betsalel) Grinberg produced *Yoysef mit di Brider (Joseph and His Brothers)* with a large chorus and ballet in Constantinople a year before Goldfadn arrived in Jassy. Generally it seems best to thread a historical path through the various assertions and anecdotes, trying to include the ones that are most often quoted with the ones that are most colorful. For Goldfadn's professional debut, it's worth accepting at least three different stories.

In his autobiography, Goldfadn records that he went one evening soon after his arrival in Jassy to a wine garden, Shimen Mark's Pomul Verde—Green Tree. He went especially to hear his songs sung by a very successful Broder singer named Israel Grodner. The thought occurred to him that the material would be much more interesting if it was integrated into a play, as he had seen in non-Yiddish plays in Western Europe, Rumania, and Russia. He sent for Grodner and they were off.

The friend who'd brought Goldfadn to Jassy tells it differently. Goldfadn was staying at his house, having just arrived in Jassy, and one day, all dressed up, walking stick in hand, he was on his way out to start making contacts for

Avrom Goldfadn (1840–1908),
the father of professional Yiddish
theater.

the newspaper when the friend's wife blurted out, "What do you need a
newspaper for? There's already a Yiddish newspaper in Rumania, and the
editor starves to death seven times a day. If you start another paper, you'll both
starve together. Listen to me: Jews need a theater—that's what you should do.
Your sketch in *The Jewess* was like a play. Put it on, so we'll have a Yiddish
theater, a theater like other people have, not what Grodner does."

Goldfadn, so the story goes, took off his top hat, took off his white gloves,
took off his frock coat, and said, "Your wife has given me an idea. We're going
to be shoveling in the gold coins." He sent for Grodner, who he knew was
playing in town, and very soon thereafter he was writing away at a Yiddish
play.

Grodner, naturally, has his own story. For years Rumanian actors, including Jews who played in Rumanian theater, had been coming to see his cabaret
act. After the show they would kiss him and beg him to use his talent by acting
real theater, proper dramatic theater. But he always answered that he had no
plays to act in.

Israel Grodner was an enterprising young man. He had begun his working
life as a cigarette-maker, which may be how he got the nickname of Yisrolik
the Cig, and from that quite ordinary origin he had worked his way up until
he eventually became one of Europe's best-known Broder singers. He had very
little education, but a great deal of natural talent for singing and mimicry. He
was also a clever businessman. Ignoring the small towns, he used to come into
a city, hire the largest playing area available, build a raised platform for a stage,
and set up numbered benches. He posted printed announcements that the
famous Grodner would perform the best songs of the beloved folk poets

Zbarzher, Zunser (themselves both Broder singers), Linetski, and Goldfadn. And he made a point of singing funny numbers instead of the serious, even lugubrious ones that Broder singers often favored. So he certainly had the practical experience and the energy necessary to develop something new.

When Grodner heard Goldfadn was in town, he was of course interested to meet the man whose songs he sang. He proposed to Goldfadn, who he heard was broke, that if the famous poet would participate in the show, they would attract a big crowd. They could charge more and then split the profits. From this meeting between the poet and the Broder singer, Yiddish drama followed.

What everybody's story does agree on is that Goldfadn himself appeared that same week at Shimen Mark's Green Tree café and was a terrible flop. Dressed in his frock coat, white gloves, and top hat, he stood up in front of the crowd of working people out to drink wine and have a good time. He began to read a poem about the Jewish soul through the ages. Dead silence. Believing, as he himself ruefully admitted later, that they were simply too overwhelmed to applaud, he gave an encore: more silence. He gave another: people started to whistle and boo, and some even started toward him, apparently to beat him up. After all, they had paid extra because of him and they were being cheated. He had to be bundled home in a carriage, out of harm's way.

Gordner saved the day by jumping up onstage in such haste that his false beard hung half off. He scolded the audience for their ignorance and bad manners; they didn't care. He placated them at last with funny stories and songs, including Goldfadn's own "The Merry Hasid." It was an object lesson for Goldfadn, who kept his public's tastes in mind ever after.

Despite this failure, Goldfadn was stage-struck. He saw that he was no actor, but the very next day he started writing Yiddish plays. And for the rest of his life he devoted himself to writing and producing. He created a whole theater. He conceived, wrote, directed, produced, publicized, promoted, and painted scenery. In the process, he shaped the repertory, acting style, and even the theatrical life style that were to characterize Yiddish theater from then on and in all parts of the world.

Goldfadn's work reflects the crucial last quarter of the nineteenth century, when the Yiddish community was breaking with tradition but still dependent on it for nourishment. This was a period of transition between folk culture and the modern world, between folk and modern art.

Yiddish folk art was essential to Goldfadn's career. The jesters were an early influence on him. In fact, his father's nickname for him when he was a boy, in the 1850s, was "Avromele *badkhen*" ("Little Abie the jester") because he so enjoyed listening to *badkhonim*. He imitated them by playing with words and making rhymes. Another early influence were the Broder singers; it is probable that one of the watchmakers in Goldfadn's father's shop was a part-time Broder singer. The boy began to write tunes and lyrics in the popular mode, and soon his songs became familiar to the working people around his home town of Alt-Konstantin in Russia.

Actually, Goldfadn was brought up in a *haskole* household. His home was middle class, and his father a committed member of the Enlightenment movement that was steadily widening its influence among Russian Jews. From his youth Goldfadn was aware of such manifestations of *haskole* as the plays being translated into Yiddish and Hebrew and the amateur plays being written in those languages. He was acquainted with Western history and literature, and he shared the *haskole* conviction that Yiddish culture had to develop its own secular aesthetic.

In the 1860s Goldfadn went to the Zhitomir Rabbinical Academy. This was one of the crown schools established in the hopes of training Westernized Jewish leaders who would lead their people toward assimilation. The Zhitomir Academy was especially known for its lively intellectual life. One of Goldfadn's teachers was Avrom-Ber Gotlober, the passionate *maskil* and author of *The Bridal Canopy; or, Two Weddings in One Night.* Gotlober reinforced Goldfadn's enlightened convictions and especially his instinct for Yiddish as a literary language—just as rich as Hebrew and more suited to the portrayal of Jewish life. Gotlober and Goldfadn also shared a love for popular folk tunes. The man and the boy used to ramble the countryside together, collecting these tunes and singing them for fun.

By coincidence, at the Zhitomir Academy some ten years before Goldfadn's time, two schoolboys had composed and presented several musical comedies in Russian and Yiddish for the benefit of soldiers wounded at Sebastopol. They had been a great success among Jewish merchants and Russian soldiers garrisoned in town. Everyone at the academy remembered these productions, or had heard about them, and many were intrigued by the idea of shows in Yiddish.

Then in 1862, a new headmaster arrived, a scholar named Slonimsky. His wife was an energetic, sophisticated lady, fresh from big-city *haskole* social life. She brought with her a manuscript copy of Shloyme Etinger's play *Serkele.* Reading the play aloud in the familiar living-room fashion of the *maskilim,* which had become so widespread a custom that publishers were printing and selling plays in Yiddish for reading, was not enough for Madame Slonimsky. She felt bored in provincial little Zhitomir and wanted to make a splash, so she directed a "real" production of the play, with student actors. Young Goldfadn played the title role. He was also stage manager, property man, and improviser of scenery and costumes. This was his first theatrical experience, and it was a rare one for Yiddish boys in those days.

At that time, Jews, especially middle-class Jews like Goldfadn, were expanding their intellectual horizons as a result of the permissive policies of Czar Alexander II, absolute ruler not only of Russia but also of areas that are now Poland, Lithuania, and other Eastern European countries. Crown schools like the one at Zhitomir were part of a larger policy of access for Jews to a greater number of schools and universities. Goldfadn's stint at medical school in Vienna exemplified greater freedom to study and travel. His correspondence with Sholom Aleichem, Peretz, and Linetski exemplified the growing brotherhood of secular Yiddish writers. His association with a number of Yiddish newspapers and journals exemplified the increased freedom to set up printing presses.

As intellectual possibilities widened, traditional Yiddish-speaking society was breaking up, changing, becoming dislocated. Goldfadn was of the generation that saw places and things their parents had not dreamed of and were buried in cemeteries far from home.

Goldfadn's plays tell us a lot about his times. They are not great or profound literature; Goldfadn rarely claimed they were. But the best of them are touching, stirring, lyrical, comical. They tap the communal sources of Purim play, folk song, and poem, and they channel that energy into a more complex form. Unlike most of the Yiddish dramatists who rapidly appeared to compete with him, Goldfadn remained true to his source. Thus many of his plays have a freshness, energy, and theatricality which time has not diminished and which accounts for their frequent and successful revivals to this day.

The early plays Goldfadn devised in Jassy were hardly what we consider scripts. He handed plot scenarios to Grodner and Grodner's boy helper. The little company, which Goldfadn later described as an actor and a half, operated like the Italian commedia dell'arte, with which Yiddish folk theater had so many original similarities. Goldfadn made up the plot, wrote the songs, and explained to the actors the characters they were to play. Then the two actors, like *badkhonim*, had to improvise their own words and actions.

One of the first such plays, which he built around a song he had already composed, was a comedy about a drunken *hasid*, that favorite target of *maskilim* and Broder singers. A *hasid* (played by Israel Grodner) and his wife (the boy helper, Sakher Goldstein) quarrel, sing, quarrel some more. In the second act the *hasid* is tricked by a boy (also Goldstein) who pretends to be a girl and makes a fool of him. Goldfadn later wrote he'd forgotten the title of the piece and that it wasn't even a play, but rather "a—I myself don't know what to call it—a mess, a kind of mix-up, an absurdity." All the same, the audience was astounded and delighted, evidently not so much by the play's merits as by the fact that it was identifiably a real play, not a Purim play or just a skit, it had more than one song integrated into the action—and all in Yiddish. They loved the novelty and yelled for more. The author got busy giving them what they wanted.

Goldfadn was showman enough to catch on to what his audience would respond to. From Jassy he and his two actors went to Botosani, Rumania, but there they couldn't perform because the Russo-Turkish War had just broken out and officers were shanghaiing likely recruits off the streets. For a few weeks neither audiences nor performers dared to show themselves in public. But while the three were holed up in the attic of the café where they were to perform, Goldfadn prepared a new comedy about the blundering of some Jewish draftees who couldn't adjust to army life. This was a standard subject for Broder singer monologues. As soon as the coast was clear they began to perform it downstairs in the café, and it was a great success. (The war turned out to be lucky for Goldfadn since it brought a potential audience of prosperous traders to Rumanian cities.)

When Goldfadn first began to write out his plays in neat Yiddish script in notebooks, they were of little literary value. Yitskhok Leyb Peretz was later to reproach him: "If I had had your talent, I would have constructed my dramas and comedies around much more significant and revealing aspects of Jewish life." But Goldfadn answered all such charges in his autobiography and in various articles, claiming with some justice that his audience, at least in the early years, could not have absorbed any more sophisticated material than he gave them: a song, a slapstick, a quarrel, a kiss, a jig. When he tried to offer them higher drama they were resentful, felt cheated, didn't understand; they demanded a good laugh over a glass of wine to help forget their troubles. It was no use giving a child a marble statuette, he pointed out, when the child is crying for a crudely painted wooden doll. If fate had made him begin the Yiddish theater for Rumanian laborers and peasants rather than among the *maskilim* of Warsaw or Odessa, then—he explained—his job was to begin at his audience's level and elevate it.

In the *haskole* tradition, Goldfadn justified his plays as didactic instruments, however popular and even crude their form. He was gradually educating his Jews both to the art of drama and to enlightened ideas. His established role as a poet of the people and his emerging role as a showman were both informed by his *haskole* sense of social responsibility. He later described himself as reflecting: "Since I have a stage at my disposal, let it be a school for you. You who had no chance to study during your youth, come to me to see the faithful pictures I will draw you of life . . . as in a mirror . . . you will take a lesson from it and improve by yourselves the errors which you make in family life, and among Jews, and between Jews and their Christian neighbors.

Frontispiece engravings from
Avrom Goldfadn's early plays:
*The Grandmother and the
Granddaughter; or, Basye the Do-
Gooder (left)* and *The Fanatic; or,
The Two Kuni-Lemls.* In the first
play the grandmother has arranged a match into a rabbinical
family, but the granddaughter
loves a *maskil.* In *The Fanatic*
one Kuni-Leml is a genuine *yeshive* boy and a genuine fool; the
other is an imposter.

While you are having your good laugh and are being entertained by my funny jokes, at that very moment my heart is weeping, looking at you."

When a play finished, Goldfadn often came out himself, formally dressed, to explain the play to the audience. After The Green Tree episode he knew better than to bore them, especially since their pleasure was now his livelihood, but he read them a poem or two of his own or made a speech. He was a combination teacher, elocutionist, and barker. The tradition of curtain speeches was just one of his legacies to Yiddish theater.

In his earlier plays Goldfadn concentrated on the standard *haskole* targets of ignorance and superstition, especially among *hasidim. The Grandmother and the Granddaughter; or, Basye the Do-Gooder* has a girl elope with a young *maskil* when her grandmother tries to force her into an unhappy match for the sake of prestigious family connection with a rabbi. The grandmother, Basye, is the major character. In the end, she is left all alone and sick. A voice comes to her, promising that she will be granted a vision of the girl and her new husband, happily together, just before she dies. She has the vision—a tableau wreathed in eerie green lights—and dies repentant.

The play does not make its point subtly; nor is it subtle in style. Goldfadn still had only two actors, with a few extras as helpers and chorus, so Grodner as the grandmother naturally had many long monologues. Motivations are obvious and uncomplicated and so are the conflicts and the suspense. Still, the play's movement is brisk and unself-conscious. The two women sing solos and duets, including a musical argument which is particularly well integrated. The play made Goldfadn's point so that anyone could understand it and enjoy it, even sitting over a glass of wine.

In 1877, within a year of his debut, Goldfadn was already writing out plays of some substance, and by 1880 he had written *Shmendrik* and *The Fanatic; or, The Two Kuni-Lemls.* Similar in message and plot to Gotlober's *The Bridal Canopy,* these plays concentrated on the battle against traditional abuses, especially matches forced on young people by *hasidic* families. Their message found an enthusiastic audience. But the real reason why both were instantly favorites, and have continued to be revived ever since, is simply that they're so funny.

Shmendrik, the protagonist of the first play, is a *yeshive* student and an ass, but an ass of such a distinctive type that *shmendrik* entered the Yiddish vocabulary as a humorously contemptuous description. He is deeply stupid, but with flashes of cross-eyed, almost drunken, shrewdness. He is rude and suspicious, lazy, and intent on his infantile pleasures, especially honey cake. Jerry Lewis, whining and mugging and walking on his ankles, is a Shmendrik type. But Shmendrik has a certain charm and a mother who thinks he's a genius; she only worries that he may strain himself by overwork. In the end, the girl to whom he's betrothed manages to evade the marriage by a trick. She marries her sweetheart, leaving Shmendrik to a suitably foolish bride.

In *The Fanatic* Kuni-Leml horrifies the girl who thinks she'll be forced to marry him. He is half-blind, with a crooked leg, a limp, and a dreadful stammer, and he's hardly brighter than Shmendrik. He is the walking punch line to every joke about a matchmaker's prize merchandise. Like Shmendrik's, his name entered the Yiddish language to signify a particular kind of shambling idiot. *The Fanatic* naturally turns out well by a trick: the bride's true sweetheart impersonates Kuni-Leml for the wedding. And when the real Kuni-Leml turns up for the ceremony and confronts the impostor, he becomes terribly confused. Seeing the other's (phony) eye, leg, and stammer, he ends up accepting the impostor as the real Kuni-Leml and tries to figure out who, in that case, he himself can be.

The mode is slapstick, with songs thrown in. Kuni-Leml insists that he's not a cripple and to prove it runs across the stage into a furious pratfall. Insisting he doesn't stammer, he gets himself tongue-tied into paralysis; insisting he's got perfect vision, he triumphantly identifies his father as a ceremonial banner and the banner as his father. And he has an indignant alibi for every defeat. Nobody could call this intellectual entertainment, nor is it sensitive to character. But from a stage or a cabaret floor, it keeps you laughing.

Another perennial favorite from this early period is an operetta called *Koldunye; or, The Witch*. Goldfadn was aiming at local superstitions, belief in witchcraft being especially strong in Rumania, among Jewish and non-Jewish peasants alike. The play is a sort of fairy tale fable about Mirele, whose wicked stepmother enlists the help of a woman reputed to be a witch to frighten the girl into running away from home. But a merry wandering peddler named Hotsmakh foils the plan. Hotsmakh has his peddler's foibles, but he is a particularly lively and winning character.

By now Goldfadn was writing on a larger scale. In the second act, for example, we see a whole lively East European market day. A butcher sings about his wares. A woman selling hotcakes has a solo about her cakes and the hard life of a market woman. Buyers sing, exclaim, dance. Hotsmakh makes his first appearance in the middle of this bustle, with an amusing patter routine full of sales tricks. And then at last comes the innocent young Mirele. The audience knows that the stepmother herself slipped away the purse with which the poor girl was to do the family shopping, so that she will think it's lost and be too frightened to go home. Helplessly we watch her discover that her pocket is empty; helplessly we see the witch falsely befriend her and then frighten her and lead her weeping and protesting, in song, through the silent crowd. Right wins out in the end, in the person of Hotsmakh, but the final chorus says that there are indeed bad people in the world and they deserve their punishment.

It is true that Goldfadn was accomplishing what he had intended—weaning simple people out of cultural isolation into the non-Jewish world. Ironically, however, he was in a way accomplishing the opposite as well. For his songs, for characters like Shmendrik, Basye, and Hotsmakh, and for overall atmosphere, he drew his deepest strength from an altogether parochial folk atmosphere. He was actually entering and enriching popular tradition while he thought he was guiding his audience away from it. That paradox was to pursue him throughout his career.

During his first few years as a dramatist, Goldfadn continued to write plays aimed at enlightening Jewish behavior. These he interspersed with musical skits and pieces of all kinds that he made up in a hurry. Some plays he adapted crudely from popular French and German plays (his wife, Paulina, had a ladylike education) and some he adapted from current Rumanian hits. He had to scramble to keep attracting audiences with novelties. He once dashed off a piece about a flood to perform in a town that had just suffered one. Mean-

Scene from Goldfadn's *Koldunye; or, The Witch*, as presented in New York in 1925 by the Yiddish Art Theater. Maurice Schwartz, playing Bobe Yakhne the witch (a role traditionally played by a man), stands behind Anna Teitlebaum as the innocent Mirele; Muni Weisenfreund (later known as Paul Muni), as the peddler Hotsmakh, sits third from left.

while his output was developing from scenarios and skits into real musical plays.

The institution of Yiddish theater was growing rapidly. As Jews became more worldly, the theater's public expanded. The Russo-Turkish War brought to Rumania sophisticated Russian Jews. They had seen good non-Yiddish theater in Russia, where drama was more highly developed than in Rumania, and they could afford to patronize the theater. Goldfadn's company increased. He recruited new actors. In fact, most of the actors who were to become famous in the first half century of Yiddish theater had their first jobs with him, including Jacob P. Adler, Sigmund Mogulesko, David Kessler, and Keni Liptzin.

Goldfadn's actors came from varied backgrounds. Jacob P. Adler was a young businessman in Odessa. He hung around the Russian theater because there was no Yiddish theater to hang around. Goldfadn arrived in Odessa on tour and gave him a bit part. Within twenty years Adler was considered the Yiddish stage's greatest tragic star. Sigmund Mogulesko was a seventeen-year-old *meshoyrer* (choir singer) in a Bucharest synagogue when Goldfadn arrived there on tour. *Meshoyrerim* were sophisticated musically, and were notorious for being freethinking and irreverent. As soon as Goldfadn arrived in town he heard about the young cutup who was the life of local parties, imitating scenes from Rumanian comedies and mimicking the dignified cantor he sang for. Within a year Mogulesko had become the comic genius of his generation.

As might be expected, a number of Goldfadn's actors were Broder singers and *badkhonim*. He recruited a number of his actors from the ranks of *meshoyrerim* and cantors. Some were cabaret entertainers in Rumanian or Russian or Polish. Some were actors or singers from the non-Yiddish stage. In later years increasing numbers came from Yiddish amateur drama clubs.

Some new Yiddish actors were simply stage-struck youngsters. Maybe they had seen Russian or Polish dramas or operas. Maybe they had never seen anything like a play, except perhaps a *Purimshpil,* until Goldfadn blew into town. And they were dazzled. They were drawn to the makeshift stage; or they hung around the inn where those glamorous and worldly beings the *artistes* were staying. When the troupe moved on, they moved on with it, as chorus members or bit players or errand boys. Often this amounted to running away from home. Some pious families never did come to approve of the theater, and certainly not of the ragtag bunch who had skipped out of town without even paying the hotel bill, and had taken along their son.

Goldfadn got his earliest actors where he could find them. A sizable proportion seem to have been the lowlifes who hung around taverns and happened to be on the spot when the company needed chorus members for a night or two: cardsharps, small-time gamblers and swindlers, even pimps. Some of them stayed in the theater. Others drifted out. Once Goldfadn had the brainstorm of hiring Rumanian soldiers from the local barracks for the chorus of *Recruits*, just because they could provide their own impressive costumes.

At the beginning Grodner acted old women and Goldstein young women. As in Purim plays and various other theaters, including Shakespeare's, the audiences accepted the convention. But Goldfadn soon began to feel badly the lack of an actress, especially in the cabaret atmosphere in which his company most often performed. By 1877 there were several actresses on the Yiddish stage, all claiming to have been the first. The first may actually have been a certain Rosa, who had already sung in Istanbul taverns and thus had no reputation as a nice Jewish girl left to lose. Or it may have been Grodner's wife, since Broder singers' wives did sometimes join the act.

But most likely the very first Yiddish actress was a sixteen-year-old seamstress named Sara Segal, who became stage-struck as soon as Goldfadn and his two actors arrived in Galatz. She had a sweet soprano voice and lively black eyes. They would have been delighted to take her along, but her mother refused, so finally they left town without her. She stayed home and pined. At last her mother told her in exasperation that once she got married, she would be her husband's headache and could do whatever she liked. When the company heard the news, they deliberated. Goldfadn and Grodner were married, young Goldstein was not. Sophie (more elegant than Sara) Goldstein joined the cast at once. Subsequent remarriage to another actor in New York made her name Sophie (sometimes Sophia) Goldstein-Karp; her daughter was a Yiddish actress after her.

Goldfadn ruled the members of his companies with a heavy paternal hand —not only their performances, but their lives. He explained every role to them individually; told them where to stand onstage; planned and executed the fireworks finales he favored. He assigned the roles and planned the tour itineraries. And he demanded respect for his superior education and position. He had a grand manner and a fastidious way of fingering his pointed mustaches. When the company was flush—and often when it wasn't—he fixed himself up an office that was richly furnished, at least by comparison to the actors' crummy digs, and held court there. At the door he liked to station not one servant but two, in livery: one announced visitors and the other ushered them in. The actors spoke to him very politely, though in later years it turned out that they'd resented his authority bitterly all along, and they made him pay.

Goldfadn's plays were suited to the actors who had to perform them, so that his actors to some extent shaped the plays and thus shaped Yiddish theater. At the start, for example, Goldfadn, like Sophocles two thousand years before him, had two actors, plus a chorus. Since only two people could be onstage at a time, he had to plan very carefully how to plot his action and how to double roles. Also, his actors were generally uneducated and many were inexperienced as performers. He couldn't count on much skill from most of them and if he'd given them interesting monologues, he later explained, they themselves would not have understood what they were talking about, or remembered the words. So it is no coincidence that songs and sight gags far outweighed subtle dialogue in his early plays.

Goldfadn was clever at tailoring roles to suit individual actors, just as Shakespeare did at the Globe. For the young cutup Mogulesko he created Shmendrik. For a vivacious soubrette he created the title role in *Brayndele Cossack;* she played it all her life, and when she walked down the street people called to her by that name. For one of his earliest actresses, who was still too scared to open her mouth onstage, he wrote *The Mute Bride* so all she had to do was look pretty. Indeed, Paulina Goldfadn once commented that she thought the main reason actors remained under her husband's overbearing control was his power to give them roles with which they remained identified, vehicles that made them famous. When he couldn't come up with their wages, he promised them immortality.

Goldfadn painted his own scenery at first, with the help of Ber, a benevolent old house-painter with a bushy black beard. Asked to prepare a plain backdrop to represent a room, Ber painted yellow walls and added on his own inspiration a cozy oven with painted green smoke rising from it and looping back down to the floor. Goldfadn didn't want an oven and he certainly didn't want a loop of green smoke, but he didn't like to hurt the old man's feelings, so he explained tactfully that so much smoke inside the room might make the audience cough. But Ber, as kind to Goldfadn's ignorance, he thought, as Goldfadn had been to his, explained very gently that the smoke was only a picture. Goldfadn was stuck with the oven. Eventually the company acquired more elaborate sets, though sometimes they had to be abandoned with the actors' baggage when they crept out of hotel windows without paying the bill.

Their playing conditions oscillated between violent extremes. They played sometimes in the well-equipped opera houses with red plush lobbies which the Russian government helped maintain in many large and even medium-sized towns; at the grand Maryinski in Odessa they could expand with spectacles and an orchestra. Or they played one-night stands in drafty local theaters, where the actresses' shoulders had shivery goose flesh under their flimsy gowns and where the actors elbowed each other to make up at one mirror, by the light of a single bulb suspended from low-hanging water pipes, in a dressing room up three flights of narrow stairs from the stage. Or, more primitive still, they made do with a makeshift platform in the courtyard of a village inn. Seidy Glück, now a character actress in the Bucharest Yiddish State Theater, still remembers that once, not long after the Goldfadn years, her family planned to play in a barn, but the farmer's goat ate their scenery.

The stage effects that Goldfadn used most often were adaptable to all sorts of playing conditions. His final scenes frequently called for eerie green Bengal lights made by burning a benzine-soaked rag. He also liked visions and tableaux, offstage voices, and fireworks for his grand finales.

When Goldfadn's company were a hit in town—when, in the Yiddish idiom, they "wallowed in a *shmaltsgrub* [pit of chicken fat]"—they were everybody's darlings. Men fought to buy them drinks after the show, till dawn. Women made eyes at them from behind window curtains as they swaggered down the street. But when their show didn't catch on, or if they were competing against a company that was more of a novelty, Goldfadn and his actors slept in a hotel garret and went hungry.

Although when Goldfadn started his was the only Yiddish theater company, within a year that was no longer so. New companies proliferated. At first, most of them were made up of actors who had worked with Goldfadn and left him. Grodner quit soon after Mogulesko joined because Mogulesko was stealing his scenes. Grodner founded his own company. When Mogulesko in his turn fought with Goldfadn and quit, he joined up with the group that Grodner had founded. Then Grodner went off, leaving that group to Mogulesko, and started a third company. And the dance was on.

There are many accounts of Yiddish theater companies, all with different dates and different versions of disputes, different facts about who played which play first and where and with how much success. But anybody's account sounds like a square dance. Companies were constantly forming, taking on new members who had maybe never seen a play two weeks before, traveling, breaking up, multiplying like paramecia, reshuffling, so that people who swore enmity over a scene-stealing episode in Babroisk might well find themselves singing a love duet, or quarreling over top billing, or sharing a pitifully small salami, in Poltava (or London, or Buenos Aires) six months later. That was to be the permanent condition of Yiddish theater, and not only in Eastern Europe, but wherever in the world Yiddish-speaking Jews immigrated.

Many companies were organized simply for a single season, or a single tour, or a single performance. Others played for a season or more, but only on weekends. A "season" was generally understood as meaning from the autumn

New Year holidays to after Passover in the spring, but companies kept touring in the summer as well.

Often these were repertory companies, divided into "lines": a prima donna, a soubrette, a lover, a comic, a villain, a villainess (or "intriguer"), an older man and woman for character roles, and one or two more for spares as a plot might require. They had their own prompter, and sometimes the prompter was also the company dramatist, turning out scripts, or plagiarizing them, as best he could. Bigger companies had their own musical director, and anything from a single fiddler to a little orchestra. Sometimes they included a chorus as well, though more often they hired a chorus and extras from outside to fill their needs. Smaller companies might consist of nothing more, all told, than two actors.

Family troupes were very common, as they had been for centuries in all languages, throughout Europe and America. Yiddish actors not only recruited their wives onto the stage when they needed women, but it was also natural for actors and actresses, constantly together and constantly wandering, isolated from normal society, to marry among themselves. So a second generation of Yiddish actors grew up in theater trunks. By the age of five they were old pros at piping a little song and bobbing a little bow. Among the larger and better-known Yiddish theater families in Eastern Europe, the Treittlers, Kompaneyetzes, and Glickmans were active within five years of Goldfadn's debut. Such families might include parents, daughters and sons-in-law, sons and daughters-in-law, and grandchildren. Chances are that such a family could handle a full repertory, from soprano heroine to the man who got hit with a custard pie, plus the cashier and the boy who put up posters on walls all over town.

Often companies, whether they were family or not, were organized cooperatively. The mark system was most common in Goldfadn's day: every actor took a percentage, or a number of marks, out of the week's take. This may sound fair, but it didn't necessarily make everyone happy. Directors, theater landlords, and stagehands took their established payments out of the week's receipts before the division into marks even began. Then, since more important actors got more marks than bit players, a bit player might end his week with empty pockets. And when the company as a whole had done very little business, a mark that week could be almost worthless, so that even the most important actor might not make enough to live on. Another complaint was that most company members didn't actually see the books, so they couldn't verify how much a mark was really worth on any payday.

Another system was based on a manager, who paid wages to all the artists. He might be a businessman or perhaps the landlord of the theater building, a man with no feeling for theater at all, but only an eye for an investment. The management might consist of a partnership between two businessmen, or a businessman and an actor. With increasing frequency the manager, or one of the managers, was the star of the company. He took a cut of the gross and paid marks or a salary to everyone else. This star-manager system came to predominate, especially when America became the most active center for Yiddish theater, since it was the practice that had ruled nineteenth-century American theater.

By the 1880s Goldfadn was famous, both as a poet and as the father of Yiddish theater. But he moved through this widening world, fighting for existence like the rest. He kept touring, every season and sometimes every few days, in Rumania and Poland and Russia. Often he had to go ahead to get money so he could send for his actors. He scrambled for enough customers to pay the hotel bill. He put up posters. He contacted patrons in every little town. He even crushed a rival company that was playing Bucharest when he was: offering the rival leading man a higher salary, he stole him away in the middle of his engagement. At the same time, of course, he kept writing.

In the rough-and-tumble competition for a livelihood, other companies often took advantage of his plays. Actors who'd worked with him simply remembered lines and songs and used them. Sometimes an outsider recorded a Goldfadn play and sold it to a rival. One reason Goldfadn went to Russia in 1878 may be that he thought Russia's copyright law would protect him. It didn't help.

One particularly flagrant case of plagiarism occurred when the actor Leon Blank found that he and Goldfadn were to arrive in a certain town on the same day. Everyone had heard reports that Goldfadn had recently been having huge successes with his Biblical operetta *Akeydas Yitskhok (The Sacrifice of Isaac)*. Blank found someone who had seen the play and remembered it, songs and all. He rehearsed the play with his company, managed to open a day before Goldfadn, and stole Goldfadn's thunder and box office receipts. When Goldfadn, goaded this time beyond patience, took Blank to court, the actor blandly told the judge that the story after all was in the Bible; surely Mr. Goldfadn wouldn't claim to have written the Bible, would he?

In the early 1880s Goldfadn's plays changed. From crude scenarios built around songs, they became more complex, subtle, and dramatic, reflecting the drastic changes that were taking place in the situation of Eastern European Jews—which affected the stability of Goldfadn's troupe too.

The most dramatic change in the Jewish situation occurred in Russia, which included Jews in the Pale and part of Poland. Goldfadn happened to be playing in Odessa in 1881 when Czar Alexander II was assassinated. Under

Alexander III, a reactionary wave swept Russia, affecting Jews very harshly. Pogroms broke out in southern Russia and the Ukraine. New regulations paralyzed Jewish life with legal disabilities. In 1882 the May Laws forced more and more Jews out of the countryside into congested city slums. The quotas of Jews allowed to study were reduced, and Jews were evicted from the practice of their professions. The entire Jewish communities of Moscow, St. Petersburg, and Kharkov were marched in manacles to the railway stations and expelled. By the end of the century, 40 percent of Russian Jewry was totally dependent for survival on charity from other Jews.

Outside Russia, meanwhile, the situation was just as bad. A "cold pogrom" of legal economic persecutions made it doubtful whether Rumanian Jewry would survive. Polish Jews in Galicia were starving. Millions emigrated, most of them to the United States. The Eastern European Jewish community was in fact on its way to extinction.

Eastern European Jews were as distressed psychologically as they were materially. Not only were Jews physically leaving home, either dislocated by authorities or escaping to "Columbus's Nation"; they were also scattering spiritually. The community seemed to be becoming *Scattered and Dispersed* —the title of a play by Sholom Aleichem, which he put together in 1905 from sketches he had been publishing over the previous decade. In the play, a solid bourgeois Russian-Jewish family, with five grown children, disintegrates before the audience's eyes. One child feels himself so much a Russian that he converts to Christianity; one becomes a revolutionary, another a Zionist, another a forthright hedonist. All values and traditions are weakening, even simple respect for parents.

Under these pressures, the Jewish population's mere economic ability to support Yiddish theater became severely limited. Development ceased as Goldfadn's company and all the others had to struggle just to survive.

As the community that produced Yiddish theater and should have been its audience began to break up and emigrate, Goldfadn, like all other Yiddish artists, became a part of the vast swirling movement westward. He, too, had to keep moving to stay afloat, trying to establish companies wherever he found a potential audience. He continued writing plays, recruiting actors, training them, moving on, and starting again. His plays had their premieres wherever he happened to write them. Between 1881 and 1903 he had premieres in Lemberg and Paris, Bucharest and New York.

Yiddish actors became nomads, not just to follow their audiences, but also because they were actually outlaws. The Czar banned Yiddish theater in 1883 as part of his suppression of Yiddish culture. From then on, any Yiddish performances in Russia had to be given surreptitiously, called "German thea-

Stamped permit allowing the actor Edward Margules to perform Yiddish theater in Rumania in 1887.

ter," and camouflaged in *Daytshmerish,* the bastard Yiddish-German. (Playing in *Daytshmerish,* actors pronounced those Yiddish words they could not avoid in such a way as to sound closer to German, substituting "ah" sounds for "aw," and so on.) Companies often stationed a scout at the door to signal when a czarist spy was in the audience. When the scout gave the all-clear, they relaxed back into Yiddish. This trick didn't always work, however. Sometimes a spy got by the lookout, figured out what was going on, and rang down the curtain in midscene. Sometimes the actors slipped into Yiddish by mistake and gave themselves away. Meanwhile, playing in this Pig Latin sort of German-Yiddish gibberish was crippling for both plays and players.

Outside the law, they had to keep getting official permission to perform. Every little Russian town had a petty official who got his chance to feel important whenever a little troupe asked to perform. He might exact pleas, flattery, and bribes before letting them set up in the inn yard, or barn, or opera house. Or he might just refuse. A typical helter-skelter arrangement afflicted an actor named Fishzon, who toured Russia in 1884. He got a permit for his company to perform in Minsk, but when he arrived there the governor was not satisfied, and telegraphed the chief censor of Russia to check the permit,

while Fishzon and his company waited. Then even the affirmation of the chief
censor wasn't enough. The governor demanded verification from the national
minister of the interior—and continued to hold up performances until it
finally arrived.

At Fishzon's next stop, in Rostov, he obtained a permit to perform, but
the local police chief decided to override the permit and forbid the performance anyway, because Jews needed permits to reside in most Russian cities
outside the Pale of Settlement and the actors didn't have a permit to reside
in Rostov. They promised the police chief not to spend the night in Rostov,
but to leave town immediately after the final curtain. It didn't help. If they
weren't residents, they had no right to perform, and they had to move along.

One town had four nights of *Daytshmerish* theater every week as well as
three in Russian, because the woman who owned the theater had a lucky
combination of qualities. She was a convert from Judaism and the mistress of
the chief of police.

Most Yiddish actors moved westward out of Russia, not to return for
almost twenty years. But even in Poland and Rumania they were harassed.
Some Polish towns made do with "railroad station theater"; since stations were
outside local jurisdiction, a company could hop off a train, play in Yiddish for
a quickly collected audience right on the platform, and use the money to take
the next train out of town.

Yet even though Yiddish theater was deviled by its particular problems,
it was part of a larger current in Yiddish literature. Paradoxically, this continued to be a period of flowering for Yiddish literature, not only in Eastern
Europe but wherever emigrants brought it. A generation of writers had been
working in the language, making it into a malleable, conscious, literary vehicle.
Mendele Moykher Sforim, Sholom Aleichem, and Yitzkhok Leyb Peretz were
in their most productive years.

Yiddish writers redefined their responsibilities. It began to seem less useful
to criticize Jewish community behavior, less imperative to try to make Jews
as Western and modern as possible. Jews had been going to the logical extreme
of that position and assimilating, often even to the point of conversion.
(Conversion, moreover, offered material benefits by opening up schools and
jobs.) Now pogroms and oppressive legislation made Jews realize that a Jew
remained only a Jew, and stiffened their pride in reaction.

Nineteenth-century Romantic nationalism took shape in Eastern Europe
as Slavophilism, causing the oppression of resident aliens, including Jews. But
the Jews echoed, as always, the ideological currents of their environment. They
responded to Slavophilism with Yiddishism. True, there was no geographic
territory called Yiddishland, despite the fact that most Yiddish-speaking Jews

did live crowded into the same areas of Russia, Poland, Lithuania, and Rumania. But there was such a thing as secular Yiddishism, and to that concept it was becoming possible to feel patriotism. The Yiddish language itself became a national language, associated with pride and striving.

Just before Yiddish theater was actually outlawed in Russia, Goldfadn had had a cruel reminder of his responsibility to his public. *Shmendrik* had played in Moscow in 1880, with great success. Russians attended as well as Jews, and laughed at the slapstick. Now, in the growing wave of anti-Semitism, Russians began to yell "Shmendrik" after Jews on the street, as a term of ridicule and abuse. Goldfadn was very depressed. And as persecutions mounted, a poem dedicated to him appeared in the St. Petersburg Yiddish newspaper:

> For shame, Abie, to be asleep now
> When your people need you to be awake
> And to fight their misfortunes. . . .
>
> We have enough Shmendriks and Witches,
> Of these we have more than we need. . . .
> The jokes that we like are sharp, sharp and sweet. . . .

But Goldfadn had already begun changing his subjects to give his people what they needed. In *The Capricious Bride; or, Kaptsnzon et Hungerman* (1877), instead of making fun of *hasidic* tradition, he makes fun of the enlightened younger generation who go foolishly overboard. A girl whose head has been turned by romantic novels refuses a sensible match with a widower named Solomon and runs off with a fortune hunter. This Kaptsnzon (literally, Pauperson) woos her cynically with corny poetry and romantic nonsense, pretending that his name is Franz, like the heroes of the novels she loves, because, as he confides to a friend, "It's all the same what they call me, and I'd just as soon be 'Franz' as 'thief.' " She herself does not like to be called plain Hanele, but Carolina. After their marriage he responds brutally, "What 'Franz'? My name is Kaptsnzon. Give me my money." In Goldfadn's earlier plays, the good characters spoke a Germanic Yiddish, in the *haskole* tradition; here such *Daytshmerish* is meant to indicate affectation and dislocation from Jewish roots.

Kaptsnzon's brutality soon breaks Hanele's heart. The last scene takes place by the river. After a brief conversation with the sensible suitor she'd recklessly rejected, she runs off, and we hear a splash and her voice crying, "Adieu, Solomon." A crowd gathers and there are cries, lamps in the dark to search the river, and an anxious and mournful chorus. Solomon reappears in a boat with her corpse in his arms, and as the chorus sings, the boat is illuminated with greenish light.

Now Goldfadn also began to write dramas and operettas based on the Bible, on Jewish history and legends. His audiences were hungry for this sort of play. It was romantic escape at the same time it was a kind of supportive historical affirmation.

Bar Kokhba; or, The Last Days of Jerusalem (1883), for example, is a stirring spectacle about the hero of the last revolt of the Jews against their Roman conquerors, in the year 137. The play as a whole is somber and impressive. Immediately after the opening chorus, the high priest makes a long political speech favoring common-sense obedience to Roman commands, which Bar Kokhba answers with an impassioned call for revolt. The whole play is on such monumental lines that even the love scene between the hero and the priest's daughter Dina has him praising her as a noble flower of her people rather than for her personal charms. In one of the play's most famous episodes, Bar Kokhba tames a lion in the Colosseum and rides on its back. In another, Dina, who has been captured by the Romans as a hostage, addresses the Palestinian rebels from her prison wall. She exhorts them to fight on for independence, throwing herself down to her death at the peak of their excitement so that they will not be tempted to surrender in order to ransom her freedom. There are some lower-keyed, disturbing, subtly erotic scenes with a Palestinian named Pappus, who has turned traitor in order to revenge himself on Dina for her brutal rejection of his love.

In the end the revolt is put down. Goldfadn couldn't change history, but he structured the play in such a way that one of the causes for the Jews' defeat

Scene from Avrom Goldfadn's *Shulamis*, directed by Zygmund Turkow with the VYKT Company at the Nowósci Theater in Warsaw, 1939.

was Bar Kokhba's personal hubris. Early in the play he denounces the Palestinians for their custom of calling themselves the "children" of Israel. It is time for them to be grownups, he says, and to take their fate in their own hands, to fight for independence. But at the end, after some arrogant follies have cost him his victory, he dies in combat, saying that history waits on God's will; without God, no hero can win.

According to one historian, it was Goldfadn's rebel Bar Kokhba who irritated the Czar into finally banning Yiddish theater. According to another, the ban was triggered by the prompter of one little Yiddish company, who, in order to get rid of the competition, accused a rival company of performing a subversive play.

Other Goldfadn plays based on episodes from Jewish tradition include *Doctor Almasado*, about a Jewish physician in fourteenth-century Palermo whose skill and bravery saved his people from exile; *King Ahashuerus*, based on the Purim story; and *The Sacrifice of Isaac*.

The play from this period that is perhaps most often performed is *Shulamis; or, The Daughter of Jerusalem*, a pastorale set in ancient Judea. It's a love story in the tradition of nineteenth-century romantic Hebrew novels, especially Mapu's *Love of Zion*. Absalom rescues Shulamis from a well in the desert. They fall in love and vow to be faithful forever, calling as witnesses to their pledge the well and a wild desert cat; these will avenge any betrayal of their love. Absalom continues on his way to Jerusalem, where he was going on a pilgrimage to the Temple, and there he meets another woman. He forgets poor Shulamis, marries, and has children. But years later his two children die, one drowned in a well and the other killed by a cat. He remembers his pledge and returns to Shulamis, who has been waiting for him all along, fending off suitors by pretending to be mad. Despite its dark notes, the overall atmosphere is lyrical, light, and sweet.

These plays set in ancient Palestine reflect a further Jewish communal impulse of the times. In the 1890s the Zionist movement swelled until it took shape in the First World Zionist Congress in Basel in 1897. Throughout the 1880s and 1890s Theodor Herzl organized meetings and made speeches claiming that there was no use pretending any longer that Jews could survive in other people's countries; they needed a country of their own. With this conclusion Goldfadn increasingly concurred. He became a speaker for Zionism, especially in the late 1890s, when he lived in Paris, and his plays reflected his convictions. Of his specifically Zionist Messianic plays, the most memorable are *The Messianic Age* (1891) and *Ben-Ami; or, Son of My People* (1907). The former is a panorama in time and space of Russian Jewry, from a Ukrainian village to sophisticated Kiev, to New York, to Palestine. The hero of

Ben-Ami, Goldfadn's last play, begins as a European aristocrat, but ends up a happy farmer on Palestinian soil.

By the turn of the century, Goldfadn had created a mass of plays and songs that were the staple repertory of every acting company, every songfest or amateur recitation. Yiddish theater companies were now proliferating across Europe and America, and even in Africa, as part of the mass emigration of Yiddish-speaking Jews. A number of other Yiddish playwrights were writing with great success. But Goldfadn's works had become classics.

The most striking characteristic of Goldfadn's plays as a body is that they are totally theatrical. Built into the texts are plenty of theatrical moments; in fact, American theatrical slang actually uses a Yiddish word—*shtik*—to describe such moments. Many examples come immediately to mind: Shmendrik mugging *(Shmendrik);* Hotsmakh counting fraudulent change so fast and freely that he bewilders his customers *(Koldunye);* Dina outwitting her Roman captor by wheedling his armor and weapons from him and putting them on herself, one item at a time *(Bar Kokhba);* devilish capers and by-play between angels and demons *(The Sacrifice of Isaac).* There are tense dramatic situations: the traitor Pappus spying on Dina as she sleeps in her prison cell *(Bar Kokhba).* There are artful uses of staging: the swelling of market calls into an elaborate symphonic ballet of songs and crowd business, until little Mirele finally enters, innocent of the enemies who the audience knows are lying in wait for her *(Koldunye);* the dancing flirtation between maidens and men which draws Absalom to forget his sweetheart *(Shulamis).*

Goldfadn began as a songwriter and his cabaret predecessors, the Broder singers, were also primarily musicians. Music was an integral element in Goldfadn's theater and was to remain essential in the majority of Yiddish plays. Goldfadn would call a play "a comedy with music" or "a musical melodrama" or "a romantic opera." But what his public expected in every case was music. Goldfadn wrote that in every play he gave them, sometimes against his will, "trios, duets, solos, choruses," and all the actors had to have good voices.

The music was integrated into his plays. Songs had their place in the stories and were themselves dramatic. For example, near the end of *Shulamis,* Absalom is on his way through the desert to find his old love and make amends for having abandoned her. He meets a group of shepherds. Through them he learns that she has gone mad (though the audience knows that she's only faking). Despite his remorse and his impatience to find her the next morning, he must spend one more night in the desert. The shepherds sing a song which is at once pastoral and menacing, in which the constant refrain, disturbingly syncopated, is "sleeps not." Their voices soften and drift off into sleep, the stage grows darker and then lighter, and finally, with a rush, the action sweeps to a confrontation between the lovers—a confrontation that has been brewing since the first act, when they parted.

Similarly, when Dína, Bar Kokhba's sweetheart, spurns Pappus, the traitor sings a song of revenge which incorporates laughing in the chorus and a sort of recitative in the verse; it sounds villainous. The Biblical character Lot appears in *The Sacrifice of Isaac* and sings a song that would be appropriate for a music hall turn. The tune is merry, and the chorus to every verse confesses slyly that though he's really too old to enjoy his daughter's wedding, wine helps to heat his blood and put him in the mood for love. The song suits his obstreperously vulgar personality, as well as the Biblical account of his actions.

Many of Goldfadn's songs keep a sort of open folk-song quality, which echoes his earlier career. Even when they're sung by a full chorus to the elaborate orchestral accompaniments that later arrangers scored, both music and words reinforce the plays' special quality, which is popular, theatrical, unself-consciously Yiddish, with images often unique to Yiddish culture. Here, for instance, are the words of Shulamis as she sits of a lonely evening by the well in the desert outside Bethlehem, waiting for Absalom to return to her as he's promised:

> Sabbath, holy day, and feast day
> I say my prayers myself alone.
> I have my holy ark and there I pray.
> No one prays at it but I alone.
>
> My sad heart is there the lectern.
> None see me turn the scroll about.
> Love is there my light eternal.
> It burns and never will go out.
>
> The cantor am I, and I sing alone.
> My griefs my only choir make.
> We sing sad melodies in perfect tone;
> At happy melodies our voices break.
>
> Hope leads the prayers unending.
> We hear her even when she's still.
> We hear her crying and lamenting,
> And tears beat time. They always will.
>
> Unschooled are women, but we, too, can pray.
> Pain teaches us to read, and sigh,
> Fine commentary on love's yesterday.
> Our gallery is nearer God on high.

Enough of praying and enough lament.
Enough of weeping undisclosed.
My mourner's prayer I have to heaven sent.
God hear it! Synagogue is closed.

*(Shulamis covers her face with her hands and
weeps. She speaks.)*

Oh, there's no worse death, no worse pain
Than to hope, to wait, and to long in vain.

The lyrical melody serves the play as did the tunes of Goldfadn's contemporary
Sir Arthur Sullivan.

Though Goldfadn had since his youth a great gift for creating lilting,
hummable melodies, he could only pick out a tune on a piano with two fingers.
The melodies often came to him in the night, and once he'd been inspired,
he had to wake someone else to transcribe them for him. For this reason, he
preferred to hire actors who could write music. Mogulesko was very useful to
him, for he could arrange a score to suit a full-size orchestra as easily as one
fiddle and an accordion.

Goldfadn's musical sources were often, consciously or unconsciously, other
people's music. He drew from liturgical music, influenced by knowledgeable
cantors who had in their turn enriched their chants with elaborations of more

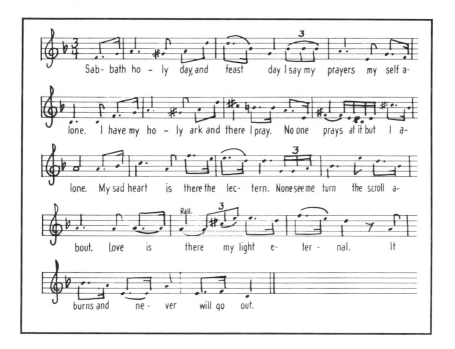

worldly motifs. He drew from the operas and operettas that were the rage in European capitals at the time: Meyerbeer, Halévy, Weber, Bizet, Wagner, Handel, and Mozart. For a while he incorporated the triumphal march from *Aïda* into one of his productions; when a local opera company presented *Aïda*, all the Jews in town believed that Verdi had stolen it from Goldfadn. He also drew from folk-song motifs, which are what his audience really preferred: Yiddish, Rumanian, Russian, Greek, Turkish, Oriental—some twenty-two distinct ethnic strains in all.

But these were only his *sources*, as he himself explained—he may not have been a composer exactly, but he was inarguably a creator. When he used operas, for example, he had to distill the tunes into their simplest form because that's what his public could hum and enjoy. In the process, he made most of them sound Yiddish.

Similarly, he transformed the plots or ideas or characters that he drew from an eclectic range of sources, so that not just the characters' names but the very atmosphere and conceptions became Jewish. For example, the character Shmendrik was evidently suggested to him by a current Rumanian hit, which Mogulesko had seen and imitated. *Recruits* used as its kernel a song about Jewish draftees that was already a staple in the Broder singers' repertories. Goldfadn also drew from the caricatures that were Broder singer material: the matchmaker, the pious ignoramus, the foolish *yeshive* student. The comic plays of the *haskole* influenced him; Shmendrik's fiancée, for example, gets out of the match much as does the hero of Gotlober's *The Bridal Canopy*. Through the *haskole* comedies he drew on Western European domestic comedies and, in some instances, on sentimental tragedies (for the mood of *Kaptsnzon et Hungerman*, for example). The suitors who line up to request Shulamis's hand announce themselves and their claims as characters did in Purim plays. *Shulamis*'s plot is a combination of Talmudic legend and several popular *haskole*-era Hebrew novels. The plot of *The Two Kuni-Lemls* echoes Shakespeare's *Comedy of Errors*, which Shakespeare in turn adapted closely from the Latin of Plautus's *Menaechmi*. *Kaptsnzon et Hungerman*'s plot has some resemblance to Molière's *Les Précieuses ridicules*. *Ben-Ami* uses George Eliot's novel *Daniel Deronda*.

As Goldfadn slowly created this repertory, slowly changing from a young to an elderly man, in character he remained much the same. He posed with expansive dignity for a photographer, wearing a fashionable Brandenburg cap. Some admirers presented him with a handsome silver-knobbed cane, and he loved to stroll past the open-air cafés swinging it and eyeing the pretty women.

He had become a sort of folk hero in both the Old World and the New.

On the Lower East Side of New York, sweatshop workers were humming his tunes to the rhythm of their sewing machines even before *Koldunye; or, The Witch* (the first Yiddish play in America) opened there in 1882. One scene that illustrates his prestige took place near the end of his life, after he had followed his fame to New York. He had an extravagant sweet tooth, and passing a fancy Lower East Side delicatessen, he went in and made up his mind, after thought, to buy a small package of imported figs. That was all he could afford; in fact, it was probably more than he could afford. But when he asked the shopkeeper the price, the man replied calmly, "What do you care?" The shopkeeper picked up a big box and went from shelf to shelf, filling it with confections. He refused to explain himself till the box was full. Then he turned solemnly to Goldfadn. "Mr. Goldfadn," he said, "I have been waiting for you for fifteen years." And he sent his delivery boy home with Goldfadn, to walk behind the great man and carry his box.

But a folk hero can be something of an embarrassment to those who have to deal with him. He was famous, yes. His portrait hung at the Hebrew Actors Union headquarters in New York. His plays were performed in Polish, Russian, and Hungarian translations. His own public, the Jewish masses, loved him. But he was broke.

Goldfadn had no solidly based community to maintain him. If he had been able to found a sort of subsidized Yiddish theater somewhere, things might have been different. As it was, he talks in his autobiography about walking down the street in various cities and hearing the sound of his music coming from the windows of comfortable bourgeois houses. People were gathered around pianos singing his songs while he kept walking, hungry, without a coin in his pocket to buy dinner. He constantly wrote and produced plays. He scrounged unsuccessfully to establish theaters in London and Paris. He wrote columns and articles, including his serialized autobiography, for Yiddish newspapers in New York and elsewhere. He tried to establish a newspaper of his own. He opened, briefly, a drama school. He gave poetry readings and speeches on any subject. He arranged benefit performances—for his own benefit. He and Paulina had to eat, and they loved good food and good wine. But he could never make much money.

And what he made he never held on to. In a letter to Sholom Aleichem, he blamed his wife for their poverty. While he floated on clouds of inspiration, Paulina was supposed to be on the ground looking after the money. But she was as impractical as he was. At a rehearsal in Philadelphia in the late 1880s, the actors Boris and Bessie Thomashefsky, observing his pitifully worn shoes, quietly went out and bought him a new pair.

It was in 1887 that Goldfadn tried his luck for the first time in the growing center for Yiddish theater, New York City. The producers of one of the major Yiddish theaters on the city's Lower East Side had brought him over from Europe as a director. There were several companies of actors in America by that time, and most of them had worked for Goldfadn in Eastern Europe, Paris, or London. When he walked onto the stage of New York's Rumanian Opera House, the actors who were assembled there to rehearse all walked out. They even picketed against Goldfadn outside the theater while he found another company and rehearsed with them. Goldfadn's overbearing ways had set up an almost Oedipal hostility among his spiritual children. Now they were asserting that they were grown up; they even had their own playwrights, and they could get along without him.

He went ahead with the show. But he flopped miserably. He was unprepared for the flash and hustle that the Lower East Side theater had taken on in five short years. His play and the production he offered seemed clumsy and corny to an audience straining every muscle to polish away any traces of the small-town greenhorn. Ironically, he couldn't present any of his better, sure-fire plays precisely because they were so popular; they'd been done again and again. Every passing company that needed an assured box office did them, and for the moment everyone was tired of them. The Rumanian Opera House fired him.

The original Opera House company returned in triumph, while Goldfadn tried to promote theaters in several American cities. At last he fled back to Europe for five years, and made bitter fun of America's "streets paved with gold."

By the time he returned to New York in 1902, it had become the mecca for Yiddish theater. At that time there were two major theater companies on the Lower East Side. One was controlled by Goldfadn's former bit player Jacob P. Adler, who was a star by then. The other was run by another star, Boris Thomashefsky. These two major theaters together gave him a weekly dole of ten dollars out of a sense of filial duty. But most of their productions were by newer, more fashionable writers.

In New York in 1907, Goldfadn completed his last play, the Messianic *Ben-Ami*. Adler bought the rights to the script but then lost interest in it. Goldfadn suffered. Naturally he longed to have the play performed. Besides, he needed the money that a production might bring in. His friends pressed Adler, who finally allowed Goldfadn to read the script to his company. The experience was traumatic. The actors squirmed and snickered through two acts, after which a minor actor took it on himself to tell Goldfadn, publicly, that the play was old-fashioned and dumb, and that Goldfadn was clearly so senile that he himself didn't know what he'd put down on paper. Goldfadn was crushed. In the less than a year till his death he kept begging his wife and friends for reassurance that he was not senile. Meanwhile Thomashefsky had stopped paying his five dollars because Adler had got the rights to *Ben-Ami.*

The very last act of Goldfadn's life was as melodramatic and sentimental a reversal of fortune as any playwright could wish. It even included the standard tearful repentance by ungrateful children around a father's deathbed. Dependent though he was on Adler's weekly five dollars, he begged and nagged to get back the rights to *Ben-Ami* and sold them to Thomashefsky. Thomashefky's cast reading was enthusiastic. Vindication became Goldfadn's obsession. He wanted a wild success for the play, to prove he was not senile, and then he wanted to die. And *Ben-Ami*'s opening night, on Decembe 25,1907, was (according to most reports) a success: applause, curtain speeches, tears and kisses, toasts and flowers. Goldfadn walked home along Second Avenue exhilarated, with an entourage of friends and fans. At his doorstep he paused to arrange a great wreath of flowers around his shoulders and then burst in like a conqueror, calling to his wife, "Paulina, Paulina, they gave me laurel wreaths. I'm not senile, Paulina, I'm not senile"—and then he burst into tears.

The next five nights in a row Goldfadn watched *Ben-Ami* from a box. During the fifth evening he felt sick, and that night he died.

Until then, *Ben-Ami*'s box office business had not been good. Despite the laurel wreaths, Thomashefsky had been strongly considering switching plays. But suddenly now, the entire Lower East Side mourned the death of the "father of Yiddish theater." A funeral procession of some thirty thousand accompanied his bier to Washington Cemetery in Brooklyn, winding out of its way to pass Thomashefky's house so the actor, who was sick, could pay his last respects from his window. Thomashefsky beat his breast publicly in the name of Yiddish theater artists: "If not for our old father Goldfadn, we none of us would have become tragedians or comedians, prima donnas, soubrettes, playwrights. If not for Goldfadn, we'd be plain and simple Jews: cantors, choir singers, folk singers, *badkhonim, goyishe* writers, clothes peddlers, machine sewers, cigarette makers, Purim players, wedding jugglers, clothes pressers and finishers. Goldfadn went out like a light in his dark room while, we, his children, ride in carriages, own our own houses, are hung with diamonds. Union members, club members, pinochle players, decision-makers, managers, sports—we're nice and warm, all of us—but our father was cold."

It made a wonderful curtain, and possibly all of it was true. And *Ben-Ami* played for months to packed houses.

4 "VAGABOND STARS"

WHEN GOLDFADN VISITED LONDON in the 1880s, he found plenty of Odessa *landslayt* (people from the same town or region), who gave parties at which he was guest of honor and who waited for weekend theater performances "as a pious man waits for the Sabbath." London was then the liveliest Yiddish theater city in the world. Actors and audiences stopped there to gather money and energy to travel farther west to the New World; many never did go farther. For a time, until New York's magnetic pull became irresistible, the London Jewish community supported not one but several Yiddish theaters. And so solidly established were both the theater and the community's sense of itself that several plays were written specifically about the London Jewish experience. London had theatrical pubs, owned by a Mr. Goldsmith and a Mr. Hershman, where actors and their *patriótn* (fans) gathered to eat, drink, gossip, and sing. Companies also toured all over England and as far north as Scotland.

In those days, most of the best Yiddish actors in the world played in Whitechapel, London's Jewish section. Notable among them were Goldfadn's early associates: Israel Grodner, the very first; Aba Shengold, a dramatic actor; the comic genius Mogulesko; the dashing Jacob P. Adler; and the tragedienne Keni Liptzin. Tiny Anna Held was in the chorus line and then won speaking parts, including Goldfadn's heroine Shulamis. (Later she became a Ziegfeld Follies beauty, internationally famous for bathing in milk and champagne.)

Another glamorous figure was Fanny Vadi Epstein. Born to paupers in a damp cellar in Warsaw, Fanny was brought to London as a child, where in the 1880s—according to legend—a minor Indian prince swept her from the chorus line to his palace in the East. (Several years later she turned up again on the Yiddish stage, bringing with her trunkfuls of such dazzling gowns that people bought tickets just to see what she'd wear next; her cultivated charm turned the hotel rooms she occupied into salons for the Yiddish intelligentsia. Warmly generous, she lavished gifts on everyone she met, till she died penniless, as she was born, in a cellar in Warsaw.)

Unlike Eastern Europe, London in the 1880s prohibited theatrical productions in wine gardens, taverns, and barns; a theater had to be officially a theater. So Yiddish theater usually did what contemporaneous avant-garde English theater was doing to avoid censorship: it set up nominal private clubs. The clubhouses, so called, were generally the back rooms of bars. Club members might pay a shilling or so a week, and nonmembers could make arrangements at the door. The club's executive committee sat at a center table nearest the little stage, and when they were ready for the curtain to rise, the chairman had only to wave a hand—or a beer glass. Towns like Jassy and Odessa had made the café atmosphere familiar to, even part of, Yiddish popular culture, and the same comfortable ambience settled in in London.

One clubhouse built especially for Yiddish theater was owned by a waddling little butcher named Smitke or Smith. The entrepreneur named his place the Princess Club and put together a fine company. Business was so good that they played regularly six nights a week. The only night off was Friday, and they could have filled the house then too, except that Smitke did not dare desecrate the Sabbath for fear of antagonizing his customers for kosher meat.

However, all this activity quickly peaked, and within a decade declined. London audiences began to assimilate and go to English theater. Moreover, in the year 1887 the London Yiddish theater suffered several crippling misfortunes. Israel Grodner died at the age of forty-six, and there was no actor of comparable stature to take his place. (The pubkeeper Hershman inherited Grodner's walking stick, which was handed down for generations till it was lost in the 1930s.)

Smitke was arrested, though not imprisoned, for holding theatrical performances in a place not licensed as a theater. Then, most seriously, a tragedy occurred at his Princess Club. Evidently a gas lamp went out one night, and in the darkness someone yelled, "Fire." In the panic to get out, seventeen people died. The shadow of the event hung over London's Yiddish theater for a long time, and business suffered.

Above all, actors and audiences kept filtering away to New York. London could not compete; it couldn't even replace the actors who continuously streamed on across the Atlantic. The actors' emigration was accelerated by the Chief Rabbi, Nathan Marcus Adler. Perhaps the actor Adler thought the coincidence of names was comical, but for the rabbi it was purely embarrassing. Yiddish theater was a constant irritation for Dr. Adler. He tried to keep an eye on it. When the actors presented the Biblical story of Hanna and her seven sons, for instance, he protested sacrilege till they substituted a new play entitled *The Spanish Gypsy*. When they blew a *shofar* (ram's horn) onstage as part of the action of Gutskov's *Uriel Acosta,* he personally had a paper *shofar* made for them, to avoid sacrilege. Now, as the actors began to lose their livelihood, he was delighted. He even paid ship fare to New York out of his own pocket for the actor Adler and several others.

By the turn of the century, London was left with only a few Yiddish theaters, primarily touring professional companies and semiprofessional and amateur club performances. Through several quirks of fate, and the constant emigration for America, London was slowly overshadowed by the Lower East Side.

The United States

Between 1881 and 1903, 1,300,000 Yiddish-speaking Jews arrived in the United States, and most of them settled in the port where they landed—New York City. Here, on the Lower East Side, was the new center of Yiddish theater.'

Probably the first Yiddish theater production of any kind in New York was *The Selling of Joseph,* organized by a house-painter one Purim in the 1860s. However, the first professional Yiddish theater production seems to have come in 1882, and to have been organized by a boy who had never seen a show in his life.

Boris Thomashefsky, an unknown thirteen-year-old cigarette-maker recently arrived from Poland, worked in a sweatshop on the Lower East Side. His fellow workers, many of them also recent arrivals, had seen and loved Yiddish theater in Europe. They sang folk songs and show songs, especially Goldfadn's, over the tables of tobacco as they worked, with the foreman and even the boss himself joining in. The workers who had the best voices sang solo, and Thomashefsky was one of these, for he had a beautiful soprano voice, which had already won him a local reputation through singing in synagogue on Sabbath mornings.

Among Thomashefsky's fellow cigarette-makers was a man named Golubok, who kept insisting that he had been a professional extra in the old country and that he had two brothers who were real actors. Everyone assumed he was lying, until one day a poster arrived from his brothers in London, advertising, sure enough, the Famous World-Renowned Golubok Brothers in Goldfadn's

Sheet music for show tunes. "A Little Letter to the Bride" is a sentimental ballad about the partings that were daily tragedies in turn-of-the-century immigrant life. "I'm an Actor" is a comic song; the "actor," who says he began his career as a sewing-machine operator, lists the Goldfadn' and Gordin roles he has played and boasts, further, that enough fruit has been thrown at him for him to open a fruit store.

Koldunye; or, The Witch. Famous or not, they were broke and stranded in London.

Thomashefsky took it upon himself to hustle transatlantic fare for the actor brothers. Golubok's tales and songs, and his own daydreams and talent, had developed in the boy a passion for the Yiddish theater. Using his gift for promotion (for which he was famous for the rest of his life), he began to search for a producer. Frank Wolf, owner of a saloon at the corner of Hester and Essex streets, in the heart of the Lower East Side, seemed ideal. Wolf had capital, and he appreciated Jewish singing, in synagogue and out. He even looked the part of a producer, sporting diamond studs in a colored shirt front. In 1882, on Thomashefsky's earnest advice, Wolf sent steamship tickets to London, to the Golubok company.

Yiddish theater arrived at the Statue of Liberty without fanfare: the Golubok brothers, four other men, and two women, all in rags. Wolf and Thomashefsky, not in the least taken aback, set about doing things in style. They rented (on Wolf's money) Turn Hall, on Fourth Street between Second and Third avenues (the same theater where the Lower East Side Jewish boys Weber and Fields had made their English-language vaudeville debut the year before). They promoted the show—*Koldunye*—and put up posters advertising the company and throwing in for good measure the "World-Famous Singer Boris Thomashefsky." They charged high prices, up to five dollars a seat, but soon sold out. With a twenty-four-man orchestra, a chorus of twenty singers recruited from several synagogues, and the choirmaster of the Thalia (an established German-language theater on the Lower East Side), their success seemed assured. Full-dress outfits were rented for the ushers, and between rehearsals, the Golubok brothers and the young Thomashefsky strolled along the Bowery, tipping their shiny new top hats to the ladies.

But opening night was a cliff-hanger, just like the Broadway melodramas of the period. According to one story, the first villains who threatened our heroes were, ironically, Jewish. There was a community of German Jews who had arrived in New York over a generation earlier and settled soberly down to be good inconspicuous Americans. Thomashefsky later described them as "half *goyim* and whole Jews." His resentment was common but unfair. In 1882 they were manfully doing their best to take responsibility for this sudden flood of exotic primitive Eastern European peasants who claimed to be their brothers. Now they heard that this ragged bunch were literally going to make spectacles of themselves before all New York by putting on a show in the Yiddish *jargón,* which to their ears was an offensive, ludicrous travesty of German. And as if that weren't bad enough, the show was to be about a crafty Jewish fortuneteller, and a Jewish peddler who sings rowdy songs making fun of Jews.

The German Jewish Committee of volunteers in charge of aiding immigrants called the Goluboks and Thomashefsky to their elegant uptown office. The actors were intimidated by its luxury. In fact, they were practically speechless anyway, since they didn't know any English, so the meeting had to stumble along between uptown German and Lower East Side Yiddish. The committee reasoned with the actors, scolded them, advised them to learn honorable trades. They lost their tempers, snapped, "Here no one makes fun of Jews" and "No wonder they drove you people out of Russia." They even threatened to have the whole bunch deported. The actors were scared, but Wolf already knew that "America isn't Minsk." "Pay as much attention to them as to last year's snow," he advised, in the words of the proverb. The show would go on.

On the great night, two hours before the performance was to begin, the streets were so crowded that the police arrived to keep order—or so Thomashefsky later claimed. People milled around, hoping for a way to sneak in or at least to catch a glimpse of an actor or an echo of a chorus. Isolated in the midst of the crowd stood wobbly platforms on which German Jewish Committee members with megaphones explained how shameful the whole scene was and urged everybody to go home. Nobody did.

Inside Turn Hall the noise and excitement were terrific. The overture began. The musicians repeated it, repeated it again. Mrs. Krantsfeld, the prima donna who was to play Mirele, was not in the wings. They knocked on her dressing room door; she wasn't there. While the orchestra kept playing the overture, Wolf and Thomashefsky rushed out the stage door and down the street to her home. There she lay on a sofa, in a kimono, a cold towel on her head. She had a headache. They begged her, they pleaded. It became clear that the committee had bribed her to ruin the show. Frantic, they offered money too. When their offer reached three hundred dollars cash down, plus setting Mr. Krantsfeld up with a soda-water stand on the corner of Division Street and the Bowery, she got up, got dressed, and walked with them to Turn Hall.

But it was too late. The chorus was gone. The orchestra was gone. Most of the audience was gone too, and the ones who were left were brawling and overturning chairs. The actors tried to start the show, but the audience wouldn't settle down. The place was a shambles. The voices of the cast quarreling backstage reached all the way to the lobby. The show was definitely over.

Some versions of the story deny that the committee had bribed the Krantsfelds to sabotage the show. Some even deny that the committee interfered in any way at all. Maybe Mrs. Krantsfeld really was sick. Maybe nobody stormed Turn Hall offering five dollars for a fifty-cent seat in the balcony. In any case,

Leading Yiddish actors in the 1890s, photographed in New York: from left, David Kessler, Krastoshinsky, Rudolph Marks, Sigmund Mogulesko, Sigmund Feinman, Jacob P. Adler.

and without a doubt, Yiddish theater had arrived in America.

Only a few months after the Turn Hall fiasco, Thomashefsky, still a boy soprano, bounced back and reorganized his company. For a while, some of their performances were quite successful, with German Jews and even non-Jews arriving in carriages, formally dressed. A few lean months followed, with the whole company back in the cigarette factory, but after that Thomashefsky and the Goluboks were able to take a lease to play weekends in a theater called the Old Bowery Garden. He added actors to his company and plays to his repertory, including several by a versatile man named Barski, a political activist whose business cards advertised his services as "Tailor, actor and playwright. Author of *The Spanish Inquisition.* Pants altered and pressed."

But in 1883 Thomashefsky was introduced to the world of competition. A whole new company was coming over from Eastern Europe by way of London—real professionals, with reputations that had reached New York ahead of them. In the course of the next three years, while Thomashefsky and his group retreated temporarily to Chicago and Philadelphia, the Lower East Side accumulated Yiddish actors, many of them good and all of them ambitious. Among the first to arrive were Sophie Goldstein, the pretty woman, who only seven years before had been Goldfadn's first Yiddish actress, and her new husband, Max Karp. The playwright-prompter-actor Joseph Lateiner came with them. Soon another group followed: the comedian Sigmund Mogulesko, the dramatic stars Sigmund Feinman and David Kessler, and another playwright-prompter, who called himself "Professor" Moyshe Hurwitz. Jacob P.

Adler and Keni Liptzin arrived on a later ship. Many of them had already worked together in various towns in Europe; in America they immediately began to perform and to compete.

At once theater became an important element of American Yiddish life. It bloomed even though living conditions were physically and psychologically grueling. On the Lower East Side, Jews slaved at piecework in sweatshops and lived in dark, overcrowded tenements. They struggled to adjust to a new society violently different from Eastern Europe, and to a new language.

Nevertheless, though the poverty on the Lower East Side was appalling, for many of the immigrants it was better than what they had known at home. The most exciting promise of New York was the chance to prosper, whereas in Europe there had been no chance at all. For a sewing-machine girl, a theater ticket or two a week might take almost half the week's wages. But if she was very careful, she might manage to buy the tickets and still scrimp out just enough to eat. Here it was possible for poor working people to have bread and theater too.

Psychologically, conditions on the Lower East Side stimulated the need for Yiddish theater to such an extent that to many sewing-machine women and men a ticket seemed almost as much necessity as extravagance. Yiddish theater was a breath of home: the music, the plot situations (especially during the first years), even the actors themselves were all familiar from the old country. It filled the new psychological gap in immigrants' lives: in the confusing shifting scramble for survival in a strange land, it substituted in subtle ways for the older communal institutions that had been the basis for centuries of Eastern European Jewish life. It was a meeting place, an arbiter of fashion, a common passion. It provided, in the form of actors, popular folk heroes. And it represented loyalty to tradition and to the community, a sort of staunch nonassimilation that still did not prevent actual full-speed assimilation—which, in the unfriendly atmosphere of Eastern Europe, had become almost impossible. For some, it took the place of organized religion, by publicly affirming a cultural-ethnic Jewishness that was elastic and didn't require any observance or piety. And it also, in a sense, reinforced organized religion by assuming many of its values.

The material of the plays, too, was comforting for the immigrants. Glorious escapist spectaculars set in a sentimentalized old country gave an evening's relief from homesickness. Other plays validated the special problems of immigrants by acting them out, making them art and convention, and thus practically a ritual. There were plays that helped teach spectators how to deal with the problems of adjustment and family dislocation, that reassured them that these were standard problems, communal problems as it were. The spectators, many of them barely literate, were going to night school at the theater.

For all these reasons people bought tickets and nourished Yiddish theater. And it thrived as well because it was not illegal in America. Artists could settle to work openly. They could use the Yiddish language, even recite Goldfadn soliloquies on the steps of City Hall. They were secure even when they were broke. They could settle in with their audiences and develop together.

And so American Yiddish theater expanded and prospered, beckoning Yiddish actors to America from all parts of the world. Actors could earn more in America. Potential audiences were bigger, and so were potential glories. And as if these lures were not enough, competitive New York Yiddish theater directors constantly scouted Europe for new talent.

For the next half century, New York had two or three (and later as many as twelve) Yiddish theaters actively performing all the time, not only in the Lower East Side, but also in Brooklyn and the Bronx. As these theaters competed to sell tickets, actors switched companies, and companies switched theater buildings, and companies and buildings switched names at such an astounding rate that it's impossible to keep all the stories straight. However, in a roughly chronological order, the theaters that were the most important in those early years were: the Oriental (on the Bowery near Grand Street), the Rumanian Opera House and the National (at Second Avenue and Houston Street), People's (on the Bowery), Pooles (on Eighth Street), the Thalia (on Fourteenth Street), the Windsor (on the Bowery), and the Grand (on Grand Street). Periodically one company or more would collapse, whereupon the losers would go on tour, or a new company would surface in New York, competing hotly for the weekend audience.

The history of Yiddish theater in New York is the story of the crazy competition between companies.

The wars, of course, included the standard arsenal of weapons, wielded with gusto. Directors tried to offer the best show, the most luxurious and convenient building, the handsomest actor, the actress with the sweetest soprano, the comedian with the lewdest wink. Rival directors dazzled the public with gimmicks and spectacles. Thomashefsky later described how it worked in the popular genre of historical operettas about princely heroes:

> If Kessler wore a big hat with a long feather . . . Adler wore a bigger hat with three feathers and a gold scarf. . . . I piled on colored stockings, coats, crowns, swords, shields, bracelets, earrings, turbans. Next to me they looked like common soldiers. . . . If they rode in on a real horse, I had a golden chariot drawn by two horses. If they killed an enemy, I killed an army.

(Yiddish impresarios were not the first to bring real horses onstage; nineteenth-century laboring-class Londoners, too, for example, liked to feel that they were getting a lot of show for their money.)

The dramatist Joseph Lateiner was typical of popular Yiddish theater *artistes* in that he had a gift and even a relish for the tricks of competition, which he had learned in the old country. In Bucharest, he once worked with Grodner and Mogulesko when Goldfadn came to town and offered him a bribe to desert them. Lateiner left his partners without giving them any notice, and on the trunk in which he had kept his scripts he left a *yartsayt* (memorial) candle. A week later, when Grodner and Mogulesko needed a new script, they discovered that the trunk was empty; the candle had been Lateiner's way of signifying the death of their company, doomed without new plays. Now, in New York, Lateiner and the rest used all the tricks they could devise and polished the practice to an art.

Producers, too, were not above creative deceptions, like attaching the title of a hit to a new play of their own. It was in this tradition that in Tel Aviv in 1975—almost a century later—a company advertised a production of *Gelt, Libe, un Shande (Money, Love, and Shame)*. This is the title of quite another play, which scandalized thousands of happy audiences half a century ago. The producer was, perhaps unconsciously, attracting customers with the glamorous associations of the old title. (No author's name appeared on the posters. The director explained to me: "It's an old play by a man named Kenig. He's dead. I prefer"—he winked—"dead authors. They're cheaper.")

Sophie Goldstein-Karp may be said to have died on the battlefield of theater competition and trickery. During a feud with Adler over which of them controlled the Grand Theatre, she found she could entrench herself legally by squatting on the premises. For a few days she worked and ate on the stage, and she slept on it at night. But the trick backfired; it was winter, the building was unheated, and she caught pneumonia and died.

Advertising, too, was full of tricks. Newspaper ads were incessant, and posters and handbills papered tenement walls. Thomashefsky advertised a play called *Rabbi Akiba and His Twenty-Four Thousand Disciples* through posters that urged: "Come and see Rabbi Akiba study Torah with twenty-four thousand disciples." But on opening night Thomashefsky came onstage alone and explained that really there was no room onstage for all those disciples. In fact, such a crowd would be dangerously heavy and might break right through the floorboards. So Akiba would have to study with them offstage, during intermission.

Not only did companies circulate handbills promoting their shows, but they also printed materials accusing other companies of plagiarism and stupidity and lack of taste. Actors insulted their rivals and mimicked their stage mannerisms right onstage, or inserted gross couplets in the middle of an otherwise serious scene. While they did it at one theater, their counterparts were returning the favor right down the street.

Throughout the nineteenth century, hundreds of American road companies were regularly crisscrossing the United States; small towns in Iowa and Oklahoma had their own little opera houses waiting for *East Lynn* or *Uncle Tom's Cabin* or *Hamlet*. And Yiddish actors, familiar with this life style from the old country, adopted the pattern of touring the American "provinces" as a matter of course. They trouped through Chicago, Philadelphia, Detroit, Baltimore, New Haven, Boston, Cleveland, Newark, Albany, Montreal, Atlanta, Toronto, and every other American city with a sizable Jewish population, and they even established stable companies in each of these cities for varying periods.

In Boston there was a company of child actors who put on *Bar Kokhba* and other plays in the 1890s. And in such cities as Chicago, Philadelphia, and Detroit, there were frequently two or more would-be stable companies in competition.

During the summer most Yiddish actors, even those based in New York, either joined touring companies or at least traded cities with other actors so as to bring the local audiences a novelty. They might even go on tour through Europe, staying as long as a year.

Of course, New York was where the glory and the action were, for Yiddish and non-Yiddish theater alike, and actors who were making enough to support themselves sometimes refused to leave it. Mogulesko, for example, stubbornly declined to leave New York for "the provinces" (Chicago), even though that meant a lawsuit by the producers who'd paid his fare across the Atlantic.

Outside New York, finding a workable theater was a hit-or-miss proposition. Sometimes a fancy place was available and the company had money enough to rent it. In Chicago, for example, Thomashefsky played in the lovely Academy of Music, where Edwin Booth himself had appeared not long before. In Baltimore, however, a company rented an elegant house called Concordia Hall and then discovered that they had made a fatal mistake. Concordia Hall belonged to a philanthropic group of German Jews, and when the actors tried to sell their tickets to the Yiddish-speaking immigrants, they were not successful. It turned out that the Germans gave charity to the immigrants. And the immigrants reasoned, naturally, that if they were seen going into the opulent Concordia Hall, they would lose out on charity doles.

Sometimes a troupe had to settle for a dingy room three flights up, off a dirty alleyway and far from the Jewish neighborhood. They might try to create a nice theater by themselves, but this, too, could bring them to grief. Thoma-

Matinee idol Boris Thomashefsky.

shefsky, one season in Chicago, worked desperately with his company to renovate a particularly shoddy hall, and on opening night the freshly varnished benches shone beautifully. At intermission, when people tried to stand up for a stroll, they discovered that the varnish had not yet dried. Thomashefsky was forced to pay for all the skirts and trouser seats that were ripped off. He stayed in town the rest of the season, nevertheless, and his audiences continued to arrive. But they were taking no chances: as they stood in line, they carried under their arms noticeable bundles of newspapers and towels.

Sometimes a troupe was invited to appear at a local synagogue or community center, with the understanding that the play would suit the hosts' convictions. Thomashefsky's company was once playing in a Newark synagogue under this agreement, when his socialist father, Pinchas, made a rousing curtain speech denouncing religious orthodoxy. This infuriated the audience, and the Thomashefskys left Newark in a hurry.

Companies were often entanglements of relatives. In Thomashefsky's troupe, for example, there traveled not only Pinchas but also Thomashefsky's sisters, his brothers-in-law, and later his wife. Between companies, crisscrossing marriages, divorces, and affairs were the norm. Thomashefsky's younger sister Emma married an actor-manager named Finkel. Finkel caught her with another man, also an actor, and shot and crippled her, but their daughter grew up to marry Paul Muni, the son of actors Philip and Sallie Weisenfreund. Jacob P. Adler married Sara Heine-Haimovitch and had an affair with Sophie Goldstein-Karp (both actresses left their actor husbands for him), and they all (and their children as well) continued to play together onstage in scenes of love and hate. To this day, in fact, a large proportion of Yiddish actors are the children and grandchildren, nieces and nephews, spouses and in-laws, of other Yiddish actors.

Landsmanshaftn

Immigrants continued to organize their social life in the manner that was familiar to them from the old country. *Landsmanshaftn* were fraternal orders of *landsmen* or *landslayt* (people who came from the same town or region in the old country), and they were a major unit of organization in the immigrant ghettos of America. *Landsmanshaftn* kept friends together in the enormous frightening world of New York. They provided services such as health care and ceremonial expenses—a wedding dowry, a funeral, a cemetery plot—for their members.

In order to fund themselves, they often gave benefits, and by the early years of this century the majority of week nights in Yiddish theater were sponsored in this fashion. Benefits became such popular occasions, in fact, that a new immigrant looking for people—maybe for his own family, whom he'd lost touch with—might get this advice: "Look in the paper for the next benefit given by your *landslayt*. Go stand outside the theater. If you don't see anyone you know, just start asking people; for sure, somebody there will be able to tell you where they are."

From these benefits came the idea for a promotional stunt of real American brilliance. The season of 1888 was disastrous for the Rumanian Opera House. Some of the actors were actually considering moving back to Europe. Then their company dramatist, "Professor" Moyshe Hurwitz, rescued business with a shrewd idea. He created a new kind of fraternal order, designed to make everyone happy, especially the Rumanian Opera House.

For weeks "Professor" Hurwitz went around the Lower East Side to club meetings, *landsmanshaft* meetings, and lecture halls, collecting subscribers to his new Order of David's Harp. A member of the Order of David's Harp was to get a special type of benefit: two dollars' worth of tickets every month to the Rumanian Opera House. He would also get seven dollars a week sick pay, five hundred dollars dowry on the marriage of every daughter, and five hundred dollars to his widow when he died. For all this he paid only one dollar to enter and then two dollars every month. Hurwitz mixed in with his sales pitch a speech about the Biblical poet-king David. A chorus in white robes accompanied him, singing psalms.

People rushed to sign up. When Hurwitz had nine hundred subscribers he rented Poole's Theater on Eighth Street near Astor Place, which was then one of the largest houses in all New York. He prepared for the gala premiere by writing a new play and organizing a splendid parade.

On August 26, 1888, Hurwitz strode like an Asiatic potentate through the streets of the Lower East Side toward his theater opening. His escort was two girls in white robes. Behind them streamed a procession of thousands of paraders, so densely packed that a man watching from the curb couldn't see through the crowd to the center of the street. The procession winding its way slowly uptown to Astor Place was like the old Purim and Simkhas Tora parades that European Jewish communities had enjoyed centuries earlier. Among the crowd there were trumpets, bands, choral groups, bright-colored flags and banners—especially the ceremonial ones that were always part of Jewish processions and in America often represented political organizations of *landsmanshaftn*. There were men on horseback towering above the marchers. Hurwitz himself rode part of the way, wearing a high hat, a sash across his chest.

The procession went up to the theater, and the lucky ticket-holders for that night went in. "Professor" Hurwitz and his escort continued directly up onto the stage, where he made a speech about the glory of the new order and let the show begin.

Business for the Order of David's Harp was wonderful. Unsubscribed seats

Jacob P. Adler's Grand Theatre on the Lower East Side of New York, around 1908.

were always snapped up. The customers themselves promoted tickets, since profits went to the good of "their" order. There were no benefit dividends to be paid out yet. For a few months, the activities at Poole's dominated New York Yiddish theater. But Hurwitz, who had always had a taste for riding in fine carriages and other forms of conspicuous grandeur, became increasingly despotic.

He came to think that the order existed solely for the sake of his theater, and then that the theater existed only for him. He argued with his partners and managers, until soon there was war in the office all the time. The managers and Hurwitz kept slapping legal constraints on one another, so that in one week the box office management might change hands several times, back and forth. Some weeks both sides paid the actors separately, and at least once in the confusion the actors got paid three times. As the order members became aware of the disintegration, they took their percentages out of the fund and went back to buying theater tickets when they felt like it. Poole's Theater's business slipped and their chief rival, the Oriental Theater, bribed away their leading actor. Soon it was the Oriental Theater's turn to celebrate and to eat again. The Order of David's Harp disbanded.

Despite its ultimate collapse, the magnitude of Hurwitz's project is indicative of the vitality of Yiddish theater as a whole on the Lower East Side. Even though Poole's Theater and many others had months and seasons of debts and near starvation, the general theater situation was thriving and stable.

The theater buildings themselves reflected this new prosperity. In 1885 a critic for the *New York Sun* had gone down to the Lower East Side to see a "quaint Hebrew" drama and had described the Oriental Theater in this way:

> . . . from without it is not a very impressive structure; nor is it within particularly gorgeous. . . . The entrance way is a short hall, flanked on one side by an apple stand and on the other by a candy vendor's table. To the left is a bar, where so-called soft drinks—ginger ale, soda, and sarsaparilla— are retailed. The auditorium is long and narrow; the stage is deep and wide. The main floor is nearly flat, and ordinary chairs bound in line by strips of pine are the substitutes for upholstered orchestra seats. There is nothing ornate about the establishment except the program, which is printed in square Assyrian *[sic]* characters.

In 1909, however, only a quarter century later, David Kessler's Second Avenue Theatre had not only comfortable seats but also a spacious foyer; on its walls were impressively wide panels molded with Grecian pilasters and hung with large mirrors and portraits of the stars; on its ceiling, painted gray and white clouds floated on a background of rich sky blue. Furthermore, this theater was built especially for David Kessler—especially for Yiddish theater.

In its helter-skelter way, American Yiddish theater had become a small-scale big business.

Vagabond Stars

At the turn of the century, while Yiddish theater was expanding in New York, there was also Yiddish theater wherever Jews were settling: in Canada, South America, South Africa, and Australia. In Europe there was theater in Russia, Rumania, Galicia, in Budapest, Vienna, Paris, and even Istanbul, as well as, of course, in London. And it was not uncommon for a Yiddish actor to have played in all these places—and not along a neat geographical route, but constantly crisscrossing. Sholom Aleichem wrote a comic novel about the life of a company of Yiddish troupers, called *Vagabond (or, Wandering) Stars (Blondzhende Shtern)*.

Outside New York, most Yiddish theater at the turn of the century was fragmented and disorganized, reflecting the difficulties of the Yiddish communities that supported it. In Eastern and Central Europe, the theater's biggest problem was the stranglehold of oppressive legalities. In Vienna, for example, a German Yiddish was permissible for performances, provided that the show was not a drama but strictly variety vaudeville, so plays had to be chopped up every few minutes by songs, dances, or acrobatics, and act curtains were out of the question.

The temporary easing of conditions in Russia in the late 1890s gave actors a lot more freedom. Fishzon and his partner Spivakovski built up a company of as many as sixty-five members, including chorus and orchestra. By 1905 Poland and Rumania had tens of troupes and hundreds of wandering actors. In Lemberg, a tall, aristocratic-looking part-time sign painter named Yankev Ber Gimpel held a virtual monopoly over stable Yiddish theater in Galicia. (Gimpel had got permission to open his wine garden café as early as 1888, by virtue of having sung forty years in a Polish chorus.) Yet new pogroms were constantly rocking the area, starting at Kishinev in 1903. Slowly, economic conditions worsened. Continuity had been destroyed and the repeated disruptions made it too difficult to start afresh, though wandering troupes did appear.

In Paris, some actors made stabs at establishing permanent Yiddish theaters, but few succeeded. A journalist from the French newspaper *La Vie de Paris* visited the neighborhood where Yiddish theater played and described the audience in 1889 as a spectacle in itself, a "sad carnival" and an "old clothes market." The same year, Goldfadn organized his Club Dramatique

Israélite Russe. It folded in 1890, started up once more, and folded again. In 1891 a semiprofessional group assembled a few ambitious productions, and in the years that followed, every few months there was some Yiddish theater in Paris, either a touring company or local amateurs.

South Africa had its first Yiddish company in Johannesburg in the 1880s. It consisted of one actor. A Goldfadn alumnus named Yankl Rosenfeld organized a group of amateurs and led them in several performances. By 1896 a few professional actors and one actress (the young wife of one of the actors) arrived from Eastern Europe by way of London and New York. Together they rented Baltic House Hall, which is variously remembered as a former circus and a former convent, and played a Goldfadn repertory for a few months, four or more times a week, to packed houses. Their audiences were Jews and non-Jews both; all the settlers in Johannesburg were starved for entertainment.

Then, predictably, a new company arrived from New York to seek its fortune. For a few weeks the two companies competed, but they succeeded only in dividing up a limited number of potential customers. Neither could survive. So within a few weeks they merged and together spent the summer touring other cities in South Africa.

While they were on the road, happily billing themselves as the only professional Yiddish actors in South Africa, a couple named Nathanson arrived

Dziganitza Theatre in Bucharest, the first and, for many years, the only stable theater in Rumania. The Green Tree Cafe in Jassy, where Avrom Goldfadn made his debut, is supposed to have looked very much like this, as did innumerable other garden cafes offering Yiddish entertainment.

from London. They were better actors than their predecessors, and a new theater regrouped around them, stimulating a larger and more discriminating audience. By 1901 Johannesburg had the Hebrew Oriental Opera Company, the Tivoli Vaudeville, and stars wandering through on tour.

It is amusing to read that the Hebrew Oriental Opera Company presented what it called "semi-sacred" pieces on Friday evenings in an attempt to placate the Orthodox Jews who disapproved of their performing on the Sabbath. "Semi-sacred" included almost any costume operetta in a Biblical setting, but for the Orthodox there was no guise that justified playacting in any circumstance, especially on Friday night. (Similarly, in 1761 an English actor named David Douglass put up posters describing *Othello,* for the benefit of Puritans in Newport, Rhode Island, as a "Series of MORAL DIALOGUES in five parts Depicting the evil effects of Jealousy and other Bad Passions and Proving that Happiness can only Spring from the Pursuit of Virtue.")

The Boer War broke out and drove all the professional actors back to England. Later the Waxmans and the Wallersteins came and stayed a few years, sometimes together and sometimes apart. Since then there have been occasional companies and periodical tours to Johannesburg, Capetown, Pretoria, and Durban.

Jews first arrived in Argentina in 1891, to work on Baron de Hirsch's visionary farming colonies. Most of them drifted to Buenos Aires, which became the main center of Yiddish theater in Latin America. In the last years of the nineteenth century, two actors who had played with Goldfadn arrived in Buenos Aires: a comedian and a lover. They formed a group of amateurs and gave several successful performances in hired halls around the city.

The early history of Yiddish theater in Argentina has a lurid element all its own. Prostitution and the white slave trade (legal in Argentina) were very lucrative professions, and prostitutes and pimps maintained not only their own synagogue, cemetery, and cafés, but their own Yiddish theater as well. They imported a young couple who had played in Galicia and London, who arrived, got married, and settled in as the directors of the Olympia Theater. The groom, Mr. Gutentag, was no businessman, so they imported another actor as manager. Inevitably the young couple didn't get along with the new manager. When they were nosed out, they set up their own theater, having an edge over their rival, since Mrs. Gutentag was the only Yiddish dramatic actress in all South America. Their rival promptly began to bring well-known stars from New York and London for guest visits. After a time of moderate competition, the two theaters merged.

But the two very different sorts of publics did not merge. The pimps were

A company of "vagabond stars" touring Argentina. Standing in the center is Hymie Jacobson; Miriam Kressyn is third from right on top of wagon.

accustomed to using the theater not only to see shows but also to meet friends, talk shop, and show off their latest merchandise. The rest of the Jewish community was outraged and stayed away. Again a second theater opened, with the sign over the door "Entrance Forbidden to *Tmeyim* [Unclean Ones]," and that solved the problem, briefly.

The ground rules for this game the Yiddish theater was playing kept changing. After the city shut down performances in the respectable people's hall, prostitution was made illegal. A former pimp stayed on in Buenos Aires and went straight, taking over the Olympia, but his past was of course known to everyone and the respectable public stayed away. He imported guest stars and promoted big shows, but nothing helped business, so at last he abandoned the attempt. Suddenly two rival theaters sprang up again, but then one collapsed after a short sprint and fled back to London. Prostitution was legalized for another round and the old gang took over once more. Though the leaders of the Jewish community formally excommunicated them, their influence dominated professional Yiddish theater in Argentina for decades. As late as 1926 a scandal erupted right in the theater, where Fanny Vadi Epstein was playing Peretz Hirschbein's drama about a prostitute, *Miriam*. The government ended the situation when it outlawed prostitution for the final time in the early 1930s.

Perhaps because Buenos Aires was so big and the Jews who arrived were at first so scattered and disoriented, the custom was for actors to peddle tickets from door to door, not only for benefits but for regular performances. It was Boris Thomashefsky who, on a South American tour, challenged this humiliating custom. At his insistence, the management advertised "tickets at box office only" and prayed that buyers would come. They did. Soon, however, the box office became a problem of another sort. Adopting the customs of non-Yiddish theater in Latin America, buyers had to tip the cashier in order to be allowed to buy a ticket—certainly in order to choose a good seat. The position of cashier in a Yiddish theater became a concession, like operating the refreshment stand or serving in the cloakroom.

This abuse lasted for some time, in Buenos Aires and in other major cities of Latin America as well. Yet it didn't stop the stars from coming, though they had more problems of their own. Herman Yablokoff recounts in his memoirs a visit to Buenos Aires in the 1930s:

> It has very often happened that the American guest star has read to the troupe [gathered for him] in Buenos Aires or Europe his new play, to which he has bought exclusive rights or which he himself created. When the reading is done, they give him the good news:
> "The play is already like a prayer that's been recited. It's been done already."
> "When? Who?" The guest star clutches his head.
> "What's the difference? The public has already seen the play."
> "The music?"
> "Also, already sung."
> The guest star feels ready to faint away. He reads them a second play, a third —the same thing. . . . If the play wasn't presented exactly as he has it, then someone has already told all the jokes and staged all the comic scenes in other plays. You might as well pack yourself up and go home. The pain is even greater when you find out that your own friends committed this sin against you— American actors, union brothers! Their excuse was:
> "So-and-so played a dirty trick on me, so I was forced to use your repertory. What was I supposed to do? Go home?"

Outside the big cities, especially in the early days of Jewish settlement, South American audiences were grateful for whatever they were offered. Elderly actors reminisced to Yablokoff:

> It's hard to imagine the joy and the festive spirit that a visit of a troupe of actors brought into the life of a provincial city, especially in the Argentine colonies. It was an event of cultural and social significance. Some of the colonists put on their holiday clothes and quit work for the days that the actors spent in the colony. They looked for an opportunity to spend time chatting with the actors. . . .

Actors passing through Jewish settlements in other parts of the world got similar welcomes. Melbourne, Australia, was always ready to enjoy a show. In Toronto, Canada, Mr. and Mrs. Michaelson, ice cream parlor owners, opened a theater in 1906 together with Mr. Abramov; a year later a Toronto real estate dealer named Charles Pasternak converted a synagogue (which had been converted from a church) into The People's Theater, and Jacob Caplan's Café catered to the vagabond stars and their constellation of fans. Even in Brussels, before there was a Yiddish press to print posters, the audiences were welcoming Yiddish troupes. All over town, in the windows of Jewish-owned shops, restaurants, and beauty salons, placards scrawled by hand on colored paper proclaimed:

> Stupendous production! Tears and laughter!
> Enchanting music! Your favorite stars!

And people bought tickets.

5 *SHUND* AND POPULAR THEATER

THE YIDDISH MASSES LOVED THEATER. They ate, as the saying went, their *broyt mit teater*—bread smeared with theater. In the 1890s, on New York's Lower East Side, many greenhorns saw their first play, *zikh gelekt di finger*—licked their fingers—and called for more. There was a community of some three hundred thousand souls, most of whom barely scrounged a living as sweatshop machine operators or rag and pin peddlers, that managed to support several theaters, several music halls, tens of little cabarets, amateur drama clubs, concerts, lecture series, social dance halls. Their appetite for theater was astounding.

They used the theater building unceremoniously, as a meeting place, just as their fathers had used the little synagogue back home to study, gossip, pray, drink schnapps, and eat black bread with butter. The theater aisles and lobbies were clubhouses where *landsmanshaftn* crowded their fund-raising machinery for theatergoing en masse. Spectators ate drumsticks from brown paper bags, cracked walnuts, and even nursed infants during the show.

In fact, the Yiddish masses savored theater so much that they were a show in themselves. Hutchins Hapgood, a non-Jewish New Yorker, exploring the Lower East Side as if it were a foreign country—as indeed it was—wrote:

> . . . the theater presents a peculiarly picturesque sight. Poor workingmen and women with their babies of all ages fill the theater. Great enthusiasm is manifested, sincere laughter and tears accompany the sincere acting on the stage. Peddlers of soda water, candy, of fantastic gewgaws of many kinds, mix freely with the audience between the acts. Conversation during the play is received with strenuous hisses, but the falling of the curtain is the signal for groups of friends to get together and gossip about the play or the affairs of the week. Introductions

are not necessary, and the Yiddish community can then be seen and approached with great freedom. On the stage curtain are advertisements of the wares of Hester Street or portraits of the star actors. . . .

And *The Rise of David Levinsky,* an excellent novel of the period written in English by the Yiddish newspaper editor Abraham Cahan, gives another glimpse:

> An intermission in a Jewish theater is almost as long as an act . . . musicians . . . were playing a Jewish melody . . . in the big auditorium. The crowd was buzzing and smiling good-humoredly, with a general air of family-like sociability, some eating apples or candy. The faces of some of the men were much in need of a shave. Most of the women were in shirt-waists. Altogether the audience reminded one of a crowd at a picnic. A boy tottering under the weight of a basket laden with candy and fruit was singing his wares. A pretty young woman stood in the center aisle near the second row of seats, her head thrown back, her eyes fixed on the first balcony, her plump body swaying and swaggering to the music. One man, seated in a box across the theater from us, was trying to speak to somebody in the box above ours. We could not hear what he said, but his mimicry was eloquent enough. Holding out a box of candy, he was facetiously offering to shoot some of its contents into the mouth of the person he was addressing. One woman, in an orchestra seat near our box, was discussing the play with a woman in front of her. She could be heard all over the theater. She was in ecstasies over the prima donna.
>
> "I tell you she can kill a person with her singing," she said, admiringly. "She tugs me by the heart and makes it melt. I never felt so heartbroken in my life. May she live long."

This then was the public whose tastes shaped Yiddish theater. They wanted what people always want from theater, and they had special needs as well, derived from their special situation as Yiddish-speaking Jews, as homesick Eastern Europeans, as hope-filled new Americans, as individuals in the general uprooting and urbanization of late nineteenth-century America. Because the Lower East Side had the most energetic and prosperous Yiddish community of the time, and one of the most densely clustered, it was here that styles of production, writing, and acting were established, to be exported to every other Yiddish-speaking community in the world.

The Audiences and the Actors

From the beginning audiences were passionately responsive to what went on onstage. Yiddish theater always kept something of the Broder singer café atmosphere, just as it kept the exuberant intimacy of the *Purimshpil.* When

From *The Big Stick*, a comic Yiddish newspaper of New York in the early 1900s, a cartoonist's impression of the same people as they behave at "American" theater uptown and as they behave at home in the Yiddish theater. At the Yiddish theater they are hissing, and yelling "Hurrah!," "Shaddap!," and "Soda!," some people read news-papers, a policeman with his billyclub breaks up a fight as an elderly gentleman munches a big sandwich, and a man in the front row takes off his shoes.

the show displeased the audience, they were ready to yell comments and hiss, as had Goldfadn's patrons at the Green Tree; if they were bored they yelled, "Get the hook!" which they had learned from American vaudeville. When the show pleased them they showed their pleasure lavishly. They might wait outside the stage door to carry an actor on their shoulders through the city streets, setting him down respectfully in front of his favorite after-the-show café. They might even treat him the way European students treated the "Swedish Nightingale," Jenny Lind: harnessing themselves to her carriage and pulling her along in triumph. They analyzed their own reactions to shows over endless glasses of tea in Lower East Side cafés. Newspapers carried not only drama reviews but also gossip columns, editorials, letters to the editor—all about Yiddish theater. When Abraham Cahan wrote in the *Jewish Daily Forward* that the popular favorite Ludwig Satz was "not really a comedian," it was considered a controversial issue. People argued the question. They even argued it at the theater while Satz himself stood onstage, singing as loudly as he could to make himself heard over the angry voices.

Yiddish actors have always been aware of the special quality of their audiences. Half a century ago the glamorous Bertha Kalish told an interviewer that the difference between starring in Yiddish on the Lower East Side and in English on Broadway was that "The American in the theater is virtually dragged along against his will," but the Yiddish fan "works with the actor or the author . . . he comes premeditatively, with keen anticipation to the theater." To this day Yiddish actors boast that Yiddish audiences are livelier, more responsive, and more loyal than other audiences.

At the same time the relationship of the Yiddish actor and his audiences has always been complicated. Actors still sometimes refer to audiences as "Moyshe"—Moses—but with scornful connotations of simple-mindedness: a dumb yokel, a coarse rube. Or they sneer the catch phrase *oylem goylem*, rhyming *oylem* (audience) with *goylem* (or golem, the legendary mindless mechanical giant). They feel for Moyshe a regal mixture of condescension and responsibility, sentimental loyalty and irritation. They feel they should be elevating his taste, and though they may not lose too much sleep worrying about this obligation, it gives many of them some uncomfortable moments. They resent Moyshe's power too; if Moyshe isn't pleased, they starve. Besides, whereas the Yiddish actor came to conceive of himself as an artist, with certain responsibilities toward his community, the masses have always related to him as to something larger. For them the actor was a cultural institution with an almost religious hold on their imagination.

Popular Yiddish theater has traditionally been an actor's theater as opposed to a writer's theater; in this it resembled popular American theater of

Kalmen Yuvelir in the typically romantic setting, costume, and pose of a star of the full-blown romantic operettas of the turn of the century.

the late nineteenth century, in which such stars as Edwin Booth, Joseph Jefferson, and James O'Neill (Eugene's father) overshadowed their vehicles. Americans, including Jews and the other immigrant groups of the era, felt special adoration for, and a passionate wish to identify with, stars of drama and vaudeville. Perhaps one reason was that the stars embodied the American idea of success. Thus, whereas very few of the hit plays of the Yiddish theater at the end of the nineteenth century are remembered today, the names of such stars as Boris Thomashefsky, David Kessler, and Jacob P. Adler remain household words in households that don't retain a word of Yiddish.

Boris Thomashefsky billed himself on posters as "America's Darling." His memoirs are a series of romantic episodes, and he relates them all with equal gusto. Nice girls and respectable matrons sent him flowers and presents, filled his matinees, and swooned in the aisles. His wife, Bessie, ran away from her parents' Baltimore home and went on the stage for love of him. When he played King Solomon, the quip was that the only difference between Thomashefsky and the real king was that Solomon had to support his harem, whereas

the actor's harem supported him. Thomashefsky fixed up his dressing room
at the People's Theater with rich furniture and carpets, tapestries and golden
mirrors on the walls, and many little lamps with different-colored shades to
cast warm, seductive light. For several decades respectable people worried
about Thomashefsky's luscious calves, which in flesh-colored tights were destroying the modesty of American Jewish womanhood.

But it wasn't just his calves. It was also his sweet voice, powerful and
unctuous, his flashing dark eyes, his soft and luxuriant masculinity, like that
of the heroes of modern romantic films from India, which appealed greatly
to Eastern European ideals of beauty. Hutchins Hapgood thought him "rather
fat . . . rather effeminate . . . phlegmatic." But a circular distributed in the
audience at one of his shows declared:

> Thomashefsky! . . .
> Your appearance is godly to us,
> Every movement is full of grace,
> Pleasing is your every gesture;
> Sugar sweet your every turn.
> You remain the king of the stage;
> Everything falls at your feet.

Thomashefsky seems genuinely to have enjoyed peacocking, preening, and
grand gestures. He played successfully in more serious roles too, but he was
supreme in musical comedy and melodrama. He portrayed young princes and
other romantic heroes through the 1920s, went on Broadway, tried other
ventures. In the end he returned to the Yiddish stage with a play based on
his own life, but the Yiddish stage had sadly diminished by then. He died in
1939.

David Kessler, Thomashefsky's rival, was tall, broad, and vigorous, with a
strong peasant neck; a vulgar good fellow, rather arrogant in his bearing. He
was a demonstrative man, who clapped an acquaintance over the shoulder
when he felt friendly, shook his hand, and then kissed him. Over a third glass
of wine Kessler started talking excitedly, even incoherently, and his eyes
burned. He was not a ladies' man; on the contrary, he was notoriously dominated by his wife. Gossips said he regularly put on an apron and scrubbed the
kitchen floor. In backstage politics, he was in his later years no match for his
own son-in-law, Max Wilner.

Kessler was a dissatisfied soul. In his earlier years, starting with one of
Goldfadn's first companies, he won favor from the crowds with his powerful
singing and emoting. But evidently, even though he was quite uneducated, he
had resources for artistry. He came to be committed to the idea of fine,
realistic drama in Yiddish, and he was capable of playing quietly, gently, and

sensitively. However, the masses who had made him a star wanted broader and more sensational stuff. Many anecdotes picture Kessler facing away from the audience during some melodramatic scene and muttering savage asides to his fellow actors, parodying the silly dialogue that "Moyshe" forced him to mouth, and cursing his fate.

Jacob P. Adler was perhaps the most colossal figure of the great three. Contemporaries always referred to his eyes: how deep they were, how magnetic, how intelligent. *Adler* is German for "eagle"; his nickname with the public was *Nesher Ha-Godol*—"The Great Eagle" in Hebrew—by virtue of his piercing glance, his strong profile, and his commanding stage presence. In his later years people raved about his mane of pure white hair. Most of the anecdotes about him give the impression of a personality which was suave, strong, and cold.

Adler's daughter Celia describes how he moved through a London park, wearing a black cloak and looking like an Oriental prince, driving aristocratic Englishwomen to pluck at his sleeve in hopes that he would look at them, just once, and perhaps grant them a smile. Adler had several wives before he married the actress Sara Heine-Haimovitch. He had a number of children; among them, Celia, Stella, and Luther all made resounding names for themselves in the theater.

Adler was already crazy about Russian theater when Goldfadn gave him a walk-on in an Odessa semiprofessional production. He was never much of a singer, which made him a rarity on the Yiddish stage, and he was much more comfortable with tears or with heroic thunder than with comedy. Before coming to America, Adler had been a star in London and a famous carouser, moving from café to café with a train of hangers-on whom he insulted in Russian and Yiddish. The first time a New York theater sent him money to cross the Atlantic he squandered it and had to stay behind. When he did arrive he spent a short period out of favor, hanging about in a dingy hotel room wearing a torn bathrobe. But soon he established a dominion that was to endure for the rest of his life.

After some twenty years of stardom, during a period of tense jockeying for control of the Lower East Side theater business, Adler fell sick. He had word published in the Yiddish papers that he was dying and that he wished to bid farewell to his beloved public. The next day was Saturday, ordinarily the big matinee day. People came to him from all over New York. Those who wouldn't ride on the Sabbath walked, some from as far away as Brooklyn over the bridge. The street outside Adler's hospital window was packed. Adler spoke to them awhile out the window and then went back to bed. Next day he sent word that he was already convalescing. To his cronies he boasted that even from a hospital bed, Adler could empty all the other shows on the Lower East Side.

Thomashefsky, Kessler, Adler, and many others were the romantic idols of the ghetto. Sigmund Mogulesko was another type of star. He was a comic. Hutchins Hapgood called him "a natural genius," with a "naïve fidelity to reality . . . perhaps the greatest talent of them all," and added: "He and Adler, if they had been fortunate enough to have received a training consistently good, and had acted in a language of wider appeal, would easily have taken their places among those artistically honored by the world."

Mogulesko's presence could make a play, his winks and nuances could make a song. He was gifted musically, having begun as a choirboy, and orchestrated many of Goldfadn's scores as well as his own. He seems to have had an unusually flexible range, from sensitive character portrayal to nimble —often obscene—improvisation. Mogulesko was a rather small man, with a warm smile for his friends, though he was not above theatrical feuding or ad-libbing so as to confuse an actor he didn't like. Clowns like Mogulesko and his successors Aaron Lebedev, Ludwig Satz, and Menashe Skulnik had a special place in the public's collective heart. In the earliest years of Yiddish theater, before drama and romance came to dominate the downstage center spotlight, they were the soul of the play.

There were also star actresses, in several categories: vivacious soubrette or hoyden, stately prima donna, emotional heroine, character comedienne, villainess. They all had to have good voices, and usually they had to be able to dance. In looks, the public favored flashing eyes, adorable smiles, and *zaftik* (juicy) figures.

The names of some of the most important actresses indicate their offstage romances. Sophia (or Sara) Goldstein, the very first actress, left Sakher Goldstein and married another actor, to become Sophie (sometimes Sophia) Karp. Bessie Thomashefsky was Boris's wife. Bina Abramovitch married the actor Max Abramovitch. Dina Stettin became Dina Adler when she married Jacob P. Adler. When Adler left her for Sara, wife of the actor Heine-Haimovitch, Sara Heine-Haimovitch became Sara Adler. Dina Stettin Adler married the portly baritone star Sigmund Feinman and took the stage name Dina Feinman. Whereas male stars consolidated their power by being star-managers— choosing plays, casting roles, controlling money—female stars generally needed powerful alliances. However, they, too, sometimes headed companies of their own.

The popular style in Yiddish acting was unsubtle, broad, and electric. Yiddish actors to this day explain proudly that if there is any one quality that sets them apart from their non-Yiddish fellows, it is the intensity and abundance of their temperament, which they also call energy, or presence. Just like the actors who strode the nineteenth-century American stage, they were bigger than life. Fans, however, customarily praised how true to life, how natural, they were. But then truthfulness is judged differently in different eras. An eighteenth-century tragedienne electrified Paris because Voltaire persuaded her to run across the stage rather than walk sedately. In her hoop skirt and powdered pompadour, reciting blank verse, she seemed to them as lifelike as Marlon Brando's mumbling and scratching seemed to later audiences. Thus when Yiddish actors were being heartrendingly "natural," they swept and stamped about, declaimed in big voices, rolled their eyes, gestured operatically, wept. The prima donnas had hysterical fits at regular intervals. The comedians milked each *shtik* till it was dry.

Most Yiddish actors at the turn of the century had very little formal education and little or no professional training. They didn't know much about non-Yiddish theater; many of them had never seen it. Those who had sung in synagogues did know about voice production and music, but even in simple voice placement the majority were ignorant. David Kessler was generally hoarse in the fourth act after having yelled through the first three.

Since the time of Goldfadn's first play, Yiddish actors had felt free to make up lines as they went along. In this they followed the commedia dell'arte tradition and indeed the repertory system in general, for learning a new play or two every week forces the actor to rely on his prompter and his wits. Sara-Sophie Goldstein-Karp was notoriously weak on learning lines. Sometimes she pretty well repeated her role line by line from the prompter, and if he sneezed she was on her own to improvise. When she played opposite Thomashefsky in a Yiddish version of *Romeo and Juliet*, they had a specially constructed prompter's box hidden next to Juliet's balcony. Unfortunately, when they went on tour to Philadelphia, where the balcony was too far away to hear the prompter, what her Juliet crooned to Romeo was a combination of improvisions and snatches of soliloquies from Goldfadn's *Shulamis.*

In typical repertory fashion, actors and their specialties—the young lover, the comic, the soubrette—were types as set as Greek masks or commedia dell'arte roles. It is true that no Yiddish actor ever became as typed as the American Joseph Jefferson, who played Rip Van Winkle and virtually no other role across the country for fully the last forty years of the nineteenth century, but Yiddish stars did nonetheless have their distinctive styles and did fight to establish squatter's rights over juicy roles by identifying themselves with them.

People were fascinated by the actors, and the more they knew about them, the more fascinated they became. They whispered and pointed as actors promenaded not too modestly along East Broadway, flicking walking sticks.

Boris Thomashefsky in a comic character role. "Green" means a newly arrived immigrant, as in "greenhorn." Avrom Shomer's *The Green Millionaire* was only one of a series of "green" plays that were the rage of the Lower East Side for a few seasons around 1910. The best known of these was *Di Grine Kusine*, or *The Green (Girl) Cousin*, whose catchy title song about the country girl with her cheeks like red apples is still sung today; other examples were *The Green Girl* and *The Green Boy. The Green Wife; or, The Jewish Yankee Doodle* was based on Abraham Cahan's story *Yekl the Yankee*, which in 1975 also became the source for the movie *Hester Street*.

One of David Kessler's *patriótn* (fans) has strayed by mistake into the People's Theater, which is Boris Thomashefsky's domain; Thomashefsky's *patriótn* have "trimmed" him as he deserved. From a cartoon in the newspaper *Der Groyser Kibitser (The Big Kibitzer).*

They gossiped about the romances between actors and actresses. They kept up with company politics and feuds, which the actors themselves sometimes referred to onstage. They were present at actors' weddings—like that of Molly Picon and Jacob Kalich—which were held onstage as afterpieces, for slightly higher-priced tickets.

All this private information only intensified the public's reactions to the plays they saw. When an actor and actress who were recently divorced from each other played a tender love scene together, the audience got two dramas for the price of one, and the emotional level was almost twice as high. When Thomashefsky had to play a father soon after his own little son had died, and broke down while singing a lullaby, the whole audience wept till the curtain had to be rung down. Similarly, at a benefit production for Celia Adler, both her mother, Dina Feinman, and her father, Jacob P. Adler, came before the curtain and embraced her together and wept. Knowing the couple had been bitterly estranged since Celia's babyhood, everyone shared the sweetly melancholy significance of the gesture. And wept.

As part of their contracts, most actors had the privilege of a benefit sometime during the season. This was a play that they chose in order to show themselves off in the starring role, casting the other parts as they wished and pocketing the profits. (Benefits were common practice for centuries in English and American companies.) For actors who were special favorites, the evenings were generally triumphs. They got box office money, applause, splendid curtain speeches, bouquets. After their first joint benefit, Boris and Bessie Thomashefsky had to hire a cart to take home the cut-glass pitchers, mantelpiece clocks, songbirds in fancy cages, and other outpourings from admirers. One woman contributed a satin hanging on which she had laboriously embroidered in delicate colors the names of all Thomashefsky's roles, surrounded by a laurel crown.

One aspect of the public's passionate commitment to theater was the phenomenon of *patriótn*—patriots or special fans of particular stars. Actors like Adler and Thomashefsky, and some lesser ones as well, could count on ovations at every entrance and gifts on all occasions from their hangers-on. Some *patriótn* took their idols' names and became known as "Adler" or "Karp." Other *patriótn* actually entered the theater professionally, as did Morris Gest, who became a successful Broadway producer and son-in-law of the famous (Jewish but not Yiddish) producer David Belasco. More often *patriótn* simply were *there*, running for coffee, hopping to pay the bill when their idol was ready to leave the café. They hustled tickets to their idols' benefits. Some slipped right into being a part of the actor's household—echoes of the disciples who clustered at a *hasidic* rebbe's court.

Young David Levinsky, hero of Abraham Cahan's novel, joins his best friend, Jake, as *patrión* of a certain prima donna:

> We would hum her songs in duet, recite her lines, compare notes on our dreams of happiness with her. One day we composed a love-letter to her, a long epistle full of Biblical and homespun poetry, which we copied jointly, his lines alternating with mine, and which we signed: "Your two lovelorn slaves whose hearts are panting for a look of your star-like eyes. Jacob and David." We mailed the letter without affixing any address.
>
> The next evening we were in the theater, and when she appeared on the stage and shot a glance to the gallery Jake nudged me violently.
>
> "But she does not know we are in the gallery," I argued. "She must think we are in the orchestra."
>
> "Hearts are good guessers."

Fights broke out between *patriótn* of rival stars. Once, for example, David Kessler opened in the title role of *Uriel Acosta,* a part for which Jacob P. Adler had been famous for years. A group of Adler's *patriótn* paraded past Kessler's theater with signs calling Adler "the only true Uriel Acosta." Kessler's *patriótn* fought back by leaning out the theater's windows and dousing them with pails of cold water. Sometimes these rivalries came to brawls, although in the Yiddish theater they never reached bloodshed, unlike the 1849 Astor Place riot, when the militia had to be called out to end a fight between fans of rival Macbeths, the American Forrest and the English Macready; twenty-two people were killed.

Often, the public naïvely identified actor and role. Once, for example, Dina (Stettin Adler) Feinman was playing a long-suffering wife. Her drunken stage husband yelled at her, insulted her, hit her, ordered her to pull off his boots. At this a woman in the audience had had all she could take. She stood up in her seat and yelled, "Don't you do it, Dina, don't you do it. You tell that bum where to get off." Similarly, when Jacob P. Adler was playing in *The Yiddish King Lear* and his daughter begrudged him a bowl of soup, a spectator couldn't bear the old man's sufferings. He was drawn out of his seat and clear down the aisle to the stage, yelling, "Leave those rotten children of yours and come home with me. My wife is a good cook; she'll fix you up."

A spectator once rebuked a young comedian bearded and costumed as an old man: "For shame, an old man like you dancing and singing like a fool." Others hissed smoking onstage on the Sabbath, absolutely refusing to allow even gentile characters to break Jewish laws, so that directors simply learned to avoid this action on Friday-night and Saturday performances.

Because of this inability of the audience to separate onstage situations from those offstage, actors fought to play virtuous characters rather than villains;

In the comedy *The Three Little Businessmen,* Rudolph Schildkraut, Boris Thomashefsky, Ludwig Satz, and Regina Zuckerberg *(left to right)* are all very excited.

nobody liked actors who played villains because they seemed to be bad people. Once the other featured dramatic actors in Thomashefsky's company complained that he'd been playing "all the Josephs"—an allusion to Bible-story plays—and they forced him to take a turn at playing a bad guy. But at the moment when he was supposed to deliver innocent Jews into the hands of a wicked king or some such evil deed, he stepped forward with a tirade defending the Jews and proclaiming that he would die for their survival. Naturally, he destroyed the play. But he consolidated his place in his audience's hearts. (When Joseph Jefferson died in 1905, shopkeepers put his portrait in their windows, draped in black; people grieved because they felt that the actor had had all the lovable qualities of Rip Van Winkle. Even today housewives who follow soap operas have been known to confuse actresses with the home-wrecking women whom they portray.)

The stars indulged in displays of personal temperament without minding how they distorted the play. For example, once when Kessler, Adler, and Thomashefsky all happened to be playing together, their personal feuding created a whole new play. Evidently Kessler started the fight by mimicking Thomashefsky while they were onstage. At that moment in the scene, which took place in a kitchen, Thomashefsky was supposed to throw a plate on the ground and break it, but he was irritated enough to break two. Kessler, not to be upstaged, broke a few himself—both of them continuing with the dialogue as written, more or less, all the while. Adler was supposed to be playing a quiet, gentle old rabbi, but he refused to be left out, so he, too, started breaking plates. By the end of the act, all the plates lay in shattered bits on the stage, and the three were starting to smash the furniture. The crowd loved it.

Sometimes even non-stars took such liberties. Once a bit player who had been waiting many years for his big moment simply stepped forward and delivered the star's major third-act monologue. He left the star literally speechless, but he got a great ovation. And since such monologues were often set pieces, like arias, it didn't make much difference to the progress of the plot.

The Playwrights and the Plays

The actors dominated Yiddish theater, but the playwrights, too, enjoyed careers that were theatrically flashy, melodramatic, and farcical. These men, the playwrights of most of the popular Yiddish drama of the late nineteenth and early twentieth centuries, were Goldfadn's younger contemporaries, his rivals throughout his lifetime, and more successful than he in his American years. They were creators and symbols of a different kind of theater from his. Their plays, and the plays later patterned on theirs, sustained the commercial Yiddish theater.

Moyshe Ha-Levi Ish Hurwitz (literally Moses the Levite Man Hurwitz) (d. 1910), who liked to be called "Professor" Hurwitz, turned up on the scene of Yiddish theater in Rumania as early as 1877, when he offered Goldfadn a play he'd written. According to Goldfadn's later account, the play was awful. Furthermore, it was plagiarized from a Rumanian source. Goldfadn was already so desperate for new material that he might have bought it despite these failings, except for the fact that Hurwitz had apparently become a Christian missionary not long before. (Christian missionaries, Hurwitz was to explain, make good livings, and his family had got tired of living on potato peels.) Goldfadn figured that for his new little theater, fighting to become accepted in the Jewish community, connection with a deserter would be disastrously poor press.

But Hurwitz was a hustler. He marched into the largest local tavern, ordered a lot of wine all round, and for the benefit of all who happened to be drinking there, Jews and Christians alike, he improvised an emotional "reconversion" ceremony, in the course of which he added Ha-Levi Ish to his name. "Professor" was a later addition, when he began to claim he'd taught geography at a Rumanian university. A standing actors' joke during his thirty years on New York's Lower East Side was that the geography professor didn't dare go uptown on the subway for fear he wouldn't be able to find his way back down. Actors also called him Professor Meshumed—Professor Convert —but only behind his back.

This reconversion stunt in the Jassy café was a very good show in itself. It was also great publicity for the Yiddish theater Hurwitz promptly set up, using benches in the courtyard of the same café. His posters promised a free glass of beer with every ticket. Finding a cast was no problem, for the floating population of Yiddish actors was already increasing. First he put on the play that Goldfadn had rejected. Then he began turning out others. In the early years he mostly followed Goldfadn's system, whereby the playwright controlled the group. But sometimes, when he went broke, he joined another troupe wandering through Rumania as actor, or dramatist, or prompter, or all three. In 1886 he arrived in New York by way of London and joined the Rumanian Opera House company, which included the actors Mogulesko, Kessler, Feinman, Finkel, and Abramovitch. He was already a known playwright.

New plays were in great demand. Regular audiences kept clamoring for them. Actors demanded them to beat the competition. So Hurwitz turned out a new play every week or so for the next thirty years. The usual term for this process is to "bake" plays—to turn them out like trays of indistinguishable buns, shaped from the same batch of dough and shoveled in and out of a hot oven. Under repertory pressure, Hurwitz sometimes left his company at curtain time on opening night without any last act. In one such emergency he provided a fourth act for a play that was set in an obscurely Oriental setting by coming onstage himself, dressed in a sultan's turban, and delivering a speech, extempore, for three-quarters of an hour. Among Hurwitz's plays were *Judah the Galilean; or, The Prince of Bethlehem, Mother Love, Monte Cristo, Elijah the Prophet; or, Millionaire and Beggar,* and *The Gypsy Woman.*

Hurwitz loved flash and swagger. When he was riding high, as on the David's Harp fraternal order that he promoted, he would keep a carriage with four fine horses and a liveried coachman. When times were tight, he scrounged and borrowed—even from the coachman—so as not to lose the carriage, whatever else went. By 1904, times were permanently bad for Hurwitz. He promoted an opera company in Yiddish and went broke. Under the strain he suffered a stroke. He lived in a miserable nursing home until 1910, when he died poor and lonely. His small funeral procession set out from a stable on Houston Street.

Hurwitz's principal rival was Joseph Lateiner (1853–1935). Ironically, despite their fierce rivalry, history now lumps their names together like a vaudeville team. Hurwitz-and-Lateiner are synonymous with vulgar dramatic baked goods of uncertain freshness. However, some critics do claim that

Lateiner was more gifted and more conscientious than Hurwitz. Among his more than eighty plays were *Ezra; or, The Eternal Jew, Blumele; or, The Pearl of Warsaw, Mammon God of Wealth; or, Koyrekh's Treasure, Mishke and Moshke; or, Europeans in America (or, The Greenhorns), Satan in the Garden of Eden,* and *The Jewish Heart.*

Lateiner became an actor and prompter within a year of Goldfadn's Green Tree debut. Soon he began translating and "Yiddishizing" plays from Rumanian and German. He wrote some plays, including two on the themes Goldfadn used later in *Shulamis* and *The Two Kuni-Lemls.* (Goldfadn's versions were infinitely better.) For a while Lateiner was with Grodner and Mogulesko in Bucharest as their company dramatist. They paid him his first fee as a dramatist: twelve francs in the form of a dozen one-franc tickets to a single night's performance. The catch was that he couldn't get rid of the tickets. At last the company's own ticket-seller took pity on him and relieved him of the twelve tickets—for eight francs—on speculation. Already Lateiner could see that a Yiddish playwright had to hustle to stay alive. Soon he left them in the lurch to work for Goldfadn, who was also in Bucharest at the time.

When a troupe consisting of the Heine-Haimovitches and the Karps arrived in America several years later, they found Lateiner there before them, stitching shirts in a shop. Since he already had a reputation, they hired him at once as their prompter and dramatist. His private library of German plays (published in pamphlets at six cents apiece) kept him supplied with plots that he could adapt at need. At first Lateiner took care over each play, and it showed. But his company needed novelty, always novelty, to draw the crowd away from the competition, and soon Lateiner's own special competition— Hurwitz—arrived in America. Both men plunged into the bakery business, until the two were almost continually bent over their respective ovens like cartoon madmen, jerkily kneading and shoveling in play after play after play.

There were other dramatists of similar accomplishment, among them Nokhem Meyer Shaikevitch (1849–1905), often called simply Schomer. Schomer began his career as a young *maskil,* peddling writings in Hebrew. An editor offered him three rubles for a story in Yiddish and, broke, he accepted, writing all night and turning up with a story the next day. He sold the astonished editor nine stories in a row and kept on writing, till he became probably the most popular Yiddish novelist before Sholom Aleichem (though on a much lower literary level).

Schomer-Shaikevitch met Goldfadn in 1876, when the former was in Rumania as a merchant involved in the Russo-Turkish War, and it was Goldfadn who first inspired him to dramatize his stories for stage production. Most of Schomer's plays, including those he himself directed with hastily put-together companies, were dramatizations of his novels. By 1889, when the Rumanian Opera House sent him money to come to America, his plays were repertory staples. Among the best known of them were *The Coquettish Ladies, The Jewish Prince, The Unfaithful Wife; or, The Bloody Idea, The Golden Land* (*Di Goldene Medine*, a common epithet for America), and *The Second Haman*. In all, he wrote hundreds of novels and dramatizations.

The plays of Moyshe Zeifert (1851–1922) were very like the others'. The main distinction is that he sneered openly at them himself, apparently getting sardonic relish out of acknowledging that they were trash. He once wrote that he'd dreamed he'd died and gone to heaven, where the recording angel judged his lifework. Although his good angel tried to excuse his plays on the grounds that he'd had a family to support, the judge found his lifework so bad that he sentenced him to twenty years in flames—to be followed by rebirth as a Reform rabbi in St. Petersburg.

Some of the other important names among the popular playwrights of the time were Anshel Shor, who was a successful manager as well, Yosef-Yehuda Lerner, Rudolph Marks, Yitskhok Oyerbakh, and Nokhem Rakov. A better category of melodrama writers includes—as we shall see in a later chapter— Max Gabel, Zalmen Libin, and Isidore Zolatarevsky.

And there were many playwrights who were primarily actors. The most significant of these was Sigmund Feinman, a very portly, melting-eyed baritone. Feinman had been a choirboy from a bourgeois Kishinev family. He was relatively well educated for a Yiddish actor of the period. While many actors could put together some gags and a song or two, Feinman was capable of somewhat more substantial efforts. He wrote a number of plays that remained popular, such as *The Jewish Viceroy; or, a Night in Eden, The Father's Curse, Azariah; or, The Valorous Hero, The Jews of Morocco, Tsirele the Rabbi's Daughter,* and *The Silent One; or, Buried Alive*. Boris Thomashefsky himself wrote or adapted a number of popular plays, including *The Polish Wedding, The Jewish Soul,* and *The Little Lost Lamb*.

"Baking" plays required certain techniques. "Professor" Hurwitz tended to make up his own skeleton plot and flesh it out with scenes he found elsewhere. In one of his plays, for example, the poor tenement-dwelling hero became violently jealous of his wife, though she was innocent, and for several minutes the couple spoke to each other in a Yiddish prose version of *Othello* —probably by way of a German translation. Lateiner, after writing a few Bible-story plays, developed the technique of taking a serious plot from somewhere and adding a farcical subplot from somewhere else or out of his own head. People in the theater sometimes called him "professor" too, meaning a medical specialist who does radical surgery. Thus a tear-jerker called *The*

Jewish Heart is interspersed with comic scenes about wives henpecking husbands. *Mishke and Moshke; or, Europeans in America (or, The Greenhorns)*, about a girl who defies her uncle in order to marry the poor boy she loves, was popular especially because of a comic elderly couple prone to malapropisms —such as *malerike* (malaria) for America.

The essence of "baking" was to add a superficially Yiddish flavor to somebody else's play, by giving it a Yiddish title, by giving the characters Yiddish names, and by setting them down in Eastern Europe or the Lower East Side or ancient Palestine. One blatant example occurred when Hurwitz learned that his competitors, at the Rumanian Opera House across the street, were rehearsing a play by a man named Weissman about Jews in fifteenth-century Spain. It was called *Don Isaac Abravanel*. Hurwitz simply rummaged up a play about a hermit by the popular German playwright Kotzebuë, adapted it violently, named it *Don Joseph Abravanel*, and managed to open it, barely rehearsed, before his rivals knew what hit them.

From such a creative process, naturally enough, the dramatic development tended to be faulty or out-and-out incoherent. And indeed the actions and ideas and characters of Hurwitz-Lateiner plays generally held together from scene to scene "the way a pea sticks to a wall"—a Yiddish expression that means: not at all.

Many of these plays were simply copied by hand, never printed. Often an actor got not a whole script, but merely his role, with cue words from preceding speeches. (The word "role" probably derives from a similar system in which individual actors' parts were copied onto rolls of paper in the Middle Ages.) As different companies played a play, moreover, the words changed; the same was true of *Uncle Tom's Cabin* and other American plays that barnstormed the country. Consequently very few texts remain from all those thousands of performances.

There's no way of knowing how many actors "baked" a play when they needed one. Sometimes they didn't bother to tell the audience the author's name. Sometimes, to attract customers, they advertised on posters that the play was by "Professor" Hurwitz or some other well-known writer. Sometimes they did the opposite: altered a play a bit and listed themselves as author rather than crediting the real author. One of Thomashefsky's greatest hits, *Dos Pintele Yid (The Essential Spark of Jewishness)*, seems actually to have been by Zeifert, who got little of the money and none of the glory.

Since the presence of actors onstage had as much impact as the lines they spoke, it didn't much matter that often they didn't know what would be coming out of their mouths next. In the 1880s, Thomashefsky set up a company in Philadelphia consisting of his brothers and sisters, their spouses and children, and his father, Pinchas. Pinchas doubled as character actor and company dramatist. He had a habit that drove his son mad. They needed a new play every week, and it sometimes happened that on the very day when they were about to open he handed Boris a final act that broke off without a conclusion. There would be several blank pages, and at the very bottom of the last blank page, Pinchas would carefully have drawn a fancy curlicue and the words "Curtain Falls." When Boris lost his temper over this, Pinchas invariably lost his, too: "Nu, you're supposed to be a star—let's see how you'll end the play. I have to write everything out for you?"

In the archives of the YIVO Institute for Jewish Research in New York there are hundreds of Yiddish plays, most of them copied by hand into ruled notebooks and scrawled over with line changes. I read a number of these plays, but they are hard to make out—not just the words, but the action. The plots are convoluted, with sections left out and characters unidentified, so that by the end of many scenes it is impossible to recall the beginning. The long speeches go on and on, in a strangulated, pompous *Daytshmerish;* and the grand finales bring together—so to speak—handfuls of obstructed plot strands that I could not make head or tail of.

That's why I was delighted to find this scene synopsis in the memoirs of an actor named Boaz Young. It is the third-act curtain of an unnamed historical operetta, evidently by "Professor" Hurwitz, and there is no dialogue; playing a hero who had been denied his rightful throne, Young improvised as follows:

> "I alone and no other have the right to the throne," I explain to the audience. The king's courtiers are trying to poison me. When I come to see the king in his palace, they serve me a certain sort of apples which are poisoned. For some reason I become suspicious and ask myself, should I eat these apples or should I not? The spectators know that the apples are poisoned and enjoy themselves when I am about to start eating them (. . . the audience played roles along with me; some yelled that I shouldn't eat and some told me to go ahead and eat.). And so, puzzling—eat or not eat—I sniff the poison. I made a long pause, expressing with my face that now I understand what's going on. I say, smiling quite coolly, "No, these apples I shall not eat!" (At these words, the public applauded strongly.) Right away I spoke the sentence, "God has given me too much intelligence for the Heavenly One to betray me now." And, leaping up upon the throne, I stood in a regal pose and cried out with great pathos, "I must and I shall become the King of Israel!" At that the curtain fell . . . [but immediately] rose again several times. When the Professor came up on the stage to bow to the audience, he complimented me and said that that was exactly what he'd had in mind all along.

The catchall term for most popular Yiddish plays from the 1880s to the present is *shund,* pronounced with a short *oo* sound, as in "wood." *Shund* means trash; popular etymology traces the word back to *shindn,* which means to flay a horse.

Shund is the sort of art that most cultures and most people like best. It is not by any means the sum of the culture. It is art for the masses. It's neither the string quartet nor the piously preserved folk song, but the commercial, mass-produced jukebox song. Songs on a jukebox may seem all alike; yet there's always a new one which is the rage. Jukeboxes used to offer not just music, but a whole spectacle of changing records and colored lights; that, too, could be called *shund.* Calendar pictures of puppies, pin-ups, and sad-eyed children are *shund.* So are soap operas, the Grand Old Opry, a lot of Broadway shows, *I Love Lucy* and *Hee Haw,* John Wayne cowboy movies, and Charlton Heston Biblical epics.

Shund in the theater feeds the human appetites for amusement, excitement, escape, affirmation. The Renaissance Spaniard Lope da Vega stated without apology that when he sat down to write his four hundred (or more) successful plays, he locked up the highbrow rules "with six keys" and concentrated on pleasing his public.

I asked dozens of people in Yiddish theater to tell me exactly what *shund* is, and I got dozens of answers, among them this: "A brother and sister, separated in infancy, meet and fall in love, but under the wedding canopy, just in the nick of time, they discover their true identities and their hearts are broken."

This detail from a flier advertises *Two Mothers-in-Law,* a comedy about cultural collision. In this scene, one of the mothers-in-law, a fashionably "modern" woman, turns up her nose at the other mother-in-law, who is pious. The actors involved are Celia Adler and David Barats as the unfortunate young married couple, Misha German, B. Rosental, Molly Picon, and "our beloved comedian" Ludwig Satz. Arch Street Theater, Philadelphia, 1917.

This happens to be the plot of Aksenfeld's *haskole* drama *Man and Wife, Brother and Sister,* and it requires no more violent a suspension of disbelief than plots by Shakespeare or Ibsen.

Another actor explained that *shund* is artistically primitive, like Jacob Jacobs, in *The President's Daughter* (produced in New York in 1972), lining up his actors at the edge of the stage, where they cranked out dialogue as if it came off an assembly line. Or like the romantic leads in *Money, Love, and Shame* (produced in Tel Aviv in 1975), who burst into a love duet only minutes after they meet.

Shund may lean heavily on insulting repartee and on puns. In *My Son the Doctor* (Tel Aviv, 1975), the father, bitterly mugged by Menashe Varshavsky, complains that instead of *nakhes* (gratification) from his son, he gets only *kadokhes* (fever, with humorous connotations); the pun is dumb, like those in television comedies or Abbott and Costello movies.

Shund is also associated with *Daytshmerish* and, more generally, a diluted, crippled, macaronic, or eviscerated Yiddish. It freely mixes everything: classical Yiddish songs, topical jokes, pilfered dialogue, irrelevant new show tunes.

Israel Bercovici, dramaturge of the Bucharest Yiddish State Theater, began his definition of *shund*—as do many other observers—by saying that it includes vulgarities, especially double entendres. Several comedies of the 1970s offer examples. The hero of *Here Comes the Groom* (New York, 1973) disconsolately rips blank pages from his diary; the audience is given to understand that these are the days when his wife refused to sleep with him. *My Son the Doctor* mentions a naked woman painted in a toilet bowl as a comical example of the depravity of hippie youngsters, and a middle-aged man shakes in every limb when his son's girlfriend wiggles up in a bikini.

To call a play *shund* is an insult. But *shund* is so elastic a concept that people can disagree over whether a certain show is *shund* or not. Yiddish actors call each other's productions *shund* in the conviction that their own are of higher artistic quality, more refined, more intellectual, spoken in purer Yiddish. The Yiddish intellectual community, endlessly analytical, endlessly verbal, spits out the term with venom in the heat of debate. All the same, though *shund* is certainly theater of the lower sort, geared to box office receipts, meant mainly to provide actors with good roles and audiences with laughs and thrills, that does not necessarily mean that it's bad theater. It can have energy, theatricality, flair, flashes of art and wit; in Yiddish theater, as in other popular art forms, what people call *shund* can be very good stuff indeed.

In the 1880s and 1890s, the Yiddish public's favorite sort of show was what we can call, tongue in cheek, "high *shund*"—melodrama-operettas. They reigned on the garishly gaslit stages of the Gay Nineties, and were the Yiddish latter-day equivalent of *Uncle Tom's Cabin* and *Pisarro; or, The Conquest of Peru.* (These in turn were picked up from a form that Pixérécourt and Kotzebuë had made the rage of Paris and Berlin in the early nineteenth century.) Such melodrama-operettas added sensation and spectacle to high romance (which the Yiddish masses were already addicted to through the *haskole* novels and *hasidic* tales they devoured by the thousands). "High *shund*" plays took place in exotic lands: ancient Judea, fifteenth-century Spain, the courts of sultans and emperors. The plots wandered on and on, providing twists and thrills; comedians turned somersaults and made vulgar puns.

Two such operettas were special hits for Thomashefsky. The plot of *Rabbi Akiba and His Twenty-Four Thousand Disciples* has the revered post-Biblical Palestinian scholar go mad and wander into the woods, where he happens to find a gypsy's daughter and fall in love. She sings him "Raisins and Almonds" (a lullaby which the author "borrowed" from Goldfadn's *Shulamis*), whereupon Akiba becomes unmad, and together they go to the Temple in Jerusalem, where the chorus performs Russian dances with balalaikas and high boots. Thomashefsky played Akiba, naturally.

Alexander; or, The Crown Prince of Jerusalem was bread and butter for Thomashefsky for twenty years after its debut in 1892. A girl named Naomi lives in a woods in Palestine with her poor father. A hunter comes by—who turns out to be Alexander, the prince of the realm—and Naomi and he fall in love. He has to go back to tend to business in Jerusalem, and she and her father (and their comic servant) agree to follow in six months. When she arrives at his palace, he has become insanely suspicious and brutally accuses her of infidelity, whereupon she faints from shock and loses her power of speech. Curtain. Alexander discovers that he was wrong. In an agony of remorse, and a long and fiery monologue, he gives up his crown and scepter. He puts on full armor, tells his mother goodbye, mounts a white horse, and gallops off to fight a war. Sensational curtain, with Thomashefsky on a real horse! Later Naomi recovers her speech. It turns out that she is really a princess, so they marry and live happily ever after.

Alexander, incidentally, figures in a classic tale of *patriót* warfare. Followers of one of Thomashefsky's rivals so resented his triumph in this role that they fed his horse an emetic just before show time.

The historical operettas are full of pageantry and fustian, creating scenes of monumental impressiveness for the audience to gape at. Here, for example, is a bit of a scene from Hurwitz's *Athalia.* It is based on an incident in the Biblical book of Kings, in which Queen Athalia and her young grandson are rivals for the throne. The boy king has been hidden away by loyalists, who are plotting their next move.

YEHOYADA [the priest]   The hour has come. Now we must speak out, Princess. The dear theft can no longer remain hidden. God's silence for so long a time feeds the pride of the evildoers in the evil that they do, and they deny the truth that God has spoken. Your grandmother Athalia wants to sacrifice to her idol Baal on our altar. Therefore let us reveal the king's son whom you have saved and whom we have kept hidden under God's protection.

PRINCESS YEHOSHEVA [the boy king's aunt]   Does the child know of his fate and of his great name?

YEHOYADA   No. He still believes that his name is Eliazin and that his mother abandoned him and that I have been a father to him out of sympathy.

PRINCESS YEHOSHEVA   Ah! What danger did I rescue him from, and what danger does he now face!

YEHOYADA   What, Princess? Does faith in our dear God tremble within you so easily?

PRINCESS YEHOSEVA   To your wisdom, lordly man, I entrust my all. I have poured out my tears in prayers to God for him. Now I ask you a question. Which of our friends will stand by you? Will Eviezer help you? . . .

Such pseudo-Biblical bombast certainly glorified the Yiddish *jargón.* It glorified the spectators' identity too, as they watched Jews wearing golden robes and crowns, and speaking Yiddish with crushing dignity. It was a marvelous new experience for the proletarian immigrant community. And the star actors, too, aggrandized their images as they strutted monumentally through heroic roles.

Since the Yiddish theater's public and budget were generally smaller than those of their non-Yiddish counterparts, their scenery lacked the really first-rate gloss of fashionable theaters in New York and Paris. They were hindered also by having to change repertory very often, so they pieced together new sets as best they could. Nevertheless, they always attempted to affect lavish sets.

In *Alexander; or, The Crown Prince of Jerusalem,* the hero's horse made a sensational entrance wearing a jeweled saddle. In a play about the Johnstown, Pennsylvania, flood, there was a scenic water wall made of blue cloth, with real water behind it, so the actors actually got wet. In *Parsifal* (in a radical departure from the usual), Thomashefvsky invested fifty thousand dollars in costumes and scenery.

As for music, that had been featured from the days of the Green Tree skits. The critic for the (non-Jewish, of course) *New York Sun* saw *Bar Kokhba* on February 21, 1885, and wrote in his review that music underlay the entire show,

vivifying even the dullest portions . . . a melodious monody which swells sometimes into a chorus of tearful and tender lamentation . . . quaint, eloquent and touching, full of heart and feeling. . . . So idealized . . . that it lifts up both play and players and creates an illusion stronger than would be possible by the most deft arrangement of ordinary dramatic materials.

A number of accomplished musicians, such as Joseph Rumshinsky, Alexander Olshanetsky, Sholem Perlmutter, and Sholom Secunda, composed scores for chorus and orchestra. Selling show tunes on sheet music and recordings was a lively industry, featuring love duets and marches, sentimental ballads about the old home town and comic patter songs (which regularly stopped a show).

Tsaytbilder (scenes or pictures of the times) were another type of play, also popular. These loosely documentary, highly sensationalized portrayals of current events were not peculiar to Yiddish theater—Broadway audiences in 1857 saw *The Sidewalks of New York*, about a fire and panic that occurred earlier that same year, and eighteenth-century Japanese saw kabuki plays about real-life love suicides—but they were a substantial part of Yiddish theater from Goldfadn's earliest years. Lateiner wrote a *tsaytbild* called *Immigration to America* soon after his arrival. Both he and "Professor" Hurwitz based theater pieces on the Johnstown flood. Hurwitz wrote a play about the Dreyfus trial. And one of his biggest hits was called *Tisa Esler*, after a town in Hungary where a Jew had recently been brought to trial on charges of having sacrificed a Christian child in order to drink his blood as part of a religious ceremony. The New York audience liked solid evenings of four hours or so, but *Tisa Esler* was so long that it had to be divided into two evenings. Part One was called *Tisa Esler*. Part Two was called *The Tisa Esler Trial*, and Hurwitz himself played the defense lawyer, talking for an hour straight, extemporaneously.

Domestic Drama

Besides the "high *shund*" historical operettas and *tsaytbilder*, there was a third form of Yiddish theater—domestic dramas. These eventually came to dominate the Yiddish stage. Plays of the cozy sort that people have laughed and cried over since Menander, they aimed at mirroring real life, and did so superficially. Domestic dramas pushed toward a satisfying conclusion at the final curtain, juxtaposed young star-crossed romances with lower-class comic characters, and indeed mixed sad and funny elements so violently that a French term for the genre was *comèdie larmoyante* (tearful comedy). They also added such standard features of nineteenth-century melodrama as: pathetic deathbeds, innocent children, rising suspense, dramatic music, stunning curtain lines, and above all, wrenching appeals to clearly defined social attitudes. (The nineteenth-century masters of this form were the Frenchmen

Poster for *The Messiah Is Coming,* a particularly sensational mixture of musical show and emotional drama, starring Ludwig Satz in an uncharacteristically serious role.

Scribe and Sardou; on the American stage, some hits at midcentury were *A Working Girl's Wrongs, East Lynne, The Octoroon,* and *The Drunkard; or, The Fallen Saved.*)

Yiddish audiences responded wholeheartedly to these dramas, getting so caught up in the characters' sorrows that they facetiously classified plays as one-handkerchief, two-handkerchief, or three-handkerchief ordeals. Another term was "onion plays." The Yiddish word for sympathy is *mit-filn*—literally "with feeling"—and the audiences "with-felt" the characters totally. The stories and the spectators' will to believe carried the *mitgefil* along, even when the actors were far too old or too fat to look their parts.

The Jewish Heart (1908) by Lateiner is a good example of domestic drama. So powerfully did it sway the masses that it set a record by running several hundred consecutive performances. Yankev, or Jacob, a poor orphaned Jewish art student in Rumania, has won a prize for a painting entitled "The Sinful Mother." His archrival, a Christian art student named Viktor Popeska, is bitterly jealous and makes strongly anti-Semitic remarks, though his mother, Madame Popeska, tries to soothe him. Act One ends with Yankev's discovery that Madame Popeska is actually his mother as well as Viktor's; she had abandoned Yankev and his father (now dead) when he was a baby and run off to marry her Christian lover and bear his Christian children.

Yankev is in love with Dina. In Act Two, according to a new edict Jews must have their parents' signatures in order to get a marriage license, so Yankev goes to acquire Madame Popeska's. Moved, Madame Popeska promises to give her signature, and the mother and her new-found son embrace. Viktor enters. Horrified by the scene, and by the revelation that his mother is Yankev's mother, as well as by the humiliation that her public acknowledgment of Jewish blood will bring to him, he threatens Yankev with a gun. Madame Popeska is torn between her two loyalties and at last refuses her signature. The curtain falls on Yankev's declaration to his weeping mother: "We remain strangers."

In Act Three Yankev and Dina have decided to emigrate to America, where they will be free to marry without anyone's signature. But Yankev has been lying sick since his confrontation with his mother. She comes now to his sickbed:

MADAME POPESKA *(Draws the curtain to* YANKEV's *bed.)* Ah, noble picture, heart-quickening appearance. My Jewish child, believe me, never has mother loved her child as I love you, my Yankev. Outcast wife, how was I able to conceive such a crime, and—and— Oh, how bitterly I now regret it. Can you ever forgive your mother, my good child, my Jewish child? *(Falls onto the bed, weeping.)*

As late as 1933, domestic melodrama was still helping the Jews of Pittsburgh, Pennsylvania, to teach their children moral lessons.

YANKEV *(Awakens. Note: She uses the familiar form of "you," du, to him; he uses the coldly formal ir to her.)* Is it you, Madame? In such a condition as this? Please rise, Madame.

MADAME POPESKA No, not until you say you will hear me out.

YANKEV Yes, but first take a seat, please. What is it you wish from me, Madame?

MADAME POPESKA Yankev, I am speaking to you as to a grown man. Yankev, you want to marry. But first I beg you to answer me: do you love your Dina? Do you really love her?

YANKEV I love her so much that I would sacrifice my life for her.

MADAME POPESKA Thank God. Yankev, you know the power of love and you will understand me. When I married your father, I was a child, fifteen years old. I didn't marry him for love. My poor parents pressed me to become a rich man's wife. Three years later, chance brought me together with my present husband, and then I, too, loved, as only an eighteen-year-old loves for the first time in her life. I sacrificed everything for him, for the emotion of my first love bewitched, enchanted me. I acted without thinking, without considering. When I grew older, the first enchantment passed. With time I recalled more and more strongly my own dear ones whom I had left behind me in my Jewish home. *(Trembles.)* Most of all I recalled my child, whom I left behind in the cradle. Ah, how often a burning longing came over me, and like a madwoman I wanted to run out into the world, run and find my child. But by then I was already also the mother of my two Christian children, and they, too, still lay in their cradles. *(Weeps.)* And this mother-heart of mine was torn in two. I did not know whom to sacrifice, or for whom. No one can imagine how I suffered in silence. Years passed, and the picture of my Jewish child did not fade, until chance brought you to me as a grown man. Now *(she kneels)*, Yankev, this sinful woman kneels before you, as before her judge. Hand down your verdict on your sinful mother. Demand the hardest sacrifice from me, and I will do it gladly, only let me be your mamma. You are a Jewish child with a Jewish heart—have mercy on your unhappy mother and forgive her, forgive her. *(Kisses his hand.)*

YANKEV *(After a strong inner struggle, presses her to his heart.)* Mother!

MADAME POPESKA What sweet, heavenly music for me to hear the word "mother" from your lips.

YANKEV *(Kisses her.)* My poor mother!

MADAME POPESKA No, not poor—I am the richest, the happiest mamma to have a child like you.

YANKEV *(He now uses du for "you.")* Now, be strong, Mother. For just as horrible fate tore mother and child apart twenty years ago, now we have found each other again only to lose each other once more.

MADAME POPESKA *(Fearfully.)* What are you saying, my child?

YANKEV   I have no other choice but to leave this place.

MADAME POPESKA   *(Screams.)* No, no, never again!

(A knock is heard at the door.)

YANKEV   Mother, perhaps you should not be seen in this house now?

MADAME POPESKA   *(Leaving.)* No power in the world can tear me away from my new-found child, from my Yankev. *(Kisses him. Exits.)*

(Enter VIKTOR.*)*

YANKEV   Who is this unexpected guest?

VIKTOR   Sir, I come to you now as one businessman to another.

YANKEV   With you, sir, I do not do business.

VIKTOR   Say then that I come to make you a proposition.

YANKEV   And if I am not curious to hear your proposition?

VIKTOR   You must!

YANKEV   I must? Apparently you forget that you are in my house, and I can show you the door as you did yesterday to me.

VIKTOR   You wouldn't dare, Jew! Remember the consequences, which could be very unhappy for you.

YANKEV   Heartless beast! Why do you pursue me so unkindly? Even into my own home your bitter hate pursued me and gives me no rest. Why?

VIKTOR   *(Excited.)* As you see, I am calm; follow my example and be calm now too. Ask me to sit down and hear what I've come about.

YANKEV   Among Jews, hospitality is holy. You are actually my enemy. However, now you are my guest. Sit down, if you please.

VIKTOR   *(Mockingly.)* Thank you. *(Sits down.)*

YANKEV   Now tell me the reason for your coming here.

VIKTOR   First, I want to be sure you are aware that the Popeska family is one of the most aristocratic and noblest in Rumania.

YANKEV   I know it. In particular, you are the noblest of the noble; you have given me evidence of that more than once. Well, then, continue.

VIKTOR   Joy and harmony have always reigned in our family. Suddenly you came and destroyed our home. Please, hear me out calmly.

YANKEV   I am calm.

VIKTOR   I have been thinking over a means whereby you, who destroyed our happiness, can make good that misfortune which you brought upon our house.

YANKEV   *(Ironically.)* "How I might make good that misfortune." Good, I am calm.

VIKTOR   I demand that you leave our land, our Rumania, as soon as possible, and leave it forever.

(Pause.)

YANKEV   Ha ha ha! That is marvelous.

VIKTOR   What is marvelous?

YANKEV   That for once we both should have the same idea. You see, yesterday, immediately after I left your house, I came to the firm conclusion to leave this sweet fatherland, Rumania.

VIKTOR   Well, then, our Rumania isn't good enough for you? All the better. Leave on your travels, but quickly. Perhaps you need travel expenses?

YANKEV   Thank you very much, I no longer need money for travel expenses.

VIKTOR   Why not?

YANKEV   Because I now intend to remain here in this land.

VIKTOR   But did you not just say that you decided yesterday to leave?

YANKEV   Yes, yesterday I reached that decision. However, today a certain person tells me that it is no longer necessary.

VIKTOR   A certain person?

YANKEV   Yes, a certain person, and no other, in fact, than our mother.

VIKTOR   Jew, be very careful how you speak. I forbid you to repeat that expression "our mother." My mother cannot also be your mother.

YANKEV   I beg your pardon a thousand times for having been born to the same woman as you. Believe me, if she had asked me, I would have told her it was better for me never to be born than to have you as a brother.

VIKTOR   Jew, who gives you the right to call me brother?

YANKEV   Once again I beg your pardon a thousand times. Unfortunately, we are, against our will, two brothers. And if you have read the Bible, you have found there two such unsuited brothers as we are: Jacob and Esau.

VIKTOR   And I insist to you that Madame Popeska, my mother, ceased to be yours in the moment when she entered the Christian faith.

YANKEV   Brother Esau, my mother never entered the Christian faith. The proof is that now after twenty years there beats in my mother's breast a warm Jewish heart.

VIKTOR   Jew! Do not insult my Christian mother!

YANKEV   Your Christian mother is now at this very moment in my Jewish house. Just a few minutes ago she knelt here before me and was overjoyed to hear the word "mother" from me, her Jewish child.

VIKTOR   Take back your damned lie. Madame Popeska would never sink so low.

YANKEV   And her Jewish son pressed her to his Jewish heart and called her mother, for she is and she remains my Jewish mother.

VIKTOR   Jew! Two of us is one too many on this earth.

(Pulls out his revolver. They struggle.)

YANKEV   Beast, do you want to cause a murder?

(The revolver goes off. VIKTOR *falls dead.* MADAME POPESKA *and* DINA *rush in.)*

To protect Yankev, Madame Popeska tells the police that she shot her own son Viktor, and they take her away.

Act Four takes place at the wedding canopy set up for Yankev and Dina. Madame Popeska is there, under arrest. At the end of the marriage ceremony the rabbi prays, at her request, for Yankev's father, the Jewish husband whom she abandoned in her youth. Overcome by remorse and joy, she dies. Yankev sings a reprise of a song he'd sung in the first act; its refrain goes: "Always

Conclusion of Act II, *Dos Yidishe Harts (The Jewish Heart)* by Joseph Lateiner, as presented in 1908 at David Kessler's Thalia Theater on the Lower East Side. Yankev, played by Kessler, has just accidentally shot his Rumanian Christian half-brother Viktor; their mother heroically seizes the gun and takes the blame.

remember your mother's song." Curtain.

Popular dramas of this sort operate by pushing certain buttons calculated to bring on tears or laughter. In Western cultures such buttons include sweethearts' love, lost innocence, mother love; in Tennessee, hillbilly songs twang on about the same subjects.

The Jewish Heart pushes scores of these buttons, touching so many deep nerves and releasing so many powerful responses that it is in effect a ritual performance. The main story, as opposed to the comic subplots, deals explicitly with Jewish identity. Yankev's transformation from passive victim of anti-Semitism to active hero, which he achieves by confronting Madame Popeska and Viktor and ultimately expresses by emigrating, is the essential action of the play. Yankev insists throughout on pride in his Jewishness. He can't reform, nor can he really destroy, his anti-Semitic antagonist, but he can disdain and diminish him. Like black heroes facing "Whitey" in plays, movies, and novels of the 1960s, he is cool, proud, and elegant; he is in control of the confrontation; he can even beat Viktor within Viktor's own code of aristocratic etiquette. Besides, Yankev is essentially a good man, and always dealt honorably with his art school rival, whereas Viktor is "heartless." This is Yankev's real victory over his tormentor—this and the winning away of his mother's heart—since the actual killing is not his responsibility. Yankev is further rewarded for his Jewishness by getting revenge on Madame Popeska for having deserted him; even better, it is revenge without guilt. In the course of such scenes, the audience vicariously gets its own back at all the Rumanians and Poles who insulted them and discriminated against them, both personally and as a group. Safe, together, and comfortable in a theater on another continent, the audience watch a Jew conquer a Christian nobleman in a ritual of vindication.

Madame Popeska, who deserted the Jewish community, pays for her sin. She has suffered all her life. Toward the final act her suffering crescendoes; she is humiliated in front of both her sons, and she has a particularly painful moment when she believes that Yankev is about to leave her. She earns forgiveness by repenting, like all the fallen women nineteenth-century audiences and novel readers liked to weep over. But in the end such heroines inevitably die.

In the wedding scene in the last act of *The Jewish Heart*, Hebrew prayers are chanted onstage. Such a device was very popular, and many plays included at least some part of a marriage ceremony, a prayer for the dead, a Passover *seder* table, or a mother blessing the Sabbath candles. Liturgic cantorial music was often used, even in Jewish vaudeville programs. Such moments of prayer evoked religious and cultural feelings which heightened whatever action was going on at the time. Prayers intensified the play by acting out an experience that was special to the community who sat together and watched it. It is interesting that the specific situation in which a parent (or surrogate parent) manages, despite obstacles, to attend his or her child's wedding, and then swoons or dies beside the wedding canopy, recurs in a number of plays and movies, such as the American-made, tear-jerking film of the 1930s, *The Two Sisters,* starring Jennie Goldstein.

The Jewish Heart enters two especially painful and interrelated areas: guilt and the mother-child relationship. Many American plays of the period, non-Jewish as well as Jewish, manipulated these raw feelings. Indeed, the experience of leaving mother behind, on the farm or across the ocean, was one of the essential American experiences of the late nineteenth century. This inevitably meant leaving behind the life style learned at mother's knee. Guilt and homesickness were constantly set overflowing in sentimental tears by such songs as "A Brivele der Mamen" ("Write a Little Letter to Your Mother"), the Irish-American "Mother Machree," and the American "Old Folks at Home." In *The Jewish Heart,* Yankev is rewarded by a reunion with his mother and, subtly, by the liberty to leave his home without guilt.

The Jewish Heart also touches on feelings about the old country. The play corroborates that leaving for America was the right thing to do. It hints at the future success waiting for Yankev. But in some scenes it deals with the old country differently, though equally effectively, by offering the sweet ache of homesickness. Yiddish theater was lavish with choruses of peasant girls in embroidered blouses, and in songs like "Mayn Shtetele Belz" ("My Little Hometown Belz"), "Rumania, Rumania," and "Odessa Mame," which praise the tree-lined streets, the outdoor cafés, the wine, and home cooking of another life. Even Cossacks in boots seemed relatively safe, from a distance, and almost evoked nostalgia. The other life seemed warmer and sweeter, the farther the audience got from it; memories of it, as of childhood, charged the play with emotion. On Broadway the equivalent was an obsession with the idyll of a farm back home: farmers' daughters and sons were ruined, or almost ruined, in the big city, or farms were saved from mortgage foreclosure.

Comedy

In a domestic drama like *The Jewish Heart,* the emotional pitch could be so grueling that audiences needed the relief of comic interludes. Every act of *The Jewish Heart* has at least one episode of a complicated comic subplot which involves Dina's father and stepmother. Here is a scene in which the stepmother, named Serke, is alone with her own newly married daughter, Rosa.

SERKE   *(Springs to her feet.)* My child, you are lost! My daughter, you are unlucky!

ROSA   What's come over you, Mamma?

SERKE   Just a few weeks after the wedding, and already he is trampling you beneath his feet.

ROSA   What are you talking about, Mamma?

SERKE   Do you think that I care about earrings? *(*LEMEKH, *a bumbling grocer,* SERKE*'s second husband, appears outside the window and stays throughout the scene to eavesdrop and comment.)* All I care about is why he should have it all his own way. My child, you are still too young and don't know that everything in married life depends on the direction you take right after the wedding. All you have to do is let him have it all his own way now already, and for the rest of your life you won't be able to do a thing with him. Follow your mother's advice, daughter. You must have those earrings, and for only one reason: so as to have your own way.

ROSA   But, Mamma, is it worth quarreling with my husband just for a pair of earrings?

SERKE   Who says you should quarrel? A woman has methods enough for keeping her husband beneath her slipper. Oh, Rosie, when I was your age, what couldn't I do with your father, my first husband, may he rest in peace! He wasn't such a broken-down creature as my current one, Lemekh. Your father, may he rest in peace, was a hero, a real man, but with one glance of my eyes I could twist that hero around my little finger.

ROSA   With one glance? But what sort of a glance could it have been?

SERKE   The glance of a young woman who is winning the victory over her husband.

LEMEKH   *(Eavesdropping at the window. Aside.)* What's this I hear? Serkele was young once too? And here I always thought that she was born an old hag.

SERKE   *(Sighs.)* Ah, child, at your age, how I used to toy with my husband, how I used to dimple for him.

LEMEKH   *(Aside.)* Serkele, dimple for me too.

SERKE   Yes, yes, Rosele. You have to know how to deal with men. For example, mine—he should intercede for us in heaven—really hated tears. So what did I do? Over every little thing I whimpered so and sniffled so that he practically went out of his mind. And that's how I got my way about everything.

ROSA   Mamma, mine can't stand tears either.

SERKE   Nu, darling, why not use that?

ROSA   *(Laughing.)* But, Mamma, how can you cry, pour out tears, when you don't feel like crying?

SERKE   Get away, you silly girl—can't a woman manage a bit of art? Give your eyes a little squeeze, and there are your tears.

LEMEKH   *(Aside.)* Oy, men! These women lead us right into the bathhouse.

SERKE   Shh, here comes your husband. Yes, my child, just give it a try the way I taught you, and let us see which of you two will win out. *(Exits.)*

*(*HERMAN, *ROSA's new husband, enters.)*

HERMAN   So here you are, Rosele. I thought you were coming with us. Why did you stay here?

*(*ROSA *turns away from him.)*

LEMEKH   *(Aside.)* Aha, the comedy begins.

HERMAN   Rosele, aren't you feeling well? Why do you sigh so sadly? Is there something you need?

ROSA   And if you found out what I needed, would that help me?

HERMAN   What sort of words are those? Child, don't you know that you are my entire life? *(Tries to caress her.)*

ROSA   How should I know that? When you refuse me the littlest thing I ask you for!

LEMEKH   *(Aside.)* She's pretty good at playing the comedy.

HERMAN   I refuse you the littlest thing? Oh, maybe you mean the earrings? Listen, Rosa, you know very well that for my part, nothing is too precious for you. I've already bought you more than one valuable gift without your having even asked for it. But this time I truly don't know what you saw in those earrings. I find them absolutely unappealing. The stones have no sparkle.

ROSA   But if they appeal to me!

HERMAN   But tell me a reason.

ROSA   Without a reason. They appeal to me.

HERMAN   In other words you've just got a crazy idea in your head. Well, I am sorry to say it, for I truly love you, but I'm never going to give way to your crazy ideas. My name isn't Lemekh.

LEMEKH   *(Aside.)* Even though he insults me, it gives me pleasure. Now, there is a man. Oy, Serkele will have a fit.

ROSA   Herman, can you refuse me such a little thing? Me, Herman? Unless—unless you don't love me. Yes, now I see it, you never did love me, you never did.

LEMEKH   *(Aside.)* She is actually crying tears. Ha ha. "Give your eyes a little squeeze, and there are your tears." But now I look forward to hearing how he'll tell her off.

HERMAN   She's crying! And I made her cry! *(Goes to her.)* Don't cry. You know I can't bear to see your tears.

ROSA   *(Crying.)* I only know one thing, that you don't love me, and I'm the unhappiest girl in the world.

HERMAN   What's come over you, child? I don't love you? *(Caresses her.)* After all, what a bad man I am, what a tyrant. How can I have the heart to make her cry over such a little thing? Her tears are not a little thing. I must really have hurt her. *(Deciding.)* Rosele, come on now.

ROSA   I won't come on. I haven't made up yet.

HERMAN   Come, I tell you. Do you know where to? To buy you the earrings.

LEMEKH   *(Aside.)* Oy, that's bad. Get out of here, you're a Lemekh.

ROSA   Let it go. I don't want them anymore.

LEMEKH   *(Aside.)* Serkele is actually a pup compared to her.

HERMAN   Rosele, you know what? You stay here. I'll just run over myself and bring them back here to you. Where is my hat? Adieu, Rosele. In five minutes I'll be back with the earrings. *(Exit.)*

LEMEKH   *(Aside.)* And here I thought that I was the only Lemekh in the world. How strongly he took his stand at first: "My name is not Lemekh." What does his wife do? She gives her eyes a squeeze and makes him into a squish.

ROSA   *(Explodes with laughter.)* Mamma, your advice was right. You have to know how to handle men. You have to get a good firm hold on them. What's he going to do, run away? He won't get there what he gets at home.

Curtain

In the end Herman reasserts himself and carries Lemekh along with him, so Serke and Rosa get their comeuppance and become happily docile wives.

Mogulesko played Lemekh. His droll winks, quavers, and capers made "Oy, that's bad" and "Get out of here, you're a Lemekh" catch phrases in every café on the Lower East Side. In another scene of *The Jewish Heart*, he sings the comedian's almost obligatory comic patter song—the *kuplét*.

Like the Gilbert and Sullivan patter song of the era, and like the parabasis of Aristophanic comedy, the song hooks on only tangentially to the plot of the play. Thus, in response to some remark, Lemekh steps to the footlights and sings a song whose chorus goes:

> Just a minute, pal of mine,
>> what's the rush, my friend?
> I'll stop your running. I'll
>> give you a kick.
> I'm gonna smack you with a
>> stick.
> Where is the fire? You're
>> gonna get burned.

The first verse of the song is about a young man who starts getting fresh with his girlfriend ("When he started creeping with his hands, this is what she said . . ."). The second verse is about an elderly cuckold who catches his wife halfway out the door with her young lover. The third is equally unrelated. (For a contemporary example, one verse of the naughty *kuplét* of *Money, Love, and Shame,* sung by a clever comedian in Tel Aviv in 1975, makes fun of Brezhnev, to the delight of an audience of recent immigrants from Russia, even though the scenes just before and after the *kuplét* are about a prostitute on trial for killing her pimp, in a setting of some fifty years ago.)

The *kuplét* took the clown out of the play framework, reasserting the primacy of the relationship between the individual performer and the audience. For the moment, the play resembled the vaudeville of the era, both Yiddish and American (and the English music hall), with its intense rapport between performer and public. (Half a century later, Jacob Jacobs is still leaning over to the audience, in the course of a *kuplét,* to commiserate with someone in the first row on his Galician accent—always good for a laugh. Another of his perennial routines is to sing a verse about a man who is cuckolded or impotent, peer out into the audience, and ask someone why his wife is laughing so hard.) The *kupletist* danced off into the wings, but the audience knew their role, and their applause draws him back to add another verse, and another, and another, while the inevitability of the chorus as punch line to each verse, and the catchiness of the tune, encourages the audience to join in and sing.*

*A *kuplét* recorded not long ago in Buenos Aires by the comedian Pinye Goldstein refers explicitly to the relationship between *kupletist* and public. ("Lebedik on Yiddish," Tikva Records T66).

> *Chorus*
> It never gets on, and it never gets off.
> The whole damn thing is really just a bluff.
> It never gets on, and it never gets off.
> You end up in the same place, sure enough.
>> You push and you pull,
>> And you think that you have got it,
>> But you aren't here, and you aren't there,
>> And what you've got is not it.
> For it never gets on, and it never gets off.
> The whole damn thing is really just a bluff.

In *The Jewish Heart*, Yankev and Lemekh speak two very different sorts of Yiddish. Putting what seemed to be nobler language in the mouths of nobler characters is not a Yiddish invention. In *Uncle Tom's Cabin*, the runaway slave Eliza says, "They press upon my footsteps—the river is my only hope. Heaven grant me the strength to reach it, ere they overtake me! My child, *we will be free*— or PERISH!" In the same play the slave girl Topsy says, "Reckon I'se goin' to dance, Boss." Shakespeare uses the same convention when his noble characters speak blank verse, while his rustic clowns speak colloquial, relatively realistic prose. But in Yiddish *shund* the speech gap is wider than in its English counterparts. Yankev speaks *Daytshmerish*—like Alexander the Great and the other princes of historical operettas—stressing the Germanic components of Yiddish over the Slavic and Hebrew, as an affected English-speaker chooses the Latinate over the Anglo-Saxon. He uses purely German words instead of their Yiddish equivalents, so that an uninitiated spectator has to guess the meaning from the context. Though to modern ears *Daytshmerish* sounds like a parody of Yiddish and of German both, to the actors and audiences it sounded finer than their workaday *mame-loshn*, Yiddish. Thus romantic actors like Thomashevsky had to master *Daytshmerish*, while clowns like Mogulesko did not.

When young David Levinsky, hero of Abraham Cahan's novel, goes to the

---

It never gets on, and it never gets off.
You end up in the same place, sure enough.

Verse
Young Abie falls in love with Sadie,
Treats her swell, just like a lady,
Swears he'll give her riches without end.
He'll buy her this, he'll give her that,
Whatever she wants, from a house to a hat.
She'll be a princess with the world to spend.
Before they're wed the lover talks with passion.
But afterwards you can yourselves imagine—

(Chorus)

Verse
Why look beyond the end of your nose?
Take Yiddish theater impresarios—
They tell you that for tickets you must dash,
They say their music is the latest,
That Pinye Goldstein is the greatest,
That compared to their set up, and their scenery,
    and their lights, every other theater is just trash.
You come, you sit, you hope, but all in vain,
For in the end they've bluffed you once again—

(Chorus)

theater, in a scene set around the turn of the century, he is perfectly satisfied by the convention.

> Madame Klesmer was playing the part of a girl in a modern Russian town. She declaimed her lines, speaking like a prophetess in ancient Israel, and I liked it extremely. I was fully aware that it was unnatural for a girl in a modern Russian town to speak like a prophetess in ancient Israel, but that was just why I liked it. I thought it perfectly proper that people on the stage should not talk as they would off the stage. I thought that this unnatural speech of their was one of the principal things an audience paid for. The only actor who spoke like a human being was the comedian, and this, too, seemed to be perfectly proper, for a comedian was a fellow who did not take his art seriously, and so I thought that this natural talk of his was part of his fun-making. I thought it was something like a clown burlesquing the Old Testament by reading it, not in the ancient intonations of the synagogue, but in the plain, conversational accents of every-day life.

Shund *in America*

Yiddish popular theater asserted Yiddish identity, and not only Yiddish, but more specifically American Yiddish. In fact, *shund* was the first art form to express the distinctively American Yiddish community. When the scenes were romanticizing past Jewish glories, the audience's identification with the characters moved them with pride and longing. And when the butcher, the rabbi, the market woman, the pants presser, and the tenement landlady made their entrances, a shock of recognition expanded the audience's delighted sense of self. Familiar representations titillated non-Yiddish audiences too; they relished seeing a typical shrewd Yankee (in *The Contrast*, 1787) or a typical New York Irish fireman (in *The New York Fireman and the Bond Street Heiress* and a string of others, in the 1850s) upon stage. It is no coincidence that New York vaudeville houses of the period, including Yiddish ones, hung huge mirrors in the lobbies to reflect the audiences. They were part of the show.

At the turn of the century Yiddish audiences were still greenhorns fighting to "ungreen" themselves. Later they were an Americanized generation struggling to cope with "Yankee" children. Both these problems became major dramatic themes. Even the simplest allusion to these problems, or to any facet of the Lower East Side experience, galvanized audiences with the feeling that the play was truly and intimately about them.

Since a new language was part of the New World, one staple situation was a dialogue of misunderstandings, half in Yiddish and half in English. This

Avrom Shomer's play *At Sea and Ellis Island,* advertised in the third week of its run, in 1911. Such plays mirrored fresh memories of immigration for an audience of immigrants and immigrants' children. The prima donna Keni Liptzin, of course an immigrant herself, had her own theater, which she billed as "The Home of Yiddish Drama." A sketch of the author, who was Shomer-Shaikevitch's son, appears opposite Mme. Liptzin's.

reflected in a comic light the daily difficulties of the uninitiated immigrant who still hasn't learned the important new vocabulary: "Hurry up," "Payday," "Hester Street," "Christopher Columbus." In *Dos Pintele Yid (The Essential Spark of Jewishness)*, the characters' inability to communicate in words is a sad and funny metaphor for the gulf which already separates their cultural experiences. An Americanized young girl believes she's speaking pure Yiddish; the Old Country Jews she's speaking to can't keep up with her New World sophistication. In the eyes of the audience, who have been through it, the joke is on them all.

Yiddish (What the Audience Hears)	English (What the Words Mean)
BENITA *Bay uns in New York, ah, Jesus Christ, Chinatown, sporting places, gambling houses—*	BENITA At home in New York, ah, Jesus Christ, Chinatown, sporting places, gambling houses—
ALL *Vos?*	ALL What?
BAYNUSH *Vus fershteyt ir nit, ferdishe kep? Dos heyst avade: besmedreshn, mikves, bikur-kholim, tsedoke-pushkes.*	BAYNUSH What don't you understand, you horses' heads? Naturally she must mean: synagogues, ritual baths, organizations to care for the sick, charity coin-boxes.

The scene ends with Benita teaching the yokels, phonetically, a song that the audience naturally understands, beginning (as the uninitiated characters mispronounce the words): "Tree cheers far Yankoo Doodle." The characters' mistakes make each spectator freshly conscious of what he has come through and what he shares uniquely with the people sitting around him; only they can get the joke. As plays about immigrants' problems became increasingly popular, what depth they lacked as plays the audience could supply from the realities of their own experience. This in itself helps account for their capacity to immerse themselves so passionately in the stories, as well as for their reverence for the actors who represented them onstage.

As the Yiddish-American community hurtled from its old-country setting into the modern Western world, their theater took the same forms as their neighbors'. But their response kept the intensity of the ritual Purim play, which was still a living tradition, and the intimacy of *mame-loshn*.

Uprooted, its social organizations, its cultural forms, its devotions, and its associations all weakening and dimming, the community tried to keep touch through theater. Theater evoked their passions through play themes, through personal identification, and through the event itself, since the gathering of so many people, speaking Yiddish, was itself an affirmation of the group's identity.

6 JACOB GORDIN

THE PLAYWRIGHT JACOB GORDIN recalls the first time he saw a Yiddish play, in 1891, at the Union Theater on New York's Lower East Side:

> Everything I saw and heard was far from real Jewish life. All was vulgar, immoderate, false and coarse. "Oy, oy!" I thought to myself, and I went home and sat down to write my first play, which at its *bris* was given the name *Siberia*. I wrote my first play the way a pious man, a scribe, copies out a Torah scroll.

Beginning with *Siberia*, Jacob Gordin wrote at least thirty-five plays—possibly as many as sixty, for he hid behind a wealth of pseudonyms—and a number of them were and still are very strong.

Gordin's monumental presence affected the Yiddish theater beyond the plays themselves. By the time of his death in New York in 1909 (one year after Goldfadn's), a number of serious dramatists and actors had begun to work in a professional popular Yiddish vein that was distinct from *shund*. Gordin's most creative years, around the turn of the century, are often called the Golden Age of American Yiddish theater. Sometimes they are called the Gordin Era, for the man left his personal mark on Yiddish culture.

Ironically, Gordin began as a conscious alien to Yiddish culture. His father was a *maskil*, and the son wrote and spoke Russian more comfortably than Yiddish. While still in his teens in the Ukraine, young Gordin started writing articles in Russian for various left-wing newspapers and worked for underground causes. Included was the independence of an area of the Ukraine from the rest of Russia, but interestingly not the civil rights of Jews; indeed, Gordin claimed that the 1881 pogroms were the Jews' own fault, because they had failed to be Russians and to live by farming. As an adult he wrote articles, stories, and sketches for important St. Petersburg newspapers (according to some reports, he wrote theater reviews under the pseudonym "Ivan"), and became well known as a socialist activist. Believing that the soil was the only answer for humanity, he worked several years as a farm laborer. When in 1891, at the age of thirty-eight, he came to the United States, he came with a group called *Am Olam* (Hebrew for "Eternal People"), who planned to establish a utopian socialist farming commune. Czarist police arrived to search his home in Russia only hours after he had fled.

Am Olam failed in America, and Gordin, though his heart was with his Russian comrades and writing in any language but Russian was laborious for him, took a regular position on one of the growing number of radical Yiddish newspapers on the Lower East Side.

He had a wife and eight children to support, and without a moment of leisure in which to acknowledge the irony of his fate, he found himself in a city office far from the soil, worrying constantly about money rather than revolution, and writing almost exclusively and with increasing intensity in Yiddish and for Jewish readers. His situation was simply a particularization of a larger irony that simultaneously affected the Yiddish community in America and Europe.

In the last two decades of the nineteenth century, after Czar Alexander III's May Laws of 1882 had taken back all citizenship rights and left assimilated Jews high and dry, official anti-Semitism grew in Russia and other Eastern European countries. Poor economic conditions affected everyone,

Jacob Gordin (1853–1909), whose plays and personality made the 1890s into a "Golden Age" of Yiddish theater.

especially Jews, and exacerbated anti-Semitic feeling. In the easier days of the 1860s and 1870s, Jews like Gordin had been drifting or rushing away from Jewishness in order to be true Russians or Poles, or else true "citizens of the world." Now there was a movement in the opposite direction, back toward their roots. The movement touched all Eastern European Jews, including many who emigrated to America. It took form as Zionism (Theodor Herzl wrote *The Jewish State* in 1896, in reaction to the Dreyfus trial); and perhaps even more relevant to Yiddish culture, it took form as Jewish socialism: the Bund.

In the 1880s, Russian-Jewish radicals suffered the first of a series of traumatic shocks when their radical comrades approved of pogroms in which Jews were massacred on grounds that it was more important to encourage the peasants to assert themselves than to protect their innocent victims. Many Jewish radicals, feeling that the post revolutionary international brotherliness was after all not going to include Jews, were groping back inward toward Jewishness. For example, A. Vayter, who later went to prison for the revolutionary activities of his youth, left politics for Jewish literature and wrote a play called *Der Shtumer (The Mute),* about a revolutionary who goes to sit quietly in synagogue. With many others the shift was much more gradual, almost imperceptible. Russian-Jewish radicals who came as political refugees to New York paralleled the ideological shift of the Jewish comrades they left behind in Russia.

By the time Gordin arrived in 1891, a sizable group of radicals was already living on New York's Lower East Side. They were the area's elite, and they were consciously elitist. Their elitism was strictly intellectual rather than social or economic, though they sometimes came from middle-class families. Some of them lived by writing and lecturing, but most worked, like the majority of Lower East Side Jews, in sweatshops in the garment trades. Bent over sewing machines, they argued about aesthetics and political philosophy and even stole glances at open copies of Karl Marx, Gorki, and Tolstoy. By night they packed the lecture halls, where they stood on tables to get the speaker's attention and to ask questions. Hutchins Hapgood described them for his friends "uptown":

> It is this class which contains . . . the many men of ideas who bring about a veritable intellectual fermentation. Gifted Russian Jews hold forth passionately to crowds of workingmen; devoted writers exploit in the Yiddish newspapers the principles of their creed and take violent part in the labor agitation of the East Side or produce realistic sketches of life in the quarter. . . . The excitement in the air causes many splits among the socialists . . . each prominent man has his "patriots"—the faithful adherents who support him right or wrong. Intense personal abuse and the most violent denunciation of opposing principles are the

rule. Mellowness, complacency, geniality, and calmness are qualities practically unknown to the intellectual Russian Jews, who, driven from the old country, now possess the first opportunity to express themselves. . . . Their poets sing pathetically of the sweatshops, of universal brotherhood, of the abstract rights of man. Their enthusiastic young men gather every evening in cafés of the quarter and become habitually intoxicated with the excitement of ideas. In their restless and feverish eyes shines the intense idealism of the combined Jew and Russian—the moral earnestness of the Hebrew combined with the passionate, rebellious mental activity of the modern Muscovite.

Much of that talk was going on in Russian. Yiddish was not the first language of these intellectuals, just as Jewishness was not their first loyalty. They looked down on the larger majority of Lower East Side Jews, simple workers from Rumania and Galicia and elsewhere in Eastern Europe, uncultured and without political consciousness, who defined themselves simply as Jews and spoke only *mame-loshn.* These intellectuals respected Russian as the language of the Russian people and as the vehicle of a great literature; they sweated to learn English: but they scorned Yiddish as the *jargón* of pietism, lullabies, and *shund.*

Predictably, Gordin and the other Russian-Jewish intellectuals had no respect for Yiddish theater. If they went to theater, they went to Russian theater, or American, or to dramas in some other language, such as the German theater of the immigrant neighborhood just north of the Lower East Side. They scorned *shund* as unintellectual entertainment for peasants who liked, in Goldfadn's own rueful summation, "a song, a jig, a quarrel, a kiss." More, they positively hated *shund* as a reinforcement of parochialism, an institution whose dramas and indeed whose total ambience stressed an unthinking attachment to Jewish community over all other values. It was the epitome of what they burned to reform. It seemed to them a caricature of all Jews, including themselves, perversely exposed for all the world to see. Indeed, any intellectual who saw Lateiner's play *The Jewish Heart* (in which the mother finds her long-lost son and the young artist proudly confronts an anti-Semite) and secretly experienced a sympathetic emotional tug hated the play all the more because it made him vulnerable to just those feelings that he was rejecting. To this day, the fear that the world is watching, and that threatening sense of personal vulnerability, seem to be part of the venom with which Yiddish intellectuals refer to Yiddish popular theater.

Gordin's comrades brought enrichment to the Lower East Side, including a proliferation of newspapers. There were dailies, weeklies, monthlies, quarterlies, most of them affiliated with a distinct political position. The radicals' influence stimulated special festival journals and yearbooks; there were humorous periodicals; there were union papers and special-interest papers about health, or about chess. The first radical Yiddish weekly in the United States *(The New Times)* was founded in 1886 by Abraham Cahan, who recognized that to teach the masses you must speak to them in the language they understand—and promptly startled everyone by switching his soapbox lectures from Russian to Yiddish. Cahan, whose background, career, and convictions paralleled Gordin's in many ways, eventually became, as editor of the *Jewish Daily Forward,* the only figure on the Lower East Side as influential as Gordin himself. The press itself was the heart of the community's cultural life.

Almost all professional Yiddish writers, including poets, novelists, and playwrights, supported themselves by writing for newspapers. The novelists printed ongoing serials; some sixty-five serials appeared between 1892 and 1898. The dramatists who were to appear in Gordin's wake, such as Leon Kobrin and Z. Libin, were developing their eye for drama and ear for dialogue through writing realistic sketches of the sort Hapgood mentioned. One of Gordin's earliest newspaper pieces was just such a vignette. It had a large proportion of dialogue, which was perhaps Gordin's way of coping with writing for the first time in what had been for him almost exclusively a spoken language. (Indeed, the fact that Yiddish was much further developed as a spoken than as a literary language may be relevant to the instinctive attraction so many Yiddish writers have felt in drama.)

Gordin's sketch caught the eye of another Yiddish writer, who dramatized the piece for Mogulesko. Gordin then came to the attention of several artistes. They were looking for fresh material, and Gordin seemed promising.

Intellectuals were not encouraged to write plays. "Professor" Hurwitz, Lateiner, and a few other *patentirte* ("patented") company dramatists turned out a steady supply of historical operettas and domestic melodramas and fought to keep their dominion against ambitious newcomers. They prompted the actors to behave like fraternity boys hazing unfortunate candidates for admission. Pros referred to would-be playwrights as *yolds* (suckers). When an author came around trying to sell his new play, the actors might insist that he copy it out (by hand, of course) all in red ink, or in green ink. They might contrive to cover him with soot by brushing against him accidentally on purpose as he read his play aloud to them. They might ask him to read it onstage while they moved toward the back rows, asking him at intervals to read louder, until they slipped out one by one, leaving him shouting like a *yold* to an empty house.

Nevertheless, there was some movement toward a theater beyond *shund.* Not only were there intellectuals ripe to be drawn into the Yiddish theater if the right plays were performed, but the masses, too, seemed ready for more

A melodramatic rendering of ideological conflicts in the Jewish community. Boris Thomashefsky, in modern western dress, has just pulled himself free of a chain labeled "Assimilation" and is following his heart back across the ocean to traditional Jewish life. The play, by Avrom Shomer, is *Ha-Tikva*, which is Hebrew for *The Hope* and is the name of the Zionist anthem. The small print at the bottom of the poster gives directions to the theater by bus, subway, and elevated railway from all parts of New York City and from as far as Passaic and Jersey City. 1931.

ambitious works. Perhaps they were growing accustomed to theater itself. Perhaps another reason was that they were settling in as Americans: an increasing proportion of the Lower East Side had ungreened itself. Critics in Yiddish newspapers were calling for something better than *shund*, and some actors, too, were getting restless. They were becoming aware of the finer varieties of theater in the world, especially through their Russian contacts and through their neighbors' German-language theater. Jacob P. Adler, in particular, was eager to aim higher.

One important result of this restlessness was the different use to which Yiddish theater put foreign dramas. Hurwitz and Lateiner had grabbed plots from German, French, or Russian plays, and from Broadway hits too, and "Yiddishized" them by making superficial adaptations. But now, in addition to this brutish use of generally undistinguished plays, managers and actors were beginning to choose well-known plays and present them either in adaptations *(The Taming of the Shrew* became *The Pretty American)* or in relatively faithful translations.

Here is a partial list of the plays that appeared in more or less recognizable Yiddish versions between 1890 and 1905: Shakespeare's *Romeo and Juliet, Macbeth, Othello, Coriolanus, Hamlet, Julius Caesar, King Lear, The Merchant of Venice, Richard III;* Molière's *The Miser;* Schiller's *Maria Stuart,*

William Tell; Goethe's *Faust;* Lessing's *Nathan the Wise;* Dumas's *The Lady of the Camellias;* Ostrovsky's *Belugin's Wedding;* Gorki's *Children of the Sun;* Tolstoy's *The Awakening, The Power of Darkness;* Hauptmann's *The Weavers;* Zola's *The Blind Wedding;* Ibsen's *A Doll's House, An Enemy of the People, Rosmersholm;* Strindberg's *The Father.* Yiddish theatergoers also had Verdi's opera *Ernani,* Meyerbeer's *Les Huguenots,* Strauss's *The Gypsy Baron.*

If actor-managers were looking for material, Gordin was, as always, looking for a way to support his children. The editor Philip Krantz arranged to bring the parties together, in a restaurant on the Lower East Side. Gordin made an impressive entrance. Tall and handsome, dashing in the darkly romantic Russian style, with deep-set eyes and thickly curling black hair and beard, he was a man of imposing presence. On this occasion, he wore his usual soft broad-brimmed black hat and neat but shabby black suit. He walked with immense dignity, grasping a walking stick, which he waved for emphasis when he spoke.

Under his confident manner he felt uncomfortable. He had never been to the Yiddish theater, but imagined, as he later recalled, that every Yiddish actor was a boor who was as likely as not to wipe his nose on his sleeve, jump up on the table, and recite gross ditties. Instead he saw gentlemen in top hats and silk shirts, looking "sensitive" and speaking intelligently. (Among those "gentlemen" were Jacob P. Adler, David Kessler, Sigmund Mogulesko, and Sigmund Feinman.) Gordin said to himself: If Yiddish actors are really just like other actors, why shouldn't Yiddish theater be like other theaters? Politically he believed in an *Am Olam* in which Jews would rise out of their backward, isolated state and join everyone else in international brotherhood and enlightenment; his conception of Yiddish art followed from his politics.

His new friends invited him to attend his first Yiddish play, which, as we have seen, horrified and inspired him. He resolved, like "a pious man, a scribe," to write a whole new kind of Yiddish drama. He called his first play *Siberia,* and it opened on the Lower East Side in 1891.

The rehearsal period for *Siberia* was war: Gordin in one camp, the actors in the other, Adler in the middle. On the first day the actors were already transposing his wholesome Yiddish dialogue into *Daytshmerish,* because an actor felt cheated saying only a skimpy line like "Reb Berl, why do you want to make me unhappy?" Besides, the actor knew that his audience would feel cheated by such untheatrical language. So he automatically substituted something like this: "My dear most honored Mr. Berl, sir, when commences the lion to roar in his cage, when snaps and springs the tiger, when tears and bites the leopard, then shall justice triumph in the heavens and the pure spirits of

Jewish patriots shall resound, 'Hear, O Israel.' " Gordin would not permit it.

On the second day, a new battle. Gordin discovered that Kessler was planning to sing operatic selections with a large chorus in the middle of the action, again as a matter of course. Gordin would not permit it.

On the third day, Gordin refused to permit Mogulesko to insert into the second act the *kuplét* that was every comedian's right. Mogulesko and Gordin stood on the stage glaring at each other and yelling in a mixture of Russian and Yiddish. Mogulesko had the stronger voice: "Get out, you black beard, you anti-Semite—don't even breathe in this theater!" Mogulesko gave the management an ultimatum: either Gordin left or he would. Everyone in the cast but Adler sided with Mogulesko. Besides, since Mogulesko was the comic favorite of the Lower East Side, he was the one who was necessary for a box office success. So Gordin left. They rehearsed and opened without him.

On *Siberia*'s opening night, the audience was the usual *shund* audience, munching apples and waiting to be entertained. The play seemed dry to them. They squirmed and giggled. At last, after the second act, Adler stepped in front of the curtain with tears in his famous "eagle" 's eyes. "I stand before you," he said, "ashamed and humiliated, my head bowed with shame, that you, my friends, are unable to understand a masterpiece by the famous Russian writer Jacob Mihaelovitch Gordin. Friends, friends, if you only understood what a great work we are playing for you today, you wouldn't laugh and you wouldn't jeer." He wept.

The audience was very impressed. They applauded Adler's speech. Then, when the third act began, they paid respectful attention, and they were moved. Toward the conclusion, when Mogulesko as the comic servant said a heartbroken farewell to his master, who was being sent back to Siberia, the whole house wept.

That night Mogulesko and the other actors began to catch on that Gordin's plays were good for them, since they gave them meatier roles with characters and scenes that allowed them to move audiences deeply. And at the third night's performance, when Gordin, having finally received a written invitation from the stars, did appear at the theater, the actors joined the audience in giving him an ovation.

The Golden Age of plays and productions had begun.

A few weeks later Gordin turned up at Thomashefsky's theater. At first no one recognized him. They treated him as they treated aspiring playwrights on the Lower East Side: with no respect whatsoever. Gordin, however, was still serenely unaware of Yiddish theater politics and fashions. He held his new script, and he waited. And soon somebody recognized him as the famous Russian writer who had just won ovations for *Siberia,* and came bursting into the rehearsal, shouting, "That's no *yold*—that's Jacob Gordin." The company were flustered and respectful. But soon they recovered their usual brash manners, especially when they found he'd come to offer them something. Looking pointedly at the slim book under Gordin's arm, the director asked, "Is that all?" Gordin looked him up and down before replying, quietly, "It's enough."

The director offered Gordin sixty dollars for *The Pogrom in Russia:* a good price. Gordin accepted. He only stipulated, rolling the *r*'s in his heavily Russian-accented Yiddish and shaking his finger for emphasis, "Will you play the play exactly the way I wrote it? Tell the truth. You won't change a word?" They promised. He also arranged to take a bit part in his own play, partly because the role called for a Russian and partly because he needed the extra five dollars a week he would earn.

Gordin had learned what to expect. During the rehearsal period of *The Pogrom in Russia,* he watched the cast like a hawk. He chose the costumes himself, crushing the actors' taste for tinsel in favor of realistically poor peasant clothing. When they begged for musical interludes, he granted them Russian folk songs which the characters might realistically have sung. Once the direc-

The familiar horse and wagon with which Aba Kompaneyets, founder of the Kompaneyets theatrical family, advertised his productions through the streets of Warsaw. On the right of the wagon is a poster advertising Jacob Gordin's play *Mirele Efros,* in Russian above and in Polish below.

tor tried to sneak in a *kuplét* with a dance. Gordin didn't say a word. He picked up his script, put it under his arm, and started out of the room. The actors had to run after him and coax him back, swearing never to do it again.

For this opening night people arrived who had never imagined they would set foot in a Yiddish theater. At Gordin's entrance as a Russian policeman, the place went wild. People yelled, "Hurray, Gordin!" and threw their hats in the air. Sudden stage fright struck Gordin dumb, and he stood staring down at his feet till Thomashefsky hissed him his lines from the wings. Then he recovered himself. The play won an ovation after every act and a mild riot greeted the end.

The next morning Abraham Cahan proclaimed in the *Jewish Daily Forward* that a "new chapter" had begun in Yiddish theater.

An incident that night illustrated the principal ideas in that chapter. Onstage the scene was a kitchen of a small Jewish home in Russia. A Russian policeman (Gordin) sat at the little table. He spoke Russian, because that was the language that a Russian policeman realistically would speak. The housewife put fish and schnapps in front of him. As he began to eat, the actress turned toward the audience: "He should only choke on it." In 1892 Yiddish actors were used to ad-libbing asides to get a laugh, and a sly insult to a czarist policeman was bound to please the crowd. But this time the veteran actress, Bina Abramovitch, got a reaction that nothing in her twenty years on the Yiddish stage had prepared her for. The policeman slammed the table with the butt of his whip and jumped up, overturning his chair, spilling the schnapps in his fury, and yelling, "No, no, *no!* That's not in the script!" In defending his play, even if he had to destroy the performance—and the scenery—Gordin was asserting two principles that were revolutionary in the Yiddish theater. One was respect for the play as a serious literary endeavor. The other was realism.

Gordin's Plays

Jacob Gordin was a good, not a great, dramatist; the classical Yiddish writer Yitskhok Leyb Peretz went so far as to call Gordin's plays, on the average, "partway between art and *shund,*" and to prefer Goldfadn's unpretentious folksiness. Gordin was a good, not a great, thinker. What *was* unquestionably great about him was the role he played, through his dramas and his moral authority, in transforming Yiddish theater. He made the intellectual elite feel that a theater in the Yiddish language could be their concern and even their pride. And as these intellectuals entered the theater, first as audiences and then as artists, the theater itself inevitably rose in quality.

Gordin did not write an entirely new sort of play. In form, his plays were a refinement of the domestic melodramas that Hurwitz and Lateiner and the rest had been turning out for years. Yet they seemed to his fans, as they drank tea at their favorite cafés after the show, like an intoxicatingly strong fresh wind. These three scenes from *Sappho* illustrate both what was old and what was new about them.

Sofia Fingerhut, later called Sappho, is a beautiful, intelligent young woman with the high romantic principles of the New Woman of her generation. She works in a photographer's studio in Odessa. She is to be married to her sweetheart, Boris, a photographer. In this scene, early in Act One, her parents and younger sister Lisa look on and bicker as the tailor fits her wedding gown.

> *(Odessa. Parlor of the Fingerhut apartment.* SOFIA *has been singing Russian songs offstage behind the dialogue. Still singing, she enters, bows to the tailor, and examines the wedding dress he has brought for her. She is wearing an outfit that is not expensive, but very tasteful and original.)*
>
> SOFIA   A wedding gown! A gown which you try on joyfully, put on tearfully, and take off fearfully.
>
> FINGERHUT [SOFIA's father, a would-be man about town, who spends his days in cafés, playing cards with his cronies.]   Where do you find out things like that?
>
> SOFIA   *(Laughs.)* From novels. Now we'll see. Herr Fingerhut, turn your back to the audience. *(Runs to her father and turns him to face the wall.)* Let the gown be tried! *(Throws off her robe and puts on the dress.)*
>
> TSHERNE [SOFIA's mother]   *(Helps her.)* Sofia—the tailor—ay, girls today! Tfoo, curses on them. *(Spits.)*
>
> SOFIA   One's own husband, a doctor, and a ladies' tailor don't count as men. Isn't that right, Herr Tailor?
>
> FINGERHUT   What are you asking the tailor for? Ask the tailor's wife.
>
> SOFIA   *(At the mirror.)* I love a dress that's sewn with taste, with a lovely line that doesn't scream but speaks to the eye. It's pleasant to please everyone, and a pretty dress is a powerful method of pleasing. The woman who doesn't use that method is like a hunter who goes out early in the morning into the woods to shoot wild animals and leaves his gun at home. Ha ha ha. Yes, in fact a woman is always in the woods among the wild beasts, and she must always keep her gun handy at her side. Shoulder arms! *(Pretends to shoot.)* Bang, bang, bang! *(Sings a snatch of an air from* Les Huguenots, *which begins "Pif-paf": hunting noises. She says to the tailor)* Yes, the dress is better now. *(Takes the dress off.)*

LISA [SOFIA's younger sister]   Thank God, success at last, after only fifteen fittings. *(Sits down to sew her own dress.)*

SOFIA   You're a fool. You have to fit and try the wedding gown so it's right before the wedding. After is too late. *(Changes clothes.)*

FINGERHUT   Fräulein Sofia, may I in the near future turn my face back to the audience? I must talk business with you. If you understand me, I—uh—

TSHERNE   You gave him pocket money just a few days ago—a few days. When was it? Sunday or Monday? A memory! Tfoo, curses on it! *(Spits.)*

FINGERHUT   When I say that I took nothing, you may be sure; my word is holy. Sofia, I need to be shaven. The father of the bride needs a smooth chin. I need a little pack of tobacco. And today I am going to treat myself to tea in the front of the Paris Café. Let them know what sort of man Matias Fingerhut is—a plague on their fathers' graves.

SOFIA   *(Takes a purse from her handbag.)* This is what's coming to you. *(Gives money to the tailor.)* This is what's not coming to you. *(Gives tailor more. He thanks her.)* And you, Papa, I have given two twenties this week already.

FINGERHUT   You say you've given me already? Hem, how can it be that I don't remember?

SOFIA   On the contrary, *you* tell *me* how it can it be. Ha ha ha. But never mind. You're the bride's father, after all. Here. But don't stay long in the café. A bride's father is supposed to sit at home, not in Paris.

FINGERHUT   *(Puts on his top hat.)* Fräulein Sofia, merci. Monsieur Tailor, we will make the journey together. Lisa, tie my cravat á la Garibaldi de Pompadour.

LISA   *(Rudely.)* They'll recognize you that way too.

SOFIA   Come here, I'll tie your cravat—how do you say it?—á la Garibaldi de Pompadour. Ha ha ha! He's right. As long as a person lives, he should hold himself like a fine gentleman. *(Ties her father's cravat.)* Mama, he looks like he must have been a shocking heart-breaker in his day.

TSHERNE   Yes, and he never did any *other* work in his life. . . . *(FINGERHUT bows majestically, top hat in hand, and exits with the tailor.)*

SOFIA   *(Goes over to flowers.)* Oh, my, nobody watered the flowers today. *(Takes water from carafe.)* If I were rich, I'd fill the house with flowers. The most expensive furniture doesn't make a room as pretty as flowers do. *(As she waters, she sings the same Russian song as before.)* Other brides cry before the wedding, and I sing. . . . They want to get married, so why do they cry? Me, I sing, and —Mama, I would give five years off my life now not to have to get married.

TSHERNE   What is all this, silly?

SOFIA   *(Sighs.)* Well, it's—I don't know. . . . But now it's too late. All over now. Ehh! *(Sings another phrase of the same song.)* You know, Mama, that's the song a Russian bride sings. . . .

Bertha Gersten, in the title role of *Mirele Efros* by Jacob Gordin, confronts her weak-willed son and defiant daughter-in-law. Still from film made in New York in 1939.

Now the final scene of Act One. Sofia's friends have come to congratulate her; the wedding is to be the next day. But meanwhile the audience, and Sofia, have overheard Boris telling Lisa that she is the one he really loves.

(The parlor is full of guests.)

SOFIA   It isn't proper, I believe, for a bride to sing, and just because it isn't proper, that's why I'm going to do it. This romance is a setting of the words of our Russian poet. It's called "The Suffering Flower." I like the words very much. *(Declaims while* BORIS, *her fiancé, accompanies her with the melody on his guitar.)*

> "In the shadow of a high old tree
> Bloomed a lovely flower, delicately.
> Suddenly a lightning bolt split, sharp, the tree.
> The flower stood, her head bowed, dry and starved.
> The sun still rises, dawns are still as bright,
> The birds still sing with joy, life still rings out.
> The flower stands in silence, pressed by suffering's weight.
> She weeps with pain. She feels unhappy, cold."

ALL   Bravo, bravissimo! *(Applaud.)*

BORIS Now gather your strength, I'm going to give you a concert. Attention! Hey! *(Flings his hair back dramatically and plays.* LISA *listens closely, suddenly weeps and runs off impetuously.* BORIS *puts down his guitar and runs after her.)* Lisa, Lisa! What's the matter with you, silly? *(*BORIS *exits. Everyone is astounded. We hear his voice, then a loud kiss. He leads her by the hand back onstage.)* Nothing's the matter. Part nerves, part my music. *(Quietly to* LISA.*)* Be a smart girl. *(Sits down.)*

TSHERNE Girl, what did you start to sniffle for, out of a clear blue sky? Tfoo, curses on you! *(Spits.)*

FRADE [SOFIA's aunt] Don't worry, you'll get married too. There are no convents for Jewish girls. . . .

*(*LISA *cries harder.)*

TSHERNE I'm asking you, what are you crying for? My girl, you've seen an evil spirit.

*(*LISA *covers her head, weeps harder. Pause.)*

SOFIA *(Smoking a cigarette, very calm.)* So then, you don't know why she's crying? I know. Lisa is crying because she knows that I won't be getting married tomorrow. She's not going to dance at my wedding. *(Some people laugh.)* It's no joke. I'm not going to marry Boris. I regret it today. Tomorrow is too late for regrets. *(Everyone is astounded.)*

TSHERNE What's the matter with you today? Tfoo, curses on you. *(Spits.)* What regrets?

FINGERHUT What kind of a game is that? In that kind of game you lose your stakes.

SOFIA It's a bitter game, but you can only play a hand with a suitable partner.

MELEKH [SOFIA's uncle, a rich fish merchant] If you mean me, a fig for you and your father together.

FINGERHUT Oh, shut up. Sofia, what kind of deal is this? This match? Matias Fingerhut's daughter? All Odessa knows I'm making a wedding.

SOFIA Your deal remains a deal. Your daughter is getting married—I mean *that* daughter. Your son-in-law remains, the photography shop remains, and I remain independent, so I can work and give you money. You—we're making a good business arrangement. Boris Stavropolski! You love my sister, and I don't want to rob my sister of her happiness. You will be a happy couple.

BORIS *(Confused.)* Sofia, heaven help you, what's come over you? I can't understand you. What makes you talk like this? So what, I like to play around a little with her, any man would do it, but I swear to you—

SOFIA You just said that you're in love with her. If that is the truth, why should I rob my sister of her happiness? Why should I unite myself with a person who will not belong to me with his entire soul, with his entire life?

BORIS   No, it wasn't serious. Believe me, Sofia. You must not believe—

SOFIA   You want me to believe that you are not to be believed? I know it, and I tell you that if you have lied to her, I will not be the wife of a liar. So, now. Tomorrow we will dance at my sister's wedding. Lisa, I would have given you my wedding gown, but unfortunately it would not fit you. Never mind, in Odessa you can find anything for rent, and renting is more practical and cheaper. My room you can have just as it is. *(With tears.)* I fixed it with taste; every object had a meaning for me. I dreamed it would be a nest. Never mind, your true love will be able to bloom in a strange nest. But enough lament—I'm no longer a bride, and the match is no longer a match.

BORIS   Sofia, remember what you're doing! You have openly, in front of people—

SOFIA   When a person does something, he must feel that he is right to do it, and if he is right to do it, he must do it openly in front of the whole world.

BORIS   But heaven help you, Sofia, how can you? Have you forgotten?

SOFIA   I have forgotten nothing. The whole world must know that too.

BORIS   What are you trying to do? *(Prevents her from speaking. She frees herself.)*

SOFIA   Yes, the whole world must know that too. I . . . must become a mother. I am not ashamed. I loved the man. And one who loves faithfully must have faith, must believe, must sacrifice everything in the world. Yes, I had faith and sacrifice. That will not force me to marry him when I feel and understand that I must not be his wife.

TSHERNE   Oy, *vey iz mir* [woe is me]. What a misfortune. *Vey iz mir.*

MANITSHKE   [Young girl] What does it mean? What is she saying, Mamma?

FRADE   Quiet. You don't have to know. Come home, Melekh, come home.

MELEKH   Home! Dragging the trout out of the cooking pot.

(All the guests stand, look anxiously at SOFIA.*)*

FINGERHUT   What have you done? Be smart. A clever mamselle tells such things?

SOFIA   I come out openly before the whole world and say that I was blind, I made a mistake, it is my error and my misfortune. It is nobody's business. I take all the responsibility. Strangers with their piety and righteousness, with their laughter and mockery, will not force me to stifle, to bury, the truth and to act against my feelings. If I am to be a mother, I can care for my child by myself. Nothing frightens me. I will be free and honorable in my actions, honorable the way I understand it, not Aunt Frade's way and Uncle Melekh's and all the rest!

FRADE   *(Insulted.)* Come, girls, come. And five minutes ago I made fun of Lempert's daughter Doba, who got herself in trouble. I didn't remember you shouldn't mention hanging thieves when there's a hanged man in the family. Home!

(All SOFIA'*s friends get dressed to leave.)*

SOFI   You're running away? You're already ashamed of me too? Ha ha ha. A little pinch in the dark is all right with you, but open love, open, as our true feelings command us—that's a scandal. Yes, it will be very bitter for me to know that people are ashamed around me. But it would have been much more bitter to feel that I should be ashamed of myself. *(Laughing and crying.)* Monsieur Fingerhut, this is a little à la Garibaldi de Pompadour, hm? Never mind. And if the "pure ones" run away, that doesn't frighten me either. Only it's hard for me to feel that all I hoped, all I waited for, all my sweet dreams— Oh, oh! *(Lets her head fall onto the table, and weeps bitterly.)*

Curtain

Several years pass between Act One and Act Two. Sofia has had Boris's baby and continues to live with her parents and to work to support them all. Boris and Lisa are married and living abroad. The fish merchant and his wife, Melekh and Frade, have gotten a fiancé for their silly daughter Manitshke by the fairly common method of putting a penniless young man through school on the understanding that he will marry the girl when he finishes. The fiancé, whose name, significantly, is Apollon, is a pianist. He has just returned from his studies to go through with the bargain, and it is obvious to the audience that he and Sofia are soul mates; only *she* can appreciate his piano-playing and cosmopolitan spirituality. She scrupulously avoids encouraging his interest in her. But that evening he comes to her home.

SOFIA   *(Alone in dressing gown, hears a weak ring at the door.)* Someone is ringing? Who can it be so late? *(Goes to door.)* Who can it be? . . . Apollon, you?

APOLLON   Yes, it's me. Forgive me, I took the liberty— I have come to you as I would come to a good comrade if I felt as I feel today. And I tell you as I would my comrade: Friend, I'm far now from everything I call home, food, sleep, worries, trifles, usual interests. On a night like this I would want to hear music, talk about what is honorable, pure, and far from the dirty reality, far from our miserable life. I would want to cry. Comrade, friend, don't drive me away. *(*SOFIA *covers her bare arms with a shawl, indicates a chair to him, and herself sits down in a corner far from him, frightened and worried. She sits so deeply back in her*

Bertha Kalish as the broken-hearted heroine of Jacob Gordin's *Kreutzer Sonata,* rereads an old love letter she keeps in a book of Tolstoy. This English-language production was given on Broadway in 1906. By the time Mme. Kalish autographed the photograph, twenty-one years later, she was nearly blind.

armchair that she looks like a child. Pause. It's so quiet that we hear the ticking of a clock.)

CHILD'S VOICE   *(From another room, half asleep.)* Aunt Sofia, who's in there with you? Oh! I don't want you to— Come here!

SOFIA   *(Starts up. Quietly.)* The child!

Curtain

Apollon pursues and wins Sofia despite her genuine efforts to resist. It is he who names her Sappho, after the poetess. She braves the abuse of the entire community for him, but he weakly marries Manitshke and has a child by her, while still continuing to see Sofia. In the end Sofia resolves to move to another city with her little daughter and to start a life alone, but independent and with dignity. Boris comes home; he has nursed Lisa through a long illness till she died, and now, a sadder and wiser man, he wants to marry Sofia and give his daughter a home. At first she refuses but at last, and mostly for her daughter's sake, she agrees. The end.

Here in *Sappho,* as in the old-fashioned domestic melodramas, rising suspense explodes punctually for a climactic curtain. There are romance, sentimentality, grand speeches, music. There is "tearful comedy": pathos alternating with comic effects. In other words, Gordin still generates most of his power the old way.

Still, the overall impression is of another league altogether from Lateiner's *The Jewish Heart.* Gordin's first reaction to *shund* had been that it was "far from real Jewish life." So now his effort was to look freshly at the realities of Jewish life and put them on the stage. He adopted a form that was ubiquitous on European and (later) American stages of the mid-nineteenth and twentieth centuries. Perfected by Eugène Scribe and Victorien Sardou, it was known as the "well-made play": a melodrama that has been tightened until it ticks along like a machine, stringing together its sensational effects while the complicated plot resolves itself with inexorable logic. Although the events and characters are rather obviously manipulated, incidents are connected so as to make sense: to seem to happen the way things really do. Almost all Gordin's plays, though relatively loose and operatic, are fashioned after well-made plays. The form was already familiar on the Lower East Side, but Gordin used it with a new intelligence and sensitivity.

Truthfulness and reform had been the intentions of serious European dramatists of the 1860s. Alexandre Dumas *fils,* and after him Émile Augier, wrote "thesis" or "problem" plays, well-made plays that dealt directly with aspects of reality which dramatists had previously considered unfit for art: corruption in business dealings, for example, prostitution, and venereal disease. They specifically aimed to expose social problems and bring about their correction. Ibsen stretched the form to a further degree of thoughtfulness and moral perception in *Ghosts* and other plays of the 1870s and 1880s. Before the turn of the century, Zola in France, Hauptmann in Germany, and Tolstoy in Russia were shocking their audiences with their unprecedented truthfulness. Problem plays crossed to America almost a generation after they appeared in Europe. In the 1890s, while James A. Herne was writing the most realistic plays that Broadway had yet seen, his New York contemporary Jacob Gordin, who had watched the latest Ibsen, Zola, and Hauptmann plays in the elegant theaters of St. Petersburg, was doing the same—and with greater popular success— downtown on the Lower East Side.

Sappho is soap opera, but its ending is a far cry from the splendidly improbable conclusions of *shund,* the rhetoric of operetta curtains, or the dramatic deaths in the final acts of melodrama. True, Lisa's death is suspiciously providential. True, the tacit rules on the Lower East Side, as on Broadway, would not have permitted Sappho to end up happily with another woman's husband, especially not while her child's father was alive. (Only George Bernard Shaw was daring enough for that in 1892; most writers and audiences were not.) Gordin's realism seems limited today and his plots artificial, but still, despite the rather obvious manipulations, his scenes do indeed reflect everyday realities, the complicated human efforts to get along—as opposed to the almost ritual simplicities that operate in *shund.** Gordin had a fondness for moralistic, unnaturally centripetal endings, but usually on the heels of realistic dramatic episodes. In his play *God, Man, and Devil,* the hero repents and tidily dies for his sins. But first he yields to a range of human temptations: sinking morally, he becomes mad for money, leaves his wife for his pretty young niece, and shames his old father.

The Yiddish public, after their initial indifference to *Siberia,* came to realize that Gordin's realism did indeed suit their innate tastes. Since the time of the Broder singers, they had enjoyed the portrayal of authentic social types, and even in fantastical operettas, as Hutchins Hapgood observed, the audiences savored bits of reality, glimpses of genuine local types, and murmured with delight, "So natural . . . so true"—their highest praise. The Yiddish masses also loved the newspaper sketches and vignettes that mirrored life as it honestly was on the Lower East Side. Many of these sketches were written by men who were later to turn their talents to playwriting.

Gordin not only derived a lot of his realism from European and Russian dramatists (he especially emulated the romantic, sensational, almost operatic mode of Tolstoy, Gorki, and Ostrovsky); he also took license from them, pushing his realism into the realm of grotesquerie. The atmosphere of *God, Man, and Devil* is compounded of superstititous spells and curses, hints of the diabolical, constant references to the bitter cold, shadows and thunder, the senile songs and rhymes of a tipsy old *badkhen,* madmen and idiots, a bloodstained prayer shawl—and a single sweet fiddle playing psalm melodies.

Hutchins Hapgood described another dark play this way:

> *The Slaughter . . .* is the story of the symbolic murder of a fragile young girl by her parents, who force her to marry a rich man who has all the vices and whom she hates. The picture of the poorhouse, or the old mother and father and halfwitted stepson with whom the girl is unconsciously in love, is typical of scenes in many of these plays. It is rich in character and milieu drawing. There is another scene of miserable life in the second act. The girl is married and living with the rich brute. In the same house is his mistress, curt and cold, and two children by a former wife. The old parents come to see the wife; she meets them with the joy of starved affection. But the husband enters and changes the scene to one of hate and violence. The old mother tells him, however, of the heir that is to come. Then there is a superb scene of naïve joy in the midst of all the sordid gloom. There is rapturous delight of the old people, turbulent triumph of the

---

*The Broadway producer David Belasco also employed a kind of selective realism—his stage could be set with an actual interior from a Childs restaurant, down to the last spoon, with faucets pouring real water—but his characters continued to stand in spotlights downstage center, posturing wildly and delivering grand, affected speeches.

husband, and satisfaction of the young wife. They make a holiday of it. Wine
is brought. They all love one another for the time. . . . But indescribable violence
and abuse follow, and the wife finally kills her husband, in a scene where realism
riots into burlesque, as it frequently does on the Yiddish stage.*

Avrom Goldfadn, smarting badly because intellectuals dismissed his plays
as old-fashioned, found Gordin's realism shocking.

Do you know the difference between Gordin and me? [Goldfadn demanded
rhetorically]. I looked for good qualities in Jews, especially the decencies of
family life, and put that on the stage. He, Gordin, looked for all bad qualities
in Jews—thievery, murder, swinishness—and put all that on the stage. He
especially desecrated the Jewish family. . . .

Gordin was often denounced for the "thievery, murder, swinishness" he put
on the stage, as were the European writers who called themselves realists and
naturalists. Since Gordin's characters and settings were most often Jewish, the
accusation was especially bitter, for the Jewish community has always worried
to desperation about the image it presents to the gentiles. Gordin, always the
old revolutionary, rather enjoyed the abuse.

For once Goldfadn found himself an ally of the *shund*-baker "Professor"
Hurwitz. In their circle "realism" was a dirty word. "They're yelling Gordin!
What's Gordin?" Hurwitz asked shrilly. "He's a dramatist? They talk about
his prose. On the stage the same prose as in the street . . . Did you ever hear
such a thing? Put Hester Street on the stage?"

Certainly the plain Yiddish Gordin's characters speak, at least in his better
plays, is far from Hurwitz's bombast. Some characters, like Sofia and Apollon,
speak a more German Yiddish than the others, but they stop short of *Daytsh-merish* and in fact mix in a lot of Russian. Conscious intellectuals of the day
did still feel that a Yiddish that stressed the language's Germanic components
was finer than vulgar Yiddish, so that too was realistic dialogue in its way. Satan
in *God, Man, and Devil* addresses God in a superdignified Germanic Yiddish,
but when he comes to earth disguised as a lottery ticket peddler he speaks as
juicy a Yiddish as anyone else. Beyond its role in the dramas themselves,
Gordin's Yiddish was a declaration that Yiddish was no longer to be considered a *jargón* but rather a language among languages and a conduit to universal
culture.

Another element in Gordin's realism is his characterization. In *Sappho*,
it is true that most of the characters are indicated, as in *shund*, by a comic
"humor" or verbal tic (a dramatist's trick that goes back through commedia

---

*This melodramatic mode of ranting, hysterics, and murders—unabashed emotionalism for per-
formers and audience—has its closest relative in traditional contemporaneous Sicilian melodrama
—a similarity explored by the critic Stark Young. —N.S.

dell'arte and Ben Jonson to Greek masks). Fingerhut is always and only the dandified parasite; Mrs. Fingerhut superstitiously spits and curses; Melekh the fish merchant predictably sees the world in terms of fish. However, Fingerhut is a relatively well-observed modern social type, which had not previously been seen onstage, and the major character, Sappho herself, is infinitely more solid and rounded than, for example, Madame Popeska in *The Jewish Heart.* What's more, we see her character develop as her life goes on.

Gordin wrote roles, not plays, commented David Pinski, one of the most important Yiddish literary figures of the twentieth century. Many critics have agreed. For a gala in honor of the tenth anniversary of the opening of *Siberia,* Gordin—never modest—prepared a one-act sketch called *The Gallery of Types.* It consists of characters detached from his plays appearing one at a time to pay tribute to their creator. Sappho brings Gordin flowers and says she is there to honor him "as Sappho, as a woman, and as a human being." Fingerhut uses his fractured French on the master of ceremonies and tries to touch him for a few dollars. The "Jewish King Lear," named David Maysheles in Gordin's adaptation of Shakespeare, is led on blind and talks about his disillusionment with the world. A henpecked husband from still another play stays only a moment, flinching every time he hears a noise offstage, and escapes into the wings just in time to avoid his wife, who enters from the opposite side. All these characters present themselves like Purim play characters, to the master of ceremonies and to the audience. The audience recognized them instantly and caught every allusion they made to their ongoing lives within their respective plays.

Gordin's Actors

The audience also instantly recognized the actors who had identified themselves with Gordin's roles. Hapgood had remarked on Yiddish actors' "remarkable sincerity" and "direct and forcible expressiveness." Even "in the general lack of really good plays, they yet succeed in introducing the note of realism. To be true to nature is their strongest passion, and . . . even in a conventional melodrama . . . often redeems the play from barrenness." Now Gordin had given the actors characters that could stand alone: roles that were deeper and more complex than any available in Yiddish plays up till then. Pinski confirmed what the actors themselves felt—that Gordin wrote his roles for actors rather than for audiences. The actors expanded in their craft as they played these roles, achieving successes of a new and intoxicating sort.

Jacob P. Adler, who loved Russian theater and loved speaking the Russian

language—especially with cronies over caviar and vodka at late-night cafés—
was Gordin's first champion in the theater. In 1893 he went so far as to try
to establish a theater entirely for Gordin plays and translations of fine non-
Yiddish plays, but his company could not survive without lighter and more
vulgar plays to nourish the box office. One reason Adler welcomed Gordin's
plays was that Adler was the only star with no talent for low comedy and not
much of a singing voice. Also, he had the perfect Gordin blend of monumental
presence, explosive temperament, and—at psychologically crucial moments—
a quiet simplicity that seemed (at least by contrast) to be heartrendingly
natural. He could switch from a whisper to a roar to a silent tear, rocketing
his audience up and down on an emotional roller coaster. As Gordin's "Jewish
King Lear," he made himself close to divine on the Lower East Side.

David Kessler was another "Gordin actor." He chose Gordin plays whenever he could and tried as manager to include them in his repertory. A number
of intellectuals preferred Kessler to Adler. They raved about his strength and
sensitivity, which grew as he played roles ranging astonishingly from Apollon
to Hershele Dubrovner (the Faust-character hero of *God, Man, and Devil*)
to the brutal husband in *The Slaughter.*

Jacob P. Adler and Sara Adler in a sensationalized problem play, *The Great Question*
by Zalmen Libin. The "great question" refers to birth control. On this poster for the
Arch Street Theater in Philadelphia, 1916, the note in the bottom left corner announces "Staged and presented by the great stage architect J. P. Adler."

Many actors, like Leon Blank and Morris Moshkovitch, clearly improved their abilities when playing Gordin roles. The combination of the vehicles themselves and the dignity that Gordin's authority vested in them refined the actors' native presence and temperament into something very fine. Boris Thomashefsky, the first time he played a Gordin role, won the critics' admission that he was a much more intelligent actor than they had previously thought. And Sigmund Mogulesko, as Fingerhut and in a wide range of other roles, developed from a comic into a character actor with "the most felicitous instinct for characterization," although, as Hapgood remarked, "he had no ideas about realism or anything else."

Under Gordin's influence, the Yiddish theater acquired serious actresses, the four most impressive being Bertha Kalish, Sara Adler, Ester Rokhl Kaminska, and Keni Liptzin.

Kalish began as a giddy chorus lovely in Gimpel's Garden Theater in Lemberg. She was stolen from Gimpel's (as were countless others) by American talent scouts, and made her way up to featured roles at a rapid rate. She sang on the non-Yiddish Polish stage as well, and there were rumors that jealous actresses, both Polish and Yiddish, tried to poison her. Kalish's talents lay in her grace and stately elegance, her playful femininity, and the womanly wisdom she seemed to possess—particularly when she spoke Gordin's words. Gordin was once in her dressing room admiring her as she brushed her wealth of long dark hair. "Write a play for my hair," she coaxed him coquettishly. So he wrote for her, according to the story, one of his most popular plays, *The Kreutzer Sonata.* She also played Hershele Dubrovner's innocently adoring niece in *God, Man, and Devil.* Gordin wrote *Sappho* especially for Kalish, and when she left the Yiddish stage few other actresses dared to attempt "her" role.

Kalish went on the Broadway stage, playing Maeterlinck's *Monna Vanna,* which had brought her fame in Yiddish, and a translation of *The Kreutzer Sonata,* among other roles. She succeeded fairly well on Broadway, though the Americans never gave her the sheer adoration that her first public had. The Yiddish theater missed her, and she made frequent guest appearances on the Lower East Side. In her last years she was almost totally blind; her daughter had to lead her onstage and position her there; but once the curtain went up she managed to give the impression that she could see, and she performed as effectively as ever.

Sara Adler had as her trademarks her temperament, her very dark hair, and her smoldering expression. She was the wife of the actor Heine-Haimovitch when she fell in love with Jacob P. Adler, sold her jewelry for him, and finally

Ester Rokhl Kaminska, the "Mother of Yiddish Theater," in the title role of *Mirele Efros* by Jacob Gordin, in Poland in 1909. Her daughter Ida Kaminska appears here as the heroine's grandson Shloymele. The family was to continue the tradition when, several decades later, Ida Kaminska played Mirele Efros and her daughter Ruth played Shloymele.

married him. They appeared together in many Gordin works. Gordin wrote *Without a Home* especially for Sara Adler; she played the emotional role of an immigrant woman who suffers, and eventually goes mad, because her husband and son adjust to American ways but she cannot.

Before Ester Rokhl Kaminska made her debut in Poland, she was a high-spirited, stage-struck milliner's assistant who loved singing and dressing up. Her parents heard that she was getting too interested in the theater, and told her to come home from the big city to their village; like a good girl, she came. When they died several years later, however, she returned to Warsaw and applied herself with awesome intensity to learning roles. She played Goldfadn and *shund* heroines throughout the years when Yiddish was illegal, learning how to turn Yiddish into *Daytshmerish* and how to pack up her make-up box quickly and get out of town. It was principally in Gordin roles that Esther Rokhl Kaminska was to win for herself the popular title "mother of Yiddish theater."

Ester Rokhl married Avrom Yitskhok Kaminsky, who owned and managed the first stable Warsaw Yiddish theater, a drafty circus building in an inconvenient neighborhood. She spent most of her life on the road, however, as manager and star. The Yiddish public and even Polish and Russian critics called her the Jewish Duse, after the reknowned Italian actress, because of the truthfulness and simplicity with which she portrayed Jewish types, principally in Gordin roles. Yiddish writers and intellectuals were proud to be her friends, though she herself was not at all an intellectual. Rather, she was a gentle, warm-hearted "mama," like the roles in which she had her greatest successes, and one of her life's major satisfactions was seeing her daughter Ida play the parts she had created.

Keni (or Kenia) Liptzin ran away from home as a young girl to join one of Goldfadn's earliest troupes. She starved on the road in Eastern Europe and in London, and then moved on to New York. Liptzin was a tiny woman with big bright dark eyes. She wore elegant clothes and sparkly jewelry: earrings with brilliants, rings that stiffened her short fingers, tiny shoes with jeweled buckles. She carried a lap dog, as fashionable ladies did, and petted it. But such pretty tenderness was not her most striking quality. Rather, she had strength, even hardness. She had intelligence too, though she was almost entirely uneducated. It was Gordin who educated her, perhaps even shaped her, through the plays that he wrote for her. The best-known of these was *Mirele Efros* (called *The Jewish Queen Lear*).

Liptzin was married to a successful publisher, so she did not, like most Yiddish theater people, have to make her ventures pay. Almost every season she put on a play or two by Gordin or translations of plays of some literary quality. She was a star-manager; she was free to hire talents to suit the play and could be relatively aloof from company strivings and politickings. And if her offerings were too intellectual to draw crowds, her husband made good her debts. Thus she managed to remain true to the Gordin ideal in a way that no other actor or entrepreneur ever could—including Gordin himself.

Actors identified themselves with Gordin roles as they did with *shund* roles. Sometimes they owned the roles legally by having commissioned the play or by buying the rights later on. Sometimes they simply established squatter's rights. When Ester Rokhl Kaminska toured America, theatergoers enjoyed the battle between two established Mirele Efroses: the American Liptzin and the Polish Kaminska. Generally Liptzin was considered to have won, since New York audiences preferred her grand manner to Ester Rokhl's lower-keyed naturalness.

In New York, where Gordin kept an eye on his creations, the actors not only respected him; they were scared of him. One night he slipped into a theater to watch a performance of one of his plays and caught Mogulesko ad-libbing jokes. He stood up in his box and bawled Mogulesko out, for all the audience to hear. Another time he went backstage and slapped the portly and extremely dignified Sigmund Feinman for a similar offense. European actors who had never even met him came similarly under his spell. They were as much in awe of Gordin as *hasidic* disciples were of their rebbe. They sprinkled their conversations with aphorisms from his plays, as if they were quoting proverbs or holy Torah. Many even started making up aphorisms in his style. Ester Rokhl called him her messiah; his plays and philosophy of drama had "raised her up from the dust," she said, and made her an artist. When he died, actors, especially in Europe, mourned that with him gone, it was "back to the wooden swords and paper crowns" of Purim plays and *shund*.

Gordin the Teacher

As a revolutionary, Gordin had wished from the start to elevate, liberate, and enlighten the masses. As a playwright, he simply focused his attention on the *Jewish* masses. He broadened his conception of enlightenment to allow for a degree of ethnic identity, and made his forum the theater. His didactic impulse was in keeping with much of Jewish art—from the simplest Yiddish folk tales to the dramas of the nineteenth-century Enlightenment to Goldfadn himself.

Gordin brought secular Western learning to his audiences. The Lower East Side stampeded for education; adult night schools were packed, and Philip Krantz (the editor who engineered the restaurant meeting between Gordin and the actors) published a series of volumes in Yiddish on every subject from the pre-Columbian Indians to modern medicine. Gordin's plays were night classes too: In *Sappho*, Apollon calls Sofia by the name of the Grecian poetess and then explains (to Sofia *and* to the audience) who Sappho was; he also explains the source and symbolism of his own name. *God, Man, and Devil* takes its premise from the Faust and Job stories: God and Satan wager on the corruptibility of a pious Torah scribe named Hershele Dubrovner, and the action of the play puts him to the test. The prologue takes place in heaven, and the devil says explicitly to God: We've been through this before, in the cases of "your loyal servant Job" and "the learned Dr. Faust." Thus the ignorant are introduced to Goethe and Marlowe. In *The Kreutzer Sonata*, the heroine carries around Tolstoy's book because, she explains, it tells a story somewhat similar to her own romantic heartbreak.

Gordin even justified his hack-work translations and adaptations, such as *Rosie*, from Schiller's *Kabale und Liebe*, on the grounds that he was putting his audience in touch with the high points of Western culture, and making them cosmopolitan. And indeed he was, though evidently not fast enough to prevent an enthusiastic first-night audience at Thomashefsky's production of *Romeo and Juliet* from calling for William Shakespeare to come out and take a bow.

When Gordin aimed to teach moral values, they were primarily ones that were directly congruent with his political views. In *God, Man, and Devil* and *Dementia Americana*, it is above all greed for money that destroys the heroes. Similarly, *The Lunatic* shows how materialism destroys the creative spirit. In *A Russian Jew in America*, the villain is trade unionism as a capitalist tool. *Sappho* and *The Kreutzer Sonata* preach women's right to human fulfillment, one of Gordin's pet crusades, and a daring new morality. *Without a Home* shows the breakdown of family values in immigrant tenements as well as the necessity for adjustment to modern situations. In *The Jewish King Lear*, Gordin points out the *haskole* moral that the old ways must give room to enlightenment: the loving daughter goes to the university while the ungrateful children are hypocritically Orthodox Jews. Many parents took children to see *The Jewish King Lear* and *Mirele Efros (The Jewish Queen Lear)* to teach them the consequences of treating their parents badly; one banker on the Lower East Side swore he could tell when these plays were on, because the next morning always brought guilty sons and daughters mailing money orders to their parents in the old country.

Gordin taught his morals straightforwardly, so that at times—at the expense of realism—his characters become almost allegorical figures: Sofia-Sappho is good; Apollon's wife and his father-in-law, the fish merchant, are bad. Often Gordin used symbols as unsubtly as the Jewish *magid* (itinerant preacher) used his metaphors. In *God, Man, and Devil*, before the devil sells him the lottery ticket, Hershele Dubrovner plays psalm melodies on his fiddle. As he becomes rich and corrupt he stops playing, but at his last moment, when he repents his sins, he plays once more. The fiddle is explicitly the voice of his soul, which is silenced for a while but not forever. (As the devil himself concludes ruefully, "Money only lets you seduce, abase, and cripple a man; you cannot destroy him entirely.") Similarly, Hershele's booming factory weaves prayer shawls. His best friend's son is injured at his loom, under sweatshop conditions, and dies. This is the incident that finally brings Hershele to repentance, and it is with the bloodstained shawl the young man was weaving that Hershele finally hangs himself. Such symbolism is theatrical and effective, rather like Ibsen's in *The Wild Duck* or *The Master Builder*.

Gordin's moralizing was part of his stature as a rebbe for the intellectuals of the Lower East Side. He wrote constantly in journals, exhorting Jews toward ideals of justice, enlightenment, self-respect, socialist brotherhood. In 1900 he was a founder of the Educational League, one of the institutions dedicated to evening classes for workers. He raised money for it, recruited faculty, taught classes. Whether he lectured on socialism, Jewish history, theater history, or anything else, the hall was always packed, and not with listeners but with disciples.

Gordin was a founder in 1897 of the Freie Yidishe Folksbiene (Free Yiddish Folk Theater), a reading and discussion club dedicated to creating a better Yiddish theater. Amateur drama clubs already existed in New York, Baltimore, and other cities. Now they proliferated, training a new generation of artists and reformers. Many of them called themselves Jacob Gordin clubs. In 1901–02 Gordin put out a newspaper called *Teater Journal un Familien Blat (Theater Journal and Family Paper)*, and in 1904, *Dramatishe Velt (Drama World)*. Several other Yiddish theater periodicals came out in America in the next few years. Through his influence, the intelligentsia came to associate the higher life of the mind with an ideal Yiddish theater.

Gordin's Critics

However, as time went on, Gordin the playwright did not retain the adoration that Gordin the leader did. Gordin's reforming urge sometimes boomeranged. Often he couldn't resist going beyond symbols to out-and-out harangues, which were, of course, neither realistic nor interesting. Or he dropped realism altogether so that simple characters made splendid philosophical speeches and turned intellectual aphorisms. Newspapers were printing more serious theater critiques than ever before, largely through Gordin's own influence, and this review of *The Purity of Family Life* (1904) was not atypical:

> The leading feminine role was not a role at all, but a collection of propagandistic speeches. Madame Liptzin, who played this role, had nothing to play . . . instead of an actress, she had to be a speechmaker.

Critics had other complaints too. They criticized plots that were derivative, clumsy, or improbable. The Warsaw critic Dovid Frischman was especially savage in accusing Gordin of taking great tragedies and reducing them to sad stories. His eight children and the harsh finances of the Yiddish theater made it inevitable that Gordin "bake" a lot of plays, and that some of those plays be as mediocre as these titles indicate: *Murder on Madison Avenue, Ida; or, The Treasure of Poland, Capital, Love, and Death, Mohammed; or, The Jews of Arabia, Galileo, Martyr for Science.* (Some of these he credited to a fictitious "Doctor Jacobi from London.")

A few years into the twentieth century, the critics said that his plays were old-fashioned. The European avant-garde, though not yet the American, had moved beyond his innovations.

In Prague between 1910 and 1912, Franz Kafka saw Gordin plays performed by a third-rate company on a makeshift stage in the cheerfully seedy Café Savoy. He was so impressed that he used Gordin plots, speeches, and gestures in a few of his stories. Kafka was perhaps drawn by the dark, sensational atmosphere of some of the plays. He enjoyed the monumental theatricality, and was sufficiently detached from Yiddish culture so that even *shund* plays or acting style didn't make him feel threatened or angry. Furthermore, he was evidently groping for some Jewish identity at that time, and felt, as he explained in a letter to his fiancée, that even when you find these plays corny and laugh at them, you laugh at them "because you love them." But Yiddish literary leaders like Abraham Cahan in New York and Yitskhok Leyb Peretz in Warsaw were not groping for Jewishness—they were offended by *shund*. Gordin had said that Yiddish drama could be modern art, and that's what they demanded.

Gordin could not tolerate criticism, however constructive. It was an article of faith with him and his supporters that his plays were as fine as Ibsen's, or better. He took to answering the smallest newspaper critique right from the stage, between the acts or after the final curtain. He had a special feud with Abraham Cahan, though Cahan gave him, on the whole, balanced and even sympathetic reviews, refusing only to consider Gordin one of the world's great dramatists. He denounced Cahan *ad hominem,* and caricatured him in *The Russian Jew in America* as a cynical union boss who puffs a cigar and snickers, "What do I need a brain for if I have a constitution?" (At this line on opening night, Cahan stood up in his box and blurted out in Russian, "It's a lie!")

In rhetorical fashion, Gordin described his contributions to Yiddish theater:

> Judith [i.e., the Jewish masses] had a sickly undeveloped little daughter. The child grew up uncared for, wandered in the rubbish, wore gypsy rags. I raised her up from the rubbish heap, took off her rags and dressed her in the clothes that children from decent families wear, washed her dirty little face and showed the world her charm and intelligence. I gave her presents. . . . The presents maybe aren't worth much, but nobody was giving her any that were more valuable, better, more costly. Instead of gratitude I often hear from the mother insults and curses, and she often perversely permits me to put the child back in her old rags. But she remains my beloved. . . . She and I seem to have nothing in common, however we are one body and one soul. She doesn't care about me. . . . I know: when I fall, her bought-for-money friends will dance on my body and she'll remain indifferent. If I died today, she'd forget me today. . . .

And indeed, as a playwright his day was ending. In 1904 he tried to manage a theater that played his own repertory. He went broke. The community of Russian radicals was beginning to break up. Their Lower East Side was peaking and starting to disperse. People were learning English and moving away.

Meanwhile the masses, who had all along enjoyed "a song, a jig, a kiss, a quarrel," had their ranks swelled by a new rush of immigration. A wave of pogroms beginning at Kishinev in 1903 sent over a whole wave of Jewish peasants who knew nothing of drama. Yiddish music halls prospered as never before. There were silent films for a dime on the Bowery and Second Avenue. The New York depression of 1903, too, drove people to prefer escapist entertainment over more strenuous stuff. By Gordin's death in 1909, no company was so foolhardy as to expect to make money from a Gordin play; actors indulged themselves in a Gordin role only when they had a benefit, and even then they ad-libbed for a laugh and added music for spice.

Moyshe, the quintessential mass audience, receives his supplicants: Keni Liptzin lays her Liptzin Theatre at his feet (above its door the legend "Gordin Plays"); Kessler, his Thalia Theater (also with a repertory of "Gordin Plays"); Thomashefsky, his People's Theatre (legend: *Who Is Guilty?*, a successful melodrama); and, at the far right, Adler offers his Grand Theatre ("Gordin Plays"). Liptzin is costumed as Mirele Efros, Kessler as Hershele Dubrovner, and Adler as the Jewish King Lear, while Thomashefsky wears the tights, cloak, and feathered hat of the operetta hero. All four stars are trying to win Moyshe's favor; meanwhile, on the left, a manager bows low.

Evidently the masses had respected but distrusted Gordin all along. Russian, radical, atheist, intellectual—to many of them, he was too alien. They considered Goldfadn the father of Yiddish theater (though they didn't support him financially either), for Goldfadn conceived of his plays as expressions of a Yiddish folk spirit: something of their own. Gordin, on the other hand, vowed openly to make Yiddish theater secular—a national theater in its own national language. Goldfadn expressed the masses' feeling that Gordin was somehow a traitor:

> What he has done to my child! He took my beloved child, my Jewish child, my Benjamin, and converted him! He defiled my holy of holies. He's just a missionary [i.e., away from Judaism], how does he come to Yiddish theater?

Even "Professor" Hurwitz felt himself more Jewish than Gordin, more literally "popular" both in his attitudes and in his dramaturgy. Hurwitz liked to refer to Gordin with heavy irony as Jacob Mihaelovitch, meaning that Gordin was really a Russian—or tried to pass as one. He also called Gordin the Black Jew; that was the title of a Gordin play, but Hurwitz was slyly alluding to Gordin's beard and to his anti-Semitic heart.

Would Gordin's most loyal *patriótn* have predicted that the Gordin plays that remain most popular are *God, Man, and Devil* and *Mirele Efros?* These two plays reinforce, most broadly and simply, Jewish values. Moreover, *Mirele Efros* is in form one of the more old-fashioned of his melodramas. And the extremely strong and interesting *God, Man, and Devil*, with its prologue in heaven and chorus of angels at the end, is akin in form to Goldfadn and even the Purim play. Thus not only did Gordin influence Yiddish drama; it influenced him; and what was strongest in Yiddish popular theater actually absorbed Gordin, as ongoing repertory, back into itself. Gordin wrote good plays—some still being performed in the last decade, in Yiddish as well as in Hebrew and Polish translation. But in retrospect it seems that his greater contribution was precisely that he broadened the definition of Jewishness, making it possible for a wider range of people, and especially the Russian-Jewish intellectuals, to include themselves fruitfully in the definition.

Gordin suffered from throat cancer for several years before he died. He took a trip to Eastern Europe, partly to try to control his plays, which were beginning to be pirated and performed there. There was little hope of royalties, but he was desperate to limit the mangling of the scripts which inevitably occurred. He wrote a series of articles about his trip. But he could do nothing to ensure that his plays would be performed the way he wrote them.

Back in New York, he rehearsed a play called *Dementia Americana*, starring Bessie Thomashefsky, whom some supporters called the most realistic actress of all. His mood during rehearsals was so tense that the actress tried to comfort him. "Don't worry. After all, this is not your first play." "No," he answered, "but it will be my last." Meanwhile, Abraham Cahan was publishing a series of retrospective critiques which all but demolished him; Gordin's *patriótn* later claimed that the articles killed him.

On his deathbed, Gordin cheered up briefly when friends talked to him about revisiting the lively cafés of Odessa. But soon he lapsed into silence. His final words are supposed to have been *"Finita la commedia."* The *New York Theatrical Mirror* reported that his body lay in state on the stage of the Thalia Theater, banked with flowers; that there was no room in the building for all the people who wanted to pay their last respects; and that ten thousand people followed his coffin on foot, stopping at the Educational League and the Theater Circle and crossing the Brooklyn Bridge to his grave.

Gordin would have enjoyed Leon Kobrin's tribute:

> I see him still, stepping through the streets like a palm branch. His baronial beard hangs with a festive dignity over his broad chest. His eyes like two fires, sharp as knives; in his right hand a stick, and in the left—one of his plays. He passes, and the actors tremble when they catch sight of him. People who know him say, "There goes Gordin," and those who don't know him look after him and say, "What a good-looking man."

7 THE NEW REPERTORY

In the 1860s, young Sholem Yankev Abramovitsh took the pseudonym Mendele Moykher Sforim (Little Mendel the Book Peddler) because he didn't want any of his learned Hebraist colleagues to know that he had begun writing in the "rejected daughter," as he called Yiddish. By 1909, when Mendele celebrated his seventy-fifth birthday, millions of Yiddish readers referred to him with love and respect as *der zeyde* (the grandfather), because through his novels, essays, and plays, and through his influence on other writers, he had developed Yiddish as a literary language.

Jews celebrated their *zeyde*'s seventy-fifth birthday with parties all over Eastern Europe. There were festivities also in the Americas, in Johannesburg, and in Melbourne—wherever Jews had migrated and established new Yiddish literary centers. They were celebrating the growth of a modern Yiddish literature, which seems from our perspective to have appeared with magical suddenness.

One of the number of creative outbursts of the era was the convention in Czernowitz, Rumania, in 1908, at which Jewish writers from Europe and America gathered to discuss the Yiddish language. Delegates talked about standardizing grammar, spelling, and diction, which varied sharply from place to place. They made speeches, held seminars, debated with passion such questions as: Was Yiddish the Jewish national language? What was its relationship to Hebrew, which was developing as a modern vernacular along with pioneering Zionism? Was the "rejected daughter" a language at all? The verdict was that Yiddish was *a* national Jewish language, though not, perhaps, the only one; and that a language, in any case, it most certainly was.

The Hebrew writer Ahad Ha'am dismissed the Czernowitz convention tartly as a Purim carnival, but he missed its significance. For the Jews of Eastern Europe and their relatives who had migrated elsewhere, the words "Yiddishist" and "Yiddishism" now described a creative cultural identity.

Yiddish drama, too, was enjoying a major upsurge. In 1909 David Pinski published his small book entitled *The Jewish Drama.* He described the history of Yiddish theater as a play in three acts:

The first act was the era of Avrom Goldfadn, the father of Yiddish theater, and of his contemporaries the *shund*-bakers, "Professor" Hurwitz and Lateiner.

The second act was the era of the Russian revolutionary dramatist Jacob Gordin. (These two eras overlapped: Goldfadn died in 1908, Gordin in 1909.)

The third act was modern, serious Yiddish drama. This was the future, and Pinski claimed that the future had already begun: The first professional Yiddish theater company committed to performing only plays of serious literary value was established in 1908 in Odessa, the gay cosmopolitan city on the Black Sea, and center of Yiddish intellectual café life in 1908.

The Eastern European Jewish community and its outposts in America and elsewhere coalesced around a variety of ideologies. Besides religious orthodoxy, which remained a major force, two of the most significant ideologies were Zionism and radical political thought (socialism, communism, anarchism), which were combined in varying degrees. Zionism was associated with the Hebrew language; Labor Zionism expressed itself in Yiddish. Radical politics were articulated primarily in Russian and Polish, the languages of Jews of the middle and upper classes. The political ideology which became most closely associated with Yiddish as the language and culture of the masses was Jewish socialism, called the Bund.

In the late nineteenth century, Eastern Europe underwent its industrial revolution, acquiring an increasingly impoverished urban proletariat. Most Jews were proletarian workers, and many of them turned to politically subversive convictions, especially socialism. However, Jews were proletarians with special disadvantages: they were settled by law within the Pale of Settlement, transplanted brutally as the Pale contracted, and squeezed into a diminishing range of jobs. The anti-Semitism of the 1880s further cut them off from their non-Jewish counterparts. Their response, like that of the Russian-Jewish radical intelligentsia, was to turn for support back to their own kind.

The Bund was a socialist party specifically for Jewish workers. It was founded in 1897 through a series of strikes led by former rabbinical students in Vilna. Whereas socialist activity was generally conducted entirely in Polish or Russian and was officially, like Marx himself, against religious identification in general and Jewishness in particular, the Bundists addressed themselves to the Jewish situation and in Jewish terms, and—after early hesitation—their speeches and pamphlets were in the vernacular of the masses, Yiddish.

At its peak in 1905, the Bund was actually demanding cultural autonomy for the Jews of Russia, their own schools in their own language. The Yiddish-speaking proletariat, with their own organization and their own young leaders risking Siberian imprisonment for their sakes, developed a new, strong sense of cohesion and worth.

In this exciting atmosphere of cultural nationhood, Yiddish language and literature bloomed, especially in the areas that are now Poland and Russia. (In Dublin in the same years, a similar interaction led the intellectuals who founded the Abbey Theater to make a conscious attempt to revive Gaelic as a symbol and instrument of Irish national spirit.) Many literary and theatrical ventures took the name *Folks,* meaning "of the people"; the Folk Stage, for instance, the Folk School, the *Folk Journal.* It was an era "of the people" and for Yiddish writers and thinkers, the early years of the twentieth century were a time of intellectual exhilaration.

Of course, it was also a time of starvation, uprooting, and massacre by marauding troops, with the Russian-German battle line moving forward and back through the heart of the Pale. Yiddish writers wrote about poverty, not only because it was a socialist theme, but because poverty was all they saw, and they themselves were hungry. Yitskhok Leyb Peretz supported himself meagerly all his life as a clerical worker at a desk in a tiny cubicle; and when he took a young writer under his wing, he often first helped to find him a bowl of potato soup and an old overcoat against the Warsaw winter.

Still, astonishingly, Mendele's "grandchildren" kept writing. On paper scraps in Siberia and in notebooks in Galician villages, lying on a ragged mattress in a Warsaw cellar or nursing a single glass of tea at an Odessa café table, they kept on. Yiddish had its journalists and belletrists, essayists and critics, novelists and poets and playwrights.

Soon, with the vast geographical dislocations of Eastern Europe's Jews, Yiddish literature became international. Yiddish writers in Europe published in New York newspapers; Yiddish presses in Cracow published play scripts written in Buenos Aires (though they didn't always let the authors know), and for the benefit of Warsaw readers, plays written in New York were printed with a short glossary of American "Yiddish" words, such as *downtown, union, shop boss,* and *wages.*

Yiddish writers traveled back and forth, though their direction most often was from Europe to America. American Yiddish publishers offered better fees than Warsaw publishers could, just as American producers could afford to send talent scouts to Bucharest to scoop up the prettiest leading ladies. America offered political freedom and relative prosperity, and even political activities could be carried on in Yiddish. So a lot of writers immigrated to America, where their colleagues welcomed them in cafés, waiting impatiently to continue an argument or a chess game they'd left off in Warsaw.

It takes one's breath away to comprehend the floods of words that suddenly poured out in the decade before, during, and just after World War I. Some statistics that help to imagine it are the newspaper circulations. The very first regular periodical in Yiddish appeared in Russian in 1862, as a supplement to a newspaper in Hebrew. But in the years just before the First World War, Russia had, by some counts, as many as fifty Yiddish dailies, weeklies, monthlies, and annuals, many of them illegal. In Warsaw alone two papers claimed to sell 100,000 copies each, daily. New York's first Yiddish newspaper appeared in 1885, and by 1916 New York Yiddish dailies had a combined circulation of some 646,000. That doesn't include the weeklies, quarterlies, and the rest. These newspapers were of all political affiliations, from anarchist to conservative, and they printed not only news but serialized fiction, sketches and poetry, advice columns and correspondence, essays and editorials. (In addition, newspapers of Jewish interest were simultaneously being printed in Hebrew, as well as in Russian, English, and the languages of all the countries with large Jewish communities.)

The father figures of modern Yiddish literature were still producing— Mendele Moykher Sforim and the younger Yitskhok Leyb Peretz and Sholom Aleichem—and a new generation of important writers was busy too. Peretz, the most adventurous of the three, personally lavished his warmth and energy on any young writer who struck him as promising. In person or through tireless correspondence, he gave them advice and encouragement. On the door of his little Warsaw apartment hung a sign giving the hours when he officially "received." But the initiated knew that he was "at home" till late every evening, and they started to arrive as soon as he was due back from his office. "Come," he habitually greeted them. "What goods have you got to show me today?" Then he settled himself to listen to their latest efforts.

Novelists since Dik and Schomer-Shaikevitch in the nineteenth century had found enthusiastic Yiddish readers. Now many new ones appeared, including David Pinski, Sholom Asch, Leon Kobrin, Joseph Opatoshu, and I. J. Singer.

The development of Yiddish poetry was also striking. Alongside the folksong-like lyric strain, which continues to this day, several distinct schools of Yiddish poetry appeared, most notably in New York. The so-called sweatshop poets, such as Morris Rosenfeld, gave way to more thoughtful and sophisticated poetry: Abraham Reisen (a protégé of Peretz); the nature poet Yehoash, who made a translation of the Bible into Yiddish, the crown of his lifework; Abraham Liessin, Joseph Rolnick, and many others.

In 1907 a coterie of poets called *Di Yunge* (The Young Ones) made a violent stir when they published their first works in New York. Among their leaders were Moyshe Leyb Halpern, Mani Leib, Moyshe Nadir, Zisha Landau, and I. I. Schwartz. When the group called themselves *Di Yunge,* the name conveyed youth, courage, adventure, and progress. When older writers referred to them, the tone of voice was different, and *Di Yunge* seemed to mean simply "young and brash." *Di Yunge* announced that only new writing was worth reading and only new values worth considering. (Meanwhile the Dadaists were shocking Paris with similar pronouncements.) They tried to evoke pictures and feelings rather than social and moral ideas. A decade later came the *Inzikhistn* (Introspectivists), led by Glanz-Leyeles, Minkoff, and Yankev Glatstein, and inspired by Peretz. They went further still and, like their non-Yiddish avant-garde counterparts, their poems were floating swirls of freely associated images.

Criticism as a literary activity was going on furiously during this entire time. The Czernowitz conference was only one example. People were writing, thinking, arguing at meetings, feuding in letters to the editor. Literary criticism, generally with attention to the political and sometimes even moral implications of a given work, went on with the sort of passion one nowadays associates with young critics only—but then, in a sense, the whole profession of Yiddish critics was young. In this period, a great number of Yiddish writers earned reputations as critics which they maintained for decades to come: Dr. Alexander Mukdoyni (in drama), Dovid Frischman, the historian Shimon Dubnow, Ba'al-Makhshoves (Hebrew for "Man of Thoughts," pseudonym of Isidor Eliashev), Avrom Coralnick, Shmaryahu Gorelik, Shmuel Niger, Nakhman Meisel, and others.

This was an era of belletrist journals of all sorts, in Yiddish as in French and other European languages. Some of these journals were politically affiliated, some had vaguely liberal stances, and a few were aggressively dedicated to art for art's sake—a radical position in Jewish cultural life. Like the journals of this period in Paris, these were often eccentric and short-lived, but they were feverishly earnest.

Yiddishists had even reached the intellectual stage of studying their own folklore, in a range of anthropological projects paralleling similar enterprises in the non-Jewish cultures of Europe. Peretz collected folk legends, told them to his friends, recorded them, and used them as material for his own stories. S. Anski went on a three-year expedition in the Ukraine, gathering folkways, some of which he put together in his play *The Dybbuk.* Marek, Ginsburg, and

Yehude-Leyb Cahan researched folk songs. In 1908 Spector and Bernstein published a collection of over four thousand old proverbs.

New Yiddish Drama

Naturally, Yiddish drama was part of the explosion. In 1909, to use Pinski's formulation, the first act of Yiddish theater history (Goldfadn, Hurwitz, and Lateiner) was still holding center stage. Indeed, the Lower East Side audiences were less responsive to serious art than they had been in Gordin's high years. There was lots of *shund*, both operetta and melodrama. Many hacks had joined Lateiner and "Professor" Hurwitz, both of whom were still alive, in pleasing the crowds. There were even fashions in *shund*. One season New York had a craze for plays about prostitution and the underworld; the best was Zolatarevsky's *Money, Love, and Shame,* starring Bertha Kalish. Another season brought a run of comic operettas "in green": *The Green Girl Cousin (Di Grine Kuzine*—it rhymes), *The Green Bride, The Green Groom.* ("Green," of course, is slang for "greenhorn" or newly arrived immigrant.)

Some popular playwrights, however, like Isidore Zolatarevsky, Zalmen Libin, Max Gabel, and Anshel Shor, had a more refined sense of style and structure than their colleagues. In dramaturgy, if not in moral authority, they were as close to Gordin (Pinski's second act) as they were to the *shund*-bakers. The ongoing Yiddish repertory also included some of Gordin's and Goldfadn's plays, which already were treated like traditional classics. And meanwhile there was the new crop of dramatists: Pinski's third act.

They had trouble getting their plays on professional stages. Drama as literature developed some years before the commercial theater could or would follow it. For that reason, in Yiddish theater as in other cultures, the intellectual dramas were performed by amateurs or under institutional auspices more often than they were produced by the big-time impresarios of Warsaw or New York. Leon Kobrin had a typical experience when, at the turn of the century, he took his first play to a theater on the Lower East Side.

Kobrin was already well known for his realistic stories when, holding tightly to the script of *Minna; or, The Ruined Family from Downtown,* he found the manager backstage bent over his account books. Young Kobrin said timidly that he'd written a play.

"Comedy or drama?" asked the manager, much too busy to waste words.

"Comedy," Kobrin risked, for the play had both comic and serious elements.

"We do only dramas here, never comedies."

A few weeks later, Kobrin nerved himself to try again. This time he knew the right answer. "It's a drama," he said.

"We do only comedies here, never dramas."

Kobrin protested that he'd been told that—The manager interrupted him. "We don't do plays by *yolds.*" Period.

All the same, *Minna* did get on a stage, in a Jacob P. Adler production, though it was drastically adapted by Jacob Gordin. Kobrin, and the other young playwrights, kept writing.

They were encouraged by the increasing stability of Yiddish theater as a profession and a business, and by the development of an educated proletarian audience. These developments occurred both in America, the Yiddish theater mecca, and in Eastern Europe, where harassment had replaced flat prohibition. Pinski had a further theory. He attributed the new interest in drama to the fact that most of the new dramatists were educated in the Russian tradition—in Russia, writers had just begun to consider playwriting as seriously as they did writing in other forms, and Yiddish writers shared their concerns.

Russian drama, after centuries of importing and imitating Western European fashions, suddenly leaped forward at the end of the nineteenth century to be a rich and a lively part of the European avant-garde. In Russian theater (as in European theater as a whole), the turn of the century was a period of extraordinary energy and innovation in both playwriting and production. Besides spectacles and burlesques, sentimental melodramas and farces, there were serious attempts to picture life situations realistically. There was the naturalism of Tolstoy and Gorki and the subtle observation of Chekhov. There were the Russian symbolists, expressionists, and other genres that were a twentieth-century reaction against realism. The Russians Andreyev, Evreinov, and Blok had counterparts in Poland (Youshkevitch), in Czechoslovakia (Werfel), in Germany (Kaiser, Toller), and indeed in every part of Europe (Yeats, Maeterlinck, D'Annunzio, Strindberg). Yiddish dramatists, nurtured by Russian culture, felt themselves to be a part of all these new aesthetic movements.

Most new Yiddish dramatists experimented with more than one of these styles, so that for many of the best of them it is difficult, even misleading, to try to isolate a characteristic form. It would be a similar distortion to connect any one dramatist with a single message or point of view or subject.

During their lifetimes too, most of the new Yiddish dramatists lived in both Eastern Europe and America. Most of them made several of these switches: from Slavic literature to Yiddish; from Hebrew literature to Yiddish; from Bundist activist to less active sympathizer; from religiously Orthodox to radical; from an antireligious to a positive attitude toward Judaism; from Europe at war to America at peace. Several of them "lay in prison" either in

Poster for a Yiddish translation of Maxim Gorki's *Lower Depths*. The title is also given in Russian and in English translated as *Night Lodging*. The bottom section of the poster advertises a benefit for the director Maurice Schwartz. 1919.

their youth or in their later years. A survey of the major third-act dramatists is a kaleidoscope, testifying to the creative expansion of the Yiddish arts.

Leon Kobrin

Leon Kobrin (1872–1946) belongs in the second (Gordin) act almost as much as in the third. He was much younger than Gordin, but their lives touched, and his best play is more like Gordin's than like those of his contemporaries.

As a boy in Russia, Kobrin preferred Russian to Yiddish. He had read a little Mendele and Peretz in translations, but, as he recalls in his lively memoirs, he thought of Yiddish as fit only for "simple tales for servant girls and ignoramuses." At fifteen he was writing short stories in Russian.

Kobrin came to America in his early twenties. He lived by milking cows in rural Pennsylvania, then by drudging nights in the hot, damp cellar of a bakery in Philadelphia, then by turning out piecework in shirt and cigar factories in New Jersey. Eventually, like Gordin and partly through Gordin's influence, he turned toward Yiddish literature. He joined the Free Yiddish Folk Theater club on the Lower East Side and published sketches in the Yiddish press. Meanwhile he continued working in a laundry, supporting his wife and child on a total of about a dollar and a half a week. In 1899 his novel *Yankl Boyle; or, The Village Youth* established him as a major young writer.

It was around this period that he tried to peddle *Minna; or, The Ruined Family from Downtown.* Within the next few years he wrote *The East Side Ghetto,* which was widely welcomed as the first really accurate picture of tenement life; *Sonia from East Broadway,* and other realistic though melodramatic plays. Like Gordin, he continued to aim for realistic observation of conditions around him. For that reason, one of his last plays, written decades later, was about a new neighborhood, a section where more prosperous New York Jews had been moving from the Lower East Side. *Riverside Drive* is the story of a man who has established himself in America, married the American-born daughter of a Reform rabbi, raised children who speak only English, and in the 1930s at last sends for his old parents. They are pious countryfolk, and to them their son, his family, and the streets of New York are all alien. There are comic scenes in which all the characters speak different languages. But the deeper difficulties of communication are of course not funny, and in the end the old couple return to Europe, where they feel they belong.

Kobrin wrote some twenty plays, many of them dramatizations of his own novels or stories and some translations or adaptations of other people's works. Although most of them were about American Jewish life, the best known and most successful remains his dramatization of his own novel *Yankl Boyle*, sometimes called *Der Dorfs-Yung (The Village Youth)* or, in translation, *The Child of Nature*.

Yankl is a strapping young man, the handsomest fisherman in his Russian village on the Dnieper River, and the best singer and dancer. He is the "child of nature": naïve, inarticulate, perhaps even simple-minded. His family and that of his girl cousin Khayke are almost the only Jews in town. Yankl has no religion, beyond local superstitions, and barely speaks Yiddish. Since childhood, it has been vaguely assumed that he will marry his cousin, but he loves a Russian peasant girl named Natasha, who works at his father's inn. "You're pretty," he tells her in Russian, adding between his teeth his favorite curse: "The wolves eat you up!"

Yankl's father lies dying, terrified that the devils will torture him for having been a bad Jew. As his shadow moves on the bare wall beyond his bed and peasants drink and sing in the next room, he tries to make Yankl promise to marry his cousin and be pious.

David Kessler in the title role of *Yankl Boyle (The Village Youth)* by Leon Kobrin.

FRUME [YANKL's mother]   Yankele, your papa is dying. He won't forgive you.

NOKHEM [YANKL's uncle, brother of the dying man]   Yankl, your papa is going to strangle you. It's no kidding around, I'm telling you.

YANKL   *(Stares wonderingly at father.)* My father's going to strangle me? Me? Him? *(Gestures toward sick man and laughs.)* He's going to strangle me?

YESHAYA [YANKL's father]   *(Pulls himself up on pillows, feverishly.)* Yes, yes, I'll come from the grave to strangle you, from the grave—Goy! Goy! Goy! *(Falls back on pillows with a groan.)*

YANKL   *(Huddles away from him in fear.)* Papa—

FATHER   Yankl, be a Jew, a Jew— If not, I won't be able to rest in my grave.

(YANKL looks at him, frightened.)

UNCLE   *(In YANKL's ear.)* You hear? It's no kidding around, I'm telling you. He's going to strangle you, and that's all.

(YANKL stares around, more and more confused, bewildered, frightened.)

MOTHER   *(Goes over and strokes YANKL's head.)* Yankl, make your father happy. What's the matter with Khayke?

YANKL   *(Voice trembling.)* For God's sake, what do you want from me? *(Sobs piteously, walks to the side, and weeps into his sleeve. From the next room, the sound of loud singing.)*

FATHER   Oy, oy, make them stop singing. To die among *goyim—gevald*, help, where are the Jews?

MOTHER   *(Runs to door, calls.)* Please, have mercy, be quiet. My Shayke can't hear.

(Silence. KHAYKE enters with another Jewish man. YANKL wipes his eyes on his sleeve and looks angrily at KHAYKE.)

KHAYKE   *(To YANKL's uncle, her father.)* Oh, Papa, why is Yankl so angry? *(YANKL glares at her more angrily still.)* Papa, oh, Papa, look how he looks at me, like a wolf.

Yankl gives in. Immediately, at the bedside, the families settle the dowry and carry out a simple betrothal ceremony. The father is sinking. Everybody is praying and crying.

NATASHA   *(Enters, whispers to a man.)* How is Shayke?

HIRSH BER   Shh. Dying.

NATASHA   Yankl is crying—ah, my poor darling.

HIRSH BER   Just got engaged to Khayke, and now he's crying for his father.

NATASHA   *(Frightened.)* Engaged? Khayke? . . .

[YANKL's father dies. His mother screams and weeps.]

YANKL   Papa! *(Falls to his knees beside the bed, crying.)*

ALL   "Blessed is the righteous judge." [This is the traditional formula when someone dies.]

*(*NATASHA *looks at the scene with big, frightened eyes. Automatically crosses herself.)*

This is the first-act curtain.

Yankl is tortured. He believes that his father will suffer in hell if he marries a gentile; he also believes that his father's ghost may return and punish him. All the local Jews, who are as ignorant as he is, keep him in terror. But he loves Natasha. At last, when he learns that she is pregnant with his child, he kills himself.

This play is vivid, grotesque, sensual. It intermixes superstitious terrors and groans and the highly colored metaphors of a traditional preacher with coarse songs and shouts. The dialogue is full of Russian words and curses, Russian songs and dances. This is realism, powerfully heightened and sensationalized.

Mendele Moykher Sforim

All three of the classic masters of Yiddish literature were alive and productive at the start of the twentieth century—Mendele Moykher Sforim, Yitskhok Leyb Peretz, and Sholom Aleichem. Mendele was "the grandfather" already and was writing forms other than drama. His *haskole* plays *Di Takse (The Meat Tax)* and *Der Priziv (The Conscription)* were far behind him though after his death his novel *Masoes Binyomin Hashlishi (The Travels of Benjamin III)* was dramatized and successfully performed. But his younger contemporaries Peretz and Sholom Aleichem were writing plays with an eye to a living stage.

Yitskhok Leyb Peretz

Peretz (1852–1915) did his writing in the cold Warsaw dawns before it was time to leave for his job selling cemetery plots at the Warsaw Jewish Community offices. Evenings he received guests, read, corresponded, and was the soul of Yiddish cultural projects. He seems to have managed without any

Program and souvenir album for the Folksbiene's production of *Vos in Fidele Shtekt* by Yitskhok Leyb Peretz (New York, 1948). The portrait is of Peretz. The Folksbiene, an amateur company, identifies itself on the cover as Workmen's Circle Branch 555.

sleep. He was a vivid, volatile personality, given to flash floods of enthusiasm. The twenty-four dialogues and plays he wrote differ strongly in style.

Peretz wrote one-act plays about the Jews of Warsaw, as sharply observed as his short stories. *Shvester (Sisters),* for example, is about three poor young women. The eldest is a widow with starving children. The other two are servant girls, of whom the older, Nekhama, is already seduced, pregnant, her reputation ruined, and her manner hardened. When the eldest calls her shameless, Nekhama snaps back:

> You know what, Mirl? Do what I tell you. Make me a wedding. Break out your nest egg: a dowry, wedding expenses, clothes. Have you got it? Can you do it? No? Then shut up!

Nekhama steals the youngest sister's boyfriend in order to protect her innocence, for a little while longer, from the same ruin as her own. Ester Rokhl Kaminska played Nekhama in Poland, and Bertha Kalish played her in New York.

Another of Peretz's plays, *A Frimorgn (Morning),* pictures poverty and despair in a slum basement. In still another, *A Kvores-Nakht (A Cemetery Night),* a young wife goes to sob on her mother's grave because her husband has beaten her.

The Vilna Troupe's production (1928) of Yitskhok Leyb Peretz's *Night in the Old Marketplace*. In this scene the dead are dancing.

. . . Why did he do it? You don't think, God forbid, that he doesn't love me? You don't think, God forbid, that I came to complain about him to you? Or that I want you to tell it for me, up there where you are? No, God forbid, never.

He did it from hunger, Mama! And because I didn't want to cry. But I did want to! God is my witness, I wanted to. I couldn't. I was like turned to stone. Frozen! And he says: "A woman whose husband can't feed her screams, scolds!" And a black fire lit up in his eyes, and: "You're going to scream!"

Until at last he beat her out of his own rage and frustration, and ran out of the house. That was two days ago. She doesn't know where he's gone and is afraid he may have harmed himself.

At the other end of the spectrum, Peretz was drawn to symbolism. The playwrights he most admired were Maeterlinck and Strindberg, Wyspianski and the other Romantics of the Young Poland movement. He associated simple realism with the plays of Gordin, whom he considered old-fashioned and overrated. Many of Peretz's stories were fantasies, and he wrote several symbolist plays, which might better be called dramatic poems: *In Polish oyf der Keyt (In the Synagogue Anteroom), Di Goldene Keyt (The Golden Chain),* and *Bay Nakht oyfn Altn Mark (Night in the Old Marketplace).*

The Golden Chain begins when a rabbi, seeing the spiritual deterioration of the world and especially of Jewish tradition, refuses to say the prayer that ends the Sabbath on Saturday evening. He wants to hold on and create an eternal Sabbath. The play follows four generations of his descendants. The chain linking Jewish generations, as symbolized by his family, is broken by the rationalism of his children, but there is hope of forging it together again. Many critics consider this Peretz's greatest work, at least to read, but it has not had a successful stage career. It was, however, performed several times after its premiere in 1906 by Ester Rokhl Kaminska's company in Warsaw. Peretz never gave up hoping that audiences would find it exciting to watch on a stage. He wrote and rewrote it; three Yiddish versions exist, and one in Hebrew.

The German director Max Reinhardt called *Night in the Old Marketplace* "a rare specimen of a universalist-symbolist play" and considered producing it. Peretz once described it as a "dream of a fever night." When friends urged him to make it less a poem and more a play, with a tighter plot and more distinct characters, Peretz insisted that the truly Yiddish style, which would one day be acknowledged as such, was all in cryptic hints, and in interpretation of what is hidden.

In the old marketplace, ghosts of such living beings as a poet, a street-walker, and a water-carrier mix and dance. The leader of the revels is a ghostly *badkhen*, who whistles three times and calls the others out this way:

> With a whistle opened wide
> The shadowy door.
> *(Calls out.)*
> Hey, stiff starched side,
> Two and two make four.
> Soap bubble and ironing board.
> Golden weight and silver trust.
> Come, dear guests!
> And all those who truly must
> Believe in themselves, in life.
> From dream,
> Foam,
> And clouds into clumps woven and beat,
> His dear name's dizzy cheat!
> Come and glide!
> You we invite
> To a stroll by night!
> Come fly, come fly!
>
> Hey, you, open an eye.
> Show your teeth,
> Your ivories. . . .

The action ends at daybreak when the *badkhen* calls, "Into the synagogue!" and they all disappear. Alexander Granovsky was to adapt this play and produce his vision of it with music as a "tragic carnival" of disconnected pictorial episodes at the Moscow Yiddish State Theater in 1925. The director David Herman also adapted and produced it.

When Peretz died, 100,000 Jews followed his funeral procession through Warsaw. The Polish newspapers didn't mention it.

Sholom Aleichem

Sholom Aleichem (Sholem Rabinovitsh or Rabinowitz) (1859–1916) wrote a number of plays at the start of the century. In addition, he wrote many short stories in the first person, or as somebody pouring his heart out to "Mr. Sholom Aleichem": such monologues were naturals for reading aloud and remained staples of the recital stage. His dealings with professional theater were rarely happy; New York theater managers, he said, haggle over a play as cattle dealers haggle over an ox. Many of his plays were chiefly performed by nonprofessional or semiprofessional companies.

Among his humorous one-acters, whose titles hint at their content and jolly style, are *A Doctor, The Divorce,* and *Mazel Tov.* The most substantial of his one-acters is *Mentshn,* a word that means either simply "people" or, as in this context, "employees." A major character is the servant Daniel, described this way in the stage directions:

> . . . an elderly house servant, a steward and overseer of the *mentshn* in the household. An old bachelor, who wants to look young. Wears a red vest with brass buttons, checked trousers, a green tie. Thinks highly of himself and speaks sternly to his inferiors; diminishes and speaks weakly to his superiors.

In an early scene, a servant girl named Liza has just been fired, in disgrace, ruined by her master, the man of the house. In the kitchen, Daniel is paying out her last wages. She is crying. The cook, Rikl, is urging her to take a job that has been offered her far from home.

> RIKL [The cook, a merry soul in an apron]   *(Spoon in her hand.)* It's your chance to provide yourself with a dowry . . . to have a household of your own, little fool, and keep your own *mentshn.* . . .*(To* DANIEL.)You know how I hate to mix into other people's business. But this is her chance to provide herself with a dowry. What a pious little calf she is, you know it.

> DANIEL   *(Looking sternly at her through his spectacles.)* Who's asking your advice? Your work is at the oven. Set another three places at the table. Madam's relatives are coming down right away; poor relatives, so we have to give them dinner in the kitchen with the *mentshn.*

> HERTS [Elegant manservant: frock coat, white vest, nice mustaches]   They should consider themselves lucky it's not with the dogs.

The girl who is to be the new maid, and her parents, enter and take off their coats. Rikl and Herts make fun in whispers of their clothes and manners.

DANIEL   Sit right down here at the table; you can eat too. Rikl! Serve the food.

(Girl's father washes ritually, makes grace loudly. HERTS *makes the responses.* RIKL *laughs.*

In comes MADAM GOLD, *mistress of the house. As soon as she appears, the kitchen turns upside down:* RIKL *rushes for the oven.* HERTS *gets busy with the plates, bangs the spoons, throws the forks.* LIZA *jumps up and slips out.* DANIEL *throws off his spectacles, stands up, becomes shorter by a head. Girl's father stops eating.)*

MADAM GOLD   *(Standing on the steps above the kitchen.)* Rikl! Give them something to eat and a glass of tea. *(To the girl's mother.)* I forgot to ask you what her name is, your daughter

MOTHER   *(Giving the familiar form.)* Riva.

FATHER   *(Giving the Biblical form.)* That means Rivke.

MADAM GOLD   Riva? Rivke? Not nice. Rebecca. Rivetshka. *(Giving the familiar Russified form.)* Her name will be Rivetshka.

MOTHER   You like Rivetschka, let it be Rivetschka! Who would give you advice? She's yours.

FATHER   My words exactly. Just so it's good for her here, and she doesn't lack for anything. *(Quotes in Hebrew.)* "Not the interpretation signifies, but the deed."

MADAM GOLD   That depends on her. If she is a good worker, it will be good for her; if she's a bad worker, it will be bad for her.

DANIEL   If she's a good worker, it will be good for her; if she's a bad worker, it will be bad for her. *(Signals to* HERTS *and* RIKL.*)*

HERTS and RIKL   *(In chorus.)* If she's a good worker, it will be good for her; if she's a bad worker, it will be bad.

HERTS   *(Aside.)* The bad year I wish for them!

MADAM GOLD   My *mentshn* have never complained about me yet.

DANIEL   Our *mentshn* have never complained yet. *(Signals to* HERTS *and* RIKL.*)*

HERTS and RIKL   *(In chorus.)* Never complained yet.

HERTS   *(Aside.)* That's how many plagues on their heads.

Beneath the energetic repartee it becomes clear that the impotent bitterness of the *mentshn* against their masters' tyranny is the major thrust of the play. Rikl's husband comes to the kitchen to visit for a minute; no one wants to hire a married *mentsh*, so Rikl and her husband and their daughter each serve in separate households and see each other only in rare moments snatched from work.

Later Fanitshke, a former serving girl, appears. They haven't seen her since she was ruined as Liza was. Now she makes a flamboyant entrance, elaborately dressed and made up, chattering about her fiancé in affected French phrases and laughing uncontrollably.

RIKL   *(To* HERTS.*)* I think she's a little too happy.

HERTS   I'm afraid she's had a few to drink.

FANITSHKE   Ce n'est pas vrai! I don't drink! I don't drink liquors, I drink wine! Champagne, parole d'honneur! *(Takes out a cigarette.* HERTS *lights it.)*

HERTS   So you have a fiancé already, Fanitshke?

FANITSHKE   . . . What "Fanitshke"? No more "Fanitshke"! Fania Yefimovna . . . All the officers—and the generals—know only Fania Yefimovna. Et basta! . . . Two students beat each other up over Fania Yefimovna, parole d'honneur! They beat me up too, see? *(Rolls up her sleeve, shows a blue mark.)* See, look . . . ha ha ha! *(Laughs hysterically.)*

RIKL   *(Takes her hand, sits down near the oven next to her.)* But just tell us, child, where have you been all this time? Why haven't we seen you?

FANITSHKE   What is there to tell? I've told you everything already. Only what goes on in here *(gestures to her heart)*—that is no one's business! Ha ha ha! . . . And upstairs there, what's new? *(Points to the stairs.)* Liza's fired, that one's new? *(Points to* RIVETSHKA.*)* They keep firing and hiring new *mentshn?* Always new *mentshn!* Ha ha ha! *Mentshn!* Ha ha ha! What are you all making faces for? What are you looking at me for? Because I'm laughing? Ha ha ha! I'm happy, so I laugh. . . . Ha ha ha! *They* should only be happy the way I am. *(Points upstairs.)*

HERTS   Amen.

FANITSHKE   Or even half as happy.

HERTS   Amen . . .

Madam Gold catches Fanitshke and Herts dancing and orders Daniel to fire the entire staff for "messing up" her house. At this Daniel's control snaps. His voice rising, his eyes filling with tears, he tells the others:

Come! Come away from here! We aren't allowed here. Who are we? What are we? . . . We're nothing. . . . We're *mentshn. Mentshn* is what we are. *Mentshn! Mentshn!*

Another play of Sholom Aleichem's, *Groyse Gevins (The Big Win,* also called *The Two Hundred Thousand),* is a merry play, produced frequently; in

1975 it appeared in Tel Aviv and New York. It's the story of a simple tailor whose life and character change temporarily when he thinks he has won a lottery jackpot of 200,000 rubles. It has lively apprentices, comical villains, something of the atmosphere of Dekker's *The Shoemakers' Holiday,* and romance, together with a clear message about the unhappy effects of money.

Shver tsu Zayn a Yid (Hard to Be a Jew) is another of Sholom Aleichem's plays that are often performed. In it, two students, one Jewish and one Russian, trade places for a year to see whether it is indeed hard to be a Jew. After considerable blundering and merriment, and naturally a romance, the Jew is arrested for his part in the romp, ending on the dark note that has been lurking under the fun. *Tsezeyt un Tseshpreyt (Scattered and Dispersed)* is an allegorical panorama of the Russian-Jewish bourgeoisie at the turn of the century; in a single family, the grown children are respectively an intellectual, a Zionist, a hedonistic man about town, and so on.

Besides writing plays, Sholom Aleichem dramatized many of his stories and novels for the stage. (Directors often used his writings as a basis for adaptations without his permission.) Of these, *Tevye the Dairyman* is known best now, for its musical descendant, *Fiddler on the Roof,* though the original dramatization was a repertory staple in New York, Russia, and Rumania, and also a movie starring Maurice Schwartz. Other dramatizations of Sholom Aleichem novels include *Stempenyu; or, a Jewish Girl,* about the love affair of a small-town violinist (played by Boris Thomashefsky); *The Outcast; or, Samuel Pasternak,* and *Yosele Solovey. Blondzhende Shtern (Vagabond Stars)* tells the romantic adventures of members of a traveling troupe of Yiddish actors in the early Goldfadn era.

Herald flier for *Dos Groyse Gevins (The Big Win* or *The Jackpot),* also called *200,000,* a comedy about a man who thinks he's won 200,000 rubles in a lottery. The portrait at the center is the author, Sholom Aleichem. The Eden Theatre is the building originally built by Maurice Schwartz as his Yiddish Art Theater. The ad for benefits is traditional.

Sholom Aleichem came to New York in 1914 and, after two years spent miserably trying to make a living through writing for the Yiddish theater and press, died there in 1916. Almost all the Jewish shops and factories on the Lower East Side closed to honor him on the day he was buried.

Sholom Asch

Sholom Asch (1880–1957) was the first Yiddish dramatist whose plays established a reputation outside the Jewish world. At the age of nineteen, upon Peretz's urging, he switched from writing in Hebrew to writing in Yiddish— "Peretz freed me from the chains of Hebrew" was how he later put it. He was already becoming known as a Peretz protégé and a Yiddish novelist when he wrote his first play, *Mitn Shtrom (With the Current)*, about a *yeshive* scholar who leaves wife, child, and pious studies in order to look (in vain) for a new kind of Torah, which will satisfy him spiritually. *With the Current* was produced first in Polish, because in 1904 no Yiddish theater in Poland was competent to attempt it.

In the next few years Asch wrote *Meshiekhs Tsaytn (The Messianic Era*, also called *A Dream of My People)*, about a patriarch who goes to Palestine, though almost none of his children or grandchildren have the strength or faith to follow him. This play was produced in Polish and Russian as well as in Yiddish. He dramatized *Kiddush HaShem (Sanctification of the Name—*an expression meaning martyrdom) from his novel about seventeenth-century Cossack pogroms. Another historical play was about Sabtai Tzvi, the false Messiah of the seventeenth century, and a third, *Amnon and Tamar*, was set in Biblical days. Asch portrayed contemporary Jewish life as well. He dramatized *Motke Ganef (Motke the Thief)* from his rich, vigorous novel about the underworld, and *Uncle Moses* from his novel about love and money in the Lower East Side garment industry; Maurice Schwartz starred in a film version.

Asch's most famous play is *Got fun Nekome (God of Vengeance)*. Max Reinhardt produced it in Berlin in 1907. It appeared in German in Vienna and in English on Broadway, where in 1923 it was closed down by the police for immorality. The protagonist, Yekl Shabshevitz, owns a whorehouse and lives above it with his wife, a former prostitute, and their adolescent daughter. He believes he has succeeded in his mad efforts to keep his daughter absolutely innocent; he is about to dedicate a Torah scroll and find his daughter a respectable bridegroom. The daughter, however, is fascinated by the life downstairs. Without altogether understanding it, she develops a lesbian relationship with one of the prostitutes. After a delicately erotic scene in which the two women pretend they are a piously betrothed young bride and groom, they run off together with a pimp. Seeing that his attempt to keep his daughter from being contaminated by his business has not worked, Yekl rages savagely against God. *God of Vengeance* had success as both scandal and play. Yekl was played by such powerful stars as Rudolph Schildkraut and David Kessler.

"I am not a Jewish artist," Asch often said. "I am a universal artist." In the 1930s and 1940s, drawn to Christianity, he published a series of Christological novels which detonated considerable controversy among his Jewish readers. Some fifteen years later, Asch settled in Israel, and he died there.

David Pinski

David Pinski (1872–1959) was another of Peretz's protégés. He had a good secular education in Moscow and Vienna, and later studied at Columbia University in New York. He had migrated to America in 1899, after distinguishing himself as one of the first Yiddish writers to address himself directly to the miserable situation of urban workers. He wrote novels, stories, and essays, and worked as editor of various periodicals.

Soon after coming to America, Pinski wrote his first play, *Yesurim (Sor-*

Isaac Samberg in the title role of *Motke the Thief (Motke Ganef)* by Sholom Asch.

rows), a one-acter which immediately won the prize in a competition run by a dramatic literary club called the Jacob Gordin Circle. In the same year he wrote his first three-act play, *Isaac Sheftl*, which tells the story of a peasant with artistic sensibilities, whose impoverished environment has let him develop only far enough to be a petty inventor and then frustrates him into destroying his machines and himself. Soon afterward Pinski wrote *The Mother*, also a grim play, naturalistic in mood, about a widow who loses her children's love when she remarries; this was written as a role for Keni Liptzin.

The Kishinev pogroms of 1903 shook Pinski into a closer consideration of Jewish identity, especially that of Eastern Europe. He wrote *Di Familie Tsvi (The Family Tsvi)*, which was performed and discussed frequently in the years that followed. In a Russian city, a bourgeois Jewish family waits, trembling. A pogrom is brewing. The patriarchal grandfather, Reb Moyshe Tsvi, rises to the moment, even welcomes the chance for martyrdom, and at first expects his family and fellow Jews to join him in a sort of holy army. They will die in defense of the Torah scrolls, which the rioters will certainly burn. The play records Reb Moyshe's successive confrontations with representative elements of the Jewish community, beginning at the dinner table with his businessman son and his three grandsons: the Bundist, the Zionist, and the assimilationist. Next he rushes to the synagogue.

Act Two begins with this scene. Two beggars stand at the lectern near the Torah scrolls in the dark synagogue. They are studying Talmud, and even when they chat, they lapse into the Talmud singsong chant.

FAT BEGGAR   I've got such a sweet place to hide that if I were only good and full of food like I always am at the end of Passover I could lie there days and days and no one would find me.

THIN BEGGAR   Where, exactly?

FAT BEGGAR   Right here under the synagogue. See?

THIN BEGGAR   Where the pigs crawl under?

FAT BEGGAR   So what's that to me? I'm not going to eat them.

THIN BEGGAR   I'm only asking.

FAT BEGGAR   Besides, you can drive the pigs out and ask them politely to excuse you, and have even more room. See?

THIN BEGGAR   Room for a lot of Jews.

FAT BEGGAR   *(Back to Talmudic singsong.)* And even for Jewesses too.

THIN BEGGAR   *(Talmudic singsong, swaying, looking into Talmud.)* So, then? Where are we up to?

FAT BEGGAR   *(Singsong.)* We're up to—we're up to where a bite of something would be very nice.

REB MOYSHE   *(Enters wearing fur hat and long coat. Kisses the mezuza.)* Holy congregation, forgive me for—. *(Interrupts himself.)* The synagogue alone? The —synagogue—alone!*(He hears the* BEGGARS *swaying and chanting. Blissfully.)* No, Jews are sitting and studying Torah! Thank you, God, that I lived to hear it. Your children are being beaten, and they sit and study your Torah. *(He goes forward and sees the beggars. The bliss disappears from his face.)* Only they! God, how great is thy people Israel! The worst of them become the best.

FAT BEGGAR   Good day, Reb Moyshe. Did you say something?

REB MOYSHE   Good day, children, and thank you. I was just about to open my mouth to curse, but I heard you studying and my curse became a blessing.

FAT BEGGAR   Who did you want to bawl out?

REB MOYSHE   Who? The cowards, the weaklings, the faithless, those who care about themselves, not the synagogue. *(Sits down, tired.)* I ran here and saw before me a synagogue full of Jews. You hear, children, I ran to synagogue and thought that the synagogue would be full of Jews. I saw young and old before me, men, women, and children. My heart went out with joy and I rejoiced, and was ashamed to arrive the last, and I wanted to ask them to forgive me: "Holy congreg—"

FAT BEGGAR   That's how it should have been.

REB MOYSHE   It should have been, shouldn't it? And I come into the synagogue and open my mouth, and don't believe my eyes—no Jews. A fearful thought ran through me, and a curse lay on my tongue, an unholy curse. But you took the curse from my mouth, and God's blessing fall on you. May he give you life as you gave life to me. *(Stands up and raises his voice.)* Ah, Israel is not abandoned, Israel is not abandoned. If they over there, those heretics of mine, had seen you, how embarrassed they would have been! What is all their might against your might? What is their power, what is all their power and all their battling, against you, you sitting here now and studying Torah? *(The* BEGGARS *look at each other furtively and shrug their shoulders.)* But, children, you must show that your strength is not only for studying the Torah, but also for defending it. Like a stag to water, that's how we Jews must run to study Torah, but we must be like lions to defend our purity from unclean hands. We must fear no enemy, however great. For to die for our purity, a martyr's death to sanctify the Name—can there be a sweeter death?

But why am I talking to you and disturbing your study? Study, children, study. I will prepare everything myself. I know where our iron tools are. You will be armed and strong, you will be strong. *(Hurries out the door.)*

FAT BEGGAR   Do you understand what he's talking about?

THIN BEGGAR   Why shouldn't I understand?

FAT BEGGAR   If—may the hour never come—if they attack the synagogue, we should be the soldiers of God and stand up in defense of purity.

THIN BEGGAR   Ye-es, it would be a great thing to sacrifice your life to sanctify the name. You call that nothing much?

FAT BEGGAR   You tell me, could you do it?

THIN BEGGAR   I'm only talking. I'll tell you the truth. I'll be dead of fright before they ever get to the synagogue.

FAT BEGGAR   And I'm going to be lying with the pigs so fast, I won't even remember how I got there.

Reb Moyshe's last confrontation is with townspeople huddling in the forest. No one is willing to fight at his side except, at the end, his assimilationist grandson, who does it for the wrong reasons. It becomes clear that something proud and noble—Judaism itself—is as aged as a very aged man and will die with him, even though the Jews of the town may survive. Pinski explained repeatedly that this was not just another "pogrom play"; its subtitle is "The Tragedy of the Last and Only Jew." The play has a lot in common with Gordin's melodramas. Events move along with a certain heavy logic which comes from the characters themselves: how they are destined to behave. Reb Moyshe Tsvi's grand speeches are impressive curtains.

Pinski wrote a number of historical plays: *Rabbi Akiba and Bar Kokhba, Beruriah, Yokhanan the High Priest, Alexander and Diogenes.* He also wrote several plays about contemporaneous social conditions.

His plays about sensual love include *Yankl der Shmid (Yankl the Blacksmith),* later made into a movie, which is about a virile blacksmith who gets into trouble by wanting his wife and his neighbor's wife as well; it ends happily, however. *King David and His Wives* recalls five love episodes of King David. Among them are David's love for King Saul's daughter when he is a boy, for Bathsheba when he is a man, and for the maiden hired to keep him warm in his old age. *Professor Brenner* is about an elderly man who loves a much younger woman, but must face the fact that her admiration for him is not an adequate basis for a marriage. The atmosphere in these plays and in such others as *Gavri and the Women, The Dumb Messiah,* and *Mary Magdalene* is human, realistic, relatively low-keyed, and psychologically valid.

Pinski's best-known play, and probably his best, is *The Treasure.* Even before its Yiddish premiere, Max Reinhardt produced it in German in 1920. The same year the Theatre Guild presented it on Broadway in English. Tillie is the daughter of the gravedigger, one of the poorest men in a Russian-Jewish village, where everybody is poor. Lively, shrewd, and imaginative, she sees in the few gold coins her half-witted brother found in the cemetery evidence of

Sweatshop setting on a poster for the Yiddish Art Theater's production (1921) of *Rags (Shmates)* by H. Leivick. Maurice Schwartz's portrait appears superimposed on the tower of his theater, the Madison Square Garden, on Twenty-seventh Street and Madison Avenue. Celia Adler's photo is the second from right.

buried treasure. Soon the whole village is drunk with the rumor. The middle act of the play takes place in the cemetery at night. A constant orchestrated flow of townspeople stumble in twos and threes across the graves, scared of ghosts, calling to each other in the dark, bickering over the money they haven't found yet. The ghosts themselves appear, briefly; they are amused. In the end, the village finds there was no treasure, and they are badly disappointed, for the comedy is played against their very real poverty. But Tillie has had some days of glory, and as long as they lasted she has had credit enough to enjoy fancy clothes and a desirable suitor. Celia Adler played Tillie in English for the Theatre Guild.

For many years Pinski was president of the Yiddish division of the international writers' organization, P.E.N. He lived most of his life in New York, but spent his last ten years in Israel.

H. Leivick

H. Leivick (1888–1962), whose real name was Leyvik Halpern, was expelled from his *yeshive* at the age of fifteen for reading Mapu's romantic Hebrew *haskole* novel *Love of Zion*. Two years later he joined the Bund and spent many years in Siberia for political activities, an imprisonment he described in a 1959 autobiography, *In the Czar's Prison*. He arrived in America shortly before the First World War and there wrote many poems and plays. He wrote for the daily *Der Tog,* but for most of his life made his living as a paperhanger.

Leivick's most renowned play is actually a dramatic poem: *Der Goylem (The Golem),* a blank-verse retelling of the legend of the mechanical man created from clay by a rabbi in Prague in the seventeenth century to defend Jews from an accusation of killing Christian children for their blood. In the end, the golem gets out of control. He becomes too human, desires the rabbi's daughter, and begins to get violent and kill people. The rabbi returns the golem to clay. The Habima Theater performed *The Golem* in Hebrew in Moscow in 1925. The first Yiddish production came two years later, also in Moscow. It was later performed in Polish and English. Some years later Leivick wrote a sequel to this play: *The Salvation Comedy—The Golem Dreams.* He wrote other dramatic poems or poetic dramas, including *Hirsh Lekert,* about a martyred revolutionary, *Sodom, Abelard and Heloise,* and, much later, after World War II, *In the Days of Job, A Wedding in Fernwald,* and *The Miracle in the Warsaw Ghetto.*

Some of Leivick's early plays were produced by Maurice Schwartz in the 1920s. The best known were about capitalist conditions on the Lower East Side: *Shmates (Rags)*, *Bankrupt*, and *Shop*. Abraham Cahan serialized *Rags* in the *Jewish Daily Forward*. Here is the opening scene of *Shop*. ("Bankrupt" and "shop" are English words which were absorbed into Yiddish. "Shop," especially, meaning the working place of a great proportion of the Lower East Side men and women, appears in the Yiddish dialogue; all other English intrusions have been underlined at their first appearance.)

(A garment industry <u>shop.</u> Barred windows. Right, two <u>cutting</u> tables. . . . Left, the <u>designer's</u> worktable, the <u>finishers'</u> table. Between these, the <u>pressers'</u> table. Between the cutters and pressers, tables piled high with fabrics, dresses and trousers, making a wall which divides the shop in two. Big time clock by the door; each worker puts in his card as he enters.

When the curtain rises, we see an odd picture. Old LAZAR is cleaning the shop with a long broom. The empty <u>machines</u> are turning noisily. It seems that the old man turned on the electricity and is enjoying the results. He dances as he cleans, heavily and comically. The clock shows a quarter to eight in the morning. Enter WOLF, one of the <u>bosses.</u>)

WOLF   *(Frightened.)* What's going on?

LAZAR   *(Confused, runs quickly and shuts off the electric power, turns back, stammers like someone caught sinning.)* It's just something.

WOLF   What's that? "Just something"?

LAZAR   Nu, forgive me. It's really wrong. Just a sort of foolishness. Sometimes it gets lonesome here. So I do it. Forgive me.

WOLF   No, I don't forgive you. What do you mean, turning on the electricity? You'll break the machines. All the needles.

LAZAR   You're right. Never again.

WOLF   *(Sets to work at cutting table. Spreads out fabric, cuts with shears.)* Senile. *(LAZAR turns.)* How many times have I told you that you have to clean up a shop in the evening after work, not in the morning.

LAZAR   Nu, don't yell at an old friend, Wolf.

WOLF   Again friend, again comrade. I've told you fifty times: don't call me friend or comrade. So we were "neighbors" in Siberia; so what? . . . Such dust—all the devils take it! If you clean up the shop in the morning once more—!

LAZAR   All right, shh, don't yell.

WOLF   How many times have I told you you should speak to me properly, call me <u>mister.</u> People come in, <u>businessmen,</u> and there you are in the middle with your "you,"* "friend." Why is it with *Mr.* Gold—

LAZAR   Mr. Gold is a *mister,* a native. What am I to him, and who am I to him?

WOLF   I'm a *mister* too. No more "at home in the old country." I'm like Gold too.

LAZAR   But how can I—

WOLF   No arguments. <u>That's all.</u> Unless you don't care about your job. *(*LAZAR *laughs sadly.)* You're still laughing?

LAZAR   *(Confused.)* Nu, not at all, just the opposite; let it be *mister. (Pause.)*

WOLF   They make me sick, *landslayt. (Pause.)* Instead of this, tell me what the shop is talking about. About the general <u>strike</u> that's coming?

LAZAR   What do I know?

WOLF   The workers must talk about me, probably. No?

LAZAR   What's to talk?

WOLF   Just, I mean, about me. That is: a boss. The shop hates me, probably, right?

LAZAR   I haven't heard that.

WOLF   You haven't heard? You don't want to say. You hate me too, I see that.

LAZAR   It isn't nice to make fun of an old comrade.

WOLF   Nu, enough of your cleaning up.

*(*GOLD *enters. Man in his thirties, stern and cold. Counts his words. Uses a powerful glance. Looks down on workers. Uses any means to an end. However, when he feels he's losing, he doesn't crumble but gives way and remains the same. When old* LAZAR *sees him, he runs far upstage with the broom.)*

GOLD   What's the argument?

WOLF   A senile old man. I tell him to listen in to what the shop is saying about the strike, and he—

GOLD   *(Interrupts.)* Not necessary.

WOLF   It's important to know what the shop is thinking.

GOLD   The shop doesn't think.

WOLF   But there's going to be a strike.

GOLD   So? I'm not letting any <u>union</u> up here. . . . *(Pause.)* As far as I'm concerned, they'll be working here during the strike. You, maybe—

---

*LAZAR has been addressing WOLF in the familiar second-person form: *du* (thou). WOLF tells him to use the formal, respectful *ir* (you).

WOLF   What—me?

GOLD   This is no union shop, and it isn't going to be. You maybe feel like giving in to them. I don't have to give in to them. My conscience is clean.

WOLF   Who says I'll give in to them?

GOLD   The former Bundist is scratching inside you.

WOLF   Maybe I still am a socialist.

GOLD   *(Mockingly.)* A socialist. *(Pause.)* No wonder the shop has no respect for you.

WOLF   Not everyone has a face like yours, that never smiles.

GOLD   You don't smile to a shop. *(Pause.)* What's a shop? Workers. *(Goes nearer to him.)* Look at the collar a person can wear! Dirty! A business establishment is a business establishment! Not a little prayer house, not a Bund meeting.

WOLF   Stop it.

GOLD   And those greenhorns of yours, I don't need them in the shop. . . .

WOLF   What can I do? Acquaintances, *landslayt*—they come begging for work.

GOLD   A shop doesn't need acquaintances. Negroes, Italians, Chinese. A shop needs hands. *(Pause.)* Let the strike begin tomorrow, even. *(*BARAKAN, *the designer, enters, greets them, and goes to his worktable. . . .* HYMIE, *a cutter, enters.* GOLD *goes quickly over to him, puts a hand on his shoulder.* HYMIE *smiles.)* How are you, Hymie?

HYMIE   Thanks, Mr. Gold.

GOLD   How's the family?

HYMIE   Thanks, Mr. Gold.

GOLD   You talked to me about a raise.

HYMIE   I'm a family man, four children.

GOLD   Go in the office. *(Sees* MINNA, *a sewing machine operator, entering.)* Here's your lady with the gray eyes.

Wolf's "lady with the gray eyes" despises him for betraying his socialist principles. The play works out relationships between people and ideologies. Jacob Ben-Ami directed the premiere of *Shop* in New York; he played Wolf, and Jacob Adler's daughter Stella played the gray-eyed lady, Minna.

In Tel Aviv today there is a small house on a tree-lined street. It serves as a coffeehouse for Yiddish writers, with rooms for meetings and lectures and space for evenings of Jewish culture. It is named, in Hebrew, *Beit Leivick*— Leivick House.

Osip Dimov

Osip Dimov (1878–1959) wrote for the Yiddish stage, though through much of his career he wrote in Russian. Although his real name was Joseph Perlman, he began under a Russian name as a Russian writer and kept the pseudonym for the rest of his career. He had very little Jewish education. His first play, *Every Day*, was performed in Russian, then in German by Max Reinhardt, and eventually it was made as a German film.

The wave of Russian pogroms in 1903 made Dimov conscious of his Jewishness. In the next years he wrote, in Russian, *Shma Yisroel (Hear, O Israel)* and *Der Eybiker Vanderer (The Eternal Wanderer)*. However, it was not until after he arrived in America in 1913 (brought over by Thomashefsky, who had seen *The Eternal Wanderer* and had it translated into Yiddish) that he started writing specifically with the Yiddish stage in mind.

Dimov wrote over thirty plays. Many were translated from Russian into languages besides Yiddish: Polish, German, Hebrew. *Yoshke Musikant (Yoshke the Musician,* also called *The Rented Bridegroom* or *The Singer of His Sorrow)* was performed by the Vilna Troupe in an adaptation by the poet Yankev Sternberg, with Joseph Buloff in the title role. It is a lyrical fantasy about a fiddler who loves a serving maid. She loves a card-playing wastrel. Yoshke wins a fortune in a lottery, but deliberately loses it at cards to the wastrel so he can afford to marry the girl. After this sacrifice Yoshke goes mad from a broken heart.

Among Dimov's other plays were *Di Ervakhung fun a Folk (The Awakening of a People)*; the trilogy *The World in Flames, Jerusalem,* and *The Town Spirit*; and *Bronx Express*. The last was performed at the Astor Theater on Broadway in English. Some of these plays were directed by Thomashefsky or Maurice Schwartz, some by Dimov himself. Often characterizations were so sharply drawn from real persons that actors were embarrassed to meet their originals on the streets of the Lower East Side.

Peretz Hirschbein

Peretz Hirschbein (1881–1948) wrote his first plays in Hebrew: *Miriam,* about a prostitute, and a number of others, which were published but never performed. Then he moved to Warsaw, where Yitzkhok Leyb Peretz took him under his wing, drew him to Yiddish, and introduced him to Sholom Asch,

Jacob Ben-Ami as Levi-Yitskhok reads the name which Bertha Gersten as Tsine has written on her slate, in Peretz Hirschbein's *Green Fields.*

to the poet Abraham Reisen, to the writers Yankev Dineson and Hersh Dovid Nomberg, and to the rest of his circle. Peretz frequently put up Hirschbein on his leather sofa and even fed him. Hirschbein, himself starving, wrote about the starving Jews of Warsaw; he earned the nickname the "cellar poet," for writing "cellar dramas." By 1908 he had written several plays in Yiddish, including *Tsvishn Tog un Nakht (Between Day and Night)* and *Eynsame Mentshn (Lonely People),* a one-acter after Gorki. Most of his plays from this period were symbolist.

In 1908, urged on by Peretz, by the Hebrew poet Bialik, and by the literati of Odessa, he organized in that city the first professional Yiddish art theater. For the next two years he traveled with them, and started writing and producing a group of lovely pastorales of Lithuanian-Jewish rural life: *A Farvorfen Vinkl (A Secluded Nook), Der Shmids Tekhter (The Blacksmith's Daughters), Di Puste Kretshme (The Idle Inn),* and the trilogy that begins with *Grine Felder (Green Fields).*

The hero of *Green Fields* is Levi Yitskhok, an unworldly young scholar. He has wandered into the countryside, where a Jewish farmer hires him to tutor his sons. Tsine, the farmer's daughter, a healthy, artless country girl, is worried because a neighbor wants Levi Yitskhok for his own household.

TSINE Oh, if only I could do something to make you happy to stay with us! You know what—when you're done eating, you'll come out into the fields and see how I bundle up the hay. I take a bundle this big up on my head, and all you can see is my feet underneath. Tell me what you like to eat. . . .

AVROM YANKEV [Her young brother] *(Enters.)* Here, I've got a board and a piece of chalk. The rebbe's going to teach me how to write my name.

TSINE   Me, too, rebbe. Write my name. I want to see how my name looks written out. *(LEVI YITSKHOK writes "Avrom Yankev" in big letters.)* That's my name—so long?

LEVI YITSKHOK   That says Avrom Yankev.

TSINE   I beg you, write my name—Tsine. *(He writes.)* Oy, little mamma mine! Look, now I'll erase it and you write it again.

AVROM YANKEV   You're crazy.

TSINE   Write, I beg you. *(LEVI YITSKHOK writes. She erases it again.)* Now once more. I just love to see you write.

LEVI YITSKHOK   That's silly.

TSINE   Me, I can see already that you're not going to go away.

In the next act, some time later, Levi Yitskhok is sitting alone outside the farmhouse. He is sniffing at two apples which Tsine climbed a tree to get for him but which, by Jewish law, must not be eaten at that time of year.

(TSINE comes out of the house, bringing a board on which something is written in chalk.)

LEVI YITSKHOK   What's that?

TSINE   Read what's written on it.

LEVI YITSKHOK   But that's not Avrom Yankev's writing.

TSINE   It's mine. *(LEVI YITSKHOK looks wonderingly at the letters. Reads.)* "Tsine, daughter of Reb Noyakh."

TSINE   Nu, well, who wrote it?

LEVI YITSKHOK   Not Avrom Yankev.

TSINE   Erase it.

LEVI YITSKHOK   Why should we do that? It isn't good to erase a name.

TSINE   I beg you, erase it. Wipe it off, that's right.

LEVI YITSKHOK   Ha ha. You're being childish. Nu, well, there, I've erased it.

TSINE   Now close your eyes. *(He does. She takes chalk from her pocket and writes.)*

LEVI YITSKHOK   Now?

Leah Noemi as Gitl, mother of the heroine Tsine, in the Vilna Troupe's production of *Green Fields* by Peretz Hirschbein.

TSINE   Just for a little bit, keep them closed. Now. Nu, what do you see written?

LEVI YITSKHOK   My name—Levi Yitskhok. Who wrote it?

TSINE   Me.

LEVI YITSKHOK   It's not possible.

TSINE   It is, too, possible.

LEVI YITSKHOK   I'll erase it and you write it again.

TSINE   Close your eyes again, then. *(He closes his eyes. She writes his name again in big letters. He keeps his eyes closed. She quietly steals up close to him and gives him a kiss. She runs away into the house.)*

The audience is not surprised when in the next act he asks the farmer for Tsine as his bride.

All Hirschbein's pastorals were performed often, especially by Yiddish art theaters. An adaptation of the Levi Yitskhok trilogy played every weekend through the winter of 1974–75 at the semiprofessional Folksbiene art theater in New York, and a charming film of *Green Fields* is still in circulation. The film was produced in 1937 on location among the farms of upstate New York. In one scene Tsine's family and the family from the neighboring farm meet on a country road. Both families are riding in horse-drawn wagons. Since the film company could afford to hire only one horse, they cleverly made do by showing his front half with shots of one family and his back half with the other. Hirschbein also wrote a number of one-act plays in a similar mode, including *Raisins and Almonds,* whose title refers to the song Goldfadn wrote for his play *Shulamis* a generation earlier.

Hirschbein had the looks and manner of a poet; A. Lutsky, himself a poet, wrote with teasing affection that even when Hirschbein asked for a radish, he somehow managed to ask for a radish "symbolically." At the same time, Hirschbein was proud of his extraordinary physical strength and loved to astonish people by bending a silver half dollar in his bare fingers. Hirschbein spent a lot of time on the move. He went to Argentina to work on a Jewish farm settlement, then in 1914 came to New York. After further years of traveling, as far as Africa, he moved to California, where he died.

Other Dramatists

A number of other playwrights belong by rights in a survey of Yiddish drama, but I mention only three as representative:

Fischel Bimko worked as a prompter in a Yiddish theater company, among many other jobs. He wrote over twenty plays of all sorts, of which the most esteemed were *Dembes (Oak Trees)* and *Ganovim (Thieves).* His strongest characters are simple earthy people, like the passionate heroine of *Oak Trees,* for whom a father and son come to blows. *Thieves* was first produced by the Vilna Troupe in 1919 in Yiddish and later in Israel in Hebrew. *Oak Trees* was most recently done in 1975, by the Workmens Circle amateur group in Tel Aviv.

A particularly interesting play of Bimko's is the salty *Amerike Ganef* (a wry expression meaning, roughly, *Thieving America* or *American Thievery*). At the conclusion, the protagonist, a pimp newly arrived from Poland, becomes drunk with patriotism.

> FETER [Uncle, a term of address for a pimp] . . . I'm as good as any Jew you see here. They came to America kosher and got *tref* [nonkosher]. I came *tref* and I go out kosher. . . . All . . . who were thieves, knife-stickers, throat-slitters, purse-cutters, America made out of them <u>shoemakers</u>, <u>watchmakers</u>, <u>clockmakers</u>, <u>dressmakers</u>— and whatever other <u>makers</u> there are. *(Street demonstrators offstage are heard singing "My Country 'Tis of Thee." His excitement rises.)* If I go thieving here or doing bad to people, my name isn't Smart Velvel. I'll live and I'll see, and anyone who doesn't let me—*(gestures.)! (Grabs his wife.)* Our America! *(Exit.)*

SHEYGITS [Gentile, or Smart-Aleck, one of his gang]   *(Grabbing one of his girls.)*
If you walked at home, here you ride a carriage. *(Exit.)*

YUNG [Kid, another of his gang]   *(Grabbing the other girl.)* An upside-down
world, America. *(Exit.)*

Alter Kacyzne (1885–1941) began as a photographer, but wrote in many
literary forms, including drama. His best-known plays are *Prometheus, Herod,*
and *Der Dukes (The Duke)*. In a preface to *The Duke*, which deals with a
legendary Polish duke who converted to Judaism and was martyred for it,
Kacyzne wrote: "I was more concerned with the social Yiddish drama than
with the personal drama of the convert himself." Kacyzne was shot and killed
by Ukrainian Fascists in 1941.

Mark Arnstein acted with a Yiddish amateur company from the age of
fourteen. At twenty-two, he wrote his first play, which was in Polish. His most
famous work, *Der Vilner Balabesl (The Little Vilna Householder)*, was performed first in Polish and soon thereafter in Yiddish. His career continued in
both languages. He directed many Yiddish plays in Polish translations, believing that this built a bridge between the two cultures. In 1922 he produced
several of his comic one-acters in California in English, including *Mayn Vaybs
Meshugas (My Wife's Craziness,* also called *Nobody Home)*. The same year
he organized a Yiddish amateur troupe in Argentina and toured South America. He is believed to have died in the Warsaw ghetto.

Overview

Out of this kaleidoscope of people and plays some constants do emerge.
Most of these dramatists began their lives and careers in Europe, but many
ended up in America; all of them were born in the nineteenth century and
died in the twentieth; several lived to see World War II, the destruction of
the Yiddish-speaking community which was their readership, and the founding of the state of Israel. Educated in Europe (though few of them formally),
they were aware of the experiments of their non-Jewish literary colleagues.
Many began by writing in a language other than Yiddish: Russian or Polish
or Hebrew. Most of them wrote in forms other than drama and thought of
themselves as writers rather than as dramatists.

Pinski had described the young writers who, in 1909, he expected to be
the "third act" as being genuinely Jewish in content. He meant that they were
to develop stories out of intrinsically Jewish situations rather than adapting

non-Jewish plays by superimposing Jewish settings and characters upon them. Peretz's young wife in *A Kvores-Nakht (A Cemetery Night)* is at her mother's grave, for example, because it was a Jewish custom to go there for advice or —as she mentions—to send complaints or messages to God. Dimov's Yoshke Musikant lives in a *shtetl,* and all his friends are typical *shtetl* figures: the woman who sells chickens, the men who sells cemetery plots, the wedding fiddler.

These writers' plays often deal with Jewish problems, such as pogroms, loss of faith, assimilation. Jewishness per se was a conscious preoccupation for many, though not all, of their major characters. The other major preoccupation was politics from a leftist perspective, for Yiddishism was bound up with reforming political consciousness. To express such concerns, these writers tended to construct their dramatic conflicts not so much between individual personalities as between social groups or generations, as represented by characters who function allegorically. In Leivick's *Shop,* one character is a typical boss; another is the former revolutionary corrupted by capitalism; a third is the voice of his reforming conscience. In Pinski's *The Family Tsvi,* every character argues his own political solution. In *Yankl Boyle,* ignorance and superstition, embodied in most of the Jewish characters, push Yankl toward his doom, while his native instincts are clearly those of the free, healthy spirit. This approach is presentational rather than representational. It resembles Purim plays and Brechtian expressionism rather than the subtly internalized psychologizing that was a dominant strain in many of the serious dramas of twentieth-century Europe and America.

Perhaps the reason many Yiddish dramatists tended to make Jewish concerns a deliberate program, with concepts acted out even in realist plays, was that they couldn't take a national drama for granted. Unlike most European cultures, Yiddish had not developed a drama naturally over the centuries. Nor had it developed a thematic vocabulary out of which an artist draws gestures, associations, and conventions that are common to his audience. Many of the truly national motifs that were available, such as Purim plays or traditional pieties, were already so old-fashioned that they no longer fully represented the larger audience. Furthermore, they had been popularly vulgarized through association with *shund.* Within the forum of Yiddish theater, religiousness itself tended to be a romantic notion, or even a metaphor for secular nationalism. It was no longer the powerful villain it had been in plays from the *haskole* through Gordin, in years when pious repression was more of a threat in real life. In *The Family Tsvi,* for example, Reb Moyshe is a little mad, a little ridiculous; in *Green Fields,* Levi Yitskhok is touchingly naïve. What modern Jews had in common, if religion was taken away, seemed to these dramatists to be conflicts of loyalty and self-image, political concerns, and a negative identity—i.e., they were not exactly Russian, Polish, or American. Playwrights couldn't simply picture human behavior, and trust that a distinctively Jewish drama would emerge. True to the traditional Jewish view that art's function is didactic, these playwrights consciously tried to forge a theater to deal with Jewishness.

The new Yiddish dramatists shared the traditional Jewish awareness of history as a continuum: *The Family Tsvi, The Golden Chain,* and a number of other plays deal explicitly with the Jewish experience as it changes in time. Often they use the family as a microcosm of that larger experience. Many of these writers put plays in Biblical or other Jewish historical settings: Leivick's *The Golem* and Asch's *Sanctification of the Name,* for example. They have a sense of the Jewish experience as a dramatic panorama, ranging over eras and ideologies.

Even the plays that were most popular in translation were commentaries on society and social relationships. A few pungent comedies like Gogol's *The Inspector-General* and Molière's *The Imaginary Invalid,* a few dramas like Ibsen's *Ghosts* and *An Enemy of the People,* pop up in repertory after repertory. On the other hand, *Hamlet* almost never does (except in an adaptation called *The Yeshive Student,* which makes drastic changes from Shakespeare's original), and the Greek high tragedies never do. Yiddish theater has never been drawn to the ancient tragic view of man's character and fate. The critic A. Mukdoyni speculated that the reason was Jews' always having so many problems from the outside world that they gave less attention to inner conflict. Furthermore, Jewish tradition emphasizes community rather than the individual. Besides, classical tragedy demands a protagonist who is a king, and Yiddish life offered no viable equivalent. In any case, the tragedies written in or translated into Yiddish are not "high," insoluble, and inevitable, but rather based on a whole other world view. (In form, too, the non-Yiddish plays most often translated tend to the opposite extreme from the classical: romantic, active, free, and colorful.)

At the same time, however, some of the Yiddish playwrights explored individual motivations: Pinski's men and women, for example, Bimko's, Asch's, Hirschbein's. Like modern Western drama, the Yiddish drama had discovered Freud (though psychology was rarely its primary concern). And as if part of a latter-day Renaissance (during the Renaissance each European nation had developed a sense of nationhood, established its vernacular as a vehicle for its own modern literature, and freed art from its role as servant to religion), Yiddish literature focused increasingly on the classical humanist subject, the individual human being. Painters and sculptors, poets and dramatists, used Jewish modes and forms to express individual visions or to investigate those human responses which are individual and universal.

These "third act" plays tend to have certain theatrical qualities. They are more often dark, heavy, and grotesque than bright and brisk. Some of their weight comes from the abstract concepts that the characterizations are carrying. The frothy artificial drawing-room genre is as alien to them as that social milieu was to Yiddish culture. Their humor tends to come out of plot or character type rather than from verbal felicity. Maybe one reason is that the characters tend to be proletarians or country folk, so their speech has vigor and juice rather than elegance. In general, there is a fondness for largeness and risk, an almost operatic quality, rather than the smaller, lighter, more flexible tone that we associate with modern drama.

If one were to choose the contemporaneous modern playwright with whose works these writers' plays had most in common, it might be Eugene O'Neill. Like them, O'Neill experimented in a wide range of styles. The effort he made to deal with ideas is the source of both the strength and the heaviness in many of his plays. The atmosphere of his plays, like theirs, is sometimes comic, less often happy. Although unlike Yiddish writers he was interested in psychology more than in sociology, his characters sometimes came from social groups that had not previously appeared onstage. The fact that O'Neill and the Yiddish dramatists were writing simultaneously in the United States explains some of their similarities; they were responding to similar stimuli. O'Neill's sense of belonging to a victimized minority, the Irish, is also a factor.

Pinski further described the "third act" writers as refusing to "let the actors lead them by the nose." Certainly most of the group first had their plays performed by earnest bands of amateurs—in this, too, they resembled O'Neill —or simply published, and only later saw the plays produced professionally. Thus they were relatively independent of individual stars or box office managers. However, as long as the commercial theater offered these writers their only hope of professional production, it was inevitable that they would often be led by the nose by actors. Kobrin, for example, complained in 1915 to an English-language magazine of Jewish interest that it was impossible for a serious writer to have his plays done as he wished in the commercial theaters of the Lower East Side.

> . . . only the other day I had an experience that was to me most heartrending.
> I was compell⌐d to leave the theater after the first act of one of my own plays.
> . . . I could not stand the desecration any longer. The child of my brain was so
> horribly mutilated before my very eyes that it was hardly recognizable.
>
> You see, in the Yiddish theater the life of a play is extremely short. It is taken
> on the road, the actors improve upon the dramatist's original conception, and

to save actual financial expense, two or three characters of the play are elimi-
nated. What can be left of a play when commercial exigencies dictate that a
number of essential characters be dispensed with?

Music was another grievance. Goldfadn had wanted no music at all in his
last play; Gordin fought for the same austerity; they both lost that battle, and
the crowds continued to impose their demand for music on the commercial
theater.

But these new playwrights did find stages of their own. Most of their plays
were done by small, serious "art theaters": professional, semiprofessional, and
even amateur—like the very first Yiddish art theater of Odessa, organized in
1908 by Peretz Hirschbein.

Art theaters immediately became part of the flowering of Yiddish culture.

8 THE ART THEATERS

In 1910, Yitskhok Leyb Peretz, with one of his characteristic whirlwinds of enthusiasm, terrified the Jews of Warsaw by renting the biggest concert hall in town for an afternoon seminar on Yiddish theater. Warsaw was the Yiddish literary center in Europe, with one of the largest concentrations of Jews, but anti-Semitic feeling was high at the time and Poles were actually boycotting Jewish stores. It seemed like looking for trouble to go outside the Jewish neighborhood and make oneself conspicuous. But there was no arguing with Peretz when his mind was made up. He arranged a panel to speak on the history of Yiddish theater, on Yiddish plays, and on performers and audiences of present-day Warsaw. The speakers were all intimates of his: the critic Mukdoyni and the writers Yankev Dineson and A. Vayter. Peretz himself would introduce them and give the summation—if Polish mobs or police had not broken up the place by then. In the days before the conference, the scheduled speakers muttered to each other consolingly that in any case no Jews would have the nerve to show up.

When the four arrived at the Philharmonia Hall, however, they were overwhelmed to find that so many thousands of people waited outside that barely half could get in. Peretz, intoxicated with the occasion, got carried away and made all his speakers' main points in what was supposed to be only a graceful introduction. His own passion was infectious, as always, and applause shook the Philharmonia when he roared a war cry: "Let no Jewish foot cross the threshold of the old *shund* theaters! We will destroy the old theater, and on its ruins we will build the new Yiddish art theater!"

The destruction of *shund* never happened, of course, and never will in any culture. But Peretz, with his healthy flair for dramatizing his ideas and himself, was formulating the battle line for Yiddish theater as he had for Yiddish literature. The Yiddish proletariat was not to be left (as were the masses of other nations) to stew in vulgar entertainments. Peretz insisted that the very lowest Yiddish theater should have some artistic merit, and that the highest should be, by any intellectual's standards, art. In the first two decades of the twentieth century, forces both inside and outside the professional Yiddish theater succeeded in establishing the "art theater" as a fact of international Yiddish life.

As of 1910, Yiddish culture lacked three vital elements that were integral parts of all other European cultures with fine national theaters: First, it lacked an established tradition of performance, as well as schools for training continuing generations of practitioners. Second, it lacked state support, which gives institutions like theaters and drama schools financial stability. Third, the Yiddish intellectual and social elite did not value their "national" theater enough to include it among the cultural treasures to be maintained and advanced as a matter of course.

Russia, France, Germany, and other European countries had developed these three elements gradually, as part of their larger national histories, and now the Yiddish community, particularly the intellectuals, attempted to catch up. They telescoped the process for Yiddish theater into a few brief years, and they pushed as well to modernize Yiddish culture as a whole. They imposed attitudes and criteria belonging to other nations upon the expanding possibilities of modern Yiddish theater, while for subsidies from a nonexistent Yiddish state they tried to substitute voluntary funding by individuals and communal bodies. Naturally, they were influenced by what their fellow intellectuals were doing on the non-Yiddish stage, particularly by the aesthetics and principles that shaped the so-called art theater movement.

Yiddish art theaters were part of the wave of little art theaters that had a strong effect on European drama beginning in the 1880s, and reached America almost a full generation later. The first significant art theater was founded in 1887 by a clerk in the Paris gasworks, André Antoine. With no expectation of making money, barely hoping to break even, but for sheer love of the art, he and a group of mostly nonprofessional actors set up the Théâtre Libre, a tiny stage in a tiny building at the end of a dead-end street. They committed themselves especially to naturalism, hanging a raw bloody side of beef onstage when the action took place in a butcher shop, and turning their backs to the audience when it seemed natural for the characters to do so. Antoine was especially inspired by the works of Émile Zola, who pioneered literary naturalism and "slice of life" dramas. He was the first to stage Zola's plays and dramatizations of Zola's novels.

Other small theaters appeared in Europe in the same period, all created by people dedicated to reforming or transforming the theater of the time. In 1889 Otto Brahm founded the Freie Buehne in Berlin. In 1891 J. T. Grein founded the Independent Theater and opened it with Ibsen's *Ghosts,* which the lord chancellor had banned from the London stage. Grein went on to be the first to produce George Bernard Shaw's plays in England.

The Moscow Art Theater, founded in 1898 by Constantin Stanislavsky and Vladimir Nemirovich-Danchenko, was also part of this wave of reform. Naturally, of all the art theaters, this one most directly influenced Yiddish theater, which was attuned to the intellectual life of its East European environment. The Moscow Art Theater was the first to produce Chekhov's plays as the author had envisioned them. In interpreting modern realistic drama, Stanislavsky's group evolved a vividly lifelike method of acting which was to have a widespread effect on modern Western theater, especially in America, where Yiddish immigrants helped to spread it.

Although most of these independent art theaters were more or less committed to realism, there were some groups and individual theorists who explored other, antirealist visions. In 1893 Aurélien-Marie Lugné-Poë, for example, opened the Maison de l'Oeuvre with the premiere of Maurice Maeterlinck's symbolist *Pelléas and Mélisande.* Jacques Copeau devoted the Théâtre du Vieux Colombier to his own fantastic creations. In Dublin, Lady Gregory and her circle established the Abbey Theater, with special attention to the symbolist masques of Yeats, as well as the realistic dramas of Synge. And the Moscow Art Theater experimented with various nonrealistic modes, such as constructivism, again shared by Yiddish compatriots.

What all these groups had in common was a determination to provide a better kind of theater than the commercial establishment and, if possible, to influence the commercial theater. Often they were almost religiously serious about their mission. One example of the changes they introduced was Stanislavsky's daring to turn the houselights off while the stage was lit; previously, fashionable Moscow audiences had enjoyed drinking, gossiping, and inspecting each other's gowns to the accompaniment of a play. The groups issued manifestoes, lots of them, repudiating the mindless sensationalism and superficial realism of commercially successful hits. They valued ensemble work and denounced star actors and their personality cults. They were in service to the production as a whole, which usually meant the conception of the writer and/or the director.

"Sweeping Out" Yiddish Theater

Yiddish theater had its young idealists too. At the turn of the century, Jacob Ben-Ami, still a boy and fresh from his grandfather's farm, was appalled by the *shund* he saw in nearby Minsk. Local and traveling Russian companies, some of them subsidized by the state, offered Minsk residents an alternative to Russian *shund*. In contrast, Yiddish shows offered only a range of operettas, farcical burlesques, and melodramas in *Daytshmerish*. Even the Gordin repertory had barely reached Minsk yet. Jews of cultivated taste went to the Russian theater. The youngster wrote in his diary: "I am going to learn from Russian theater, and then I will sweep out Yiddish theater with a broom and make it beautiful." Only a few years later he was part of the first Yiddish professional art theater, and his career was bound up with the development of Yiddish drama.

While Ben-Ami was still a clever *yeshive* boy, adults were calling for the reform of Yiddish theater in Eastern Europe. While he was still playing hooky to watch tightrope jugglers and hurdy-gurdy dancers at peasant fairs, or to sing in the Russian opera house chorus, Yiddish critics were pointing out the lack of Yiddish art theaters. (Critics' voices were shriller in Eastern Europe than in America because the contrast between Yiddish and non-Yiddish theater was more acute: the Polish and Russian theaters were more adventurous than the American, while the Yiddish theater in Poland and Russia was far more backward.)

In the years just before Peretz's panel at the Philharmonia, literary clubs in cities and even villages all over the Yiddish-speaking world sponsored series of lectures and evening courses about Yiddish and non-Yiddish theater. Yiddish periodicals popped up, with names like *Theater, Art and Theater,* and *Yiddish Drama.* Dr. Yitskhok Sziper wrote a valuable two-volume history of Yiddish theater up to the mid-eighteenth century. Journalists used reviews of plays as excuses for theoretical essays about drama. Interest was bubbling especially among the young, proletarian, self-taught intelligentsia. In America, Jacob Gordin was a major influence in these circles.

Nevertheless, when such theater-lovers had the price of a ticket, their options remained basically the same: professional *shund,* amateur theatricals, or drama in Russian. Mendele Moykher Sforim did not expect a flowering of Yiddish drama to parallel that of Yiddish literature: "You can't expect to transform a village stream into the River Dneiper." But a lot of his colleagues refused to accept his analogy.

One representative effort of the time was the ambitious Theater Society founded in Warsaw by Mukdoyni and Vayter. It was modeled on a Yiddish literary society that already had branches throughout Eastern Europe. On the advisory board were Peretz, of course, and such important figures as Sholom Asch, Abraham Reisen, Hersh Dovid Nomberg, Yankev Dineson, Mordekhay Spektor, with Mendl Elkin an active participant.

Vayter was a silent vibrating wire of a man. He was one of many Jewish revolutionaries who, after 1905, had their noses rubbed in the essentially anti-Semitic feelings of their comrades and returned almost as new converts to Yiddish culture, swelling the Yiddishist cultural excitement of the period. Now he lived without a passport, without a job, under a false name, because the Czar's police were hunting him. He wrote *Der Shtumer (The Mute)* and other plays about his experiences.

For almost a year Vayter gave himself over entirely to the Theater Society. He wrote letters and rode trains to towns all over Eastern Europe, begging funds, founding local branch committees, actually starving himself for the price of train tickets and stamps. He called the Theater Society "my one bit of hope to build something, for the years when I was busy knocking down."

The Theater Society came to nothing. The group promising the biggest potential support in money and influence was the aristocratic St. Petersburg Jews. Peretz himself took on the mission of approaching them, but recklessly he antagonized them. They made the mistake of welcoming him formally at a banquet in his honor with speeches in Russian rather than in Yiddish (which some of them did not know). Peretz listened for a while. Then he pushed abruptly to the head of the table, biting his lower lip and literally trembling with rage. The guests expected a graceful acknowledgment, full of Peretz's famous wit and charm. Instead they heard a long, cold speech beginning: "Jews who welcome a Yiddish writer in the Russian language will never build Yiddish culture. They won't build a Yiddish theater; they won't even build a Yiddish barn, because even a Yiddish barn must be built in the Yiddish language." Mukdoyni, bitterly disappointed, claimed that Peretz was acting not on principle, but only because he was furiously humiliated at having had to sneak into St. Petersburg, where Jews could rarely get residence permits. In any case, Peretz's explosion alienated the Theater Society's best hope. Miserable conditions before and during the war doomed it.

Vayter eventually turned himself in to the Czar's police and served a term in Siberia (his second); he was shot in 1919 in his Vilna apartment in a Polish police raid.

Meanwhile, though the Theater Society had foundered, other experimental groups kept popping up. The time was ripe.

In 1908, Peretz Hirschbein founded his Yiddish art theater. He had been prowling restlessly around Europe, writing and occasionally acting a role in one of his own dramas. Hawkishly handsome and intelligent, he was ready for whatever adventure turned up next. When he stopped off at the Princess of the South, as he called Odessa, the lively intellectual circle led by the Hebraist H. N. Bialik decided that here—at last—was the man to found a Yiddish art theater.

Hirschbein resisted all his friends' coaxings and pressures to found the theater. He protested that there wasn't enough repertory and there weren't enough suitable actors. He pointed out that although you could now legally perform in Yiddish, you still couldn't put up posters in Yiddish, and you had to write plays out in German and send them to St. Petersburg to be censored. Still Hirschbein was hankering to give it a try. As young actors and actresses (Lazar Freed, Miriam Orleska, Leah Noemi) gravitated toward the theater they'd been waiting for, the Hirschbein Troupe (taking Stanislavsky's Moscow Art Theater as their model) began performing in and around Odessa.

News about the troupe, which was praised in the Russian press as well as the Yiddish, reached Warsaw. Peretz and others raised money for the group, which was always broke, to come for a guest engagement. Warsaw's Jewish intellectual elite turned out for the opening and were charmed by the personal freshness and intelligence of the group, whom they got to know and made much of. One night Mendele Moykher Sforim came to see the youngsters and later visited them backstage. They were nervous at meeting the great man, but when he approached them he beamed benevolently and greeted them with the prayer *"Shehekhiyonu"* ("Bless you, God . . . who has kept us alive, sustained us, and allowed us to reach this happy occasion").

On the Warsaw tour the group performed a strictly "literary" repertory: plays by Sholom Aleichem, Sholom Asch, and Hirschbein himself. The latter two productions seemed amateurish and dull to the Warsaw audiences, who had built such hopes around the enterprise. But Sholom Aleichem's *Mentshn* was a great success. And what really distinguished the production was the firm energetic attack of the young director David Herman, and young Jacob Ben-Ami's performance as the elderly butler, Daniel, changing from an obsequious servant, when the lady of the house visits the kitchen belowstairs, to the staff martinet when she leaves.

Ben-Ami, since his youth as a stage-struck *yeshive* student, had begun his career by playing tiny parts in Russian in Minsk. There a Russian director had offered to recommend him for Stanislavsky's famous Moscow Art Theater academy. But that meant converting, since Jews rarely got residence permits to live in Moscow, and Ben-Ami had refused. It was an awkward interview, since the director himself had got where he was by converting, long ago. Ben-Ami joined a Yiddish troupe which was passing through town and needed a prompter in a hurry. For the next few years he played small parts and then —though one director fired him, predicting that he'd never become an actor —bigger and bigger parts. He went to Russian theater. He studied Yiddish literature. By the time Hirschbein founded his Odessa art theater, Ben-Ami was ready to play leading roles and try his hand at direction.

The Hirschbein Troupe broke up in 1910. Hirschbein wanted out of the trouper's life and back to his writing and wandering. The troupe had made its point; the thing could after all be done. The actors scattered. Ben-Ami became director for a serious amateur group in Vilna; his route eventually took him on to New York, where he was an important part of later developments in the professional Yiddish art theater.

Meanwhile it seemed logical that the next step to creating a Yiddish art theater was to find even more Yiddish actors. One of these reformers' biggest problems, besides lack of money, was lack of actors. Most of the older professional Yiddish actors in Eastern Europe had spent their careers dodging police, speaking a mangled *Daytshmerish*, always moving on. Their powers lay in energy, personality, improvisation. They sang, strutted, and winked at the women in the back row. They ranted themselves hoarse in melodramas loosely adapted from Hurwitz-Lateiner adaptations. Mukdoyni claimed that half of them were totally illiterate. He said that the men spent their offstage time drinking and playing cards while the women, who were actresses solely because they'd married actors, dressed like servant girls and left their cooking pots only long enough to appear onstage and sing their songs.

He was exaggerating. Ester Rokhl Kaminska was then leading a company through Eastern Europe, and though the "Jewish Duse" was not an educated woman, she was intelligent, gifted, and sincere. There were many capable actors touring with Yiddish companies—American Yiddish stars like David Kessler, and Jewish stars of German and Russian theater like Rudolph Schildkraut and Paul Baratoff. Juicy Gordin roles, as always, had a startling way of making an actor more of an actor than he himself expected. But the theater reformers were impatient with these older professional actors, and the feelings were mutual.

Hirschbein in particular had no patience with popular, professional Yiddish theater. He couldn't understand how the great Yitskhok Leyb Peretz could occasionally sit for a whole evening of *shund*ish singing and dancing. (Peretz felt that the singing and dancing were innocently folksy, whatever the actors' intentions, whereas performances of Gordin were simply bad melodrama. Peretz was even known to walk out and wait in the lobby during the dialogue and come back to his seat for the musical numbers.) But Hirschbein was not the sort of young man to tolerate the sentimental inconsistencies of his elders. "The whole theater atmosphere," he later recalled in his memoirs, "—the acting, the language, and the content—it all gave me a headache before the end of Act One. Our people were blinded by love-of-what's-your-own. One evening you might be stimulated by Polish theater, which was on a very high level in those days, and the next evening you went to bathe in this homey theatrical bathhouse."

And so with these prejudices, the theater reformers set out to establish their own stable Yiddish dramatic academies in order to train their own young actors. In the years before and after the Philharmonia symposium, Warsaw saw two serious dramatic schools take root.

In both schools, the classes included Yiddish literature and the history of world drama as well as movement, voice production, make-up, and other practical skills. Among the founding teachers in one or the other or both were Mukdoyni, Mikhl Weichert, Sziper, and the young director David Herman. The students were mostly young working people who had educated themselves through night classes and continued to work in factories or shops. The schools were always scrounging, not only for money—the teachers were not paid enough to live on—but even for places to hold class. For a while a tailor shop was the classroom, and students tried to rehearse scenes between the work-tables. Sometimes class couldn't begin till nine or ten at night; the students, who all had to get up early for work, waited patiently while Weichert made the rounds of schools and union halls looking for an empty room for a few hours. Neither of these two schools lasted fully two years.

Amateur Theater

But at the same time other "schools" were blooming—amateur theatrical clubs. They were training future actors—and writers and audiences. They were actually expanding and developing a better drama, and they were to be the principal source of the Yiddish art theater movement.

Yiddish amateur theatrical clubs had existed a long time. In Lodz, for example, in the 1890s, weavers regularly performed Goldfadn's *Bar Kokhba*, setting up a stage on empty beer barrels with a white sheet in front for a curtain. Lodz remained a particularly vigorous proletarian theater town, so that professional actors were proud when they could call themselves the darlings of Lodz. This sort of theatrical was a feature in New Orleans, Cape-town, Harbin—everywhere that Yiddish-speaking Jews formed a community.

In towns that went months and months between visits by a professional company, amateur theatricals were a happy source of entertainment. In cities with a fairly steady diet of professional Yiddish theater, these clubs often offered a distinct alternative. For although some amateur groups put on frivolous or even vulgar operettas, possibly to raise money for a charity, most groups in principle and practice held sternly to a "literary" repertory. Thus a professional company might be offering *The Jewish Heart* or *The Dancing Rebitsin* (rabbi's wife), while down the street amateurs wrestled bravely with Andreyev, Ibsen, Mendele, Leivick, or Pinski. The amateur groups were part of the popular drive for self-education. They were also related to the rise of Yiddish literature, and were often affiliated with literary clubs.

Informally connected with these amateur performers were the other groups concerned with Yiddish theater. There were, for example, the claques of *patriótn,* who became knowledgeable about theater by hanging around their idols. More significantly, *kultur-tuers* (literally "culture-doers") made it their business to watch out for Yiddish theater. (A *kultur-tuer* is an intellectual who, though he may support himself by any trade or business, takes active responsibility for maintaining the community's cultural life, usually including the language itself, and helping it to progress. That such a term exists is indicative

The Artistishe Vinkele (Artistic Corner), an earnest and active drama club, in Warsaw around 1916.

of the high value the community accorded to the concept.) *Kultur-tuers* had rescued Goldfadn's first company when it was stranded, and some continued to have a soft spot for the sometimes bedraggled professional representatives of Yiddish culture.

Club members were tough critics for traveling professional companies. Sometimes their verdict decided whether the professionals had a successful engagement or limped away with barely train fare to the next town. Occasionally visiting stars brought only skeleton companies and recruited their minor players from local talent, which meant from the amateur club. There were times, too, when drama clubs came to feel that their town was their private territory, and on a few occasions they evidently made the touring professionals pay for the privilege of appearing or else disturbed the performance.

Many of the amateur clubs were affiliated with political organizations. Quite a small town might have simultaneously a chapter of the Bund, of the communists or anarchists or social democrats, several varieties of Zionists, and several separate trade brotherhoods. Amateur theatricals served as a social activity to attract new members, and their productions might be more or less subtle propaganda. Hershel Rosen, who acted in the politically oriented art theater Artef in New York in the 1930s, remembers occasions when politics and amateur dramatics mixed and exploded. In his Polish village, when he was fifteen, a scuffle broke out between his group, who were Bundists, and a Zionist group who had come from the next town to perform. Rosen's group defended their territory. Instead of Act Three, there was a free-for-all. The boys were arrested and nearly sent away to prison.

The first decades of the century brought a fruitful proliferation of amateur clubs. By 1910 in Poland, there were 360 such groups in the provinces, as well as a number in Warsaw. Of these, the best known is the Arts Corner, directed by David Herman. Groups functioned in the rest of Eastern Europe; sporadically in Vienna, London, and Paris (where Goldfadn directed one for a while); in South Africa, Australia, and South America; and in the United States.

Often these amateur groups were very amateurish indeed. But it's astonishing how hard they tried. They wrote to critics and to the professional Yiddish actors' union, asking for advice about everything from repertory to make-up. They hired professionals as directors. The actor Jonas Turkow wrote a handbook for amateur directors, and it sold well. At last the actors' union actually sponsored an organization to keep all these clubs in touch with one another. The organization aimed to give the clubs advice, make sure that the professionals they hired were really qualified, help them buy supplies as thriftily as possible, and steer them through the twisty corridors of censorship and government permits.

Amateur theater shaded sometimes into professional. Most amateurs stayed amateur and enjoyed themselves. But a number of individual club members did join professional companies and formed a strong element in the new generation of actors. And occasionally a whole group turned professional. In fact, the company with probably the most dazzling and longest-lasting reputation among Jews and non-Jews in the whole history of Yiddish theater began as an amateur group in Vilna, Lithuania. These were the serious youngsters who spent their evenings working with Jacob Ben-Ami, when he was fresh from his inspiring years with the Hirschbein Troupe, and with other directors. In those early days they called themselves the Organization of Yiddish Artists, or by the acronym, in Yiddish, FADA. Later they came to be known simply as the Vilna Troupe.

The Vilna Troupe

During World War I Jews were much better off in the areas the Germans occupied, like Vilna and the rest of Lithuania, than in the areas that were variously czarist (later postrevolutionary) Russia or independent Poland. In

The original Vilna Troupe in 1918. Seated left to right: Lares, Kowalsky, Kadison, Mazo, Walter, Nakhbush. Center row left to right: Shneyur, Balerina, and, far right, Tanin. Big man standing in center is David Herman, and woman standing at far right is Noemi.

Russia and Poland, an upsurge of anti-Semitism added to the misery of citizens at war. There, the repression of Yiddish theater was even harsher than before, since now companies couldn't even get on by calling themselves German theater. The Germans, on the other hand, lifted repressions in the areas they controlled. They actually plumed themselves on being above the barbaric prejudices of the East. Besides, they were homesick for a language related to German. German officers went often to Yiddish operettas, which starred German prima donnas imported especially for them. Some of them made friends in Yiddish intellectual circles.

In occupied Vilna in 1916, the amateurs of FADA took over an old wooden circus building. It was filthy and dilapidated. The stage floor had broken boards. A throne of gilded wood tilted out of the wings on a splintered leg. Puddles of rain water came through the roof and iced over. The landlord let FADA use the building rent-free for fear that otherwise the Germans would requisition it as a stable, but he never heated it. Even after they cleaned it up, the actors had to warm their grease paint by holding it next to electric light bulbs; they spread it on their faces with fingers stiff from cold.

At FADA's obligatory opening performance for the occupation officers, they presented a Sholom Asch comedy called *The Landsman* and Peretz Hirschbein's *A Secluded Nook*. The German officers and local intelligentsia were delighted. The group performed regularly, both Yiddish plays by Gordin and Pinski and translations of Schnitzler, Sudermann, Artsybashef, Yushkevitch, Molière, and O'Neill. They toured the towns around Vilna. Wherever they went, people had already heard of them.

They worked hard. Most of them stopped their jobs and devoted themselves to being the *Vilner Trupe*—the Vilna Troupe. They carried wood for the little ovens that heated the audience, though not the dressing rooms. They put up their own posters. They got only a few rubles each week, and they were hungry, but then everybody in Vilna lived off ration cards, and everybody was hungry. Except maybe the occupation officers. When at an afternoon rehearsal, in the middle of a sentence, an actress fainted, nobody was alarmed. She'd had no breakfast or lunch. So somebody found her a baked potato and a glass of water, and in fifteen minutes the rehearsal continued.

The Vilna organized themselves formally with a managing director, M. Mazo, an artistic director, David Herman, and committees of actors to confer on repertory and casting. They took on such additional members as Joseph Buloff, who'd acted in Russian theater, and Miriam Orleska, who'd been in Hirschbein's troupe.

Despite the high caliber of individual actors, the Vilna Troupe's emphasis was on ensemble work. Their performances struck the special spark of a company of artists drawing out the best in each other. Following the Stanislav-skian ideology (and before Stanislavsky, that of the Meininger Company, which pioneered ensemble work), the actors exchanged roles, going from a lead one night to a bit the next. Yiddish theater was suffering even more than the European theater from the star system, so this shift was especially revolu-tionary. Also Stanislavskian was their program of flexible realism, in which the actors aimed to use themselves to create another character, rather than to dramatize themselves. The director's conception shaped the overall produc-tion. This was the era when directors like Max Reinhardt were transforming European art theater, but until now most Yiddish theater had got by with no directors at all—except the star, who decided where everybody should stand. The Vilna Troupe had not only David Herman, who had studied at Polish and Viennese drama schools and had directed productions for the Peretz Hirsch-bein Troupe and other Yiddish and non-Yiddish ensembles; they had several other directors as well.

The Vilna Troupe reflected the emergence of serious Yiddish literature. They conceived of themselves in connection with literature, as interpreters of plays and nourishers of the young Yiddish drama. They were revolutionary in their attention to the literary quality of each play, word by word. And they startled and delighted the intelligentsia with yet another innovation: Despite

Vilna Troupe in the 1920s in a play about modern industrial life. The expressionist scenic construction is labeled FABRIK (factory).

all the varieties of Yiddish noted at the Czernowitz convention, the Vilna
Troupe all spoke in the same accent and dialect. Most of them were natives
of Vilna, but even those who were not made a conscious effort at unification
in the Lithuanian (Litvak) dialect. For the first time audiences had the aesthetic experience of a consistent pronunciation and didn't have to strain to
believe that all the characters onstage were supposed to be related.

Ester Rokhl Kaminska saw the young company when she and they crossed
paths on tour. She urged them to come to Warsaw, which was the big time.
After some trouble getting a travel permit (for Lithuania was effectively cut
off from Poland), they arrived in Warsaw in 1917. It is an indication of how
far they'd come already that they arrived in their own train. Peeping through
the curtain on opening night, they saw in the first row the glamorous faces
of Yiddish culture. It was a glittering turnout: Hersh Dovid Nomberg, Yankev
Dineson, Noah Prylucki, Hillel Zeitlin. Critics from other Polish cities came
for the occasion. Only Peretz was missing: he'd died two years before.

For their Warsaw debut, the Vilna Troupe presented Kobrin's *Yankl
Boyle*. Papers printed reviews the very next morning, which was unusual.
Dineson began his review: "Mazel tov, Jews! Mazel tov, we have a theater!"
The review in the Bundist daily began: "We have a Jewish art theater!"
Dineson had always been unconvinced that there would ever really be a good
Jewish theater; he had gone along with efforts only out of personal loyalty to
Peretz and general optimism. Now he addressed the Vilna Troupe at a glitter-
ing banquet in their honor. "You have made us," he said, "believers."

Jews and non-Jews gave them banquets and sent them flowers. Their base
remained Warsaw now, but they toured the provinces triumphantly in their
private train. Townspeople and bands met them at the local stations; sometimes more than one organization turned out with a band, and the two bands
—possibly one a Bundist band and the other a Zionist—tried to drown out
one another from opposite sides of the platform. People shoved for the honor
of carrying actors into town on their shoulders, and the actors learned to wear
old trousers for the ride, since people sometimes reached up and snipped a bit
off a trouser cuff, just for a souvenir.

The Vilna Troupe were very aware of themselves as an institution. In the
haskole tradition, they felt that they were introducing many in their audiences
to literature and art, which was true. More, they realized that the quality of
adoration lavished on them came from more than their artistic achievements,
though these were praised even by non-Jewish critics all over Europe. For the
Yiddish community, part of the excitement was for what the Vilna represented. The Yiddish community, especially the intelligentsia, saw itself in its
theater; that is one reason why discussions of Yiddish theater so often touched

raw nerves. In the Vilna, Jews saw Yiddish culture's dazzling explosion into modern times. The Vilna Troupe were purely and proudly Yiddish. They seemed a vindication of Yiddishness, and all the praise from non-Jews was sweet balm for the ache of the Jewish situation in Eastern Europe in the twentieth century.

A *dybbuk* is a creature of Jewish legend, a wandering soul that enters a living person's body and haunts it. In 1920, so some critics later observed, a *dybbuk* entered the Vilna Troupe. What happened was that the troupe presented a play called *Between Two Worlds; or, The Dybbuk* by S. Anski (Solomon Zeynwil Rapaport). It was their greatest success, and they were identified with it ever after. It was with their production of *The Dybbuk* that they influenced other theaters, especially Yiddish theaters. And with it they set a direction for themselves.

The original motivation for the production was more sentimental than aesthetic. Anski had tried for years to persuade the company to produce his play, and though they had considered it, they finally changed their minds, to his great disappointment. But when he died, they mourned him as a friend and decided to prepare *The Dybbuk* quickly to present at the traditional ceremony thirty days after his burial.

Anski was popular among the Yiddish and non-Yiddish intelligentsia. He was a big man, broad-boned and rather hunched, whose personality combined mature conviction and childlike charm. His socialist agrarian beliefs led him to work for years as a farm laborer. Though many of his best stories were about Yiddish life in rural villages, his early writings were in Russian, including the original version of *The Dybbuk*. His first comedy, *In a Conspirator's Apartment*, was performed by friends at the annual ball of the Russian revolutionaries' colony in Bern. Anski's major contributions were actually not in fiction or drama, but in his explorations of Yiddish folklore. Between 1911 and 1914 he was part of an expedition through tiny Yiddish villages deep in the Ukraine, collecting handicrafts and recording legends, songs, and sayings that were disappearing. From the motifs and legends that he amassed, Anski composed *The Dybbuk*.

The plot of *The Dybbuk* is simple. A young couple are betrothed by their fathers at birth, though they never know it. They grow up, meet, and fall in love, for their souls are destined to marry. When the girl's father decides to marry her to a rich suitor, the young man, a *yeshive* student, invokes dangerous forces through mystical *kabala* and dies. The girl's wedding goes on, but under the wedding canopy she swoons and from her mouth comes her dead sweetheart's voice, claiming her as his rightful bride. She is possessed by his spirit. Her father takes her to the court of a wonder-working *hasidic* rabbi. The rabbi

A still from *The Dybbuk* by S. Anski, filmed in Poland in 1938 under the direction of Michael Waszynsky. The bride, played by Lili Liliana, dances with the beggars. This scene, for which both the Vilna Troupe and Habima productions were famous, was filmed in a grotesque expressionistic style like theirs. *The Dybbuk* has also been filmed in Hebrew and has been performed on stage in many languages, including Bulgarian, Ukrainian, English, and Swedish.

succeeds at last in driving the *dybbuk* out by lighting black candles and preparing his court for a solemn exorcism. The *dybbuk,* who is presumed to be present in the rabbi's court though invisible to mortal eyes, surrenders at the threat of eternal excommunication from the Jewish community. But though his spirit must leave his bride's body, it remains in her soul; she dies, and her spirit joins his in death.

David Herman, himself raised in a *hasidic* family, made *The Dybbuk* a symbolist masque: mystical, lyric, and grotesque. The play text has relatively little dialogue, so the production emphasized stylized ritual pantomime and dance, choral speaking, and mass action. This production style was attuned to the avant-garde constructivism with which Meyerhold was experimenting in Russia. (In 1922 Stanislavsky's pupil and colleague Vakhtangov directed a quite similar production of *The Dybbuk,* in Hebrew translation, with Habima, a Hebrew-speaking theater associated with the Moscow Art Theater.) Herman's approach also had an affinity with the Neo-Romanticism that was a dominant Polish mode. It was also, in a way, a return to the folk pageant of the Goldfadn era and, before that, to the Purim play.

As an embodiment of Jewish tradition or folk-consciousness, *The Dybbuk* was an idealization of pure mystery. Only a few years before, it would have been psychologically impossible, among Jews struggling to free themselves from orthodoxy. Now, on the other hand, as even political ideologies were dimming as an alternative faith, and as life seemed so miserable and dangerous that faith would have been a great comfort, a degree of escapism and nostalgia contributed to the magic of *The Dybbuk*. Besides, the play affirmed that Jewish cultural roots existed and were as beautiful as those of any other nation. Jewish audiences loved it. And since these Jewish roots were far enough away to be transformed into dynamic, sophisticated art, the play thrilled non-Jews too.

The successful operetta composer Joseph Rumshinsky went to see *The Dybbuk* and later described it in his memoirs.

> . . . even though a quarter of a century has passed since I saw that performance . . . , it seems to me now as if it was only yesterday, so deeply did the performance engrave itself on my memory. Every scene, every movement, all the tones of voice of those then-unknown actors still sound in my ears, and I see the whole performance vividly. . . .
>
> The Eliseum Theater . . . was long and narrow, with crude benches, and gave the impression of a Russian barracks. I sat on a hard bench. It became pitch dark. Before me I saw an old *tales* [prayer shawl] soaked in tears. In the thick darkness I saw a tall young hasid, with a prayer book and a candle. He looked afar off, there where nothing comes to an end. When the second curtain rose in the prayer house, I heard broken, torn sounds, an unclear melody; notes which moan; ecstatic communing with God; notes which are drawn from generations and generations, slowly, very slowly. They sing slowly and rock with nervous speed.
>
> This lasted quite a long time, before they spoke the first word. It was almost like a big overture, but without an orchestra. And I must admit that no orchestra in the world and no composer could draw one in, into the mystical hasidic atmosphere, better than did the movements and the torn notes of these Jews. . . . I don't call them actors, not because I don't consider them actors, but because they were more than actors. . . . I didn't feel that I sat in a theater but rather something that I have never seen or heard before or since.
>
> The whole time of the performance I felt a pleasant shiver. My thoughts were divested of the weekday [i.e., as opposed to Sabbath]. I forgot everything and everyone. . . .
>
> The dance, the death dance—I will never in my whole life forget it. . . . One person, who was not distinct enough even to be sure if it was a woman or a man, but some sort of figure, swept, writhed, turned in an odd, irregular rhythm. . . .

Rumshinsky is referring to the episode before the wedding when the bride, in her gown, must dance with the local beggars who come to share the feast. Grotesque and increasingly malevolent, they whirl her around till she swoons. This episode was also a high point in the Habima production.

The Dybbuk took Warsaw by storm. The Polish tram conductor who drove

The Vilna Troupe's production of *The Dybbuk* by S. Anski was so popular that special postcards with scenes from the play were sold. In this scene the father, played by Leib Kadison, listens as old Frade, played by Leah Noemi, encourages the possessed bride, played by Miriam Orleska.

regularly past the theater at show time used to call out not the name of the street but simply, "Anski." Increasingly the *Dybbuk* atmosphere attached itself to all the Vilna Troupe's plays. They became identified with *The Dybbuk* and so did Yiddish theater as a whole.

Although the Vilna Troupe played in more than one style, working especially for Stanislavskian realistic characterizations, the expressionism of David Herman's *Dybbuk* became their most characteristic mode. The same became true of most other Yiddish art theaters of the period. The two most prestigious Yiddish theaters in the world, the Vilna and the Moscow Yiddish State Art Theater (GOSET), were both associated with expressionism, as was the Hebrew-speaking Habima; that in itself was enough to connect expressionism in the public imagination with Yiddish theater of the finer sort. Furthermore, expressionism is a strongly didactic form: it can act out abstractions. The Germans and Russians had already used it to teach radical politics—itself a congenial association for Yiddish theater. Yiddish playwrights and directors were drawn to expressionism as a way of dealing with abstract problems, including politics. The traditional broadness of Yiddish acting style also made expressionism seem appropriate.

There is another possible explanation for the attraction that for decades continued to draw Yiddish artists, including theater artists, to expressionism. Expressionism seems to have afforded them a symbolic way of dealing with the exotic traditions and confused loyalties that comprised their Jewish identity. Religious piety remained the only absolute metaphor for Jewish identity, but it had to be stylized, for stylization makes something seem powerful, but from a distance. Expressionism therefore served as a modern ritual to replace the traditional ones that had become worn or commonplace.

With *The Dybbuk* as the jewel of their repertory, the Vilna Troupe toured Europe, winning high praise from critics everywhere. In Rumania, King Carol requested a special performance of Dimov's *Yoshke Musikant.* Queen Wilhelmina of Holland came to see them in Amsterdam. In Brussels, the municipality ordered the train station specially illuminated for their arrival, and the minister of education was among the dignitaries on the platform to greet them. On a later visit to Belgium, Queen Elizabeth came to see Asch's *Sanctification of the Name.* In England, Germany, and France, both Jewish and non-Jewish intellectuals bought tickets.

A lot of seats remained empty, however—except for performances of *The Dybbuk,* which audiences demanded everywhere. On the whole, the Jewish masses in Western Europe were proud of the Vilna Troupe, but preferred to spend their money on less demanding entertainments. The Yiddish community offered no solid support for the Vilna Troupe's maintenance. Inevitable tensions within the group exacerbated their difficulties. The Vilna Troupe was bound to disintegrate.

In 1924 the Vilna arrived in New York, where every glittering name in the Yiddish community came to welcome them. There the group splintered. Each splinter toured, claiming to be the "real," the "original" Vilna Troupe, a title that continued to carry enormous prestige. (To this day, people say respectfully of one actor or another that "Oh, he was a *Vilner.*") Ten years later there were companies calling themselves the Vilna Troupe on the strength of one member who had belonged for a while to one of the splinters. The principal of these Vilna Troupes remained based in Warsaw and New York.

By the 1920s, Yiddish theatergoers in Eastern Europe had professional art theaters in their own language—Yiddish. These theaters in turn made it possible for talented Yiddish playwrights and actors, and demanding audiences, to aim high in their art without abandoning Yiddish for other languages. The Yiddish art theater movement simultaneously elevated Yiddish culture in the Soviet Union; in Paris, Vienna, and other Western European cities; and in North and South America. Every Jewish community, in its own way, honored its art theaters and measured itself by their achievements.

9 THE SOVIET YIDDISH STATE THEATERS: GOSET

In the 1930s, when Soviet Yiddish cultural activity had reached its peak, Shloyme Mikhoels, principal actor of the Moscow Yiddish State Art Theater, looked wistfully back to 1919: "In the era when worlds perished and new worlds took their place, a miracle occurred, a tiny miracle perhaps, but for us Jews it was big: the Jewish theater was born."

Almost as he spoke, Soviet policy had begun crushing Jews and Jewish culture. In 1948 Mikhoels's body was found buried in bloody snow on a street in Minsk; in 1952 the doors of the Moscow Yiddish State Theater were bolted. The miracle was over.

Ever since Goldfadn, Yiddish theater in Russia had followed its own course. For a generation after the czarist ban of Yiddish theater in 1882, Russian audiences saw only Purim plays or furtive wandering German-Yiddish troupes. Then, after the turn of the century, conditions eased. In 1908 Ester Rokhl Kaminska took her "literary" company from Warsaw as far as St. Petersburg, where they were a huge success in Gordin plays, which no one had seen before. In the same year, Hirschbein founded his art theater in Odessa. A new prohibition clamped down temporarily in 1910, but in 1913 there were a number of relatively stable Russian-Yiddish theaters, including three in Odessa.

But years of revolution and war totally disrupted the lives of Russian Jews. In 1915 the Russian government expelled hundreds of thousands of Jews from the Pale of Settlement; most of them eventually settled farther east. In 1917 the Pale was officially abolished. Then the redrawing of national boundaries at the end of World War I meant that some three and a half million of the

Jews still living in the Pale area suddenly became citizens of Poland, Lithuania, and other bordering states. The two and a half million who remained Soviet citizens, mostly in the Ukraine and White Russia, suffered simultaneously the Polish invasion of the Ukraine under Marshal Pilsudski, anti-Semitic pogroms, and the Russian civil wars—all between 1918 and 1921.

Life was a nightmare for Yiddish actors trying to survive in these territories. People were starving, Jews and non-Jews alike; no one had money for such luxuries as theater tickets. Transportation and communication broke down; one troupe took several months to travel from Kiev to Odessa, a trip that ordinarily took fourteen hours. Pogroms flared up, destroying actors and audiences together.

Malvina and Albert Segalesko were in a little troupe that had the bad luck to be passing through a town when a pogrom was initiated. Their description of it is recorded in the memoirs of the actor Meyer Broude. Malvina begins the story:

The voices of the Jews out in the street kept getting louder. When we looked out the window, we saw that the pogrom-makers were already at our hotel. Our fear got stronger. There were ten of us . . . plus the children. Podlubna didn't want us to stay all together in one room, so he went down and hid in the courtyard. Now they were inside the hotel, and now we could hear their footsteps and the clang of their swords. The door gave a jerk outward, and five soldiers stood in front of us with guns and naked swords in their hands.

"You're all actors?" one of them asked Segalesko.

"All Rumanian actors." Segalesko showed his Rumanian passport. [He was the only troupe member who had one.]

One of the pogrom-makers, from Moldavia [part of Rumania], took the passport, examined it, and said, "They're Rumanians, all right."

"Let them sing something," another one calls out.

"Let them play something on the piano," says a third.

Albert, my husband, sat down at the piano.

[Her husband interrupts.] Do you think I know what I played? My fingers trembled on the keys.

[She continues.] "Sing something for us," all the pogrom-makers were shouting.

All of them sat down, with their naked swords, and the actor Ribalski stood up and started singing some kind of aria. The pogrom-maker from Moldavia gave a yell for us to sing in Rumanian, and I started to sing. I don't remember what I sang. The voices of the unfortunates on the street mixed with my singing. And when they started to yell for me to dance, Albert started up a dance tune and off I went dancing. Can you imagine such a scene on the stage? I'm dancing and from the street come the awful voices of the wounded. From the attic floor above come the screams of Jews being shot, and I dance. We heard Podlubna's voice very clearly from the

courtyard, and Albert is playing a catchy tune on the piano and I keep right
on dancing.

[Albert finishes the story.] Suddenly we hear a whistle from the courtyard
and all the soldiers ran out on the street. I stopped playing. But Malvina is still
dancing. When I went over to her and told her that they were gone, she fell
over and we could barely revive her. . . .

Later, when we went down to the courtyard we found Podlubna's body
hacked in pieces.

Eventually the revolution brought socialization and relative security to all
theaters in Russia. Russia had a tradition of theaters subsidized and supervised
by the state or by local noblemen. Since Goldfadn, Yiddish theater had existed
as best it could in the interstices of this network. Now it became an official
part of a large, increasingly organized Soviet system. That was a wonderful
advantage—for a while.

The new government envisioned a society in which every separate element, theater included, followed the same basic principles and operated to
form a perfect whole. It perceived that theater was an important tool for
education and propaganda. In 1918 the Commissariat of Education's new Arts
Department established a section for theater. Its functions were to create
many new theaters, so that all the people could enjoy them, and to start
transferring management of all theaters from private owners to the state. The
head of the section was Trotsky's sister. In 1919 a Central Theater Committee
took over the long-range campaign to integrate and control the thousands of
autonomous theaters all over Russia. It was a long campaign.

Revolutionary nationalization was no boon for the established theaters. On
the contrary, they had already been protected under the Czar, their audiences
were primarily the middle and upper classes, who were used to theatergoing,
and they suffered increasingly from the controls that went along with the
subsidy. But for the thousands of new theaters aimed at new audiences, many
of whom had never been inside a theater before, nationalization was wonderful. The proletariat and peasants could enjoy theater. Separate ethnic groups
gained their own stable theaters: Ukrainian, Armenian, Latvian, Tartar.

Jews were among the new groups that benefited enormously from nationalization. In 1919 it seemed miraculous that a Yiddish theater could even exist
openly; how much more so that it be actually protected by the government.
The Russians subsidized many Yiddish theaters, providing steady income for
the actors and a budget for equipment. By the mid 1930s, which was the peak,
there were some twenty Yiddish state theaters in Soviet Russia. Some of these
were fully subsidized on a large scale in their own buildings. Some were smaller
repertory groups touring the provinces on fixed circuits. Some were teams of

only a few singers and reciters on a very small budget. There were even three Yiddish drama schools, also part of the state system. After the constant struggle, it seemed the Messiah had come at last and the vagabond stars could settle down.

It seemed especially miraculous that official Jewish institutions could exist in Leningrad (formerly St. Petersburg) and Moscow. These cities had been outside the Pale. Under the czars they were specifically forbidden to most Jews. A few years before the revolution, young Jacob Ben-Ami had been unable to consider entering the Moscow Art Theater school because he would not have been able to get a residence permit to live in Moscow. These residence permits were the subject of books and plays: Sholom Aleichem's *Hard to Be a Jew* milks wry comedy out of a student's frantic attempts to finagle a residence permit so that he can continue at the university. In one popular Lower East Side melodrama, lovely Bertha Kalish played a virtuous girl who registers for a prostitute's yellow ticket so she can stay in St. Petersburg and study medicine: prostitutes, lawyers, doctors, and some extraordinarily successful merchants were almost the only Jews allowed in. As late as 1916, even so popular a figure as the blue-eyed, flirtatious operetta singer Clara Young barely got permission to perform in St. Petersburg, and then had to bribe the police five thousand rubles for permission to stay in a hotel the night after the show.

The aristocratic assimilated Jews of Moscow and St. Petersburg had always had enormous prestige in the Jewish world. Their acclaim of Ester Rokhl Kaminska was her boast ever after. They were the ones to whom Peretz turned to subsidize his Yiddish theater—and then antagonized because they spoke Russian to him, not Yiddish. It was in these cities that, in the first years of the revolution, the jewels of a new Soviet Jewish theater were produced.

One new Russian-Jewish theater was the Habima (Hebrew for The Stage), a Hebrew-speaking theater. Originally organized as an amateur group by Nahum Zemakh and David Vardi, it was attached as a separate studio to the Moscow Art Theater and placed under the guidance of Stanislavsky's favorite pupil, Vakhtangov. Without knowing a word of Hebrew, Vakhtangov created with the group his own interpretation of Anski's *The Dybbuk,* Leivick's *The Golem,* and several other productions. He welded Habima into an ensemble. They were based in Moscow, but played with great success across Russia, Europe, and America till 1931, when most of them settled permanently in Tel Aviv.

The other Jewish theater was the Moscow Yiddish State Art Theater (in its Russian acronym, GOSET), also called the Moscow Yiddish State Chamber Theater. GOSET was to be the pride of Russian Jewry. In 1919 the

Yiddish Section (Yevsektsia) of the Commissariat for Jewish Affairs, as approved by the various other committees dealing with arts, education, etc., planned a studio to train actors for a new Soviet Jewish theater of high quality. They gave the responsibility for building this program to a young director who had been born in Moscow, but was expelled, with the rest of the Jewish community, when he was a baby a few days old.

Granovsky Organizes the Moscow Yiddish State Art Theater

Alexander Granovsky grew up among the cosmopolitan Western influences of the city of Riga in Latvia. He went on to study theater in St. Petersburg in an era when Russian experimentation was electrifying Europe's avant-garde. Although Stanislavskian realism was still very important in Russia and Europe, the newer influences that directly shaped Granovsky as a director were nonrealistic. He was closest to the formalist experiments of the Russian director Meyerhold. Meyerhold's concept of "biomechanics" defined actors as highly trained vehicles for the director's large stage vision, rather than as intuitive impersonators of realistic characters. (This concept echoed Gordon Craig's seminal book *On the Art of Theater.*) Meyerhold was continually innovative in his creation of theatrical events. He wanted to stun and electrify the spectators through all their senses, and he visualized the event occurring onstage in a sculptural nonrealistic environment which he called "constructivist." In his twenties, Granovsky studied and lodged in Germany with the eclectic director Max Reinhardt, another great influence on him.

Granovsky came home from Germany to a Russia intoxicated with theater. There were amateur theatricals, theater journals (in those hungry days when every scrap of paper was precious), ceremonial pageants galore—a theatrical explosion. Theater was part of the people's revolution. It used clowns, acrobats, singing and dancing, parades: the traditional broad folk forms of the people. The government had lifted all censorship, and this dazzling freedom, unheard of in Eastern Europe, further released outpourings of celebration for the new era.

Like Vakhtangov, Tairov, and other young directors, Granovsky used a large-scale nonrealistic style, a combination of avant-garde and folk art, to express the excitement of the new ideology. Before coming to GOSET, he staged some grand proletarian pageants and circuses. They were in the Russian language, of course. It was then that Yevsektsia assigned him to start a Yiddish studio.

Just as the society had amputated the past in order to begin afresh, so the

new Yiddish theater felt the need to break with the Yiddish theater of the past.
The break seemed especially imperative since Yiddish culture was identified
with religion, nationalism, and bourgeois capitalism, all enemies of the revolution. Granovsky deliberately chose young actors who had never worked in
professional Yiddish theater and thus were uncontaminated by what seemed
to him its naïve, clumsy, limited realism—as well as by its political associations.
He was going to train them from their ABCs. He was also going to train (or
retrain) his audience, who had seen mostly old-fashioned Yiddish theater or
no Yiddish theater at all. Only the language would remain the same.

This was perfectly in accord with the party line. For knowledge of the
Yiddish language was to be all that distinguished the Soviet citizen who
happened to be Jewish from his non-Jewish comrades. The citizen would reject
religion and parochial folkways—or, like Granovsky, perhaps had barely ever
had them. The language would be separated from Jewish cultural identity. It
would be reduced to a desensitized code, a system of communicating by
sounds. In the Ukraine and White Russia, there were schools, newspapers, and
even law courts in Yiddish—all scrupulously secular. Yiddish writers went so
far as to avoid to their best ability the Hebrew component of the language,
because of its religious and ritual connotations.

A Yiddish language purified of cultural identity was as acceptable to the
revolution as was Ukrainian, Armenian, or any other Soviet tongue; it even
had proletarian associations (as opposed to Hebrew). However, unlike Jews,
citizens who spoke Ukrainian or Armenian had no need to purify their language of cultural associations. Ukrainians and Armenians had home territories;
Jews had only a spiritual territory, which was being secularized away. Ukrainians and Armenians also had cultural autonomy; but in 1921 the membership
list of the Jewish Socialist Bund, part of the heart of the Jewish self-image,
was simply absorbed into Yevsektsia, and later Yevsektsia itself disappeared
into the Communist party. Zionism was flatly forbidden as political loyalty to
a foreign country.

Thus for the first production of the Yiddish studio, Granovsky chose to
present Maeterlinck's *The Blind:* a symbolist play, with no Jewish content or
associations, translated from the French language into the Yiddish. The program for *The Blind* explained the choice in this manifesto:

> We don't agree with those who say that the Yiddish theater must stay with a
> specific repertory and dares not step out of that standard. . . . We hold that the
> Yiddish theater is first of all theater in general, a temple of light and beauty and
> creativity, a temple where the prayers are raised in the Yiddish language. . . .
>
> The duty of our theater . . . is the duty of world theater. Only the language
> differentiates us from the others. . . .

A typically bold and balletic pose
from GOSET's high-spirited adaptation of Avrom Goldfadn's
Tenth Commandment, directed
by Alexander Granovsky.

„Tanzpaar aus der Hölle"
(Jn Granowskys „Das zehnte Gebot")

The young group, though obviously promising, seemed at first to be missing something. It didn't strike a spark. It did not yet have a distinctive style
or purpose. Significantly, the manifesto had also asked:

> What will our theater be like? Which gods will it serve? That we cannot answer.
> We don't know our gods. . . . We are looking for them. . . . And that is our
> program.

In the first few years, as the group looked for its "gods," some students
dropped out, some were dropped, some new ones came. The group went on
tour, came home to St. Petersburg, moved to Moscow. Meanwhile, although
the search for gods couldn't very well lead them to the synagogue, nevertheless
it led them as inexorably and perhaps as unconsciously as a divining rod toward
the Eastern European prerevolutionary Yiddish tradition—back toward the
cultural associations of the language they were speaking.

This searching and this journey back are visible through GOSET's early
productions. After Maeterlinck, they tentatively tried some specifically Jewish
plays. They presented Sholom Asch's Biblical drama *Amnon and Tamar* and
Gutskov's drama of Spanish Jewry, *Uriel Acosta;* the latter was an old war-

horse vehicle for Jacob P. Adler and others of the more ambitious stars of the commercial Yiddish stage. It was as if they were circling their true source. Then in 1921 they tapped that source, releasing a flood of energy and warmth, as they made theater out of their personal revolution.

The breakthrough came when Granovsky created a program which he called *Mazel Tov*, based on texts by Sholom Aleichem. In the next few years, works by Sholom Aleichem, Yitskhok Leyb Peretz, and Mendele Moykher Sforim—the three classic Yiddish writers—were to provide material for GOSET's most memorable productions. Thus this revolutionary theater was using texts that evoked and sometimes even celebrated the old Russian-Jewish ways: the ways of the actors' own childhoods, which they had repudiated. For *Mazel Tov*, GOSET associated itself with another artist who used the old Jewish motifs: the painter Marc Chagall looked at the old world in a vivid new way.

Chagall was one of the group of young Russian-Jewish painters and sculptors who were making themselves known at that time. Many were to be associated with the theater, including Altman (who designed the sets for GOSET's *Uriel Acosta* and Habima's *The Dybbuk* and, as head of the Fine Arts Committee of St. Petersburg, designed and staged the celebration of the first anniversary of the revolution), Rabinovitch, Rakov, and Falk. (Some non-Jewish painters worked with the Yiddish theater too.) Chagall, whose parents were *hasidim*, had painted some years in Paris and established a reputation. He had served as Commissioner for Beaux-Arts of Vitebsk, and had already designed stage scenery. When the company went to see him, he understood at once what they meant by searching for their "gods."

> I was in Vitebsk when Granovsky and his studio came to ask me to come to Moscow. Mikhoels and the other actors were still green students and everything was still in Reinhardt's style with a little bit of Stanislavsky.

As designer, comrade, and inspiration, Chagall was to help them achieve their own distinct identity.

It is appropriate that a painter should have been so important to GOSET. Formalist theater like Granovsky's was more dependent on a painterly or sculptural vision than on verbal resources. Besides, a language wrenched and sanitized of associations was bound to lose some of its power and be relatively sterile—or else threatening. Predictably, everyone who saw the Sholom Aleichem production Chagall designed, as well as the productions that immediately followed, was most struck with how it looked: the shapes and colors, and the patterns of movement onstage.

For the Sholom Aleichem evening, Chagall created the theater's environment. The company had just then moved into an unheated little building, on a side alley, seating only ninety. Chagall painted murals on the interior walls. He created the atmosphere of a Purim carnival. His subject was a swirling dance of Sholom Aleichem characters, or Yiddish folk musicians, *Purimshpilers,* circus acrobats, all floating over the crooked roofs of a little Yiddish *shtetl* in the style for which he is still known. He also created the scenery and costumes and even the make-up.

Mikhoels remembered his zest for the job.

> On the day of the premiere, Chagall came to my dressing room. He laid out his paints and set to work. He divided my face in two halves, coloring one green and one yellow; after all, we have the expression "he looked green and yellow" [meaning sick or uneasy]. Chagall raised my right eyebrow two centimeters higher than the left. He extended the creases around my nose and mouth over my whole face . . . to emphasize and bring out the tragic situation of the character. . . . Suddenly Chagall's finger hung in the air over my face, uncertain. Something disturbed him. He put the finger to my eye, took the finger away and moved back a few steps, contemplated my face and said sadly:
> "Ach, Solomon, Solomon, if only you didn't have a right eye, there's so much I could do."

In the course of painting the theater, the make-up, and the scenery, Chagall selected the palette for GOSET's major creations. These creations had the same essential elements as his paintings: the folksy material of the past (as seen, distanced, and commented on in the present); the styles of the revolution (both popular circus and avant-garde expressionism); and enormously energetic, wholehearted attack and verve. To these elements GOSET under Granovsky added a conscious commitment to the new communist ideology.

All these elements clicked and coalesced in Granovsky's Sholom Aleichem evening. The group were such a success that the authorities gave them a new building, which seated five hundred; when they moved, they took Chagall's murals with them. The authorities also raised their subsidy and allowed them to take on more members. Fortified by official approval and their momentum, they approached their next venture with gusto.

This time their target was Avrom Goldfadn's *Koldunye; or, The Witch.* Granovsky used Goldfadn's script for his own purposes, just as he'd used Sholom Aleichem stories and as Chagall used Mikhoels's face. He billed the production as "according to" Goldfadn. He added music by Leyb Pulver and poster-bright designs by Rakov. He introduced whole scenes of dialogue, changed parts around, and left parts out. He used the original naïve plot as a spine for the evening's events and as an ideological foil for his own statements. And he called it, simply, *The Witch*.

In the directorial style of Craig, Meyerhold, and Reinhardt, Granovsky used the actors' trained bodies to convey his vision. They threw themselves with mad agility up and down the constructivist ladders and platforms, which suggested *shtetl* roofs and marketplaces. As described by an eye-witness:

> They climbed the steps, four at a time, scaled the scaffolding, perched on the highest platforms, threw their checkered legs up in the air, propelled themselves into empty space without ceasing their laughter or their laments. Jumps, somersaults, pirouettes, tumbles in every position . . . universe in motion.

The production was a sort of Purim carnival, in both its high spirits and its use of Jewish tradition. Mikhoels himself came from a pious home which had been visited yearly by Purim players. As the peddler Hotsmakh, he drew on traditions familiar to him: *badkhonim, marsheliks,* and *Purimshpilers.* Other sources Granovsky used were the commedia dell'arte and its Russian echo, Petrushka, which had infiltrated Purim plays.

The emphasis on choral movement and ensemble work was typical of formalist theaters of the era. Part of GOSET's aesthetic value was its expression of a political ideology that emphasized the group over the individual. Mikhoels specifically wrote that "instead of the situations of individual souls, half-words, half-tones, we need definite social convictions and passions."

Indeed, aggressive revolutionary purpose unified the seemingly chaotic spectacle. For even though the old ways provided material and form for the production, the production's whole point was to destroy the old ways. Goldfadn's characters were shown as grotesque or mechanical. Granovsky created specific lines and incidents to reinforce this perspective. Goldfadn's original third scene, for example, takes place in the *shtetl* marketplace, and here Granovsky inserted a light-hearted funeral procession for the burial of old Yiddish theater, with this dialogue:

> "Charity saves from death." [This is the traditional chant of a funeral procession.]
> "Dead? Who died?"
> "The old Yiddish theater!"

All this was spoken in the modern Hebrew accent of the Habima, as a spoof of them.

Similarly, when the witch casts a magic spell, the scene becomes a parody of Kol Nidre, the most solemn of Jewish prayers from the Yom Kippur (Day of Atonement) holiday. While casting the spell, she gets so carried away that she rips off one of Hotsmakh's ear locks, whereupon he goes into mourning for it in the traditional fashion of mourning for a loved one. He sits on the ground, lights a mourning candle, and wails, in the melody reserved for lamenting the destruction of the Temple: "My poor ear lock has become a widow."

Another example of this ferociously offensive parodying of tradition is Granovsky's use of Goldfadn's lullaby from *Shulamis,* about the little goat who went to market to sell raisins and almonds. The lullaby was so widely beloved that it had become virtually a folk song in the generations since Goldfadn wrote it. So any distortion of it was abrasive. Granovsky deliberately used that shock and rewrote the lyrics as social comment:

> A Jew went off to market.
> What did he have to sell?
> Not raisins and not almonds—
> Speculators know him well.

In *The Witch,* Granovsky's theater set up a conflict of ideas rather than a conflict between or within characters. The constant tension of this conflict was the inner drama of all GOSET's early successes. The group was hurling itself against an adversary that was still vital to them; the adversary was not only objective but also internal, for they were trying passionately to destroy the culture that had formed them. And if the enemy had not seemed so rich, lively, and tough, the fight would not have been so exciting and creative. (Similarly, Chagall was interested in Mikhoels's face for the sake of the patterns he could make upon, and in conflict with, its natural appearance.)

Audiences were galvanized by *The Witch.* The acting out of revolution, hostility, the sense of mission and, on some level, their internal conflicts, released a degree of energy that seemed more powerful than any experience a spectator could have while watching a story about individuals and their little problems. As part of the larger revolutionary excitement, these youngsters and their audiences were positively drunk on what they were allowed to make fun of; they were drunk on freedom and power, on youth and on history. The actors' wholeheartedness made them frisky, like Chagall's pun painted out in green and yellow on Mikhoels's face. But the perfect synthesis of Granovsky's intellectual intentions with his creative style made *The Witch* and the major projects that followed more than just political statements or youthful high jinks; it elevated them to art.

Granovsky's next production used Sholom Aleichem's play *The Big Win* (or *The Two Hundred Thousand*) as raw material, adding music and text and changing it at will. The original version tells the story of a simple tailor who thinks he's won the lottery jackpot. The two hundred thousand rubles take him away from the labor which was satisfying to him, put him into an

A scene from Yitskhok Leyb Peretz's *In the Synagogue Anteroom,* presented by the Yiddish State Theater of White Russia. The constructivist set and the actors' expressionist make-up, costumes, and movements are also typical of GOSET and other avant garde theaters of the early 1920s.

elaborately vulgar nouveau-riche mansion, and lead him to try to marry off his daughter to a rich suitor instead of the tailor's apprentice whom she loves. So it's a happy ending when the prize money is gone, and all the characters turn back to their old simple lives. Sholom Aleichem pictures Shimele (Little Simon) Soroker the tailor and all the others with amusement and affection; they are good people at heart.

Granovsky came at the play from a different direction. He made it an attack on capitalism. Whereas in the original Shimele used much of his new wealth for charity, Shimele as played by Mikhoels abandons and betrays his proletarian brothers. Granovsky contrasted the exuberant world of the simple *shtetl* folk with Shimele's new-found bourgeois friends, who move and speak like robots, monotonously repeating, "Two hundred thousand" and such oblique phrases as "When it comes to credit, I'm the banker" and "When it comes to synagogue honors, let it be in my synagogue."

Like *The Witch,* this production stressed choral movement and speaking. It, too, had élan and infectious humor. It, too, was a production about politics. As the matchmaker, for example, Binyomin Zuskin played a poor hanger-on of the bourgeoisie, forever on the go, promoting a living, trying to ingratiate himself with the people with money. Repulsive and pitiable in his social position, awesome in the energy he calls on to survive, he is the *shtetl* type called a *luft-mentsh* (air-person), one who has no regular income but survives as well as he can, making deals. Granovsky's free-floating production punned on the word *luft-mentsh,* having Zuskin make his entrance into Shimele's little house by parachute.

However, Granovsky's use of his actors was subtly different here from in *The Witch,* perhaps because of the difference between the original texts. Mikhoels played the tailor not as an abstract figure, but as the intensification of a real person, Shimele himself. He pantomimed sewing and cutting and hummed to himself. His proverbs, his tunes, his inflections, his gait, became sensations and were imitated in Jewish homes far outside Moscow. People recognized Mikhoels on the street and greeted him, "Comrade Shimele, how are you?" Similarly, the actress Sara Rotboym, who had played under Max Reinhardt and David Herman, managed to combine in her portrayal of Shi-mele's wife, Eti-Meni, both the bounding coarseness of the nouveaux-riches and a certain appealing, almost wistful, naïveté.

The climax of GOSET's activities as an angry arm of the revolution came in 1925, when Granovsky presented *Night in the Old Marketplace (Bay Nakht Oyfn Altn Mark)* "according to" Yitskhok Leyb Peretz. Granovsky billed the production as a "tragic carnival." Moyshe Litvakov, editor of the Yiddish party organ *Emes (Truth),* called it a "chaotic panorama." The morning after the premiere, a critic described it this way:

> In this "tragic carnival" the theater says goodbye mercilessly and angrily to the "past-its-time world of the Jewish middle ages." Everything that the Moscow Yiddish Theater has made a point of in its previous offerings is in this perform-ance brought to a high point, to a monumental sternness and compact-ness. . . .
>
> Two short acts, not connected by a concrete subject, scenes continuously changing, no real unity . . . Two parts: The Dead and Dying City, and The Resurrected Cemetery.

Until his death (eight years before this production), Peretz longed to see this work on a stage, but never did. A poem of about one thousand words in all, with no story and no real dramatic roles or episodes, *Night in the Old Marketplace* scared commercial companies off. In 1928 David Herman di-rected it in Warsaw, trying for a version as close as he could manage to Peretz's intentions. Granovsky, on the other hand, recreated the play in the image of the revolution. In the course of over a year of rehearsal, he chopped out lines and characters and added new ones. He used a character in the original, the ghost of a *badkhen,* as the central figure, and further divided him into two figures: a dramatic one played by Mikhoels and a lyric one played by Zuskin.

The split mirrored the *badkhen's* multiple functions in the old Jewish community.

The stage was done in somber shades: black, brown, gray, dirty white, tones of grimness and decay. The constructivist set evoked the old cemetery and the old marketplace—a way of life darkened and oppressed by centuries of poverty and tradition. The actors' dress suggested skeletons in rags, debris from rotting graves. They were the ghosts of all the old Jews: peddlers and musicians, *hasidim* and *maskilim*, prostitutes and thieves.

The dead stream from their graves to the marketplace. The *badkhen* calls to them:

> Live what you did not live!
> Feel what you did not feel!

Two ghosts marry under a black wedding canopy. The *badkhen* makes his wedding address, screaming, "To hell, to hell!" A beadle's voice calls the ghosts:

> Holy spirits, time for prayers!
> All who were burned, all who were drowned,
> All who suffered, who were frozen found—
> Time for prayers, time for prayers!

When ghosts call out to God, the *badkhen* interrupts them, screaming, "Your God is bankrupt!"

It was a sort of requiem for the old world, which had given way at last to the new bright promises of revolution. GOSET was never again quite so savage.

In 1926 Granovsky once more approached Goldfadn. This time he left barely more than the title. *The Tenth Commandment (Loy Sakhmoyd)* came out a free-wheeling, fantastical, satirical political circus. The action took place on heaven and earth. Characters spoke by telephone to the grave of "Miss Rachel." (Rachel was Jacob's wife and the symbolic mother of all the Jews; her grave has always been a holy place in Palestine.) Jewish capitalists and English policemen wore colorful and very intricate costumes and milled about in a set which included a Café de Paris.

Around this time GOSET also did Jules Romains's *Monsieur Le Trouhadec saisi par la débauche* and other texts of no intrinsic Jewish content.

GOSET's next production went back once more to the well of Jewish heritage, but this time evidently with more sympathy than anger for the prerevolutionary Jew. This was *The Travels of Benjamin III (Masoes Benyomin Hashlishi)*, which Granovsky dramatized in 1927 from the novel by Mendele Moykher Sforim.

Mendele's *The Travels of Benjamin III* is a tragicomic saga of a poor Quixotic Jew named Benjamin (played by Mikhoels) and his Sancho Panza (played by Zuskin), another poor Jew named Senderl Di Yidene. Benjamin believes that there is another, better place than his impoverished, coarsened *shtetl,* and despite the jeers of their wives and townsfolk, they set off on the long, weary, hungry, dangerous journey. They end up back home, not because that's where happiness was all along, but because that's life—or that was life in the bad old days before the revolution. In the meantime their saga on the stage, as in the novel, is full of painful observation and wry, grotesquely human comedy.

Ever since *The Witch,* when Mikhoels played the peddler Hotsmakh and Zuskin played the witch, the Moscow Yiddish Theater rested its brilliant ensemble work on these two actors as upon two pillars. Mikhoels was a short, stocky man, balding, with a face that was intelligent but pudgy, almost squashed together. Onstage, however, he became a creature of flashing grace and moving depth. Zuskin was built like a peasant, tall and broad. He was full of fun; as a youngster in his hometown in Lithuania he had been an amateur *badkhen* and he enjoyed quips and mimicry. In his acting he continued to draw types for his characterizations from people he had known in his youth. The saying about him was that onstage he could appear to be any size he wished.

In *The Travels of Benjamin III* these two actors created individualized characters and brought out by their interplay the humanness and misery of the characters' lives. As a member of the company later recalled:

> The slow passivity of Senderl [whose nickname, Di Yidene, means The Old Woman] emphasized the active alertness of Benjamin. For several minutes, Senderl scolds Benjamin for his senseless restlessness; when Benjamin strikes out, Senderl retreats. Here they come, at the end of a hungry day (their last groschen were stolen from them) to a poor inn and must lie down on cold bare benches; broken down, exhausted, each one lies down with his own little *krekhts* [groan; also the wailing note in a cantor's singing]. Even in that *krekhts* the two actors underline the individuality of their characters. Senderl pours out a continual stream of "aii, aii, aii . . ." Benjamin holds it in, masters the hunger and pain in his bones with calling out a few times "Oy-oy."

The acting, the dramatic episodes, and the music made this production a high point in GOSET's history.

A shift was occurring, perhaps unconsciously, in Granovsky's vision. In 1928 he created a new Sholom Aleichem montage, this one based on the

Two stills from a film, based on Sholom Aleichem material, about a big business venture in matchmaking. Shloyme Mikhoels sits on a bench; his hat, umbrella, and satchel are the marks of his trade as *shadkhen* (matchmaker). The train carries a *shadkhen's* merchandise; the car being unloaded is labeled "Fat Ones," while the next car down is labeled "Rich Dowries."

luft-mentsh Menakhem Mendel. Granovsky was using the same sources as Sholom Aleichem, but from a different perspective. He made Menakhem Mendel not only a tool of the bourgeoisie and an enemy of the proletariat, but also a victim himself of the old capitalist order. In this period Granovsky directed the group in a film based on the same material. He called it *Yidishe Glikn,* a usage that means both "Jewish Luck" or "Happiness" and "Jewish Livelihood." In film as onstage, Mikhoels made Menakhem Mendel a touching Chaplinesque figure; in the 1920s, Chaplin was practically a cult figure for artists all over the Western world. (Like most of the other Yiddish films made in the Soviet, *Yidishe Glikn* has disappeared, though a copy may yet be in a Russian archive.)

After seven successful years experimenting in one direction, Granovsky seemed to be becoming less strenuously cerebral, less athletic, more at one with his textual material. His productions were definitely nonrealistic still, but they used characters less as ducks in a political shooting gallery and more as people. Perhaps he was close to exhausting the fruitful possibilities of anger.

GOSET was ready to move aggressively into a new period, with a new theatrical style and a new emotional approach. They had been most successful with classical sources; now they looked for a new direction through some younger dramatists: David Bergelson, an impressionistic novelist; Moyshe Kulbak, poet and author of the two-volume novel *Zelmenianer;* Peretz Markish, who read his expressionistic poems to enthusiastic crowds in Paris and Berlin and was a passionate Stalinist; and others of a whole generation of Soviet Yiddish writers. GOSET was finding its creative gods.

In its first seven years GOSET had become an important cultural institution. Moyshe Litvakov dedicated a whole book to it: *Five Years of the State Yiddish Chamber Theater.* GOSET had wide audiences, including so many people who didn't speak Yiddish that laughter came in two waves: first from those who understood the jokes, and then from those to whom they had to be explained. It nurtured several of the smaller Yiddish theaters in lesser cities, lending them designers and other personnel and giving advice. It influenced Yiddish theaters in other countries, who imitated GOSET productions as well as they could without GOSET's subsidy.

In 1928 the government sent them on tour to France, Germany, Holland, Belgium, and Austria to show off what the new civilization was accomplishing. The tour was a triumph. But 1928 marked the end of the theater's "seven fat years." The lean years were coming.

During the tour the theater suffered a loss from which it never really recovered. Granovsky remained in the West. Eventually his career was to take him to Hollywood, which must have been as far as anyone could get from revolutionary Moscow, and he died there in 1937. In Russia, his name came off all posters; his films disappeared permanently from all screens. Without his vision and authority, his company, all of whom had been proud to be his students and his instruments, felt orphaned and betrayed. Later they simply envied him.

Soviet Yiddish Theater Struggles

The year 1928 marked the end of the New Economic Policy. Stalin and the Communist party began their new Five-Year Plan. They called for a "dictatorship over literature," which meant harsh times for artists. Each theater was administered by a council, and its manager was usually a party member. In the next few years Russia had some eighty thousand party censors and control officers watching literature, including drama. Plays went through a double censorship process: after the script was approved, censors came to the dress rehearsal, and they could still forbid the play to open if it seemed in any way politically unwholesome. Even nonpolitical art was considered by the censors to be offensive; it was art for the bourgeoisie, not for a proletariat engaged in building a communist nation.

The Moscow Yiddish Theater discovered that in all possible ways it was breaking the rules of the Communist program. It had neglected to present a play that would celebrate the tenth anniversary of the revolution. It was erring in its repertory, which was chauvinist and reactionary, for it leaned on Yiddish classics showing the Jewish past. And its art was experimental and formalist in style instead of "popular simple realistic art, suitable to the masses . . . the only art befitting the great epoch and socialism"—what came to be called socialist realism.

Soon GOSET was disoriented. They had lost their leader, their repertory, their style and technique. They had lost every element that was their identity. They had lost their ideological sureness. As a result, they had also lost the contagious headlong exuberance that was their greatest charm.

They scrambled for a footing. Mikhoels took over Granovsky's position, as well as continuing to act major roles, and the Central Committee sent them temporarily a Russian director to help set them on the right path. But it was a slippery effort to keep their footing from then on, and in the end they did not succeed.

In 1931, the year that a national conference officially described dramatic art as a "weapon of the working class," the Moscow State Yiddish Art Theater finally got an acceptable play onstage. *Four Days* was about a small band of

Bolsheviks in Vilna. Proletarian heroes, they hold out to the death against the antirevolutionary forces, till finally they kill themselves with their last bullets. The actors did not distinguish themselves, nor did the production as a whole. But it was ideologically acceptable. The same was true of the other plays in the early 1930s, including most notably *The Deaf Man*, a dramatization of a novel by David Bergelson, which was also produced in the early 1930s by David Herman in Warsaw. GOSET dared to hope that though they had lost their old glitter for good, the lean years were over and they had proved their right to exist.

From the mid 1920s to the early 1930s, some twenty professional Yiddish theaters were established by government grant. In a period when purges, trials, terrors, and suspicions were beginning to grip Russia, the Ukraine alone had eleven Yiddish theaters. There were theaters in Kharkov, Kiev, Odessa, Krementshug, Nikolayev, Dnepropetrovsk, Baku, and Tashkent, and an especially fine one in Minsk. There was a company traveling between Kharkov and Vinnitsa, and one traveling around Smolensk. A stage in Kharkov just for one-acters. A children's theater in Kiev. Three theaters at farm cooperatives *(kolkhozes)* in the districts of Kalinindorf, Stalindorf, and the Crimea. The Jewish area Birobidzhan had its own stage. Moscow, Kiev, and Minsk had drama schools attached to their theaters. There were also smaller, less formal entertainments and amateur groups. The proliferation continued until 1935; in that year, while GOSET celebrated its fifteenth anniversary and hoped for better days, Soviet Yiddish theater ended its expansion and began to contract.

Even at the height in 1935, however, these theaters, like all Russian theaters, were hard-driven to find repertory. They were supposed to do plays that conformed to the precepts that a Central Committee Special Resolution "about the repertory of drama theaters and measures of its improvement" was later to enunciate:

> Dramatic literature and the theaters must reflect in plays and performances the life of Soviet society in its incessant surge forward, and contribute fully to the further development of the best sides of Soviet Man's character. . . . Playwrights and directors must make Soviet youth spirited, optimistic, devoted to their country, believing in the victory of our cause, unafraid of obstacles, and capable of overcoming any difficulties. The Soviet theater must also show that such qualities belong not to a few elect ones or to heroes but to many millions of Soviet people. . . . The Soviet theater owes all its successes, all its achievements, to the Communist Party and its wise, truly Marxian solution of problems.

In practice it was hard to write plays that fully and in every subtle particular followed this program. Soviet playwrights were becoming dumb or stupefied by constant criticisms and their own earnest self-doubts. Russian thea-

ters increasingly put on either classics, or dramatizations of best sellers, or
potboilers. One category of potboiler showed sensational goings-on at the
imperial court, on the rationale that they were exposés of the bad old days.
Yiddish theaters had a special problem, since whereas other ethnic theaters
in far-flung provinces could succeed in a pinch with Moscow hits in the local
language, Yiddish theaters were primarily in cities where people could go see
the hits in Russian.

Theaters, Yiddish and non-Yiddish, were also increasingly pinched by the
pressure toward the style called socialist realism. The party declared socialist
realism "historically superior and qualitatively a new step in the development
of the arts." In practice, socialist realism made both writing and acting simple-
minded, posterlike, uniform, and insipid. Mikhoels and Zuskin were relatively
weak in the roles they were being forced to play. Not only were they trained
as actors in quite another style, but the roles themselves were empty; the actors
could bring no conviction to them.

One way to avoid party criticism was to put on classics, though doing too
many of those rather than new Soviet plays was also politically suspect. It was
especially good to find a classic play that could be interpreted as showing class
conflict or the decadence of the bourgeoisie, in a manipulation of the vehicle
not so very different from Granovsky's own use of Goldfadn, years before. So
in 1935 the Moscow Yiddish State Art Theater put on Shakespeare's *King
Lear.*

King Lear turned out to be one of the company's most memorable productions. They found in it roles that they could play wholeheartedly. When they
toured with it in Europe, Gordon Craig wrote: "Since the time of my teacher,
the great [Henry] Irving, I can recall no such acting performance to move me
so deeply, as Mikhoels' playing King Lear." Zuskin played the Fool.

The company next chose *Boytre the Bandit (Boytre Gazlen),* a play by the
novelist Moyshe Kulbak about a proletarian Robin Hood figure in the oppressive days of Czar Nicholas I. Explaining, justifying, desperately explaining,
Mikhoels described the new piece in an article in *Izvestia:*

> The author brings out the legend of a folk thief and avenger, Boytre, a runaway
> recruit, who becomes a leader of the poor masses.
>
> As a corrective to some of its earlier productions, which idealized the past
> in mild, lyrical tones, the theater is trying in this production to bring out the
> weight of the misery and hate of the Jewish masses for their oppressors . . . in
> order to give the Soviet spectator a historical people's history, saturated with real
> social suffering. . . .

But the critics disapproved sharply. One, who had in years gone by praised
Chagall highly, now excoriated his influence and Granovsky's (though Gra-

novsky's own name was never exactly mentioned), and said all the theater's plays were backward-looking and showed medieval, dirty, crippled Jews. He also accused Mikhoels, Zuskin, the designer Tishler, the author Kulbak, and the collective as a whole of formalism, expressionism, nationalism, and pessimism—all alien to proletarian culture. This amounted to a serious political rebuke.

Boytre the Bandit brought contradictory consequences to the company. An odd incident happened during its short run in 1935–36. Lazar Moisevitch Kaganovitch, a Jew who was very high in Stalin's government, came to the play. The actors whispered and trembled in their dressing rooms, and they were even more scared when during their curtain calls he was conspicuously not in his box applauding. But then they were all hustled, still made up, into the lobby, where he took a position in front of them and lectured them sternly.

What this high official actually accused them of was altogether unexpected. Why show these old, dirty, crippled, benighted Jews? he demanded. Where on their stage were the new Soviet Jews, building new lives? And where were the Maccabees? Where was Bar Kokhba?

So forbidden had such nationalist-chauvinist heroes been that the older members of the company thought their ears were deceiving them. They stood quietly and listened, met each other's eyes furtively, and kept their mouths shut. The younger actors, children of the revolution, didn't know who Bar Kokhba or Judah Maccabee were. They assumed they were Soviet Jewish proletarian heroes of the revolution.

Ironically, ten years later Kaganovitch was to be a leader in protesting that Jews did not in fact want any culture or language separate from that of their Russian brothers. Why at this moment did he push the Yiddish theater into two productions dealing with Jewish history and Jewish heroes? And why did he even protect them against the political criticism of those productions?

This was the period when Stalin encouraged a general ransacking of the formerly forbidden past to bring back Russian heroes for the masses. A play about Ivan the Terrible, who was certainly no "people's patriot," won the Stalin Prize. Movies were full of military exploits by czars. A quip going the rounds had a child asking his father as they came out of a film about Peter the Great: "Tell me, Daddy, which other czars belonged to the Bolshevik party?" Unexpectedly, the Yiddish theater was allowed to share this trend, and to appropriate, in a narrow era of grace, their own—Jewish—heroes.

The only Jew who did not benefit from Kaganovitch's visit to *Boytre the Bandit* was its author, Moyshe Kulbak. Kulbak was a loyal communist; he had come home from Vilna to share in the revolution, and he had deliberately shifted from the expressionism of his early poems to the socialist realism that marked his later novels and plays. Soon after *Boytre*, Kulbak was arrested and sent to a slave-labor camp, where he was tortured and died. Jews remarked that his loyalty had helped him *vi a toytn bankes* (as much as cupping helps a corpse). Typically, the authorities officially denied even his arrest, so that it was unknown outside Russia till long after his death.

Half a century earlier, in response to Russian anti-Semitism and the demoralization of Russian Jews, Goldfadn had written plays of a heroic Jewish past. Now, when Russian Jews again needed encouragement, and, in fact, Kaganovitch seemed to be sanctioning such productions, GOSET responded as Goldfadn had—with comforting visions of Palestine, offering Goldfadn's plays *Shulamis* and *Bar Kokhba.*

GOSET presented *Shulamis* "according to Goldfadn" in 1937. Pulver arranged music based on Goldfadn's original melodies. Mikhoels concentrated on evoking the play's lyrical freshness. The company fell to rehearsing *Shulamis* with an enthusiasm, even a ferocity, that they had lost in the preceding years. Throughout the rehearsal weeks, however, they were subjected to the NKVD's inexplicable tyrannizing. Actors, both professionals and students from the GOSET studio, suddenly disappeared into the cellars of the NKVD. A few hours later Mikhoels would replace them. The rehearsals went on.

Rehearsals also brought a threat beyond immediate arrest. As the actors expanded artistically, they felt themselves losing the control over their own thoughts and the feelings that they had so painfully curbed. The production had a similar effect on audiences. The setting in ancient Palestine, the figure of the old priest, Shulamis's father—even Goldfadn's beloved old tunes themselves—were like warm sunshine on the Jews' numbed sense of national pride and common history.

As always, the artists tried to justify themselves to the authorities. *Shulamis*, they said, was a light little operetta, a love story, not to be taken seriously. The romantic legend on which its plot is based, they explained, had equivalents which had been presented by other ethnic Soviet theaters. Moreover, *Shulamis* was the most operatically ambitious play the company had ever attempted; they had chosen it in order to develop musically. They did not elaborate to the authorities, of course, the collective Jewish memories that *Shulamis* evoked.

The critics let them alone, so the company ventured a step further, putting on *Bar Kokhba*, about the Jewish hero who fought the Romans. The company went all out with monumental operetta staging, including battles onstage. As with *Shulamis*, the audiences loved it.

But with *Bar Kokhba* they had gone beyond prudence, especially since critics still referred back to the *Boytre* fiasco. So to mark the twentieth anniversary of the October Revolution, the company got busy turning out an acceptably optimistic picture of contemporary Soviet Jewish life. Mikhoels introduced it; in this production, he said, "our duty" is

> to show not only the hero but also the society. Above all—the family in which the new hero grew up. In other words—"The proletarian nest." . . .
>
> In *The Ovadis Family* must be shown the beauty, the strength of the people, who have at last made a solid foundation for their feet. . . . With *Ovadis* we are going to reveal a new gallery of strong people, heroes, who will for the first time, in honor of the twentieth anniversary of the October Revolution, make a play the way a play should be.

The Ovadis Family (Di Mishpokhe Ovadis) by Peretz Markish takes place in Biro-Bidzhan, the farming community set up to be entirely Jewish. Markish made the bleak place look like paradise. The play showed the standard conflict, old generation versus revolutionary youth. In their secret hearts, Jewish spectators seemed actually to have identified with two minor characters who were politically unreconstructed: an ignorant pious grandfather and a Zionist. But the critics were satisfied.

In the next few years the theater did a number of other plays purporting to show modern Soviet Jewish life: L. Resnick's *Donya,* S. Halkin's *Aaron Friedman,* A. Vevyorke's *The Steppes Are Burning.* They tried for the correctly cheerful tone. But most of the plays came out sad.

Jews and non-Jews, Russian playwrights had reason to be sad. Russia still had many good actors and good companies, but an All-Union Committee of the Arts with a Central Direction of Theaters had made control over theater activity tighter than ever, and now it encompassed the vast Soviet. After 1938 companies were no longer allowed to hire new personnel. In these years there were thousands of arrests and executions of artists, musicians, actors, directors, writers; among the writers who were taken away at this period were Isaac Babel and Mikhoels's friend Osip Mandelshtam, both of them Jewish. The Meyerhold Theater, Zavadsky Theater, Tairov's Chamber Theater, and other fine institutions suffocated under the shifting regulations, the censorship, and the attrition of personnel.

Meyerhold himself was denounced for formalism (defined as a style which was politically decadent and detrimental to the people's revolution) and removed from his theater. The only one who dared to give him work was Stanislavsky, now an old man. In 1938 Meyerhold was called up before a tribunal to make public confession of his crimes against Soviet art. It was a dramatic scene and he was a worthy hero. When it was his turn to speak, instead of the usual confession, he stood up and defied them all. Socialist realism was making the formerly glorious Russian theater "stupid and dreary,"

Scenes from *Laughter Through Tears,* filmed in Russia in
1928. The movie was directed by Gricker Cherikover with
screenplay, adapted from material by Sholom Aleichem, by
Gricker Cherikover in collaboration with I. Skvirski. The
sound was added in 1933.

he said. Three days later the man who had brought new energy and ideas to modern Western theater disappeared into Siberia, never to be seen again.

The government policy, never avowed, now included the deliberate, systematic extinction of Yiddish culture. Of the total of eighteen professional Yiddish theaters that had functioned in Soviet Russia in 1933, twelve were left, and the number kept dwindling. Moyshe Litvakov, spokesman for Jews in the party since the revolution, had been purged in 1937.

In the last month of 1939, in the face of this oncoming destruction and in symbolic resistance to it, Mikhoels played perhaps his greatest role, in a play commemorating Sholom Aleichem's eightieth birthday.

The play was a dramatization of Sholom Aleichem's stories and monologues about the dairyman Tevye, his wife and five daughters, and his faithful worn-out horse (all familiar to us from *Fiddler on the Roof*). The company's approach was realistic rather than expressionistic; they played without any grotesque, colorful make-up. They even tried to use authentic period costumes and sets. In the course of tracing the fates of the five daughters, the play gave a panorama of the hard life of the poor Jew at the turn of the century: one of the daughters suffers grinding poverty, another marries a revolutionary and follows him into Siberian captivity, and so on. In the end Tevye's wife dies and he himself is forced by an edict expelling Jews to leave his little town and his few poor possessions. He even has to sell his last companion, the horse, who looks at him reproachfully, as if to ask: Is this the reward for all my efforts? —a comment, of course, on the life of the man himself. A motif for the production was the folk melody that Tevye hummed as he left the town: "Fregt di velt an alte kashe . . . chiri biri biri bam bam" ("Ask the world an old question . . .") The play was a great success with audiences.

Soon afterward, violence engulfed the theater. GOSET was playing on tour in Kharkov in 1941 when Russia and Germany began fighting. Like other theaters, they organized into concert brigades to entertain soldiers at the front and in hospitals. They were evacuated to Tashkent, without any of their equipment. There they played Peretz Markish's *An Eye for an Eye*, about Jewish partisan fighters against the German occupation. In 1943 Mikhoels and the writer Itsik Feffer were sent by the Jewish Anti-Fascist Committee to America, Canada, Mexico, and England to keep Jews there in touch with Soviet Jews.

The war brought a lot of Yiddish actors eastward into Russia. Some, like the blond revue singer Mina Bern, were in parts of Poland that Russia captured, and the Russian army sent them in brigades to entertain soldiers and the Russian people. These actors were given the same civil service ranking as other Soviet artists, according to their importance to the troupe.

In 1941 Ida Kaminska, the daughter of Ester Rokhl, fled eastward with her husband, Meir Melman, and members of their family and company. It was a harrowing trip, made on foot and in trains jammed with refugees, and she was pregnant. The group wanted to rest in Tashkent, but local authorities forbade them even to leave the train station. Nevertheless, Kaminska, Melman, and a few others did stay long enough to greet some old friends who had also been temporarily washed up onshore in the same place: the comics Dzigan and Shumakher, the operetta star Clara Young, and even Shloyme Mikhoels and GOSET. Then they had to move on to Frunze, capital of the Kirghiz Republic.

Frunze seemed an unlikely place to start a Yiddish theater. It had eighty-eight Jews in all. Its Jewish center was the whitewashed one-room house of a butcher expelled years before from his home in the Ukraine. He had managed to bring a Torah scroll with him, but he could not always gather the ten men necessary for prayers. In the next few years, however, refugees poured into Asia. Kaminska's company and others were absorbed into the local Philharmonia company, which meant that they were entitled to precious bread cards. They began with a repertory of Gordin plays and other Yiddish and non-Yiddish classics, which Kaminska reconstructed from memory, since the only baggage they had managed to save was their own skins. They also presented concert programs of music and recitation.

The Frunze group, called the Lvov Theater, was such a success that it remained even after Kaminska and Melman moved to Moscow in 1944. The Lvov Theater traveled all over Central Asia until its members were repatriated to Poland in 1946. Some of them continued to wander, however: Sheftel Zak, for example, was active in Paris before he settled in New York; Eni Litan went on playing in Israel.

Other Yiddish theaters sprang up. In 1939, Avrom Morevsky led a group from Vilna to Grodno, where they organized a Yiddish State Theater of White Russia. In 1944 an ensemble was organized in Tashkent under the direction of Moyshe Lipman. Wherever there were refugees, new semiprofessional actors from Poland and Rumania found their way into Yiddish and Russian state theaters. The excellent Minsk Theater, which was on tour in Vitebsk when war broke out, was officially ordered to Tashkent and then to Siberia, where it spent the duration of the war, producing its repertory for local people and refugees.

After the war, GOSET returned to Moscow. They worked with Bergelson on his play about the hero *Prince Reuveni.* Then they turned once more to their sources. Mikhoels published a statement about the new project:

Our task is to show that you cannot destroy a people. No matter how we may bleed, we will go on as a people, and we will continue to celebrate weddings and give birth to children. Our answer will be with a performance which will bear the name *Freylakhs* and will show a Jewish wedding. A wedding is the bond of life and bearing children, the beginning of a new life.

Freylakhs means "merry." It also refers to a dance tune for festivities with a particularly bouncy beat. The play was a lyric comedy. The critics gave it the Stalin Prize. It showed a traditional wedding, with its religious customs, relatives, musicians, and dancers, and its *badkhen*. In fact, Mikhoels gave this wedding a second *badkhen;* the two actors represented the dichotomy of the ceremonial jester who traditionally combines comedy with constant reminders of the darker side of life.

Soviet Yiddish Theater Disappears

But *Freylakhs* was a sort of whistling in the dark. Times were bad. Although government control eased a bit during the war, Stalin afterward took a stronger strangle hold than ever. In 1946 the Central Committee of the All Union Communist Party condemned many writers, such as Anna Akhmatova, and a number of periodicals, on the charges of cosmopolitanism, of showing Western influences, of experimentation and formalism. They lacked "ideological integrity."

Anti-Semitism was growing. Less than a quarter of the original Yiddish state theaters were left. The Odessa, Kiev, and Kharkov theaters were already closed. Yiddish actors trying to organize theaters, even temporary enterprises, had experiences like this one of Meyer Broude and his friend Bidus, who wanted to put on Peretz Markish's play *The Ghetto Uprising:*

> We went to the chairman of the Ukrainian Committee on Cultural Affairs for permission. He told us that first we needed to get permission from the General Soviet Committee for Cultural Affairs in Moscow.

Brouda went to Moscow and got the permission.

> When I came to Kiev with the permission from Moscow, the chairman of the Ukrainian Committee on Cultural Affairs said that the situation had changed and he could not permit the ensemble. He suggested that I take a vacant position as director in a Ukrainian theater. When I said that I could not take that position, as a group of actors were starving in Odessa waiting for me, he suggested that I disband the group. . . .
>
> When I came back to Odessa and explained that the Ukraine would not permit the ensemble, I went with Bidus to the Odessa Local Committee of the

Ukrainian Communist Party. The secretary who received us didn't even ask me to sit down. He stated categorically that he could not help us at all. When Bidus said:

"In other words, we don't have the right to work?"

He answered, "Who says you don't have the right to work? You can load coal at the shipyard."

Bidus says, "We have the right to work in our specialty. We are actors of the highest rank." [He is referring to the Soviet system of ranking.]

Says the secretary, "That's a hard job, for me to figure out with actors what their rank is. It's murky with actors. Now when you give me a pair of boots, I can judge right away if they're good boots or bad boots. But with artists—impossible."

I couldn't hold myself in and said, "If you only understand boots, you should work in a shoe factory."

He gave a yell and we ran, letting the door bang behind us. Bidus was shaking. For *khutspe* [nerve] like that we could have been arrested.

Meanwhile one of those actors waiting in Odessa eagerly accepted the offer by a kind-hearted acquaintance of enough money to get the company started. Unfortunately, this backer turned out to be a spy, and the actor went to jail for four years.

GOSET tried desperately to counteract anti-Semitism by showing Jewish partisans and ghetto fighters. They did Peretz Markish's *The Ghetto Uprising,* Itsik Feffer's *The Sun Does Not Set,* Moyshe Broderson's *Holiday Eve,* Linkov's and Brat's *The Trees Make Noise.* This last was Mikhoels's last work.

In the winter of 1948, Mikhoels and the Jewish critic Golubiev-Potapov were summoned to Minsk to see a local opera production and consider it for a Stalin Prize. Everyone sensed that Mikhoels was in danger. The Yiddish actors of Minsk took turns hanging around inconspicuously in the corridor outside his hotel room, in the hopes of protecting him. Apparently Mikhoels got a phone call at the hotel from someone claiming to be an old friend, inviting him out someplace. Whether there was such a friend, nobody knows. But the next morning Mikhoels's bloody corpse, together with Golubiev-Potapov's, was found outside their hotel. The bodies were covered with snow, and snow continued to fall. At the funeral, mourners were not allowed to come close enough to look at the bodies, but there are still whispers that Mikhoels's fingernails revealed evidence that he had been tortured before death.

For a short time Zuskin took over Mikhoels's place as director and guide. Then Stalin ordered that the theater stop calling itself a state theater and took away its subsidy. The actors got no pay. It was impossible to mount new productions. The Jews of Moscow got together a little money, enough for a few performances. Some of the organizers of that collection went to Siberia.

The Yiddish theaters of Russia dropped away. There were four. Then there were none. In 1949, Brouda writes, in Odessa,

> there was supposed to be an evening dedicated to Yiddish literature. When I arrived at the place there was no one there. The next day I ran into the writer Yermiahu Drucker and asked him why they hadn't held the evening. He gave me the news that Peretz Markish and Itsik Feffer were arrested—so what Yiddish literature was there left to talk about?

In 1949 the last Yiddish newspaper in Russia, *Eynikayt,* stopped printing. The Jewish Anti-Fascist Committee was disbanded. The doors of the Moscow State Yiddish Theater, GOSET, were locked; designers for the other Moscow theaters came and shared out the scenery and costumes.

In 1950 Binyomin Zuskin was in the hospital for an operation. Police came to the hospital, arrested him, and carried him out on a stretcher, deep in a drugged sleep. On August 12, 1952, the former amateur *badkhen* and Mikhoels's great comic foil, whom Chagall called a "treasure of expressiveness," was shot, together with most of the Yiddish writers who were still alive in the Soviet Union.

10 TWENTIETH-CENTURY AMERICA

In the years just before World War I, America had the most secure and prosperous Yiddish-speaking community in the world. For over a generation it had enjoyed the most glamorous stars of the Yiddish stage, the most polished and expensive productions. On New York's Lower East Side, home of half a million Jews, Jacob P. Adler was nearing his wheelchair years, but he was still making grand old-fashioned entrances framed in dramatic green spotlights. Sigmund Mogulesko still displayed his genius for naturalness and warmth. Boris and Bessie Thomashefsky, David Kessler, Keni Liptzin—all had played with Goldfadn and Gordin, and all were still stars. A new generation, including Molly Picon, Celia Adler, and Ludwig Satz, were joining them.

America was the source of most of the Yiddish plays popular all over the world. The staples of Second Avenue, as of the English-speaking Broadway theater, were melodramas, operettas, farces, and extravaganzas. Besides the "baked goods" which "Professor" Hurwitz, Lateiner, Thomashefsky, and the rest were turning out, and the rather more substantial plays of Libin, Gabel, Zolatarevsky, and others, Second Avenue had adaptations of Broadway hits. Within a few years the Yiddish theater was also using plots from English-language movies and radio shows. Most people asked for nothing more.

Just as English-speaking theatergoers had a marvelous choice of theaters to attend, from Broadway palaces to the spunky little Bijou Opera House in Kansas City, so, too, Yiddish audiences had a large number of theaters to choose from. They could go to the big houses on Manhattan's Lower East Side. But that was no longer their only center in New York, so they could also go to neighborhood theaters in Brooklyn and the Bronx, where they would buttonhole the manager on the sidewalk after the show and explain to him

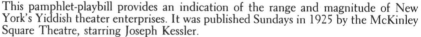

This pamphlet-playbill provides an indication of the range and magnitude of New York's Yiddish theater enterprises. It was published Sundays in 1925 by the McKinley Square Theatre, starring Joseph Kessler.

in detail what he had done right and where he had gone wrong. Occasionally they could also see Yiddish shows in buildings scattered around Manhattan's midtown area, even on Broadway itself.

There was plenty of Yiddish theater outside New York as well. The Hebrew Actors Union rule that prevented actors from auditioning for membership till they had spent several years in the "provinces" was a blessing for Yiddish communities outside New York. And even most actors who played the season in New York went touring in the summer.

Detroit, for example, had had intermittent Yiddish theater since the 1880s. There were companies based in Detroit and troupes that came through on tour. The heart of Detroit's Yiddish theatrical life was the theater run by Abraham Littman from 1914 through 1937. Littman's theater performed seven nights a week plus matinees on Saturdays, Sundays, and holidays: a total of some eighty-six plays in a thirty-seven-week season, not counting concerts and revues.

Littman's was so much a part of Detroit life that it developed its own traditions. On Saturday nights the theater would be only half full five minutes before curtain time, but there were always crowds quarreling, shoving, leaning, and elbowing around the box office, till Littman himself became exasperated and bawled them out.

"Where were you all week? From nine to five every day we were sitting, waiting to sell tickets, and you didn't come. Now it's too late."

He worked himself into a fury and slammed down his window. But his public knew him "from the old country," as the saying went; they simply stood around the lobby till he calmed down enough to stalk back and let them buy their tickets. The following week they would again wait until the last minute.

Yiddish music halls, like American vaudeville, were at their peak. While the artistes sang, waiters served wine and whiskey, and meats from the grills and ovens at the back of the hall. Roof-garden cabarets offered their patrons singing and dancing in the summertime. There was even Yiddish-English vaudeville (all male) to entertain the customers at New York's Second Avenue Baths. Resort hotels near New York, in the Catskill Mountains and New Jersey, brought in cabaret entertainers to keep their guests happy after dinner.

So the eighty thousand or so Jewish immigrants who arrived at Ellis Island in 1912—including a handsome young Russian actor named Jacob Ben-Ami —saw a lively community, having a good time in its own theaters as it continued to prosper and even to expand. They had no way of knowing that the community had actually reached its peak and was starting its inexorable decline.

In retrospect, it is obvious from the statistics that by 1912 the Lower East Side had already passed its peak population. More and more Jews were speaking English rather than Yiddish, and the flow of immigrants that constantly replaced the Jews who assimilated into American life was soon to stop short. But this was not apparent then. If on a graph one line represented the community population base sloping down, another would represent American Yiddish cultural activity continuing to rise, propelling Ben-Ami and his comrades to creative accomplishment for another quarter century, through the 1930s and beyond.

So in 1912, when Ben-Ami arrived in America, he was assured that there was a society solid enough to support the theater of his dreams. He took jobs with Bessie Thomashefsky and other popular theater companies, but he judged the Yiddish theater in America in the light of the high ideals he had brought over almost directly from the Peretz Hirschbein Troupe and from Russian theater.

Ben-Ami found in the American Yiddish theater all the weaknesses he had heard about. He discovered that the Yiddish theater shared most of them with the English-speaking theater of Broadway. The star system tended to cheapen the quality of acting—indeed, the playwright Osip Dimov ironically summed up a friend's career: "He used to be a good actor, poor fellow, but now he's just a star." The star system repressed the quality of ensemble work, and on the Yiddish stage, the stars and the union together discouraged younger talents. Producers hacked plays to pieces to keep the star center stage and to cut financial corners. Around 1910, hoping to protect the integrity of scripts, Leon Kobrin had started a Yiddish playwrights' association, but the group was so ineffectual that he compared the clout of his title as its president to that of the president of Mexico—in those days, zero. Scripts lay in desk drawers while their authors survived by writing for the Yiddish press. Producers, smoking cigars, put together deals and maneuvered in and out of partnerships, though no Yiddish partnership ever had so fierce a grip, either in New York or on the road, as the English-language syndicates such as Klaw and Erlanger, or the Shuberts (who were Jewish). Sholom Aleichem complained that theater managements handled artists as crassly as marketers handled oxen.

Amateur Theaters

FOLKSBIENE

Ben-Ami discovered, however, that in America as in Europe, though to a somewhat lesser degree, amateur theatricals provided an alternative and an enrichment to commercial theater. The motto of the Progressive Dramatic Club, for example, was "To improve, beautify, and elevate the cultural condition of the Yiddish stage." The motto of the Hebrew Dramatic League was, rather grimly, "Not to amuse, only to teach." The amateur groups also gave hopeful actors a chance to work without union cards.

In the 1880s, Boris Thomashefsky directed one of these new amateur drama clubs in Baltimore (for a handsome nine dollars a week). In the same decade eleven young men in Montreal organized the Montefiore Social and Dramatic Club. In the 1890s Jacob Gordin founded a drama study club in New York and stimulated many others. There came to be clubs all over America—in New York, New Orleans, San Francisco—with names like Jacob Gordin Circle, Goldfadn Club, Y. L. Peretz Club, Mendele Literary-Dramatic Association, Literary Art Corner, United Dramatic and Musical Club. Newark had the grandly titled Newark Intimate Theatre Group of the Young Men's and Young Women's Hebrew Association Yiddish Lyceum. Philadelphia had the Uptown Dramatic Club. Milwaukee soon had a Literary-

Dramatic Society, later called Perhift after Peretz Hirschbein, established by the rush of young refugees who arrived just after World War I; they also got together a band, a chorus, and a Russian mandolin orchestra. Chicago audiences had both the Jewish Art Players in Yiddish and a group presenting Jewish material in English, as alternatives to two professional Yiddish theaters. A New York club called East Side West Side performed Yiddish plays in English translation and published its own dignified magazine.

The amateur movement drew its vitality not only from forces and attitudes within the American Yiddish community (and from Yiddish immigrants still continuously arriving from Europe), but also from outside influences. Around the time Ben-Ami arrived from Europe the little-theater movement was sweeping America. Small towns clear across the country were putting on plays. Some of these amateur groups performed on a very high level, and some played important roles in the elevation of professional American theater in the next few years. Among these were the Little Theater in Chicago, the Toy Theater in Boston, the Arts and Crafts Theater in Detroit, the Pasadena and Cleveland Playhouses, and in New York the Neighborhood Playhouse. The Drama League, formed in 1910, organized hundreds of study groups to educate audiences all over America; *Drama Quarterly* and *Theatre Arts* started publishing; and universities began to offer serious drama courses.

A scene from Folksbiene's production in New York of *Bronx Express* by Osip Dimov.

Within the American Yiddish community, the amateur movement was propelled by both a love of theater and the impulse toward education, especially among workingmen and women. This impulse was common to the *maskilim,* to the Gordin-era Russian intellectuals, to the Bundists and other socialist groups of Eastern Europe, and to the thousands of night-school students of the Lower East Side. Whereas American amateurs tended to come from the middle to upper socioeconomic classes, their Yiddish counterparts in Europe and America ranged typically from middle class down through laborers. This was to be expected, since working-class intellectuals were such an important segment of Yiddish cultural life. And the lowest Jewish social classes—unlike their counterparts in most other Western cultures, who attended music halls and movies much more often than theater—were avid theatergoers. At the other end of the spectrum, Yiddish-speaking American Jews who became rich often moved out of the Yiddish cultural orbit and were more likely to be interested in theater in English.

By 1917 the Yiddish amateur movement in America was strong enough for a Cleveland group to invite delegates from other groups to a convention. David Pinski was formally elected president of the Organization of Literary-Dramatic Clubs. The following year a second convention was held, in Detroit, where Jacob Ben-Ami directed a special production of Osip Dimov's *Yoshke the Musician.*

One of the most illustrious Yiddish amateur groups, the Folksbiene or People's Stage, still performs today under the auspices of the socialist-oriented fraternal and cultural order the Arbeter Ring (Workmen's Circle). Formed from a series of mergers of earlier groups which already existed when Ben-Ami arrived, the Free Yiddish Folksbiene, founded by Jacob Gordin and Joel Entin, had evolved into the Progressive Dramatic Club, which then joined the Hebrew Dramatic League, which became finally the Folksbiene. It has presented at least one production, playing weekends, every winter season since 1915, a run of over sixty years.

From the beginning, the Folksbiene held strong ideals about the quality of the plays it presented. Every play had to have literary worth and moral seriousness. Among the works presented in the last sixty years have been Peretz's complex *Night in the Old Marketplace* and *In the Synagogue Anteroom,* as well as plays by Mendele Moykher Sforim, Sholom Aleichem, Abraham Reisen, Chaim Grade, Moyshe Dluzhnovsky, and others. They have also staged fifteen full-length plays by non-Jews, including Hebbel, Ibsen, Dostoevsky, Przybyszewski, Sudermann, Upton Sinclair, and Eugene O'Neill. In addition, they have given programs of one-act plays and montages of plays.

Like the amateur and art theater movements generally, the Folksbiene emphasized the role of the director. This was a sign of modernity in the Western theater and an especially revolutionary position on the Yiddish stage, where traditionally the star threw the production together. The Folksbiene hired professional directors such as Joseph Buloff, David Herman, and Leib Kadison (all of the original Vilna Troupe), Nahum Zemakh (of the Hebrew Habima), Yankev Rotboym, David Licht, and Jacob Ben-Ami. They also hired Michael Rosumani, a cantor's son who had come to America with Stanislavsky and his Moscow Art Theater.

From the start, one of the Folksbiene's problems was finding a home. In 1916 they performed at the Neighborhood Playhouse, which was part of the Henry Street Settlement, a welfare institution established on the Lower East Side by Alice and Irene Lewisohn. These two remarkable ladies, sisters of German-Jewish descent, were reluctant to let the Folksbiene in, feeling that it was better for the community to forget Yiddish and learn English. But they finally let themselves be persuaded, insisting only that every play be translated into English for them to approve beforehand. Still, on the eve of many a season the Folksbiene found itself homeless. One year they needed two thousand dollars to rent a certain theater, for weekends, in the midtown Broadway area, and by the time the Workmen's Circle Educational Division had organized an emergency committee and raised the money, the theater had been rented to someone else. In 1959 they set up a little theater in the building of the *Jewish Daily Forward*, several floors above the printing presses, and there they remained until 1973, when they moved from the Lower East Side to the midtown Central Synagogue.

In 1976 I asked Morris Adler, who with his wife Eva joined the Folksbiene about forty years ago, how he explained the group's extraordinary survival. He answered me quietly, without fumbling for words: "Purity." He and his wife (who fell in love while studying roles in a Yiddish amateur drama club in New Orleans) brought to the Folksbiene a commitment to "purity"—by which he means high aspirations: the opposite of *shund*—purity in Yiddish language, literature, and drama. Their comrades did the same. A further explanation for the survival of the Folksbiene collective is the members' sense of responsibility to the group. One veteran scheduled her daughter's wedding for a weekday so that she would not have to miss a single weekend performance. In 1949 the critic Joel Entin wrote that the Folksbiene was an "oasis in the surrounding desert of *shund* and mediocrity."

The group have developed rules that help them stay together by smoothing the inevitable human frictions. There is a minimum of squabbling over roles, for example; the director's final choices are final, but any actor can rehearse for a role he was not assigned in hope of changing the director's mind. Every member's contribution is valued, even in a season when he has no acting role, for the box office, the wardrobe, and other essential theater chores always need doing. Morris Adler, who has worked all his life in the millinery business, makes the headwear for every show, from Egyptian helmets to medieval drapery, whether he is acting that season or not. Every year the group elect officers and committees to read plays, choose repertory, and handle other business.

The Folksbiene draws support from its association with the Workmen's Circle, of which it is officially Branch No. 55, though the theater stands outside the order's formal political position. The Arbeter Ring pays the Folksbiene a yearly allowance, with a bit extra in emergencies. Moreover, by enclosing the Folksbiene in its larger organization, it provides the group with a sense of stability, a structure for resolving disputes, and a context within which a Folksbiene sympathizer can be a loyal member of Branch No. 55 without ever playing a role.

A nucleus of the Folksbiene's public, for their part, have remained engaged by the Folksbiene's ideals. When the Folksbiene has found itself in debt, there has always been some businessman proud to donate a few hundred dollars, or a few thousand. Wholesalers have given fabrics for costumes at one-half or one-quarter of the usual price. The same lumber dealer provides the wood for scenery, year after year. Such gestures testify that the Yiddish community, or at least a segment of it, has kept faith with the Folksbiene as an embodiment of the strivings of the educated Jewish worker.

Many Yiddish amateur groups, like their English equivalents, began fading away in the 1920s, and most were long gone by World War II. (Perhift, in Milwaukee, was a notable holdout.) Their influence, however, survived them. Amateur theatricals in Jewish adult summer camps endured as an institution at Nit Gedayget and Camp Boyberick, for example, long after generations of campers switched from Yiddish to English. *Pins and Needles,* the lively revue that the Labor Stage of the International Ladies' Garment Workers' Union presented on Broadway in the 1930s, was only the most conspicuous of many amateur theatricals put on by largely Yiddish-speaking workers' organizations. Even more significantly, Yiddish amateur theatricals in the first half of the twentieth century gave work and creative scope to professional Yiddish directors; they trained new professionals, such as Max Gabel and Maurice Schwartz; and they trained new audiences.

These amateur theater groups carried on the tradition of the *haskole.* They expressed the value that modern Yiddish culture places upon the individual's effort to enlighten and expand his own intellect while expanding the resources of the Yiddish language and literature.

Professional Art Theaters

IRVING PLACE THEATRE, JEWISH ART THEATER, MAURICE SCHWARTZ'S YIDDISH ART THEATER

Ben-Ami, though he worked with the Folksbiene, had his sights set beyond amateur theater. The boisterous eagerness of amateur groups was alien to him. He was reserved, elegant, sensitive, with courtly manners and a gently mischievous wit; even Yiddish-speakers called him a *dzhentelman.* He was a professionally trained artist, and what he had in mind was a professional art theater.

In Europe in the late nineteenth and early twentieth centuries, earnest amateur and semiprofessional theaters gave rise to new dramas and propelled them into the professional mainstream. The American theater followed along behind European trends, as American culture had done in a variety of ways since colonial days. So it was the naturalistic staging of Antoine's Théâtre Libre and Stanislavsky's Moscow Art Theater, the daring plays of Shaw and Ibsen, that were captivating large New York (English-speaking) audiences around the time of Ben-Ami's arrival, when European intellectuals had gone on to Reinhardt, Meyerhold, and the German expressionists. American intellectuals, who had to learn about the new art theater principles by reading articles in deckle-edged little avant-garde magazines with woodcuts on the covers, grew eager to see for themselves those principles in action: art as opposed to commercialism, dedicated collective effort under a director's guidance as opposed to *starism* (a Yiddish word), and rigid respect for the author and his text.

The situation of the Yiddish intellectuals in America was similar. Yiddish actors and writers went back and forth across the Atlantic like bees cross-pollinating. The culture closest to American Yiddish intellectuals was Russian, and Russia was the Mount Sinai from which Stanislavsky and Meyerhold, and through Meyerhold the Germans, sent revelation. Thus American Yiddish artists and audiences were in closer touch with European currents than were most of their counterparts uptown. Amateur Yiddish groups, such as the Folksbiene and later the Artef, played Gorki and Tolstoy and Hauptmann, even Ibsen and Shaw, with an amateur's enthusiasm. Professional companies played them, shamelessly adapted, because they offered stars juicy roles as well as prestige for their benefit nights. So plays by these dramatists sometimes appeared in New York in Yiddish before appearing in English on Broadway.

In fact, Yiddish intellectual audiences had had their expectations of theater raised so high that they no longer had any patience with Second Avenue's old-fashioned melodramatic curtain speeches, vulgar *kupléts,* and the broad star-oriented productions which falsified even the subtler new plays. Younger Jews were seeping rapidly out of the Second Avenue audiences too. Young immigrants *oysgegrint* (ungreened) themselves fast, and a growing proportion of Jews were actually born in America. They didn't have to be intellectual to scorn what seemed to them to be strictly for greenhorns. They were not susceptible to the popular theater's trump cards: nostalgia for the old country and a sense of being intensely at home in the theater. In fact, they resented the assumption that they could be had so easily. When they wanted entertainment they could get it more glamorously in English, on Broadway or at the movies.

Then, in the years during and right after the First World War, America suddenly exploded out of cultural isolation. New York audiences saw the Comédie Française, the Moscow Art Theater led by Stanislavsky; Jacques Copeau's innovations, and Max Reinhardt's spectacles; ravishing performances by Eleonora Duse and Chinese Mei Lan-Fang. American artists caught up with European culture, even with the European avant-garde. In fact, they became the avant-garde. Professional actors like Minnie Maddern Fiske and young Eva Le Gallienne were demanding worthy vehicles and approaching them in a new way. A whole string of earnest experimental art theaters went off like firecrackers, beginning with the amateur groups and shading into professional companies. Some of the best known of these were the New Dramatists, the Washington Square Players (later the Theatre Guild), and, somewhat later, the Group Theater.

When, in 1916, Jacob Ben-Ami organized an evening of one-act plays by Peretz at the Neighborhood Playhouse, Yiddish intellectuals recognized that the era they'd been waiting for had arrived. A production of Pinski's *Gavri and the Women* the following year was highly praised. Celia Adler in her memoirs calls what developed the Second Golden Era of American Yiddish Theater.

At the start of the 1918 season, while in Vilna youngsters were sweeping out a frozen filthy circus building and in Russia Granovsky's young actors were trying to define revolutionary Yiddish theater, a casual reader of Abraham Cahan's *Jewish Daily Forward* could assume that on the Lower East Side all was business as usual.

> Stars have changed theaters, and theaters have changed managers and dramatists. . . . David Kessler, even though the Second Avenue Theater bore his name, was to appear in Bessie Thomashefsky's theater. . . . Adler and Kessler went to work for wages. Wilner took the Second Avenue Theater from his father-in-law Kessler [after a nasty battle]. Adler wanted to reopen the theater with his old

repertoire, but Wilner wanted . . . a new play, and if it did not succeed then they would fall back on the old repertoire. They both pounced on a play from Broadway, *Just a Woman*. . . . Wilner's Second Avenue Theater is on Second Avenue, and . . . Bessie Thomashefsky's People's Theater is on the Bowery, and in between is Boris Thomashefsky's National Theater on Houston Street. [The Thomashefskys were no longer together.] Bowery and Second Avenue hurl bombs at each other. . . .

But there were signs of something else as well. A young actor named Maurice Schwartz took over the Irving Place Theatre. It had formerly housed fine theater in German, but Germans were not popular in New York in 1918, so the building was available, even though it was a little inconvenient to the Lower East Side. Schwartz took space in the *Forward* to publish his manifesto. It came out sounding like a very American translation of the statements of the Vilna Troupe and the Moscow Yiddish State Art Theater:

Can a Better Yiddish Theater Survive in New York?

For the past two years I have been going around with a plan to put together a troupe which will devote itself to playing good literary works, which will be an honor to the Yiddish theater.

I have spoken with a few actors who were enthusiastic about the idea, as well as with some writers, critics, and dramatists. We have had meetings and worked out plans, first to try it out for a summer with low-priced tickets, and so on. But as soon as it came to the money question, to the division of marks, and to who was to be the director, the manager, who should set the tone—jealousy sparked a fire in everyone. . . . And so the plan failed. And a lot of people thought we were crazy dreamers.

After two years of dreaming I have finally managed to get a most beautiful . . . little theater with a big beautiful stage, where we can put on beautiful good plays—and the main thing—where the mood will be right. . . . Now that the news is out that I have taken the theater over for ten years (with an option for another eleven), I am considered a madman, a dreamer, because the opinion reigns that that kind of theater cannot exist. They claim that the people who yell for good plays don't pay for tickets, they only ask for passes.

But the managers of theaters nowadays are nowhere near so guilty as many damn them for being. The big theaters have expenses of four or five thousand dollars a week. One flop sets them back for weeks with a sizable deficit. And therefore everybody looks for a "hit" with a "punch" to make people weep and laugh. And when the manager comes into the theater and sees the audience crying like Yom Kippur in synagogue, then he strokes his belly and goes home to sleep in peace, for he knows that this week he'll be able to pay wages and make a profit.

Besides, there is another big obstacle for good plays with literary significance. The theaters are too big. The plays get lost. A little gesture with the eye is too little. . . . A quiet moan gets lost. Then the public and even the critic

. . . say that the actor or actress has no temperament, no soul, no power of suffering, and so on. So if you want to show you have temperament, you eat the scenery. . . . In all English theaters where they put on good plays, even nice operettas, they do them in theaters of a thousand or twelve hundred seats. The spectator feels at home, he can see everything comfortably and get absorbed in it. And that gives the actor the chance to act better, for he feels that he is being paid attention to.

And that's why I want the public to have a small theater where the actors can give themselves to their art with their whole hearts, where the management and the beautiful comfortable theater and everything together can work toward one goal: to elevate the Yiddish theater from the sensational "punches" and fifteen curtain calls. . . . just to open a theater is not so useful, because presently theaters are not making such glittering profits (except for two). In order for a theater to be a financial success it must first be a moral success. And I plan for it to be a double success along the following points:

1. The theater must be a sort of holy place, where a festive and artistic atmosphere will always reign;

2. A company of young artists who love beauty must strive to bring the Yiddish theater to a beautiful fulfillment;

3. To play good dramas, fine comedies, worthy farces, and nice operettas. And if a melodrama must be played, it must have interest and logic;

4. Every play must be put on as it should be, and the author should also have something to say about his play. To rehearse enough that the actor has time to learn his role. And every play to have a full dress rehearsal with costumes and scenery;

5. The press and the theater should go hand in hand, and if the press, the people, and the theater unions give us the support we need, I am sure that the Irving Place Theater will be the pride of our Jews in New York.

Maurice Schwartz was as far from a wild-eyed idealist as the tasteful lobby of the Irving Place Theatre, with its concessionaires selling chocolates, was from the cold and drafty theaters of war-torn Eastern Europe and Russia.

Schwartz had already set the direction of his own life by his will and tenacity. Born in the Ukraine, he set out for America with his family, but somehow his mother mixed up the ship tickets and they crossed the Atlantic without him, leaving him alone in England at the age of eleven. He knew no English. A latter-day David Copperfield, he collected rags for pennies, slept in the gutter, and ate where he could. But he survived, and eventually his family was able to locate him in London and send for him.

In New York he became fascinated by the theater. He began as a *patriót* and amateur actor and then got a job with a professional company in Baltimore: eight dollars a week as an actor, with an extra dollar as stage manager, which meant gathering all the props and shifting all the scenery. (Actually, scenery in that company, he later recalled, was not complicated, for the company owned only two sets: one had a garden painted on the front and a kitchen on the back, and the other matched a palace with a saloon.

By the age of nineteen, when Schwartz was acting in a third-rate little company in Cleveland, theater had become the central passion of his life. Thus, when he heard of a secondhand spotlight being sold at a bargain, he did not hesitate to snap it up, though the company could not possible reimburse him and it meant sacrificing his entire savings—some six dollars in all. According to one legend, his big break came a few seasons later, when he was playing featured roles in Philadelphia and a leading man got sick on Second Avenue. The New York management, who had heard of him as a promising juvenile, sent him a telegram. He arrived on Second Avenue within a few hours, studied the part all afternoon, and rose to the challenge that very night.

Celia Adler tells in her memoirs that when she and Maurice Schwartz were acting together in Philadelphia, he often invited her out to lunch at Childs restaurant. He already had a rather grand manner, so she didn't suspect till years afterward that the reason he never ordered more than coffee and cake for himself was that he never had money enough for more than one lunch.

Schwartz had very little schooling, but a lot of native intelligence. When he decided in middle age to learn Hebrew, he managed so well that he could act in it and even write letters. He was also a clever mimic; he could do takeoffs on Adler, Kessler, and Thomashefsky to perfection, and was offered a lot of money to do a vaudeville turn as a mimic on the English-language stage— provided that he change his name to Maurice Black. (He didn't; he was too proud of Schwartz.)

Schwartz's personality was so strong that even now actors who reminisce about him invariably lapse unconsciously into an echo of his rumbling voice and distinctive rapid gabbling inflections. He was flamboyant, very much the actor. He smoked either heavily or not at all, was domineering and boisterous or childlike and helpless—everything to extremes. It was a combination of all these characteristics—will, shrewdness, stubbornness, ambition, passion, and charm, together with a genuine respect for what was fine—that led him to seize the moment and establish in New York a Yiddish Art Theater.

For his Irving Place Theatre, Schwartz immediately hired Ben-Ami, who was already known on the Lower East Side as a *literatátnik* (a mildly mocking term comically derived from *literatúr*). It was perhaps to be expected that the two men had a difficult personal relationship. They were opposites in so many ways. They differed in their commitment to the new principles, for Ben-Ami was already following the gospel of "European" and "modern" as opposed to "Yiddish" theater, while Schwartz's heart and training were still with tradition. Ben-Ami was a purist; Schwartz, a pragmatist. They differed in temperament and personality, and in background and education. Ben-Ami's grandfather had owned his own farm, so he was from the middle class, like most of the young reformers of the Peretz Hirschbein Troupe and the Vilna Troupe. Schwartz, as mentioned before, had an early life of poverty and insecurity. However, the two men accomplished a great deal, both separately and together. Tracing their two careers is equivalent to tracing the course of the Yiddish art theater in America.

Schwartz hired Celia Adler. Daughter of Jacob P. Adler and Dina Stettin Feinman, stepdaughter of Sigmund Feinman, she had begun in the Yiddish theater by playing child roles so winningly that Jacob Gordin himself promised to write a play for her to star in when she grew up. It remained one of the disappointments of her life that he died before he could keep his promise. Throughout her career she specialized in playing romping, innocent young hoydens and, enormous eyes brimming with tears, sensitive girls and wildly weeping mothers. She had already played with Kessler, Thomashefsky, Rudolph Schildkraut—most of the important figures in the American Yiddish theater—and in 1918 she was restless for the "old" Yiddish theater to give place to the new.

Miss Adler's husband Lazar Freed was also in the company, though they were soon to divorce. Freed was a boyhood chum of Ben-Ami's; they sang together as choirboys in their village near Minsk, and when Ben-Ami left home as an adolescent, he became prompter to a company that Freed was already acting with. As young men, they were both members of the Peretz Hirschbein Troupe. Tall, slim, and long-faced, Freed was renowned for his dreamy refinement.

Still another member of the company was a relative of Celia Adler's. This was her brother-in-law Ludwig Satz. Unlike the other young members of the group, Satz had not previously allied himself with the *literatátniks*. He already had a solid reputation as a funnyman, and though he played real character roles with the Irving Place Theatre, he was to spend most of his subsequent career back in light comedies, billed as "the man with the thousand faces" who "makes you laugh with tears and cry with a smile," (Celia Adler blamed this retreat on a devastating review by Abraham Cahan.) Satz had a round, wide-eyed face, an almost girlish grace, and gave an impression of ridiculous naïveté, helplessness, and bewilderment, especially when entangled in a *yeshive* boy's clothes.

Schwartz hired Bertha Gersten, a dark-eyed beauty who was to spend much of the next half century with Ben-Ami as his leading lady and his wife. In fact, the whole company was capable and intelligent.

The Irving Place Theatre opened with Z. Libin's *Man and His Shadow*,

Poster from the seventh week of the Irving Place Theatre's historic production (1918) of *A Secluded Nook* by Peretz Hirschbein. Sketches and engravings of the scenes decorate the poster. "Herr" Maurice Schwartz's picture appears on the lower left with notice of an evening to be given in his honor; at the top of the poster is notice of a future performance by Bertha Gersten and Jacob Ben-Ami in Ibsen's *Nora (A Doll's House)*, at which "Ladies will be admitted Free!"

a standard melodrama with no artistic pretensions. But after a few weeks the Irving Place turned to literature, and the new kind of text was to open the way to a new kind of theater. Who was responsible for this development? As usual in Yiddish theater, stories vary. But the pioneer seems to have been Ben-Ami.

When Schwartz and his partner, Max Wilner, were drawing up contracts with actors, Ben-Ami stipulated before he signed that there was to be a "literary" play performed at least once a week. And when Schwartz balked, objecting that the theater would certainly lose money, Ben-Ami took a cut in his pay check from seventy-five to seventy dollars a week as partial compensation for the expected loss. A few weeks into the season, when the Irving Place had still performed no "literature," Ben-Ami threatened to quit, so Schwartz gave him permission to try whatever he liked for one Wednesday; Wednesday was a slow day anyway.

Schwartz washed his hands of all responsibility in the experiment. After all, it was one thing to publish manifestoes in the *Forward* and something else to actually produce a sure money-loser. Ben-Ami chose *A Secluded Nook*, which had been written by his old friend Peretz Hirschbein for the Progressive

Dramatic Club. Schwartz was horrified; it was not a professional script, hand-written or typed, but a "little book," "literature," which had been published and had been acted by amateurs. He refused to act in it, though there was a role he was well suited for, and he provided no budget for sets or costumes.

A few days before the designated Wednesday, Schwartz turned up during a rehearsal and sat with the prompter, watching the end of Act One. He saw a pair of rural lovers (Ben-Ami and Celia Adler) quarrel. The lover vaults the fence and leaves his sweetheart sulking in the garden. The village madwoman passes by, singing, and depresses her still further. Her mother comes out, sees she doesn't feel well, and fears maybe she's getting a cold or maybe the madwoman has put an evil eye on her. The mother draws her inside their little cottage, gabbling as they exit the traditional formula to ward off the evil eye ("Three old women stood on a stone . . ."). The stage is empty. From a distance comes a snatch of the madwoman's song. The curtain falls slowly. It is a quiet Chekhovian curtain, far from the splendid shocks of turn-of-the-century melodrama, either Yiddish or American, which aimed to leave audiences gasping as the houselights went up. Aghast, Schwartz turned to the prompter.

"That's it?" he demanded. "That's a curtain?"

"Well, Mr. Schwartz," the prompter answered with a shrug and a snicker, "that's literature."

On that first Wednesday the house was more than half empty, for there had been no special announcement of the venture. But the few hundred spectators who were there—including the membership of a club of intellectuals who called themselves the *Shnorers* (Beggars, with a humorous connotation)—were wildly excited. They applauded the new kind of play, performed by a group of excellent professional actors. They applauded so fiercely and so long that Schwartz came in front to make a curtain speech, pointing out that he and his theater had gambled at the box office for the sake of their artistic ideals and that the community ought to support them. And so thoroughly did the community support them that Schwartz presented the play several more times on weekdays and then moved it to the big-money nights of the weekend, where it ran for a dazzling fourteen weeks in a row.

One jubilant critic wrote that *A Secluded Nook* disproved at last that the Yiddish public "enjoys chewing old mattresses." The Irving Place Theatre actors were lionized. Schwartz commandeered the role that he had been offered in the first place. Only the young playwright, Hirschbein, took no part in the festivities; he was in Canada courting his future wife, and sent back word that he was busy with something more important.

The season was not over, however, before Ben-Ami, Celia Adler, Yekhiel

Goldshmit, and some other actors were planning to break away from the Irving Place and start their own art theater. Art theaters in any language seldom last long. The collective spirit rarely endures, nor does the strength of individuals to keep choosing art over money. In this case the discontented actors complained that the Irving Place venture was not a real art theater, for Schwartz still conceived of himself as a star. Also, the company had presented thirty-five plays that season. It was a rich repertory, including plays by Shaw, Schiller, Wilde, and Tolstoy, Gordin, Pinski, Nadir, and Kobrin, as well as many less ambitious dramas. (It was no longer a list than many other companies juggled in one season.) But so strenuous a schedule made it absurd to think in terms of such basic art theater principles as long rehearsal periods, fully realized roles, letter-perfect memorization, and the development of each production into perfect maturity. Besides, there was no director to guide the process.

Backstage feuding ran so high that it infiltrated the work onstage. In one scene in *A Secluded Nook,* Hirschbein's dialogue came to take on a second level of meaning. Schwartz played a miller whose old friend, the village gravedigger, is planning to build his own mill and go into competition. As luck would have it, the gravedigger was played by a member of the anti-Schwartz faction. Schwartz's line was: "In the end, they'll be coming to us." His antagonist defies him: "You'll have a long wait till I come to you." The miller exits angrily: "Let them build." The gravedigger is left onstage without dialogue, but the actor couldn't bear not to have the last word, so he started adding a line of his own: "We certainly will build." But Schwartz topped him by repeating "Let them build" before he slammed away. The actors understood what they were really talking about and so did all those audience members who were in the know.

Sure enough, they built. The following season New York had two good art theaters, one, called the Yiddish Art Theater, at Irving Place under Maurice Schwartz and a second one formed by the dissidents at the Madison Square Garden Theater on Madison Avenue and Twenty-seventh Street. The new theater called itself, in English, the Jewish Art Theater. In Yiddish they called themselves simply the *Naye Teater* (New Theater) and trusted, as Ben-Ami gracefully put it, that their audiences would call it art.

The Jewish Art Theater drew up a set of principles which sound even closer than did Schwartz's manifesto to those of the European art theater collectives, Yiddish and non-Yiddish. First, there were no stars; roles were to be given out fairly to all actors, and all had a right to a chance at any role. No one could direct and act in the same production. No one could play a lead twice in a row, or refuse a role, including mass scenes. Even billing, that sacred prerogative of *starism,* was to be reformed, for all members' names were to be listed alphabetically on posters and ads. The company swept away the prompter, symbol and pillar of the "old" ways, and resolved to use one Yiddish dialect consistently. (The dialect they chose, the Volin dialect from an area of the northern Ukraine, is common on the Yiddish stage because its vowel system is midway between the extreme accents of Lithuanians and Poles and is thus comprehensible to all.) They set up a literary-artistic committee of two literary people (including Joel Entin), two actors (including Ben-Ami), and two painters, to decide repertory and other artistic matters. They set up a studio of students who served as extras. They even spent an extraordinary two full months rehearsing through the summer before the season began, using a hall in Coney Island, a Brooklyn seaside community where many Yiddish actors lived.

One of the actors whom the founding nucleus invited to join them was anything but a revolutionary. Rather, she was a link with the traditional Yiddish stage. Bina Abramovitch had been playing mother roles for decades. In fact, she had already won the nickname of the "mamma" of American Yiddish theater by the time she appeared in Jacob Gordin's *Pogrom* and infuriated that author by ad-libbing on opening night.

As director, they hired Emanuel Reicher, an assimilated German Jew who had studied with Reinhardt, and who seemed to be a bit uncomfortable about being linked with so conspicuously Jewish a venture. This was the first time that a professional Yiddish art theater in America had a director, in the modern sense, as opposed to a star and a business manager. It was an enormous step, and the critics testified to its results. A reviewer for the *New York Times* praised their production of *Samson and Delilah*, a play about theater and romance by the contemporary Swedish author Sven Lange:

> in a brief season . . . [the Jewish Art Theater] has already created a repertory which for richness, vividness, vigor and beauty cannot be matched elsewhere. . . . Except for the medium in which the play is presented, it is no longer the product of merely a Jewish theater. . . . The Jewish Art Theater continues to give an illusion of reality such as no theater on Broadway has yet learned to command. Its players seem to have studied the face of reality more closely and understandingly than other actors. . . . [They] depend upon an intuition. . . .

For the old broad Yiddish acting style, the Jewish Art Theater substituted Stanislavskian psychological truthfulness and realism. This trend was to become the primary force in American acting for the next half-century—as spread especially by people who came out of the Yiddish community, such as the actress Stella Adler (Jacob P. Adler's daughter) and Lee Strasberg. The "intuition" the *Times* reviewer praised could be reached by technical means; this essentially was what came to be called the "method."

Maurice Schwartz in *Sender Blank*, Sholom Aleichem's novel dramatized by Yankev Rotboym with music by Sholom Secunda, at the Yiddish Art Theater in 1940.

The Jewish Art Theater was praised by Hillel Rogoff, B. Gorin, Joel Entin, Zishe Landau, and the other prominent Yiddish critics. Although Boris Thomashefsky never came to see them, and Jacob P. Adler came only once, in honor of his daughter's benefit night, David Kessler came and applauded with all his heart.

But the enterprise didn't last. Evidently the main backer wanted to maintain the old star system, and he wanted the star to be his wife, who had, as Abe Cahan pointed out in print, a lovely figure but not much talent. The friction finally erupted in a confrontation between the backer and Ben-Ami in the actor's dressing room, where he sat taking off his make-up. Ben-Ami signed the very next day to play the lead in *Samson and Delilah* in English. The Jewish Art Theater disbanded not long afterward.

From then on, although there continued to be many literary art theater enterprises in the American Jewish community, including many rallied by Ben-Ami, the central figure of the movement remained Maurice Schwartz. His Yiddish Art Theater plodded doggedly along, season after season, from 1918 to 1950, most often in the theater he built for himself on Second Avenue at Twelfth Street (now the Eden Theatre). Not every production was excellent. Certainly the Yiddish Art Theater was as close to traditional Yiddish theater as to austere revolutionary art theater principles. But Schwartz called it an art theater, and he demanded, deserved, and received the respect that was that title's due. As Brooks Atkinson was to write in 1947—a full generation after the "Second Golden Era"—in an article covering almost half the front of the Sunday theater section of *The New York Times:*

> While Broadway managers are yielding to the fates with melancholy resignation, Maurice Schwartz keeps his Yiddish Art Theater intact in Second Avenue. Since 1918 the Yiddish Art Theater has continued to stand for something worth respecting. Yiddish theater audiences have been dwindling since the immigration quotas were fixed a quarter of a century ago, and the second generation has been slipping away from the Second Avenue stage emporium to Broadway. Like Broadway, the theater district of Second Avenue is about half what it used to be.
>
> But nothing seems to disturb the continuity of Mr. Schwartz's annual enterprises. When October arrives, Mr. Schwartz opens with something original; and unless it turns out to be conspicuously unacceptable, it keeps audiences coming until mid-season or later, when he goes on the road. Plays open and close with terrifying alacrity where everything is a feast or a famine. But Mr. Schwartz takes the thick with the thin and keeps his old gonfalon flying.
>
> Something of the traditional theater survives under his auspices. He gives his audiences story, colorful costumes, beards, lots of scenery, music and acting. For he is not afraid of the theater. If the acting on Second Avenue is not precisely in the grand manner, it has animation and latitude, with wide gestures

and excitement; and you always know that you are not in a library. Without being intolerably flamboyant, Mr. Schwartz acts with boldness, using his hands continuously, waggling an eloquent forefinger and raising shaggy eyebrows to project astonishment.

On Broadway this might be considered too rich a diet. But possibly not. . . . Mr. Schwartz gives his audiences the resonance and authority of acted theater. Whatever his vehicle may be, the Yiddish Art Theater yields the warmth and pageantry of traditional theater.

During those years, the Yiddish Art Theater presented such classics as Goldfadn's *The Two Kuni-Lemls* and *Koldunye; or, The Witch* (Schwartz played the witch), Gordin's *Mirele Efros* and *Sappho*, Peretz's *The Golden Chain*. The newer Yiddish dramatists were also represented: Asch, Leivick, Kobrin, Dimov, Kalmonovitch, Sackler. Schwartz's stage was an important force to keep them writing. It also presented a play called *The New Ghetto* by Theodor Herzl. It brought over the European Yiddish sensations that New York audiences had heard of and were curious to see, such as *The Dybbuk* in the Vilna style and *The Travels of Benjamin III* in the Moscow style.

The Yiddish Art Theater also presented plays of the non-Yiddish repertory, from Ibsen to Maupassant to Lope de Vega. Molière's *The Imaginary Invalid* was a big success. Sometimes, though, Schwartz lapsed into the old ways, adapting the play violently to his own needs, which is what must have happened with *The Miser*. Brooks Atkinson commented dryly: "Molière has collaborated with Maurice Schwartz on *The Miser*. . . . But Mr. Schwartz's contribution is the more conspicuous."

The Yiddish Art Theater's single greatest success was *Yoshe Kalb*, dramatized from the novel by I. J. Singer. The production played throughout the 1932–33 season and was revived frequently thereafter. The producer Daniel Frohman wrote of it:

> Schwartz gives in two acts and twenty-six scenes an extraordinary series of charming vignettes, romantic tableaux and brutal mass scenes, a cross-section of life that no Broadway production equals in intensity and originality.

Forty years later, it is *Yoshe Kalb* that many people think of when they think of the Yiddish Art Theater, and it is the production of 1932 against which the 1972 Second Avenue revival was measured.

Yoshe Kalb had a significant effect on the development of the Yiddish Art Theater. Schwartz tended increasingly to choose dramatizations (his own) of popular novels rather than original scripts. Furthermore, *Yoshe Kalb* plus a few other hits such as *Shylock's Daughter* (a new play based on Shakespeare's characters) cultivated in him a taste for the security of a hit and ultimately weakened his commitment to the repertory system of changing plays. Eventually the result was that the Yiddish Art Theater offered less opportunity to new playwrights and less varied experience for actors.

Thirty years after he spent his savings for a secondhand spotlight, Schwartz was still fascinated by lighting and other imaginative stage effects. He experimented with elaborate lighting plots, revolving stages, and startling masks. He employed fine designers such as Boris Aronson, Mordechai Gorelik, and Samuel Leve. He liked big effects; his 1928 production of Asch's *Sanctification of the Name* had forty-two roles and fifty extras, many of them from the dramatic studio under Osip Dimov's guidance which he annexed to the theater.

Although the company of actors was not exactly stable, Schwartz hired many of them back year after year. Several of the well-known serious actors of the American Yiddish theater played with the Yiddish Art Theater, for a while at least, and actors from abroad such as Isaac Samberg joined him for a production or a season. Young Muni Weisenfreund came to play small elderly character roles of the sort he'd performed in his parents' vaudeville skits in Chicago. When Schwartz wanted to cast him as a leading man, he was terrified to appear onstage "with a naked chin." That same season he played the dashing Russian student Ivanov in *Hard to Be a Jew,* became a star, and not long afterward made his name on Broadway and in Hollywood as Paul Muni.

Besides Schwartz's own home at the corner of Twelfth Street and Second Avenue, the Yiddish Art Theater played other houses in New York. They toured America and Canada. In Hollywood, Charlie Chaplin came to see the show and afterward went out with the company for coffee at an automat. Schwartz played London and Paris, Johannesburg and Tel Aviv.

Schwartz was always ready to try something new. He starred in several excellent Yiddish films, playing roles he had created onstage. Asch's *Uncle Moses* and Sholom Aleichem's *Tevye the Dairyman* can still be seen today. (The script girl for *Tevye* didn't know a word of Yiddish—or so the story goes.) He produced a series of children's matinees on Saturday.

Schwartz became highly respected in the English-language theater, especially in translations of Sholom Aleichem's *Hard to Be a Jew* and in *Shylock's Daughter.* He was even in Hollywood for a while, where he played, among other minor roles, a Polynesian prophet in a Twentieth Century–Fox spectacular called *Bird of Paradise.* The money he made went to finance his ventures on Second Avenue.

For always he talked about, always he returned to, his own Yiddish Art Theater. In an evolution of the old star system, he *was* the Yiddish Art Theater, and his was the hand that rang the great gong signaling the first-act curtain every night.

Maurice Schwartz's Yiddish Art Theater was the only Yiddish company ever to survive thirty years, anywhere, except the Moscow Yiddish State Art Theater (GOSET). (The Bucharest Yiddish State Theater reached its twentieth year in 1975.) Since both the Yiddish Art Theater and GOSET began around 1918 and ended around 1950, they make an interesting comparison. Each company had strengths and weaknesses derived from its historical situation. GOSET had financial security, and the resulting freedom to rehearse for months at a stretch and to commission dazzling sets gave its productions a precision and polish that the Yiddish Art Theater often lacked. GOSET had a distinct position politically and, especially in the early years, stylistically too. This impelled its work into stunning momentum and coherence. The direction of the Yiddish Art Theater, on the other hand, came of necessity from business and fashion. It expressed not principles but personality; it was guided not by a director but by an actor. Schwartz was a product of the old school which Granovsky had violently rejected. He respected intellect, but his theater was broadly emotional, rarely far from the sources and devices of the popular theater. It tended to sentimental affirmation of Jewishness rather than political statements, American razzle-dazzle rather than propulsion of ideas. Instead of structure, its strengths were breadth and variety. Whereas GOSET was squeezed to death by political pressure, the Yiddish Art Theater was free

Poster for Maurice Schwartz's film *Tevye the Dairyman*, produced by Harry Ziskin in 1939 from Sholom Aleichem's play, when it appeared in South America.

to be pragmatic and eclectic, ranging among plays of every viewpoint and, in style, from realistic to melodramatic and grotesque. And no government pressure from outside killed it; rather, it was simply eventually starved by social circumstances within the Yiddish community and by factionalism and personal feuding within the Yiddish theater.

Jacob Ben-Ami spent the years immediately after his break with the Jewish Art Theater making a smash success among the non-Yiddish New York intelligentsia. He played and directed for the Theatre Guild, for Arthur Hopkins (the first producer who dared a whole season of Ibsen in New York), for Eva Le Gallienne's Civic Repertory Company. A portrait photo in a velvet smoking jacket and flowing cravat (his costume for *Samson and Delilah*) appeared in *Vanity Fair* and other fashionable magazines. Alexander Woollcott wrote that the cocktail party question of the year was "Ben-Ami or not Ben-Ami," and compared him to John Barrymore. Barrymore called him "inspired." Mrs. Fiske spoke of his "beauty—spiritual, intellectual, technical." Stark Young called him "the most profoundly natural actor we have." From then on Ben-Ami continued to go back and forth between the American and Yiddish theaters.

Year after year, Ben-Ami toured in Yiddish, scrupulously choosing only

Jacob Ben-Ami starring as the actor in Sven Lange's *Samson and Delilah*, translated from Swedish into Yiddish, at the Irving Place Theatre, New York, 1918.

"literary" repertory. He played *Death of a Salesman* in Yiddish in South Africa, for example, and *Abe Lincoln in Illinois* and *Hamlet* in Yiddish in Argentina. To the Yiddish intelligentsia he became a symbol of high aesthetic standards; Peretz's associate Dr. Mukdoyni called him "the only tragic actor we have in Yiddish." Moreover, Ben-Ami represented the intellectuals' yearning for a Yiddish theater of fine drama, a theater judgeable by universal standards—a theater, as Gordin had proclaimed a half century earlier, "like the other nations in the world have."

It was as the knight of the Yiddish intelligentsia that Ben-Ami rode out repeatedly, together with Jacob Mestel, to try his lance, by founding art theater companies for the honor of the Yiddish theater. In 1926 they founded the New Yiddish Art Theater at Ben-Ami's old Irving Place Theater building. They hoped to establish a solid, long-lasting institution, but they lasted only one season. In 1939 the two organized a venture at the National Theater, where they were to try again in 1944. In 1939 Ben-Ami directed Gorki's *Yegor Bulitshev* for the Jewish Drama Society of Chicago and helped plan a season of literary plays there. He also set up a studio at which he, Nahum Zemakh, and Yankev Rotboym taught.

Besides the personal frictions common to every little-theater company, and the frictions between alliances in the Yiddish community as a whole, the

This still from *The Living Orphan*, filmed by Joseph Seiden in 1939, presents Lower East Side youngsters in a realistic setting.

primary reason for the inexorable collapse of company after company was lack of money due to insufficient public support. The Yiddish-speaking community was breaking up. Material difficulties, such as the move to outlying neighborhoods, interfered with faithful theatergoing; besides, art theater companies never have made much money in any language. The mass of Yiddish ticket-buyers consistently demonstrated that in Yiddish, at least, they wanted traditionally Yiddish theater; they were not interested in having what "the other nations in the world have."

During the twenties other actors who shared Ben-Ami's hopes were making similar attempts. In 1923 playwrights Peretz Hirschbein, H. Leivick, and David Pinski, and the intellectual Mendl Elkin, formed a club called the Yiddish Theater Society. They divided the active members into two committees, one primarily concerned with finances and the other with aesthetics, and soon had a membership of more than two hundred fifty. They published a monthly theater journal called *Tealit* and set up a theater studio whose teachers included the critics Mukdoyni and Niger, the historian Shatsky, and the Russian actor Richard Boleslavsky. After two years of planning, the Yiddish Theater Society established a theater to exemplify their principles and named it Unzer Teater (Our Theater). It was based in the Bronx, and its actors included Egon Brecher and David Vardi of the original Habima. Unzer Teater opened with Anski's *Day and Night,* its settings by Boris Aronson. It ran seventy-nine performances, which was a great success. Then they presented plays by Pinski and next by the younger writer Yitskhok Raboy. They visualized the Yiddish Theater Society and Unzer Teater as a solidly based institution, but their debts were swelling. In 1926 the Yiddish Theater Society, Unzer Teater, the studio, and the theater journal all sank and disappered.

In 1924 some Vilna Troupe members came to the United States and presented a season in the Bronx before they disbanded. In 1926 Rudolph Schildkraut and the writer Osip Dimov opened the Rudolph Schildkraut Theater. Schildkraut was an extraordinary figure; Reinhardt had said of him that he played great roles as well as any great actor could, but that he played small roles better than anyone. His theater did not survive either.

The 1930s saw more of the same excited plans, the same cascades of accomplishments, the same failures. The Yiddish Ensemble Art Theater formed in 1931; the New York Dramatic Troupe in 1934; and the Yiddish Dramatic Players in 1938, with members including Joseph Buloff, Celia Adler, and the writer Fischel Bimko. A production intended to reestablish a branch

Poster from the Vilna Troupe's engagement at Glickman's Palace Theatre in Chicago. The principal production advertised is of S. Anski's *Tog un Nakht (Day and Night)*, adapted and finished by Alter Kacyzne. The other two productions are Sholom Aleichem's *Hard to Be a Jew* and Peretz Hirschbein's *Green Fields*. 1925.

of the Vilna Troupe took place at the Ninety-second street Young Men's–Young Women's Hebrew Association, for one evening only, in 1936. The 1940s saw the appearance of the semiprofessional Wandering Yiddish Fraternal Folk Orders Troupe. None of these enterprises took root.

The art theaters were indirectly successful, however, in their influence on popular theater. Many popular theaters got on the "literary" bandwagon. Boris Thomashefsky, who had imported Dimov to America, presented his *Judgment Day* and other serious plays at the Second Avenue Theater. Even Littman's theater in Detroit offered "literary Wednesdays."

Yiddish professional art theaters reaffirmed the determination, first articulated by the *maskilim*, to refine, expand, and achieve recognition as a modern Western cultural asset "like the other nations have"—enlightened, energetic, cosmopolitan, and at the same time distinctive in its own national identity. This synthesis of the tribal and the universal takes many generations. Yiddish art theater made a conscious attempt to accelerate the natural process, and so far as its moment in history allowed, it succeeded.

Political Workers' Theaters

ARTEF

Another source of fine literary art theater that emerged in Yiddish, as in English, in the 1920s and 1930s was the highly political radical workers' theaters. Whereas the Folksbiene, and indeed most noncommercial groups in America in Yiddish were only vaguely committed to some political ideology (such as socialism or Zionism), or had no political associations at all, these workers' theaters defined themselves as specifically political. By far the most developed and long-lasting Yiddish workers' theater was Artef (Yiddish acronym for Workers' Theater Group), which was devoted to spreading radical politics through expressionist productions.

Artef began in 1925 as a dramatic studio under the auspices of the communist daily *Freiheit (Freedom)*, and through most of its active years it remained amateur, in the sense that its members rarely made enough from acting to live on. They agreed with John Howard Lawson, the left-wing American playwright, that it was only through "avoidance of the competitive battle of Broadway" that a collective could hope to "advance in coherence and to maintain its work on a sound social basis." In a genuine workers' theater like Artef, approved the editor of the *New Masses*, there was "emotional continuity . . . life was the life of the workers; theater was the dramatic method of presenting." As late as 1974, when one former member, Hershel Rosen, reminisced to me about Artef, he dwelt most warmly on the achievements of the collective rather than on his own small roles. Boasting sturdily, "I'm a worker, I press pants. I'm a worker," he was evoking Artef's pride in its use of art for presenting, illuminating, and enriching the life of the worker.

Although the group was never officially affiliated with the Communist party, it remained dedicated to plays of proletarian interest presented by and for proletarians. In its political aims, Artef resembled a number of non-Yiddish equivalents in America in the 1920s and 1930s, including the Workers' Laboratory Theater, the Theatre Union, the Solidarity Players of Boston, the Chicago Blue Blouses, the Rebel Players of Los Angeles—plus theaters that put on plays in Swedish, Ukrainian, and German, and three in Hungarian. There were, in fact, so many workers' theaters that at the National Festival of Workers' Theaters in 1932 fifty-three companies performed, and even more signed up the following year. These groups shared with Artef their emphasis on the group as collective (an extension of their political ideology), an orientation toward Soviet theater, and various stylistic elements, especially expressionism.

Artef was part of the traditional Yiddish impulse to educate the proletariat. The *Freiheit* had originally formed the studio that became Artef under pressure from a federation of Yiddish workers' groups who wanted a theater to serve the needs of all workers. As the special book published in 1936 in honor of Artef's ten-year jubilee told the story, in typically belligerent proletarian style:

[Before Artef] the [commercial] Yiddish theater followed the line of least resistance. This was the approach: theatergoers are simple workers, simple folks, hard-pressed Jews, exhausted laborers who have no time to read or study—Jews who just barely have time to rush through their evening prayers once in a while. These same Jews, so the story went, don't want and don't understand and don't need real art. For them it's good enough to give a jig, a tune, a bawdy joke, a little sex, mixed with some sugar-coated Jewishness and a glance upward toward Zion. All this put together made up the ugliest sort of "chop suey."

It was also a sort of insult to the Jewish masses that no one came out and denounced this horrible poison. The Jewish press didn't criticize this theater; the Jewish writers who did have anything to say didn't have a place to say it, and besides they didn't want to start up with the theater management. For this reason the situation got worse every year. And so it went till the *Freiheit* appeared. . . . The newspaper of the Yiddish worker took the matter very seriously. It set itself to exposing the whole scandal of the *shundish* botched-up theater; it set to tearing down the glories of the traditional routines—the "Oy, *mamele*" one, the "a Jewish girl needs a Jewish boy" one, the "Zion our crown" one, the "God is the only judge" one.

The attitude of the *Morgn-Freiheit* was the same in this respect as in all others—an attitude of trust in the Yiddish masses, a faith that they want to learn, that they can learn and absorb everything that is beautiful and good. Thanks to this attitude, the cornerstone was laid for a while array of cultural institutions. . . . It is no coincidence that simultaneously with the ten-year jubilee of the Artef we also celebrate the ten-year jubilee of the Yiddish workers' university and the ten-year jubilee of the proletarian schools. . . .

The Artef may pride itself . . . on its record of raising the Yiddish worker, bringing joy to the Yiddish folk masses, raising the purity of the Yiddish word, considering earnestly its obligations as a theater . . .

The *Freiheit* dramatic studio was designed to train Yiddish actors. New York had seen several attempts to establish such schools, beginning with Goldfadn's in 1888 and including Ben-Ami's, the Theater Society's, and others, but none had remained financially solvent for more than a season. The *Freiheit* studio's nineteen original students, between the ages of eighteen and twenty-five, spent their days in shops and factories and their evenings at the studio, studying voice and movement and talking art and politics. Their wages went to pay the studio's expenses and teachers' salaries. Following the Soviet system, they added a second group of students in 1928, then another—six generations, or studios, in all. These students worked independently by studio, but were available for mass scenes and sometimes entered the main group. Among the actors who began their careers in Artef studios are David Opatoshu, Michael Gorin, and Jules Dassin.

The studio began with only one teacher, Jacob Mestel. Mestel had published romantic Yiddish poetry while a student at Lemberg University, and had already been active in both amateur and professional theater, in Europe and in America, especially with ventures creating "workers' theaters." He had also taught at Ben-Ami's short-lived drama school. Soon the Artef studio acquired Michel Fokine of the Russian ballet as teacher of dance and movement. Dr. Yankev Shatsky, who had written and edited scholarly works on the development of Yiddish theater, taught theater history here as well as at the Yiddish Theater Society. The teacher of dramaturgy was Mendl Elkin, librarian of YIVO and a devoted *kultur-tuer*.

(It is no accident that Elkin's name, and Shatsky's and Mestel's and the rest, recur in these pages. Jews were constantly moving back and forth from Vilna to Moscow to Buenos Aires to Montreal, carrying with them their cultural concerns. Moreover, high-minded enterprises such as magazines, schools, and theaters were constantly being organized, collapsing, regrouping personnel, and starting again elsewhere. For an outsider who reads about Yiddish intellectual life of the period, the recurrence of these familiar disembodied names creates certain emotional effects. On one level, the effect can be comically unnerving, like the materialization of characters in *Alice in Wonderland* when they are least expected, or the Keystone Kops zipping out from around corners—"Here they come again!" At the same time, however, one is awed by glimpses of this gallant band—including, of course, many artists and *kultur-tuers* whose names have no place here—bouncing up indomitable time after time to make, once more, another try.)

Of all Artef's faculty, the make-up teacher was perhaps the most influential in shaping the young group. Young Benno Shnayder had recently come from Moscow with a group of Habima members on tour, and was currently directing an active season for the Folksbiene. His Artef students sat before their small mirrors and pots of red and pink grease paint and listened in fascination as he poured out his own excitement about the theatrical ferment in Russia in the last few years. Shnayder had been working with the director Vakhtangov under the wing of Stanislavsky himself. He was fresh from seeing the Moscow Art Theater, Meyerhold's theater, and Granovsky's Moscow Yiddish State Art Theater. He was full of the glories of the revolution and of the brilliant

Michael Gorrin and Goldie Rosler in the Artef production of *Drought* by Hallie Flanagan, in New York, 1932.

revolutionary theater. Shnayder's influence on Artef went far beyond make-up. He left the Folksbiene and stayed on as Artef's director.

The production style that Artef adopted was just then becoming familiar internationally among politically and artistically radical circles. Thus Artef's style resembled that of the Russians, including Meyerhold's theater and GOSET; it also resembled that of contemporaneous leftist troupes in other Western countries, from the American Workers' Lab Theater to the Polish Yiddish Yung Theater. The style was what became known in America in the 1930s as agitprop: formalist and constructivist, stylized and balletic. Artef's aesthetics, like its politics, were concerned with groupings and mass movement rather than individual introspection. A montage of New York critics' descriptions gives a composite picture: "color, movement and vitality" in a "heartily satirical cartoon style" (Richard Watts, Jr.); "a style of their own that has little to do with realism . . . a rhythm that runs through their plays that is the enemy of Broadway's meagre materialism" *(Brooklyn Daily Eagle)*; "refinement of inflection, perfect esprit de corps, a joyous bawdiness . . . conscious intellectualization . . . laughter, freshness and sustained emotional elevation" (Bernard Sobel, *New York Daily News*); and "a style of orchestrated performance that is one of the artistic ornaments of this town" (Brooks Atkinson).

On the Yiddish stage, this style became so firmly associated with "art"—

as were the nonrealistic approaches of the Vilna, which visited New York in 1924, and the Habima, which came in 1926—that for years serious ventures, both professional and amateur, felt compelled to adopt it. As Maurice Schwartz was later to scoff, people who fancied themselves artistic were simply "afraid to do a realistic play":

> Actors began making peculiar motions with their hands, speaking in squeaky tones, rolling their eyes, sighing at the moon, began to speak the way people are going to speak in the future, millions of years from now—"futuristically" . . . everything the reverse of natural: pointed walls and furniture, holding a walking stick upside down, jumping instead of walking, and instead of *natural* human faces—backwards noses and crooked cheeks.

(Ironically, Schwartz himself was occasionally accused of grasping at art in just this crude fashion.)

Artef took on an ambitious list of texts, looking especially for plays that dealt with either the Yiddish folk heritage or the condition of American labor. Their greatest successes came with two plays by Sholom Aleichem, which they adapted expressionistically, emphasizing the political elements in the plots: *The Big Win* and *Ristokratn (Aristocrats,* adapted from the one-acter *Mentshn).* They adapted Aksenfeld's *haskole* comedy about army recruits. They presented stirring plays about revolutionary heroes: *Hirsh Lekert* (who was Jewish), *Four Days,* Leivick's *Chains,* Gorki's *Dostegayev* and *Yegor Bulitshev.* Two of their plays showed the life of the American Jewish working-man: *In the Smoke of Machines* and *Haunch, Paunch and Jowl. Drought* by Hallie Flanagan, in Yiddish translation, was about the class struggle and had no connection with Jewishness at all. Artef kept asking for militant new scripts by American Yiddish writers, set in the immediate present. But they were hard to find.

Artef was making a name for itself. On Sunday nights, when Broadway theaters were closed, so many actors came to Artef performances that there were no seats left for the factory workers. Many such guests came back to see the same show several times over, and stayed on in the theater for the late-night sessions when actors and audience discussed the performance and the ideas behind it over coffee and cake in a friendly blend of Yiddish and English. John Garfield, who came from a Yiddish-speaking home, was one such frequent guest. Once he said, "I envy you people. You have found the way." He meant the Artef members' commitment, their searching, and their high spirits. When Garfield became an early member of the Group Theater, he was one conduit from Artef's "way" to the American professional theater. (Clifford Odets is a more extreme example of this expansion of Yiddish theater elements, as exemplified by Artef, into American theater. His plays translated the Yiddish leftist movement's passion for social reform into an English with Yiddish inflections. In a sense his plays made the American stage a new home for Yiddish theater, for they were often, as in *Awake and Sing,* set in Jewish homes among characters who were familiar with Yiddish idiom, and though they seem to be realistic, they nevertheless have an operatic quality reminiscent of Yiddish domestic melodrama.)

While the Artef company were developing artistically, they kept wandering around New York. They played in buildings on Twenty-eighth Street, Thirty-ninth Street, Forty-eighth Street, and 104th Street, as well as in many temporary homes provided by organizations. Once they even tried a cross-country tour, during which audiences welcomed them, but their unscrupulous booking agent rooked them and left them stranded. During many seasons they performed on weekends only, but late in the 1930s they had seasons when they performed every night—often still working their jobs during the day.

They always had money problems. What they got from tickets went to pay the rent, the materials for sets and costumes, and their teachers. When it didn't cover expenses, the members paid out extra and tried to stay alive. In their later years, when Artef was more secure financially, actors quit their daytime jobs, devoted themselves full-time to acting, and earned their living by sharing Artef's profits. Artef tried to pay a single member ten dollars a week and members with dependent families fifteen dollars. But the box office couldn't always manage even that much. Ironically, the most killing pressure came from their fellow workers. The unions, especially the stagehands, pressured Artef just as they pressured the strictly amateur Folksbiene and the strictly commercial Second Avenue Theater. Artef had to hire stagehands to do jobs that the members had been doing themselves, and to pay these employees substantial wages.

In 1937, when most of the American workers' theaters had already disappeared, Artef disbanded too. But in October of 1939 they pulled themselves together one last time. Even before they opened, at the Mercury Theater, they had sold over two hundred fifty blocks of tickets to unions and educational and fraternal organizations; they also sold some four thousand individual season subscriptions to their regular customers, who were delighted to have them back. A *New York Times* reporter stationed himself at the box office and described people telephoning to order tickets; first the callers placed their orders, then they scolded whoever was manning the phone for the years Artef had been away, and finally they remembered (though not always) to ask what the first play would be. After all, said the *Times*, the regulars "enjoy Artef even when they don't like it."

The *New York Post* welcomed them back:

> Some . . . years ago . . . a number of Broadway playgoers discovered right on their own doorstep such a theater as they were accustomed to seek with fervor and muddy shoes through the dark streets of Paris, or on long queues in Moscow, or in those sequestered regions of London which harbor its noted "private" theaters.
>
> That was shortly after *Recruits* was launched in a tiny theater on West 48th Street and the critics, after peppering their comments with such phrases as "an artistic ornament of the town" and "splendid ensemble acting," pointed out that though the spoken tongue of the Artef was Yiddish, their productions spoke clearly in the universal language of true theatrical art; the public found out that art and sheer fun in the theater might be synonymous and even leap over passable barriers of speech; and the Artef became an important part of the theatrical scene.

However, besides money pressures, Artef felt pressure as a leftist organization. In the 1920s and 1930s the Hebrew Actors Union and the majority of Yiddish newspapers were left of center, certainly strongly pro-labor, but they were leery of closer affiliations with the Communist party. Some Artef members claim that the *Daily Forward* actually buried their publicity. Later a number of the members were called up before the House Un-American Activities Committee, though none were indicted. Members became fearful and dropped out. In any case, once the Depression ended and war began, the revolutionary "masses" seemed a less pressing or at least a less romantic concern.

Artef disbanded during the war, then resumed for several years, lasting sixteen years in all. Even after 1953, when the group lost its coherence, members continued to give occasional performances in the old spirit. Hershel Rosen, for example, presented ventures in something of the Artef spirit and with some former Artef members, under the name Yiddish Ensemble Theater.

Another memorable theater venture in the 1930s was the Yiddish division of the Federal Theatre Project, directed by Hallie Flanagan under the Works Progress Administration, which fed thousands of artists during the Depression. Between 1935 and 1939 the Federal Theatre Project subsidized some twelve hundred productions and played to over thirty million spectators— often for free. Along with a number of other specialized groups, such as Italians and Negroes, the project included several Yiddish companies.

In New York, the Yiddish division of the Federal Theatre Project put on a *kleynkunst* revue ("a miniature theater" of music and sketches), including considerable political material, called *We Live and We Laugh*, created by

Zvee Scooler, Judah Bleich, and Wolfe Barzel. They staged Gordin's *King Lear* and Hirschbein's *Idle Inn,* both in English. They also translated English plays into Yiddish, most notably *Awake and Sing,* with a cast of vaudevillians who astonished themselves and everyone else with the talent they revealed for serious acting. *It Can't Happen Here,* Sinclair Lewis's warning against fascism, was presented simultaneously by twenty-one companies, in various languages including Yiddish, all over the country. Besides the Yiddish Federal Theatre Project in New York, there was a circuit that toured Brookline, Roxbury, Dorchester, and other small cities in Massachusetts. There were Federal Theatre Project theaters in Boston, Los Angeles, and Chicago, playing a wide range of Yiddish drama.

The project, including the Yiddish division, was killed in 1939 by act of Congress on the totally unfounded accusation of its being "red propaganda." Hallie Flanagan bitterly recalled one congressman who during hearings demanded an investigation of the playwright Christopher Marlowe, not realizing that he'd died in London some three hundred fifty years before.

Artef was one of the most powerful expressions in America of a profound element in Yiddish culture: the heart of the workingman speaking through his own *mame-loshn.* The theme emerged in theater as early as the Broder singer monologues of the 1860s that portrayed the painful lives of the "poor woodcutter" and "poor water-carrier." Half a century later, concern for the proletariat had evolved into specific political positions as well as into a generalized mode of aesthetic perception. Many Yiddish-speaking Jews channeled their traditional sympathies for the woodcutter and water-carrier, as well as their religious loyalties, into those politics and that aesthetic mode. Artef was a product and statement of this synthesis.

Writing for and About Yiddish Theater

Serious Yiddish theater had always distinguished itself from popular theater by its concern for the Yiddish word, especially the printed word as opposed to scribbled manuscripts or practiced ad-libbing. Throughout the twentieth century, serious American Yiddish theater used translated plays, plays written in Yiddish by writers living in Europe or South America, and new plays by Yiddish writers living in the United States and Canada—most often in New York. By the 1920s and 1930s many of the serious playwrights whom David Pinski had dubbed the third-act dramatists were based in America, as were very many Yiddish novelists, poets, and essayists.

Most early-twentieth-century Yiddish plays about contemporary life had been set in Europe, even plays written in America. Of the third act dramatists, as well as the still younger crop who began to write only in the 1920s and 1930s, many, like Harry Sackler, concentrated on Eastern European Jewish life, either in the present or in the romanticized past. However, the proportion of plays set in America began to rise. There was a whole genre of plays in Yiddish, as in other immigrant languages, that worked the ground of transition, introducing the characters in the old country and then following their adjustment as immigrants; Fischel Bimko's *Amerike Ganef* actually set Act One in a Polish *shtetl*, Act Two on shipboard, Act Three on Ellis Island, and Act Four in an office in New York City. An increasing proportion of plays devoted most of their attention to the American scene. In a parallel development, novelists and poets were producing works like Moyshe Leyb Halpern's volume of verse *New York* (1919), I. I. Schwartz's epic poem "Kentucky" (1925), and Yitskhok Raboy's serious novel *The Jewish Cowboy* (1942). Nevertheless, the dramatists' tendency was still to present New World life in relation to that of the old country, for the language was bound up with Old World associations; besides, it was the evocation of just those associations that drew the mass of theatergoers into the theater.

The lively American Yiddish press held on through the first half of the twentieth century as a forum where the public and the theater could argue and explain. In the early years especially, magazines appeared with names like *Di Freie Yidishe Folksbiene (The Free Yiddish Folk Stage* or *People's Stage)*, which was edited by Joel Entin, *Dramatic World,* and *Yiddish Stage.* Even in periodicals of more general interest, critics such as Natan Buchwald and A. Mukdoyni published reviews, as well as pieces about the theory and history of drama and exhortations toward the overall elevation of the Yiddish theater. Critics felt their power. Sometimes they felt their responsibility too, as Abraham Cahan did once in regard to Maurice Schwartz's young leading lady, Charlotte Goldstein. Cahan's review of *Yoshe Kalb,* written when the play first opened, had attacked her performance so ferociously that she had run in tears to Schwartz and offered to give up the role. But some months later, when Cahan returned to see *Yoshe Kalb* again, he not only changed his mind, but actually stood up in the audience during the curtain calls and apologized publicly for his earlier mistake. (English-language critics, too, reviewed both Yiddish art theater and the glossier musicals.)

Actors, for their part, wrote rebuttals of reviews, which, published in the newspapers, sometimes sparked public correspondences between actor, critic, and all other interested parties. Actors also wrote open letters appealing to the public against managers who withheld wages or otherwise treated them badly.

Celia Adler's use of the Philadelphia daily *Yiddish World* on one occasion exemplifies the continuing symbiotic bond between stars and their public,

Celia Adler and Ludwig Satz in *The Second Love* by H. Kalmanovitch. They are playing a typical "comic couple" scene, and very likely will soon sing a comic duet.

especially in the popular theater. In 1920, when she was playing a season at Philadelphia's Arch Street Theater, she wanted to leave her audience for a month, so she wrote them this open letter:

Most Honored Editor of the *Yiddish World:*

Allow me to express through your worthy newspaper my warm thanks to my managers of the Arch Street Theater for giving me their friendly permission to play a few weeks as a guest with the Theatre Guild in New York on the English stage. I will perform at the Garrick Theater in New York under the direction of Emanuel Reicher in the leading female role of David Pinski's *The Treasure* in English. I would never have permitted myself to leave a theater to which I was committed, even for a few weeks. But since by coincidence I do not play in the operetta which is the second play at the Arch Street Theater, the friendly management of the theater has permitted me to go play a role which I love very much for four weeks' time. Only then did I accept the invitation of the Theatre Guild.

I will certainly come back to Philadelphia after that performance. My first appearance in Philadelphia upon my return to the Arch Street Theater will be in Peretz Hirschbein's famous play *The Idle Inn.*

With great respect,
Celia Adler

Placated by her humble acknowledgment of her indebtedness to them, her public forgave her absence. In fact, many sent her letters wishing her luck, and some came all the way to the Garrick to wish her luck in person.

Popular Theater, Films, Radio

The background to art theaters of all sorts was the popular theater, for whatever literary drama might or might not be offered in any one season, America continued to be the capital of popular Yiddish theater. Old-time theatergoers today look back to the 1920s and 1930s and sigh for the stars they used to see. Adorably impish Molly Picon and her clever husband Jacob Kalich were singing Rumshinsky's melodies. Aaron Lebedev, a swaggering good fellow, flashed his knowing street-wise grin. Jennie Goldstein swooned plumply and wailed, as one villain after another broke her heart; later she became a jolly comedienne. Herman Yablokoff mystified his fans disguised as the singing *payats* (clown). Samuel Goldenburg played the piano onstage, his handsome profile tilted romantically over the arpeggios. Menashe Skulnik, who came late to stardom after a career of small roles and doubling as prompter, shrugged helplessly, his absurd hat perched on top of his head. Jacob Jacobs and Betty Treittler Jacobs and Rose and Nathan Goldberg continued their steady double date, season after season, at the Lenox Theater.

These stars and many more got up their own productions or played for a producer. They played on Second Avenue or in the Bronx or in Cleveland, Ohio, in music halls or in musical comedies. They stood in front of a standard living room set or an elaborate Japanese garden complete with a chorus in kimonos. The words they spoke were often silly. But the audiences were dazzled.

Yiddish theater came to include a small and rather erratic movie industry. The first Yiddish film was actually an Italian film entitled *Joseph in Egypt*. In 1913 a young actor named Joseph Green had the brainstorm of substituting Yiddish words, and showed it successfully in America and Europe at intervals for decades thereafter. After gathering experience in Hollywood, Green made his subsequent Yiddish films in Poland, where the materials and the salaries for highly skilled technicians were cheaper.

In the United States, too, especially in the 1930s and 1940s, producers such as Joseph Seiden turned out a number of Yiddish films. Many of these were rather primitive technically, shot in interiors that resembled makeshift stage settings, with little feeling for cinematic values. They were shown in theaters, either alone or with a stage show, and they were also shown increasingly under the auspices of Jewish community activities.

Some American-made Yiddish films were conceived as literary efforts. Bertha Gersten starred in Gordin's *Mirele Efros* and the star Mikhel Mikhalesko appeared in Gordin's *God, Man, and Devil*. *Tevye the Dairyman*, starring Maurice Schwartz, and *Green Fields*, produced by Edgar G. Ulmer, both used countrysides and costumes effectively to adapt to the screen what was originally stage material. In *Uncle Moses*, Schwartz portrayed a coarse businessman against an authentic background of Lower East Side sweatshops and restaurants. Judea Films presented Joseph Buloff in *The Shoemaker's Romance*, "a comic portrayal of Jewish life in the old home." *The Wandering Jew* starred Jacob Ben-Ami in "the greatest of all talking Jewish masterpieces, depicting the struggle of the Jews in modern Germany."

Most Yiddish films, however, were popular entertainments of various genres. There were tear-jerkers such as *Where Is My Child?*, starring Celia Adler, and *Two Sisters*, starring Jennie Goldstein—both ladies rolling their eyes and staggering with emotion in an exaggeration of the style of American films made a decade or two earlier. In *Bar Mitzvah*, Boris Thomashefsky sings tenderly to his child and mourns his wife, who—he thinks—was lost at sea. In *Motl the [Sewing Machine] Operator*, domestic problems follow from a workers' strike. Worldart Films Company produced *East Side Sadie*, advertised on posters as "a true incident of Jewish life in the American ghetto," which "took a year's time to produce." Some movies were happier; Moyshe Oysher bares his chest and flashes his black eyes as *The Singing Blacksmith* (from Pinski's *Yankl der Shmid*) and, on another level altogether, *Catskill Honeymoon* uses the flimsiest of plots to string together a succession of singing acts and comedy routines.

Radio was another medium for Yiddish popular entertainment. In 1926 the *Daily Forward* established radio station WEVD, named in honor of the socialist leader Eugene V. Debs. WEVD broadcast news and commentary, religious talks, songs, and comic skits presented under such titles as "The Yiddish Philosopher," "The Newsboy," "The Ballad Singer," "The Merry Cantor," "The Marriage Bureau," and "Uncle Nokhem and His Kiddies." There were Yiddish programs on a number of other New York stations, such as WMCA, WINS, WBYN, and WBNX, as well as on stations in Miami, Chicago, and at intervals in several other large cities. In 1956 there were still five stations with some Yiddish programming in New York alone and forty-one stations outside New York. (Twenty years later New York has retained only WEVD, AM and FM; stations in a few other centers, such as Detroit, Cleveland, Philadelphia, and Vineland, New Jersey, still broadcast partially in Yiddish.)

There was also a lively industry in Yiddish and Yiddish-English recordings. Records of show tunes and comic tunes sold well, and so did monologues and recitations, both comic and dramatic. Pesach Burstein sang on hundreds of

Comic scene from the film *Catskill Honeymoon*, a series of revue sketches produced in 1950 by Martin Cohen and directed by Hy Jacobson. The film is still a favorite in community centers for elderly Yiddish-speaking people.

Celia Adler in a filmed melodrama. Her infant son is taken away from her and she is confined in an insane asylum, but the happy ending comes years later when she gets out and finds him. Henry Lynn and Abraham Leff made the film in New York in 1937.

Scene from *Two Sisters*, made by Ben K. Blake for Graphic Pictures Corporation in New York in 1938. This film presents a domestic drama in a realistic setting.

78-rpm records produced by a variety of Yiddish and American companies. Sheet music, too, brought theater hits into the public's parlor.

Developments in the Yiddish Community

Throughout the 1920s and 1930s, American Yiddish theater continued to be vital and varied and to offer both popular entertainments for the large masses and serious drama for the intellectuals. However, the community that the theater served and expressed was losing coherence. The theater's social foundation was weakening. American Yiddish theater artists, especially in the literary theater, would soon resemble these cartoon characters who race off a cliff before they realize that they are running on space.

The Yiddish community lost its stability as Jews moved out of the Lower East Side, and out of comparable immigrant neighborhoods in other cities. Where there had been vitality and a complexly energetic network of institutions, there remained only the traces. For example, in 1908 a quarter of a million Jews belonged to *landsmanshaftn;* within a generation commercial insurance and, later, provisions of the New Deal replaced these orders' benefits entirely. Community pressures were diluted; in the big city it was easy for Markowitz to become Markham and Weinstein to become Winston. The very freedom of movement and the prosperity of American Jews, which had made the flowering of American Yiddish culture possible, also encouraged assimilation to take place much faster than could occur in the anti-Semitic environments of Eastern Europe. Furthermore, in the United States, as opposed to Canada or South Africa, the emphasis on "melting pot" integration accelerated assimilation still more.

In the 1920s, federal legislation drastically reduced immigration into the United States. This was disastrous for all Yiddish-language institutions, including theater. The flow of new audiences, which had always been the Yiddish theater's assurance, replenishing the theatergoers who slipped away into the Broadway theaters or movie houses or away from the city altogether, was now dammed up. Fifteen and twenty-five years later, not even the trickle of refugees from Hitler, or the upsurge of Jewish loyalties among Americans in reaction to the Nazi holocaust, could reverse this massive trend.

Yiddish actors reflected this acculturation in their personal careers. All along, Yiddish actors had been branching out into English-language theater. Schwartz and Ben-Ami played on Broadway to much applause. Bertha Kalish's accent made her an exotic heroine to the American public. Thomashefsky played in an English-language production of *God of Vengeance* in 1922.

Menashe Skulnik in the title role of the *Straw Soldier*, his famous characterization of an inept army recruit—a stock comic figure on the Yiddish stage since a Goldfadn sketch of the 1880s.

Molly Picon was a hit on Broadway as she had been in the cafés of Paris and Vienna. Charlie Cohen took his comic routines to the London Palladium. Joseph Buloff sang in *Oklahoma!* for years. Menashe Skulnik went back and forth between languages in his later years; Zvee Scooler and David Opatoshu still do.

Sometimes the "American" theater offered better roles. Sometimes it simply offered the only job available at the moment. With time, not only did economic incentives increase, but psychic ones, always present, were reinforced, for any success on the outside—in the majority culture—brought an actor enormous respect within the Yiddish minority's world. Besides, whether they realized it or not, people living in America seemed to come inevitably to the American respect for big undertakings, for new inventions, and for success, and Yiddish theaters—at least Yiddish art theaters—were rarely any of these.

Some Yiddish actors, like Paul Muni and Stella Adler, both raised in America, switched to American theater and never came back. Increasingly young people raised in Yiddish homes went directly into English-speaking theater; an astonishing proportion of American theater, film, and television people are from such backgrounds. In the mid-1920s, a group of them formed a Jewish-English theater guild. Among the members were Eddie Cantor, Al Jolson, George Jessel, and Houdini, and the first chairman was the producer Jed Harris. Jacob P. Adler came to the opening meetings, in a Broadway

Typical sensational melo-
drama of the 1930s. The poster indicates the Yiddish public's awareness of "American"
life; the sultry heroine's name
is Mae 'East.' The poster also
gives a glimpse of the interre-
latedness of Yiddish actors:
Wilner was in David Kessler's
family; Fishzon was part of
the Fishzon family who
toured Russia in the 1890s;
and "the daughter" and "the
gigolo" are in real life Mr.
and Mrs. Hollander. The
"cantor," the "gay widow,"
the "sexton" and the top-hat-
ted "wayward son" seem to
belong to the obligatory
comic subplot. Distributed
simultaneously with this poster was a duplicate printed
entirely in Yiddish.

theater. Already old and feeble, he arrived late, but as he entered, the speaker
stopped and everyone stood and applauded him to the stage. The membership
were warmly acknowledging their roots.

The gradually weakening hold of the Yiddish language was a symptom of
the community's difficulties in remaining coherent. Institutions to teach children Yiddish after public school hours were still increasing through the 1920s
and 1930s, perhaps in an attempt to counteract the enfeeblement of Yiddish
in the children's English-speaking daily environment, but in the next decade
they began to decline. The number of Yiddish daily newspapers remained at
eleven into the 1930s and then began to fall. (So, too, it should be mentioned,
did the number of American newspapers in English and other languages.) The
growth of Zionism made Hebrew seem not only more prestigious than Yiddish
but also more adventurous, and the establishment of the state of Israel in 1948
made it seem more practical as well. The Nazi slaughter of the Jews of Eastern
and Central Europe destroyed the base of the world's Yiddish speakers, leaving
outlying communities with no home soil from which to draw cultural nourishment.

Naturally, theater mirrored the threat that English might overshadow

Yiddish completely. As early as 1920 the Jewish Art Theater included English synopses in its printed programs, and not only for the non-Jews in the audience. In fact, the company was pleased to provide the synopses, for they were a sign that the theater was drawing the young people who ordinarily ignored Yiddish theater entirely. However, people generally prefer to go to plays in a language they understand, so Yiddish theater inexorably lost potential customers.

In popular theater, "potato Yiddish"—a corrupt version diluted with English words and Americanisms—had replaced *Daytshmerish* as a sign of low cultural standards. In 1932 in *Tommy My Boy* (the title itself is English), Louis Freiman's dialogue blithely applies Yiddish grammatical rules to English words and gets *mir hobn gehaykt* for "we hiked" and *ticherin* for a female teacher, as in the compliment: *Di ticherin iz di meyn boss.* By 1948 *Cue* magazine was reviewing *What a Guy!*, starring Menashe Skulnik, as a "bilingual laugh riot." (Ironically, Abraham Cahan may be said to have encouraged the process of corruption, though it would have happened anyway, for he deliberately incorporated many English words into the language of his *Daily Forward,* in an effort to help his readers learn to be Americans—and to this day there are Yiddishists who have not forgiven him for it.)

It is interesting that in the nightclub entertainment at the Catskill Mountain resorts, the so-called Borsht Belt, which was famous for its vulgarity, the punch lines stubbornly remained Yiddish, even while the comedians used more and more English in their build-ups. The intimate dirty words that outsiders didn't know were the "punch"; alone together, the audiences were, in the American metaphor, letting their pants down.

Meanwhile, of course, intellectual Yiddishists screamed in pain and made plans, in (as the Artef anniversary album put it) "an attitude of trust in the masses," to preserve Yiddish as a literary language and Yiddishism as a high culture. Art theaters considered themselves front-line fighters against "potato Yiddish." Artef had a special teacher who not only lectured on literature, but actually taught Yiddish to the largely American-born fifth and sixth studios. YIVO and YKUF (the Yiddish Cultural Association), the Workmen's Circle and the Farband (Labor Zionist Alliance), all sponsored Yiddish learning in the Yiddish language.

Beyond its dependence on the Yiddish language as a cohesive force—a vulnerability it shared with the community as a whole—Yiddish theater had material problems that were specifically its own. In the 1930s all American theaters were in trouble—the Depression, the competition of movies and radio, the falling-off of the road—but Yiddish theaters had extra financial difficulties, which continued into wartime and beyond. As Jews moved to neighborhoods as much as an hour from the Lower East Side, it became inconvenient to travel to the theater and back. It was especially hard for working people on week nights, for shows still lasted till midnight; as the average Yiddish theatergoer reached middle age and beyond, traveling became even more of a problem. The situation was compounded by the reduction of local theaters in Brooklyn and the Bronx.

The system by which Yiddish theater financed benefit performances, which at one time were its mainstay, now became a financial handicap. In attempts to keep filling the house, as business got worse and worse, Yiddish theaters gave organizations discounts of 50 percent and over on blocks of tickets, with the result that it was actually the actors who ended up making the fund-raising contributions. Still another problem was that when a company felt they had found a hit show, they grabbed it and played it throughout a season; a faithful theatergoer couldn't attend more than once that year even if he wanted to (after all, the Broadway practice of long runs is geared to a much larger number of potential customers). This attrition of the repertory system, in its turn, reduced playwrights' opportunities to see their works produced and weakened the Yiddish actors' traditional flexibility in switching from role to role and type to type.

The way the actors organized themselves as wage earners tended ultimately to sabotage Yiddish theater as a viable business. Already in the nineteenth century, partly in response to the star system, Yiddish actors had begun to organize into unions. In the 1880s a small group struck successfully against

In a 1927 poster for *Oy, Iz Dos a Meydl! (Oy, What a Girl!)* Molly Picon surveys her Lower East Side domain. On tour in Buenos Aires the play was billed as *Que Muchacha!*

Goldfadn. Then in the 1887–88 season, the Hebrew Actors Union formed its Local No.1. During that period the Lower East Side was seething with labor movements, so it is no accident that this was the first actors' union in America. In fact, it was the third labor union (as opposed to brotherhood) to be founded in the United States; the first two were the typographers and the (non-Yiddish) chorus members. Actors Equity did not exist yet. The first American actors' labor organization was a group who called themselves the White Rats, and when they went out on strike in 1900, Yiddish actors went uptown to help picket Broadway and brought the strikers coffee and doughnuts. (Soon the Italians, Germans, and Hungarians organized too, indicating the lively ethnic cultures of New York's immigrant communities; the Italian Actors brotherhood still exists.)

The development of the Hebrew Actors Union was sometimes complicated because the atmosphere in the Yiddish theater was so much like a big disorganized family that directors and managers and stars could also join, at least temporarily. (Actors still enter and leave the union, depending on whether they are entrepreneurs or employees in any one season.) Naturally, the aims of the star-managers ran counter to everything the new union tried to work for. Furthermore, blood loyalties complicated the action, as when Jacob P. Adler appealed to his daughter Celia to save him by substituting for his striking leading lady. Later the union censured her as a scab, but after all, as she explained, how could she refuse her own father?

There were too many pressures for unionizing for the movement to remain weak. The mark system had degenerated. Payment by marks or salaries was often desperately low—though unionizing was never to bring much improvement on that score. Employment was uncertain from one season—almost one month—to the next. As stars controlled the companies, lower actors had fewer chances to try different roles. With the solidification of American Yiddish theater's commercial basis, it took more capital for an actor to organize his own venture. Companies competing for the public kept bringing over new talents, so that even though potential audiences increased with immigration, there were proportionately many more actors competing for work in 1900 than there had been ten years before. Another reason for organizing was that with time these actors seem to have been developing a growing consciousness of themselves as professionals, even as artists. Unionizing was one expression of that feeling.

In 1902 Local No.2 of the Hebrew Actors Union appeared, with jurisdiction over traveling companies. Meanwhile Local No.1 grew stronger and stronger. It could impose terms on managers—though, ironically, sometimes such terms as demanding salaries instead of marks actually lowered the actors'

Menashe Skulnik clowns in the center of a chorus line for the cheerfully silly musical comedy *The Scotsman of Orchard Street.* Orchard Street is in the heart of the Lower East Side.

pay. Just as significantly for the state of Yiddish theater, it could impose a tightly closed shop and keep newcomers out of the union.

Soon a so-called Chinese Wall enclosed the fortunate members of Local No.1. Actors were not allowed even to apply for membership till they had played several years outside New York City. This was lucky for provincial audiences, but frustrating for ambitious actors; Atlanta and Toronto were far from the bright lights and often, too, far from family and friends. Once the actor got permission to apply, and paid the application fee, he came to the Hebrew Actors Union headquarters on East Seventh Street to "audition" for the membership.

On a little stage in the upstairs meeting room he presented two or three numbers, of which one was in his specialty: a comic song, a tragic tirade, or whatever. Then the members voted by secret ballot. Very, very few candidates passed. Maurice Schwartz failed repeatedly. Herman Yablokoff, who later became union president, failed his first audition. According to legend, Danny Kaye failed, and Stella Adler swooned gracefully under the ordeal and had to be revived on the spot three times in a row. By the second decade of the century, fat old men and women were playing *yeshive* boys and gypsy maidens, while young actors prowled outside the Chinese Wall, and audiences began to snicker. The same situation prevailed inside and outside the Jewish Chorus Union of Singers and Dancers.

From 1903, Local No.5 represented some of the actors who couldn't get into No.1, as well as performers in vaudeville, which was just ending its heyday. Eventually there was also a Local No.18. In 1922 the actors' locals merged under the guidance of Reuben Guskin, a former barber. Guskin served his union's short-term interests passionately for many years, as when he pressured a reluctant producer first into rehiring a certain mediocre actor for the coming season, and then into giving the actor a raise, for everyone else in the company was getting a raise and "it would be a sin to shame him." Guskin had fed the actor's family for one more season. But he had done no good to the quality of the theater.

In addition, the unions were hobbling the theater which was their livelihood, in their short-sighted attempt to guarantee jobs for all. In the 1930s, for example, when Herman Yablokoff produced an operetta, thirteen separate unions presented him with their regular demands. He had to hire at least nine stagehands, ten musicians (a minimum even for nonmusical dramas), three dressers, ten ushers, two doormen for the ground-floor entrance and one for the balcony, two cashiers, a benefit manager, a general manager, a Yiddish publicity agent (an English agent would be extra), a special policeman to keep order in the box office line (even when nobody was buying tickets), superintendents, bill posters, printers, scene painters, ten choristers, and sixteen actors. In other words, he had to have a hit merely to cover all those salaries. (Unions have of course created similar problems for English-language theaters and newspapers.)

The Yiddish-speaking community, especially immigrant communities like New York, was almost entirely proletarian. Rising out of the working class almost invariably involved adjustment out of that community and into a non-Yiddish-speaking culture. So literally only "the people" were left to support Yiddish theater, to support professional actors, to provide shelter for a stage by providing actors with the money to rent one. The professional Yiddish theater was itself proletarian and truly "popular," in that it labored for daily bread and had to make its art out of that labor. Naturally, that material circumstance was an organic factor in shaping that art, and in binding art and public together.

From inside the Chinese Wall, the thrust of the Hebrew Actors Union, like that of every other organization dedicated to securing its members' livelihoods, was toward commercial success: pleasing the crowd and selling tickets. Inevitably that meant popular rather than intellectual theater.

As the community weakened around it, popular theater held its own, for the masses still enjoyed it and the stars still exerted their magic power over the mass imagination. Besides, as more and more Jews spoke English and knew their way around New York, all that Second Avenue could offer them that Broadway and Hollywood could not was precisely popular theater at its lowest and most accessible: the voluptuous sentimentality of (in Artef's scathing denunciation of old commercial theater) "Oy, *mamele,*" "a Jewish girl needs a Jewish boy," and "Zion our crown." The average age of the audiences crept upward; they were the Jews who remembered the old country of their youth, or who lived in the suburbs and remembered the Lower East Side of their youth. In a play, they loved best any allusion to matchmakers, pushcarts, old wives' spells against the evil eye, even juicy old curses, and it didn't matter what the plot context might be. For them, those "Oy, *mamele*" plays were an affirmation of their cultural roots, their very identity. Part of what *shund* seems to be, as opposed to art, is just such simplistic and self-congratulatory reinforcement of values. A scene in which a Jewish girl chooses a Jewish boy over the gentile whistling for her from his motorcycle in her parents' driveway is a ritual affirmation of self, and it is none the less effective—perhaps it is *more* effective—when in reality the spectators live very differently from their own *mamele,* eat pork, and hear the motorcycle revving up outside the window for the neighbor's daughter, or their own.

Nevertheless, in the face of the dissolution of the old Yiddish community and the sinking proportion of serious dramatic efforts to popular entertainments, community leaders—the American version of the old *kehile*—continued to conceive of Yiddish theater as having a cultural mission and to feel some responsibility for its preservation. They even tried to use the theater as a bulwark against the tide, hoping to lure young people into Yiddish theater as a way of linking them with Yiddish culture. Plays like *Green Fields* portrayed pious old country people and could serve as an educational glimpse of grandfather's world. Unconsciously such leaders seemed further to hope that the warm intimacy that the Yiddish theater experience still held for them might also envelop American youngsters and teach them Yiddish by osmosis.

In Detroit in 1942, for example, a committee of local rabbis and laymen set up a Jewish Theater Guild. The Guild sponsored a free "art evening," presented by Jacob Ben-Ami, Bertha Gersten, Jacob Mestel, Max Bozyk, Leah Noemi, and Ben Bonus. Soon afterward the Guild presented a young people's matinee of *Green Fields* directed by Ben-Ami, again free, and a performance of Pinski's *Yankl the Blacksmith.* Advertisements were put out in Yiddish and English about a forthcoming production, also to be directed by Ben-Ami, but the Guild must have run out of money, or energy, or both, for it never took place. Similarly, the philanthropist Jacob R. Schiff bought the Public Theatre on Second Avenue in 1940 and gave it to the Hebrew Actors Union so that it would remain a home for Yiddish theater. That undertaking collapsed soon after Pearl Harbor, when audiences didn't feel like going to the theater, Yiddish or otherwise. In 1949 the Jewish community of Milwaukee made a gesture of solidarity with Yiddish literature by sponsoring the Perhift amateur theater in a performance of H. Leivick's *Bankrupt;* the occasion was the author's birthday, and he came west for the occasion.

As late as 1955, a major alliance of the Yiddish newspapers and the major social and political organizations of New York (the Jewish National Workers' Organization, the Joint Board of Amalgamated Unions, the Workmen's Circle, the Yiddish Theatrical Alliance, WEVD radio, and others) got together to subsidize a revival of Maurice Schwartz's Yiddish Art Theater, which had gone under in 1950 after thirty-one years of continuous service. They held meetings and drew up bylaws. The alliance was to handle the finances and leave Schwartz free to be artistic director. They were creating, at last, a subsidized community art theater. They even guaranteed Schwartz himself a minimum wage. Almost four hundred people subscribed for season tickets. However, an unsuccessful first play, politicking over repertory, and even bickering over seating at the premiere, destroyed the attempt only twelve weeks through the season. Debate immediately filled the Yiddish press over just whose fault the failure was.

In the face of the dissolution of the American Yiddish-speaking community, Yiddish theater artists continued to follow their instincts to survive and to maintain themselves as a community. They couldn't follow their audiences to the suburbs. But appropriately for their traditional function on the Lower East Side, they evolved into a sort of microcosm of the old, highly organized Yiddish society, either the East European *shtetl* or the Lower East Side. As relatives (or ex-relatives, by divorce), as co-workers, rivals, and friends, their personal relationships wove complicated patterns that stretched over several continents and over generations. They remained almost as interdependent as the inhabitants of an isolated village. Through their unions and clubs, they provided each other with funds for hospitalization, burial, and other community benefits. They set up purely social organizations as well.

The Yiddish Theatrical Alliance developed from a group founded in 1917 by two dressers. Dressers see actors at their most intimate, and the organization was meant to help artists with problems, especially financial emergencies, and to provide insurance and burial plots. They named the group Cousins, signifying that the theatrical profession was one big family, and opened the membership to actors, musicians, chorus singers, composers, playwrights, cashiers, producers, publicists, stage mechanics, ushers, dressers, and hairdressers. Its executive secretary for half a century was the exuberant song-and-dance

פריינד בלײבען פריינד -
שיקאגאער חברים "
·June 8th 1932·

"Friends remain friends"—the motto of the "Chicagoans" club of theater people, among whose founders was Muni Weisenfreund (Paul Muni), celebrating fourth from the left on the far side of the table.

man Charlie Cohen. Its secretary was his wife Rose Pivar, the indispensably businesslike secretary to the director of the Hebrew Actors Union.

In 1935 Paul Muni and several other actors formed a group called Mir Chikager (We Chicagoans), to help actors who had been stranded on the road, usually by unscrupulous managers, to get home. Later it changed its name to Yiddish Artists and Friends and expanded its functions, publishing a monthly bulletin in Yiddish and English, arranging special performances by members and guests, and assuming neighborly responsibility for members, such as visiting the sick.

The Hebrew Actors Union itself had always had a clubhouse where members had played cards and gossiped, drunk tea or something stronger, and had kept papers and a modest library. The labor leaders Joseph Barondes and Samuel Gompers were among the outsiders who liked to drop in from time to time. But the original clubhouse was disbanded because the gambling had become too serious.

For a long time the actors were comfortable in other headquarters. The Lower East Side had hundreds of small cafés for a little food, a drink, and a lot of talk, and several cafés were especially favored by actors and by those who wanted to watch their idols at play. There was Boym's on Broome Street,

Markiz's at Grand and Forsyth, Shtark's at Second and Houston, the Mono-
pole on Ninth Street. Of these the most glamorous was the Café Royale on
Second Avenue at Twelfth Street, opposite the Yiddish Art Theater. When
an actor arrived in America, that's where he went to make his contacts. Edwin
Relkin, for decades a powerful agent and producer though he knew no Yiddish, used the telephone number at the Café Royale as his office phone. An
unknown actor trying to impress big actors went outside and placed a call to
himself, so that everyone would hear him paged by the doleful waiter who—
according to legend—became a secret millionaire on the tips he earned bringing people to the telephone. The Broadway play *Café Crown*, written by Hy
Kraft and produced in 1942, was set in, and based on, the Café Royale.

In 1945 the Café Royale went out of business. Only a club in the union
itself could come near to replacing it, so the Yiddish Actors Club formed in
the union headquarters. It provided actors with a kitchen, tables to play
pinochle and drink tea, and a little library.

There the American actors sat, uncensored and unpersecuted. In 1920,
1930, 1940, 1950, they kept on trouping, making up, and bowing. But audiences diminished.

In 1959 I saw Maurice Schwartz perform a full-house matinee of *Tevye
the Dairyman* at the dignified Forrest Theater in Philadelphia. His Yiddish
Art Theater had collapsed nine years earlier. I had never seen Yiddish theater
before, and I didn't understand all the words, but it seemed to be very corny,
very dark, and very good. In the scene where the bearded old man, broken by
adversity, sat on a low stool downstage, surrounded by shadows, mourning for
his daughter who had run off with a Russian, muttering prayers in a basso
whisper and nodding to himself through awful silences, my grandmother and
I sobbed quietly but heartily into a single soggy handkerchief, which we passed
back and forth between us.

Once the bows and applause were over, the curtain speech was as sad as
the play. Schwartz gave it all his fireworks.

"Keep Yiddish alive!" he thundered, and crooned, and his eyes flashed.

He got an ovation. But I looked around, and to my young eyes I was the
only one in the entire building under fifty.

11 POLAND BETWEEN THE WARS

IT WOULD SEEM IMPOSSIBLE that Yiddish theater could survive, much less thrive, surrounded by the miseries of Eastern and Central Europe in the 1920s and 1930s. In the aftermath of World War I, people were starving. Once, indeed, a scuffle broke out at a Yiddish theater in Poland when an actor was supposed to be eating a meal onstage and the audience suspected that he'd somehow got hold of real meat. The actor addressed them directly. "My dear friends," he assured them, "I only wish it were true."

Politically and economically, people were at the mercy of constantly shifting pressures, which could be neither predicted nor controlled. Typically, during one performance of a Yiddish play at the Lencri Theater in Paris in 1934 (a period when many refugees were passing through France, often illegally), somebody hissed from the wings that policemen were on the way to check the actors' visas. Visas were so expensive, and validating them required so much red tape and so much luck, that of all the actors in the cast only one, Zygmund Turkow, actually had official permission to work in France. When the policemen walked in, Turkow was alone left onstage, and for the rest of the evening the entire play of three acts and a dozen characters was rendered as a solo.

On a larger scale, the life of an entire town could be disoriented by political upheavals. Vilna, for example, changed regimes four times during 1939 and 1940, as Poland, Lithuania, the Soviet Union, and Germany captured the area and lost it again. For Yiddish theater in Vilna, this meant violent changes practically overnight. The Polish regime allowed Yiddish theater, under a strict system of permits and censorship. Lithuania and the Soviet Union established officially subsidized and controlled state theaters. The fourth and final regime, the German, set up the Vilna ghetto, where some theater went on, and then killed actors and audiences together.

In Eastern Europe especially, Jews were defenseless against the force of the political maelstrom. At the end of World War I (a century after Poland had been divided up among stronger neighbors), the Allies restored territory from Germany, White Russia, and the Ukraine, making Poland the fifth-largest state in Europe and the ruler of over three million Jews. In 1920 Pilsudski's army invaded the Ukraine, initiating several years of fighting in the area (formerly the Pale of Settlement), which was especially full of Jews. The massacres of local populations plus the years of unrest and rioting eventually took a toll of hundreds of thousands of Eastern European Jewish lives. During the Polish elections of 1922, as anti-Semitic feelings rose higher and higher, Jewish cemeteries were desecrated and Jews beaten up on the streets. Orthodox Jews' beards were sheared off or pulled out of the flesh by the roots. In 1936 the regime ordered the few Jewish university students who were left after quotas had been drastically reduced to sit on separate "ghetto benches" along the sides of the classrooms.

The economic effects of anti-Semitism comprised a "cold pogrom." Beginning in 1923, the Polish government retracted the subsidies to Yiddish schools and welfare organizations which it had promised to them—as to all national minorities—under the 1918 peace treaty. The government took over the industries with the highest proportion of Jewish owners and put Jews out of civil service jobs and government contracts. Unemployment became disastrously high, and was further heightened by the thousands of people displaced during the war—evacuated and repatriated, spilling eastward and westward by the thousands. People out of work not only failed to feed themselves, but they also could not give their patronage to Jewish businesses, which every day collapsed. In the mid-1920's, out of 3,000 tailoring businesses owned by Polish Jews, 2,560 had closed. By 1931, as the Great Depression spread over Europe, one out of three Polish Jews belonged to families whose head was unemployed. In 1936 the Cardinal Primate of Poland urged a total boycott of Jewish businesses. Disease followed on the heels of poverty. Four-fifths of Vilna's Jewish schoolchildren had TB or anemia. A study showed that almost half the Jewish schoolboys in Grodno were seriously undernourished.

In Rumania the story was similar. The 1918 treaty made her the largest Balkan state, with a large Jewish population. Her new territory, carved out of southeastern Russia, was the home of almost all modern Yiddish Rumanian literature. The new government promptly denationalized 200,000 Jews who couldn't prove ten years' continuous residence, leaving them without homes or citizenship anywhere. It systematically starved out the Jewish school system,

welfare services, and all the other institutions to which it had pledged autonomy and financial support. It nationalized the industries many Jews had owned
or been employed in, squeezed students out of the universities, tacitly encouraged pogroms and attacks on the streets. It forbade posting notices in Yiddish,
and it taxed Yiddish theater enterprises so highly that for years most Yiddish
theater was disguised as cabaret entertainment in teahouses.

Nevertheless, professional Yiddish actors kept on trouping. Their persist-
ence is inexplicable—unless it was an unconscious reaction to the very oppressions that should have extinguished them. They played at the dingy Lencri
in Paris, with its public men's room opening off the stage; in Brussels, where
the feeble Yiddish press tried unsuccessfully to set up a system of ticket-buying
by subscription; and in Vienna, where the *kehile* did its best to give them a
little support and encouragement. They played in Budapest, where Béla Kun's
regime subsidized a Yiddish theater for several years immediately following
World War I. They played in Bratislava on the Danube, in a kosher restaurant,
on a makeshift stage "as big as a yawn." The more venturesome among them
found audiences in small villages deep in the Carpathians. When they toured
Yugoslavia, the government helped them survive by granting them, as well as
other troupes of foreign actors on tour, special lenient tax arrangements.

Farther east, though the anti-Semitism was even more destructive, there
was even more Yiddish theater. In the Soviet Union, as we have seen, a
network of Yiddish theaters under the eye of the Central Committee was
developing as an essentially self-contained universe with its own dangers and
triumphs. Rumanian actors, often organized in small family troupes, wandered
the Rumanian countryside, as did Yiddish actors on tour from other countries.
However, the area of Eastern Europe outside the Soviet where Yiddish theater
reached its peak in the period between the two world wars was Poland, the
territory to which the Jews of the Rhineland had migrated in the twelfth
century, bringing their Germanic language with them.

Within Poland there were many nuclei of Yiddish theatrical activity.
Zygmund Turkow's memoirs of his years touring with his wife Ida Kaminska
record that even in the smallest and muddiest of provincial towns, they and
their repertory of literary dramas were welcomed by the local *kultur-tuers,*
literary club members, and theater *patriótn.* In Cracow, where for several years
the city gave five thousand zlotys to support Yiddish theater, the Friends of
Yiddish Theater organized competitions among Jewish artists for set designs
for new productions. The Lodz *kehile* helped out the Vilna Troupe when they
came through, and donated occasional subsidies to other companies. The
Lemberg Jewish community made similar contributions. Bialystok, Grodno,
and other cities had at least one professional Yiddish theater company per-

forming for them during most of the year. But the two primary capitals of Polish Yiddish culture were Vilna and Warsaw.

Vilna, known affectionately as "the Jerusalem of Lithuania," was awesomely intellectual. The Vilna Troupe made its debut there in 1920. It was in Vilna in 1925 that a new international organization was founded to promote Yiddish scholarship: the Yiddish Institute for Jewish Research (acronym in Yiddish, YIVO). In 1928 a club called the Friends of Yiddish Theater formed there and within a year boasted over five hundred dues-paying members, a number that eventually rose to seven hundred. They acquired a renovated circus building, and for a few years they got twelve hundred zlotys annually from the city as well as three hundred from the Vilna *kehile*. The Friends supported Yiddish theater spiritually as well as financially. They organized trips to the theater by youth and labor clubs; they arranged lectures and adult classes, coordinated with productions and often held in Vilna's own museum of Yiddish theater; they put out special publications and held competitions for scholarly works about Yiddish theater. In the 1930s Vilna was the home of a group of powerful young writers who called themselves *Yung Vilne* (Young Vilna). (Many of them died in the Vilna ghetto, but Chaim Grade and Wolf Younin are now writing in New York and Avrom Sutzkever edits the Yiddish literary magazine *Di Goldene Keyt* in Israel.) In the course of a single year, 1935, Vilna had the opportunity to see fifteen professional Yiddish theater companies.

The atmosphere of Warsaw was more sophisticated and worldly than Vilna's. It had many more residents enjoying its big-city excitement, and 40 percent of them were Jewish. Warsaw had many artists, many intellectuals, many cafés, and many entertainments of the spectacular sort that in New York are associated with Broadway. Even though theater buildings were in short supply in Warsaw, due to military requisitioning and the spread of movie houses, Yiddish theater between the world wars found a number of homes there: the Kaminsky Theater, the Eliseum, the Central, the Eldorado, the Venus, the Scala, as well as smaller stages in halls or restaurants and the many cabarets.

The Nowósci, a fancy new theater building which Warsaw acquired in 1926, housed primarily Yiddish theater, and is an example of the degree of economic stability and the glamour that the Warsaw Yiddish theater attained. The Nowósci was a plush place. One of the biggest theaters in Warsaw, it seated some two thousand, with room for them to stretch their legs. It had a roomy backstage area, fancy lighting equipment, two balcony levels with elegant buffets. It was handy to the heart of the Jewish neighborhood, the so-called *gas* (literally "street"), as well as to the areas where the Jewish

Nowósci Theater, soon after it was built in Warsaw in 1926. The facade extends out into wings with side entrances, and the roof of the auditorium is visible rising behind the facade.

intelligentsia gathered, and even to those favored by Jews who had assimilated. A long and varied list of Yiddish theater enterprises visited the Nowósci from its opening until the war broke out. And though the management went briefly bankrupt in 1931, the Nowósci soon gathered its fortunes together and continued to prosper.

The Nowósci is an indication that the Yiddish community of Poland had all the elements necessary for the coalescing of a full "national" theater. Despite political and economic troubles, there was a reasonable demographic stability. Warsaw and other cities could generally produce audiences in sufficient numbers; and there was a substantial identifiable cadre of professional people. Culturally the Polish Yiddish community had achieved a strong sense of itself. Through a confluence of rich, disparate forces, the community now brought into focus the didacticism of *haskole* and the folkiness of *hasidism;* the self-affirmation both of religious tradition and of Zionism; the earnestness of the Bund and of other political movements; the intimacy of the Purim play; and the energy of the Broder singers' cabaret. The Polish Yiddish community had a language; in fact, that language's literary possibilities were still in the process of expanding. History brought all these elements together in a fruitful balance—for a moment.

Artistically the Polish Yiddish theater had joined the mainstream of Western culture, for it shared the repertory as well as the writing and staging techniques of the European theater, including the European avant-garde.

"European" came to be a loaded adjective. It referred to an intention to succeed artistically by cosmopolitan standards—as applied to anything from Hamlet's "To be or not to be" to a fastidiously elegant cabaret number— rather than to succeed by milking *Yiddishkayt.* It also meant a "literary" or "better" play, such as Strindberg's *The Father,* and specifically one that was translated from another language into Yiddish and concerned non-Jewish characters.

"European" also referred to a kind of theater approach practiced by the more serious European theaters. The term was associated with Stanislavskian principles: ensemble work rather than the old domination by stars; respect for the play text as literature; discussion and analysis of the play before rehearsals began; and strong leadership by a director with a distinct conception of the production.

Shortly before World War I, a critic for a Warsaw Yiddish daily had commented apropos of a current offering: "The overall impression is that we have good talented actors, but on the stage confusion reigns. Everyone does what he wants. There is no direction." And in fact in the lower sorts of Yiddish theater the director never did replace the kind of star who, according to tradition, tells his company: "Stand to the side, don't trip over your feet, and talk loud and fast; leave the acting to me." Nevertheless, in the early 1920s in Poland, Yiddish theater acquired its own group of young "European" directors committed to "European" Yiddish theater: David Herman (the first director in the Peretz Hirschbein troupe as early as 1908, the director of *The Dybbuk* and other plays for the Vilna Troupe, and director of ambitious amateur companies in Warsaw, Stanislovov, and other places), Moyshe Lipman, Yankev Rotboym, and Jonas Turkow. In Rumania Yankev Sternberg directed the Bucharest Yiddish Theater Studio and other projects.

Polish Yiddish theater repertory benefited from the new attitude that Yiddish intellectuals developed toward their own culture. By the 1920s Polish Yiddish culture had matured sufficiently to conceive of its traditions as raw material, to be used freely for artistic purposes. In 1919 Anski put *The Dybbuk* together from folklore he had gathered in Ukrainian *shtetlekh.* Itsik Manger rewrote the *megile* and created a sensation with his cozily modernized, quaintly lyrical Purim play, conceived as though presented by latter-day tailors' apprentices. His *megile* characters were transplanted from their original Persian palace to an Eastern European *shtetl.* Proud in her silk dress and crinoline, Queen Vashti refuses to dance naked for an assemblage of kings sporting top hats and watch fobs; her homely un-Biblical excuse is that she has a toothache. She is led off to execution, lamenting that she disregarded the advice of her father, a *pan* (Polish gentleman), in order to marry King Ahashuerus, who is a drunk with a red nose. Queen Esther's young true love moons outside the palace, recalling how he begged her to brave the disapproval of her stern Uncle Mordecai and run away with him to Vienna, where he would have bought her a string of red coral beads. (This modern *Purimshpil* was delightfully staged in 1972, first in Tel Aviv and then in North and South America.)

Partly as a result of this new attitude toward traditional material, professional Yiddish theater artists now found themselves in possession of a wider repertory than they had realized. By the 1920s Yiddish theater had established its own basic canon of dramatic classics which could be revived, experimented with, interpreted in individual ways. Goldfadn, for example, was no longer simply old-fashioned. He'd been dead long enough that now he could again be dealt with. The 1920s and 1930s brought several enthusiastic and lavish productions of *Koldunye; or, The Witch*—one by Manger, with three Hotsmakhs (instead of one) to protect little Mirele against the wicked sorceress. The period also brought the first production in a generation of *Loy Sakhmoyd* (*The Tenth Commandment*, or *Ashmodai*), politically updated by employing the good and bad angels as symbols for democracy and fascism; the play appeared at GOSET in Moscow and at Maurice Schwartz's Yiddish Art Theater in New York as well as in Poland. In this period Etinger's *haskole* play *Serkele* received its very first professional production; the character of the author himself, dead a century, came onstage in an old-fashioned frock coat and top hat to read his prologue. Professionals and amateurs performed dramatizations of works Mendele Moykher Sforim had written long before his death in 1917.

Not only did the time lapse allow enough detachment to make use of these older staples of Yiddish drama, but a sort of nostalgia for the old ways evoked by old plays swayed an audience that didn't really remember them. *The Two Kuni-Lemls* was now purely a comedy about quaint *hasidim* and not an indictment of repressive *hasidic* customs. *The Dybbuk* was perceived as having been written not by a traditional Jew, but by one who had traveled about investigating disappearing folkways. Even a play by Lateiner suddenly seemed to have its charms for sophisticated eyes.

In the period between the two world wars, Polish Yiddish theater came closer than it ever had before to taking itself for granted as an institution in the natural context of its own traditions and especially its language. The era when it was necessary to prove that a Yiddish-language theater could exist was long past; the era when it would be necessary to prove that it still existed had not yet arrived.

Yiddish was simply a living language, a natural medium for a community's theater. Linguistic purity was still an important criterion for Yiddish art

Regine Zuker and Karl Tsimbalist in an unidentified musical comedy at the Lencri Theater in Paris in the 1930s.

theaters. However, Yiddish-speaking audiences were rather flexible about which language they would go to see theater in; often they understood Polish, Russian, German, or French—or all of them—so going to Yiddish theater was only one of their options. Conversely, Poles, Germans, Rumanians, and Russians sometimes came to Yiddish theater when there was an artistic experiment they'd heard about or a pretty actress whose picture they'd seen on posters. An American Yiddish company actually flopped at the Nowósci in the 1930s because the comedy they brought, originally done on Broadway, had already been a smash in Warsaw the season before; Jews and non-Jews alike had already seen it in Polish.

Similarly, many actors, such as Paul Baratoff, Rudolph Schildkraut, and Alexander Granach, had no special loyalty to Yiddish theater. They played in Yiddish as they did in Polish, Russian, or German—because it was theater. (Many Jewish actors, as opposed to Yiddish actors, made careers exclusively on the non-Yiddish stage.) And some non-Jews worked in Yiddish theaters for the same reason. Several of the sets on the Nowósci stage were designed by Polish artists. The important Polish director Leon Schiller directed Shakespeare's *The Tempest* in Yiddish at the Nowósci in 1939, one of the last productions there and one of the most ambitious.

Polish Yiddish theater further included hundreds of amateur groups, some so earnest that they hired professionals to guide them. This extraordinary number reflected the activity of hundreds of literary clubs, chorus groups, and adult education series, and the publication of hundreds of novels and poems. The ideals and personnel nourished by the amateur movement began to influence the professional theater with the kind of Russian seriousness that had previously been only for amateurs.

Audiences at professional Yiddish theater could see two-bit comedians in *The Rabbi's Dancing Daughter* or off-key prima donnas in *A Silent Heart; or, The Broken Vow*, drearily jigging in front of a primitive backdrop. At the other extreme, they could see the "European" efforts of the Vilna Troupe, the touring Moscow Yiddish State Art Theater, or the VYKT company, led by Ida Kaminska and Zygmund Turkow. True, professional theater remained a business, so professional actors kept on scrambling and hustling, hoping for a big *schlager* (hit) to carry them awhile and pay off their debts. Still, professional companies managed to bring at least one serious production per season to most of the larger East European cities, and people did buy tickets.

"European" Stars

A sampling of the actors who played at the Nowósci exemplifies the range of Yiddish actors of high quality in Poland in the years between the two world wars. Dr. Paul (or Pavel, or Ben-Zvi) Baratoff, who in 1926 was the first Yiddish star to appear on the Nowósci stage, had already established himself as a Russian actor before he could speak a word of Yiddish.

Raised in a Jewish family that spoke only Russian, Baratoff went to medical school and joined a Russian amateur theatrical club. He practiced medicine in the clinic in the daytime, and performed at night. Eventually he turned to professional Russian theater, but after the revolution he left Russia and ended up, by way of Constantinople, in Vienna. There, perhaps in an attempt to find new roots so far from home, he joined the fine local semiprofessional Freie Yidishe Folksbiene. For his debut, in a play by Gordin, he managed to learn a total of thirty Yiddish words. He used a pseudonym for a long time, till evidently he considered that Yiddish theater had become an institution of sufficient solidity and worth to deserve his professional association. He wandered continually, visiting Rumania, where his special success was as Kobrin's Yankl Boyle, the Village Youth, appearing with Maurice Schwartz in New York and Philadelphia, and acting in Berlin with Erwin Piscator's adventurously experimental company, speaking Yiddish while the others spoke German.

When Baratoff played Strindberg's *The Father* and other European plays in 1926 at the Nowósci, his Yiddish had improved considerably. It still wasn't his strongest language, but audiences were tolerant, and in any case a Russian accent carried glamorous intellectual associations. One anecdote recalls Baratoff in a scene with the Russian-Jewish actress Lydia Potoska. Both were struggling along in Yiddish. Instead of asking her; "Are you agreed [*maskim*]?" he evidently inquired: "Are you Maxim?" And she gravely agreed that yes, she was Maxim. Potoska, too, though she had intelligence and a charming smile, never did master Yiddish. Four years later she played Mirele Efros at the Nowósci, and Yiddish critics advised her to stay away from typically Jewish heroines. She just wasn't convincing, they said. She should stick to European plays.

Another figure who represented the "European" heights to which Yiddish theater was climbing was Avrom Morevsky, an actor, director, and writer. A monumentally big man, Morevsky managed to look not only dignified—even stately—but also gentle and endearingly well fed. He was extremely erudite, writing essays about theater and translating plays into Yiddish. As an actor, a former member of the Vilna Troupe, he felt his way slowly toward his characterizations till he arrived at a fine creation, which he was then able to maintain no matter how often he repeated the role. Morevsky relied always on his intelligence, rather than on his voice or temperament. For his thirty-year jubilee in the Yiddish theater, his home city of Vilna prepared a major celebration; the versatile author Moyshe Broderson wrote a play called *Shylock Laughs,* in honor of Morevsky's special interest in Shakespeare; and the Vilna Friends of Yiddish Theater put out a book of his essays, entitled *Shylock and Shakespeare.*

An entirely different type of actor was Isaac or Yitskhok Samberg or Zandberg, the delight and despair of Yiddish directors and critics and the darling of Warsaw audiences. Samberg's face in repose was stern and dark, skull-like, with a prominent jaw. He looked older than he was, and his friend Shmuel Landau, a sensitive, extremely intellectual actor who often worked with Samberg, referred to him as "the young guy with the bald spot." (Samberg called Landau, who looked younger than his gray hair indicated, "the kid with the dyed head.") Samberg was lively, warm-hearted, a hearty fellow, quick at snappy retorts and spicy jokes. He got into angry arguments and waved his hands around wildly. He had begun as a boy in the troupe of Ester Rokhl Kaminska, being distantly related to her husband, who billed young Samberg as the "Boy with the Bass Fiddle." The public considered Samberg a folk actor, one of their own.

Samberg was, in fact, a wonderful actor. He had, above all, inexhaustible energy. When he came home from long tours in Europe and America, his colleagues were awed to see that the traveling hadn't tired him; on the contrary, he appeared refreshed and immediately began preparing for a new season in Warsaw. Quite uneducated, he was clever at rehearsals, and he was also conscientious and hard-working. On opening night he was always ready with a skillful, powerful characterization. But as the play continued to run, he tended to let himself go, using his big voice for bigger and bigger effects, using his temperament for more and more sensational scenes, until he had un-balanced the play. The role had become Isaac Samberg, and indeed, so had the play.

One outlet for Samberg's ebullience was union organization. Yiddish ac-tors had begun to unionize as soon as Germany occupied Eastern Europe during World War I. A first stab came in Lodz in 1915. In 1916 a major Warsaw daily published a call to organize under this heading: "Yiddish ar-tistes, where are you?" The writer, an actor named Zishe Katz, implored his colleagues to pull themselves together through the difficult war years and prepare realistically for the future:

> even in the most peaceful and normal times, we were always without a founda-tion under our feet or a roof over over heads, like gypsies who sleep tonight in a different place from last night and never know where their tomorrow will be. We were the same old Vagabond Stars [a reference to Sholem Aleichem's novel], disorganized free-flying birds. . . .

Unionization had been attempted before, based on the Russian actors' pat-tern,

> but in the end nothing came of it. Do you know why? Even there there was trouble over "casting the parts.". . . But never mind, what's past is past. Now in Lodz, "in a blessed hour," all set down in black and white, is an organization named the Lodz Yiddish Artistes' Union. A little while ago that union's organiz-ers came to Warsaw and started to found a union which would naturally be the central organization for all Yiddish actors, since Warsaw has after all always been the center of Yiddish theater and Yiddish artists in Poland and Russia.

Katz documented that even in the Warsaw meeting, however, there was organizational trouble; like the rehearsals of old-time wandering troupes:

> You meet for a rehearsal and instead of rehearsing you set up a second rehearsal. At the second meeting you postpone rehearsing till a third. At the third you don't bother talking about it, and nobody shows up for a fourth.

The real organizational meeting got under way at last, on a bench in the Saxon Gardens, the park where Peretz still took his evening strolls. But the whole project subsided once more. In 1918, impelled by the large number of actors among the refugees being repatriated from Russia back to Poland, the union formed again. It even had its first strike, in which the head of the union confronted the head of the company he acted in, who happened also to be his father-in-law. Although the strike failed, the union was on its way.

To one of these organizing conventions that took place in Kiev, Mendele Moykher Sforim sent a congratulatory letter, which was printed in the union's periodical. He was sorry he couldn't be with them, as a parent feels sorry to miss his child's *simkhe* (celebration). Mendele expanded the sentimental metaphor with gusto. After a difficult youth, his child, the Yiddish theater, was now celebrating its marriage to the Yiddish public. He sent them a *mazel tov*, a *lekhayim* toast of wine mixed with a happy tear, and hoped to celebrate the joys of their children.

The union aimed to help actors find work. It protected their salaries and working conditions. It looked out for other benefits, including an education fund for needy members' children. It also tried to protect actors against the pressures of amateur groups who in some towns extorted a bribe to allow touring professionals to play, or kept them out of the local theater building.

The union also had aims apart from bread and butter. It was pledged to maintaining a "better" repertory—not *shund*—though this was hard to enforce or even define. It wanted to maintain standards of talent and character among actors, especially screening the "war actors"—nonactors who had taken advantage of increased audiences and decreased personnel to start trouping. In honor of Ester Rokhl Kaminska, it sponsored a theater museum connected with YIVO; the museum was dedicated in 1922 at a ceremony celebrating the actress's thirty years in Yiddish theater. It published a journal. And its headquarters at 2 Leszno Street, near that of the writers' union, was a clubhouse for tea, cigarettes, cards, and gossip.

To enter the union a candidate had to present three letters of recommendation from theater people, writers, or other *kultur-tuers*. He had to pass examinations in acting and Yiddish literature. Sometimes would-be members could speak Yiddish, but could read and write only Polish. They needed special permission from the union to work while they studied for admission. Then only after two years on probation was a candidate finally tested and accepted. The union got after amateur or semiprofessional groups that were performing as commercial ventures and pressured them to join. A considerable number of actors and entertainers got along without ever joining the union, however, which may well have been weaker and less formal than one could guess from its official statements. But in 1936, at the nineteenth mass meeting, the membership was 324, including thirteen prompters. Fifteen actors were listed as looking for jobs. The twentieth general meeting was scheduled for September 1938, but evidently conditions in Poland prevented it from being held.

(There was also, by the way, a Yiddish actors' union in France.)

Isaac Samberg was so busy in union activities that he was called "czar of Yiddish actors." He relished the name; in fact, he probably coined it himself. But he suffered, as other czars have done, from his subjects. Feelings always ran high in the union. There were meetings and factions and feuds. One day a fellow union member spit publicly in Samberg's face. His feelings badly hurt, Samberg quit cold, and no amount of pleading, which was genuine, ever convinced him to return.

The actress Ida Kaminska, as the daughter of Ester Rokhl Kaminska, the "mother of Yiddish theater," was born into a tradition. Ida played the grandchild to her mother's Mirele Efros (as Ida's daughter Ruth later did for her). Ida's father, Avrom Kaminsky, owned the Kaminsky Theater, managed acting companies, and himself wrote, directed, and acted. Her brother Joseph composed music and conducted orchestras, in Poland and eventually in Israel.

Ida Kaminska was also part of the generation that had grown up in the old Yiddish theater and itched to reform it and make it finer and more cosmopolitan. She studied in Vienna, at the university, and became a cultivated person, a "European." Though her theatrical acumen had been appreciated when she was still playing children and ingénues, for a while she planned to be a pianist and have nothing to do with Yiddish theater. After she entered the Yiddish theater as an adult, her competence at management was as important as her acting talent, her quick movements, and her clever face. Thus she headed companies, sometimes alone, sometimes with her husband. She translated and adapted plays from Russian, Polish, and French; and when the troupe barely escaped Hitler, leaving behind scripts with the rest of their baggage, she reconstructed their entire repertory from memory.

Her marriage to Zygmund Turkow neatly symbolizes the wedding of serious professional Yiddish theater with the dynamic amateur movement in a mature partnership. Turkow began as an amateur in the drama school for young working people founded by David Herman and Dr. A. Mukdoyni, and directed productions for one of the best of these groups, *Das Artistishe Vinkele* (Little Corner for the Arts), a section of the Warsaw cultural organization Hazamir. Soon he was no longer an amateur; he, his brother Jonas, and sometimes their brother Yitskhok, as well as Jonas's wife Diana Blumenfeld, joined the company led by Ida and Ester Rokhl Kaminska—and that company was strictly professional. However, Turkow continued to care about the earnest ventures of amateur groups. Thus the Kaminska-Turkow company combined two generations of professional troupers with the amateur's intention to merge Yiddish theater with the best "European" tradition.

The new combination opened in Warsaw in 1921 at the Central Theater. Ester Rokhl was not performing that evening, but she watched from a box, and after the performance she kissed her son-in-law with, as he felt, "a mother's love, a comrade's recognition, an artist's approbation, and a theater personality's encouragement." Ester Rokhl, the young couple, their infant daughter, and a whole company set off gallantly for the provinces. They took the name Warsaw Yiddish Art Theater (Yiddish acronym: VYKT), and they worked toward an art theater repertory: classics like Molière's *The Miser* and modern European plays, usually with a left-wing political orientation, such as Romain Rolland's *Wolves* and Andreyev's *The Seven That Were Hanged.* They produced both the newer Yiddish plays, such as Yankev Pat's *In the Golden Land,* and the relatively classic ones: Goldfadn's *The Tenth Commandment,* freely adapted by Moyshe Broderson, and a rejuvenated version of Etinger's *Serkele,* with Ida in the title role. They even did a Lateiner operetta, which the intellectuals enjoyed because it was engagingly old-fashioned and the larger audiences enjoyed for less elevated reasons.

Business was not always good. Molière's *Love as Doctor,* elaborately mounted in period décor with comic ballet interludes, closed soon after it

The ensemble, soon to take the name VYKT (Warsaw Yiddish Art Theater), on tour in Vilna in 1923. From left: Adam Domb, Jonas Turkow, Zygmund Turkow, Ida Kaminska. Ester Rokhl Kaminska is seated in center. Fifth from right: Diana Blumenfeld.

opened. Following an old theater custom, the company buried their flop in wry parody of an Orthodox Jewish funeral. The funeral procession was led by the producer, carrying in a box a poster from the production. He was followed by a clown, who held a charity collection box and called, in accordance with Orthodox ritual, "Charity saves from death!" Next came a few actors carrying candles. They wore costumes from the production, which happened to be particularly appropriate: courtly black doctors' suits. The rest of the actors and a crowd of kibitzers straggled behind. The procession crossed the stage out into the yard, where they laid the poster in its grave under a marker reading: *"Love as Doctor,* daughter of Molière, gone to her eternal rest." Although *The Miser* was a hit, VYKT could not survive on fine literature alone, so sometimes they turned to vehicles that were less ambitious and more commercial.

They played all over—in impoverished riverside villages where the Jewish peasants lived on "fish and theater," as well as in industrialized Lodz and cosmopolitan Cracow. They frequently had to throw together a new show or play new roles, and the prompter had to be alert to get them through. Since they rode in trains and in freight cars (once they got a lift from an army truck), they couldn't always carry much scenery. Nevertheless, they gained a reputation for thoughtful sets. Often they hired a different artist to design each new production; Zygmund Turkow himself had studied painting. They had a special man just to design wigs so that they would be authentic—an unheard-of frill in Yiddish theater. Joseph Kaminsky composed new music for them.

Life was hard. They traveled constantly. During the economic crisis, for months at a time, the Turkows were desperate to find milk for their little daughter Ruth. They played in towns so battered by years of war and bombardments that loud sound effects made the spectators hurl themselves under their seats. Inevitably company members were intriguing among themselves and bickering. The company couldn't find a theater in Warsaw. Meanwhile Ester Rokhl was dying slowly of cancer. They had to organize a benefit to pay her doctors' bills. At her funeral, Peretz's old friend Hersh Dovid Nomberg said in his eulogy:

> . . . the Yiddish theater is nomadic, disorganized, abandoned by our wealthier people and assimilated intelligentsia, pursued by outsiders, and its only support-ers, the Yiddish folk masses, now are living through a hard and bitter time of hunger and unemployment and cannot help.

In 1926, the fiftieth anniversary of the founding of the professional Yid-dish theater, VYKT was broke. To rescue them, community leaders decided that of the over 300,000 Jews in Warsaw, a thousand must buy a ticket every day—an admirable decision, perhaps, but obviously unenforceable. Yiddish periodicals devoted feature stories to VYKT. Special committees applied to the Joint Distribution Committee (the agency through which American Jews were pouring charity into the impoverished Jewish communities of Eastern Europe) and to the *kehiles* of Warsaw and other cities in largely unsuccessful efforts to get subsidies. VYKT could not gather enough solid backing to continue to rent a theater and pay the actors' salaries. In 1928 the group collapsed.

Some years later Ida Kaminska and Zygmund Turkow broke their personal partnership as well—she eventually married the actor Meir Melman—but he continued to work toward the same artistic goals they had served together. For example, he presented Leivick's *Shop* and a dramatization of Sholom Aleichem's novel *Vagabond Stars*, with song lyrics by Itsik Manger. He dramatized a novel by the respected Yiddish author Zalmen Shneyur, which the censor mangled out of recognition. In 1939, as we shall see, just before the war, he even revived VYKT.

Yung Teater

One of the major theater companies of the Polish Yiddish theater in the period between the two world wars had no stars at all. This was Yung Teater (Young Theater). The group made their first appearance on the professional stage at the Nowósci in 1929, while they were still students at Dr. Mikhl Weichert's Culture League Drama Studio in Warsaw. The production they appeared in was *Danton's Death* by the nineteenth-century Austrian Georg Büchner. Weichert chose this play about the French Revolution because it seemed appropriate in a Poland torn by battles. It was a huge production. Morevsky portrayed a powerful Danton, and Samberg, who probably had only the dimmest notion of what the French Revolution was all about, compressed his exuberance into an intensely brooding Robespierre. The scenery was constructivist, abstract, and overwhelming. So monumental was the spectacle that the youngsters making their debut were practically lost among a battalion of one hundred extras.

Two years later, however, when the group graduated from their classes, they introduced themselves loudly and clearly to the Warsaw public:

> Yung Teater is the acting collective of graduates of the Yiddish theater studio. All have gone through a systematic theatrical education, a three-year course including practical and theoretical theater studies. Now the group appears for the first time for the Warsaw public.
> Yung Teater wants first of all to reproduce the modern dramatic creations,

Yiddish and European; the life of today with its own unique rhythm, with its ideas and drives, is to find a living echo in the productions of Yung Teater.

Yung Teater makes its first step openly without outside help, impelled by its own drive and by its deep dedication to theater, believing in the creative powers of that portion of the Yiddish masses for whom theater is not merely an entertainment, but rather a means in the battle for human and social liberation.

The group felt strongly their position as the only Yiddish actors who had gone through such a training, though Yiddish actors trained at Polish studios were no longer rare. (Artef in New York, which was an American counterpart to Yung Teater, also had a consistent study program for its members.) Yung Teater members felt the honor and the responsibility of their training and continued to be consistently experimental in staging, as well as generally left oriented in message. Their "rebbe" was Weichert, a lawyer, critic, and teacher who had graduated Reinhardt's drama school in Vienna. Reserved and authoritative, he chose their repertory and directed their productions. He found them their first stage, a small meeting hall the tailors' union rented to them for weekends. There he developed an expressionistic style that made a virtue out of cramped quarters.

Yung Teater's first production, *Boston* (1933), was about the recent Sacco and Vanzetti trial. It had forty-four separate scenes, no less, and since Weichert was using a tiny room with no stage or curtain, the forty-four scenes were spotlighted in various playing areas all over the room, among the spectators, with synchronized blackouts—a technique that avant-garde groups were trying in Russia and America at around the same time. *Boston* played over two hundred times in Warsaw alone.

Another of their innovative productions was *Krassin,* a piece of reportage

Danton's Death by Georg Büchner, directed by Dr. Mikhl Weichert with the Culture League Drama Studio at the Nowósci Theater in Warsaw in 1930. Participating in that production were the apprentice actors who three years later formed the Yung Teater.

about a Soviet ship that had recently rescued an Italian polar expedition. They created an environment suggestive of a ship, inside and out, again in many crisply shifting scenes.

Mississippi, another radical, experimental production, was about race relations in the United States. Yung Teater also presented Büchner's fragmentary play *Woyzeck*, in a translation by the Rumanian Yiddish poet Itsik Manger. They didn't dare comment on civil oppression in Poland, where the authorities were especially touchy about criticism because of the Soviet revolution next door, so they chose stories about abuses in other countries and trusted that their audiences would get the point.

The Yiddish repertory was another source for them. They presented Mendele Moykher Sforim's novel *The Travels of Benjamin III*, for example, in a dramatization originally devised for the Moscow Yiddish State Theater. For this they tried acting on three sides of the room, with their audience sitting in the center.

Perhaps the most original of their creations was Weichert's own *The Tanentsap Troupe*. The Tanentsaps, who were one of the primitive family companies touring Galicia in Goldfadn's day, are supposed to be presenting Goldfadn's *The Two Kuni-Lemls*. Yung Teater had recently moved into a hall cursed with eight big pillars in the middle, and Weichert used the curse to create the environment of a barn with a central makeshift stage, boards propped on beer barrels—just the sort of theater that the earliest Yiddish actors had. He hung wagon lanterns on the pillars, and for a curtain strung up a sheet crudely painted with bright-colored flowers. There were benches for the villagers, and their reactions to *The Two Kuni-Lemls* added a third element to the play within a play.

As the Warsaw audience settles itself, so do the spectators in the Galician barn. The director, Herr Rudolph Tanentsap, in the obligatory black frock coat, top hat, and white gloves, rushes around the "theater" getting everything ready. His wife, in flashy jewelry, towering hairdo, and crocheted shawl, keeps a stern housewifely eye on the actors and on her daughter, the ticket-taker; she is a combination of aristocratic affectations and market woman. The "audience" includes the rich man whose barn they are using and who naturally gets the best seats; the laborer and his servant-girl sweetheart, who get there first and try to take those seats themselves; an Austro-Hungarian officer from a nearby garrison; a Ukrainian soldier; an itinerant Litvak *magid* (Lithuanian preacher); a *hasid;* and a policeman. The director greets them in pompous *Daytshmerish;* this is a "German" theater, for Yiddish is illegal.

The atmosphere is lively. The audience comment on the play, scuffle, sting the actors into repartee. In the intermissions the romantic tenor comes out to sing a solo, holding the edges of the curtain together behind him to mask the frantic scenery changes, but his voice is poor and he gets whistled off. At one moment the officer thinks his emperor has been insulted, and Herr Tanentsap saves the day by sticking a beard on a portrait of the Russian Czar and leading the little orchestra in the Austro-Hungarian national anthem.

Goldfadn's *The Two Kuni-Lemls* has five scenes, but the Tanentsaps get to finish only three. In the middle of the fourth, the *hasid,* who yielded to temptation and crept in to watch, though he knows he shouldn't be in a theater, can no longer bear the sinful way these Jews are carrying on. He denounces the immodesty of the women, the jokes about *hasidism,* and the whole irreligious business. The rich man chimes in importantly that it's a scandal the way the play makes a laughingstock of Jews. Moyshe the laborer won't submit; he begins to stand up for the rights of the workingman to spend his few groschen to enjoy himself as he wishes. The actors are shouted down, the orchestra is drowned out, the policeman loses patience and declares the performance over.

Now comes the climax of Weichert's play. Herr Tanentsap steps forward. He abandons his heavy *Daytshmerish* and summarizes in pure Yiddish the happy ending of *The Two Kuni-Lemls.* He talks about the life of the Yiddish actor, who has to pretend to be an artist from Vienna, has to talk *Daytshmerish,* has to be at everyone's mercy. He becomes more and more impassioned, promises that a better day will come—and is cut off by the policeman. "Performance over." The villagers leave the barn. The Tanentsaps pack up.

The Tanentsap Troupe is a lively, amusing, and moving play. It is experimental (though not the first of the genre; a similar play within a play was *The Knight of the Burning Pestle* by Beaumont and Fletcher in seventeenth-century London), and the political implications are significant. Its collective hero is the artists and the audience, who are the Jewish masses: not the gentiles, who have their own languages and cultures; and not the Jewish bourgeoisie or the Orthodox, who are enemies to the true heart of the people, as they are to Yiddish theater.

Like all Polish theaters, Yung Teater had to take every script to the censor before production. Considering the constant censorship, they got away with murder. Presumably what protected them was their artistic reputation, which was so high that members of non-Jewish intellectual circles often came to see them. Polish drama students came, and visitors to Warsaw were told to be sure not to miss them. Their artistic achievements even drew the Yiddish middle classes, who ordinarily preferred Polish theater.

Yung Teater played a close game against the censors. Sometimes it was a narrow escape, as when they changed the title *Sacco and Vanzetti* to the less incendiary *Boston* at the last minute. Sometimes it was even closer. Once a censor, who was Jewish, came to a dress rehearsal of a politically doubtful play. Everybody knew that this censor was married to a Christian woman and missed Jewish cooking. So before the dress rehearsal they made a little party, and served him plate after plate of the salty fish he craved and glass after glass of brandy. The censor, his eyes half closed in sheer contentment, barely saw the rehearsal, and what he saw he liked fine.

Another time, they arrived to play *Mississippi* in a small town known to be a restless hotbed of subversion. They learned that policemen were stationed around the theater ready to close them down at the first sound of applause, which would be interpreted as a political demonstration. They managed stealthily to pass the word around among the spectators, and the performance went from beginning to end in total silence.

But their luck couldn't continue indefinitely. In some towns the authorities flatly refused to let them play, even though their posters were already up and many tickets sold. The reckoning came in 1936.

A local organization of theater-lovers invited Yung Teater to Vilna. Cautiously the company opened with *Tanentsap,* the least overtly political of their plays. Vilna loved them, and immediately planned an evening in conjunction with the play, devoted to readings and lectures about the Goldfadn era. But that gala evening never happened. Several days ahead, when tickets were already sold, a telegram came from Warsaw ordering Yung Teater to disband. Police stood in front of the theater door.

The group ripped the top line—YUNG TEATER—off their posters, slipped away to another part of Poland, and began to play under another name. They kept moving. Meanwhile Weichert desperately tried to pull bureaucratic strings. It took him months to get an appointment with the vice-minister in charge of such affairs. By then Weichert was in such a state that—according to his memoirs—he blurted out to the minister that although an informer may have told him that Yung Teater was communist, for another thirty zlotys an informer could have been found to tell him that Weichert was "banging" an eighty-year-old woman behind the marketplace, and for fifty zlotys one to tell him that the minister in chief was a spy of the Russian Revolution. The vice-minister, luckily, was amused. Some months later the group got a permit to tour and one to play Warsaw, both under the name Young Stage, but these were rescinded, so they took the name The New Theater and fled to Vilna. It was 1937.

In that year Yung Teater returned for a ceremony to the Nowósci, scene of its debut in 1929 as part of the chorus of Weichert's mammoth production of *Danton's Death.* The Bund was giving out prizes in honor of its fortieth year of existence. It awarded a prize to Yung Teater for its high artistic conscience and social responsibility, and in recognition of the fact that the members had continued to support themselves through most of those eight years through jobs outside their art. On the prize jury were Bund officers, and representatives of the Bund newspaper, the Yiddish Institute for Jewish Research (YIVO), the Yiddish P.E.N. club, and the Yiddish central school organization. There were also prominent men of letters. Over two thousand people attended the ceremony. In connection with this prize, Yung Teater even received a token money gift from the Polish Ministry of Education. Yung Teater's day was over, but many people who remember it still insist that it was the only Yiddish theater ever to equal GOSET in Moscow.

Kleynkunst *Revues*

Beginning in the 1920s, *kleynkunst* became a voguish genre among Polish Yiddish sophisticates. *Kleynkunst* was a sort of cabaret revue, witty, gay, and irreverent, rapidly winging from music to dance to monologue to sketch. Here is a typical program which the *kleynkunst* troupe the Polish Yidishe Bande (who called themselves, naturally, the Bandits) presented in 1939: a skit in which a couple argue over what someone was wearing at a party the night before; a monologue in which a servant girl writes a letter to her sweetheart; an interlude of gypsy balalaika music; an art song on folk motifs—tailors sing, while working, about the distant romance of ivory, apes, and peacocks; two street urchins fighting over a comfortable place in the gutter to sleep the night, and finally deciding to share it; a song about a drunken *hasid;* a skit called "Two Nazis Smell a Plot," in which two Berlin officials think they discover hidden meanings in the simplest Hebrew words and phrases; a skit called "Is It Kosher?" in which a girl makes advances to a rabbi under cover of the traditional questions; a comic sketch based on the complications of the housing shortage in the Soviet; a musical scene of jealousy between a couple of Warsaw toughs.

Russian intellectuals had enjoyed groups of this kind for over a decade, most importantly two—The Crooked Mirror and The Bat—which were the rage for years and had kept big-city Russians laughing. A similar Russian group called The Bluebird made a great impression when it toured Poland in the 1920s.

The cabaret revue had been part of Yiddish theater since the Broder singers, who combined songs, skits, personal comments, and topical jokes. Concerts made up of readings and monologues together with musical interludes had been an established genre of Yiddish theater ever since. There was a *kleynkunst* review in Yiddish at Lodz before the First World War, and the poets Yankev Sternberg and Jacob Botoshanski organized one in Bucharest in 1916. (Rumania was to have several such charming ventures.) But the first revue of real style, grace, and elegance in Warsaw appeared in 1925. It was called Azazel—a Biblical word for Hell.

Azazel caught on right away. Its mixed bag of personnel—artists, musicians, writers, amateur and professional actors (including David Herman)—entered into the project with infectious zest. Their repertory included folk songs and folk tales, bits and pieces from Peretz, Sholom Aleichem, Alter Kacyzne, plus new songs and monologues and skits by some ten different humorists, including Moyshe Broderson, Itsik Manger, and Wolf Younin. The master of ceremonies was deft at putting into his patter the names of whatever guests had turned up that night at the little hall above the writers' club.

Jewish sophisticates who had always disdained Yiddish theater came to it now for the first time and saw there Polish actors and writers. The writer H. D. Nomberg and the novelist Peretz Markish hung around night after night till they knew the texts by heart. On the streets people whistled the leitmotif of the first Azazel show, a catchy tune called the "Azazel Shimmy." And the policeman whose beat took him past the theater stopped in regularly to catch a monologue that especially tickled him. It was called "The Bagel Seller," spoken in the person of a young unlicensed street vendor.

The masses, it's true, just did not take to *kleynkunst.* They preferred the good old format: a romantic story, a laugh, and a cry, with songs and dances woven in along the way. When the Polish Yidishe Bande were only just beginning, they played the small provincial city of Kalish and flopped before the show was half over. A delegation came backstage during the first intermission. "We Kalish people don't like bits and crumbs. If you can play whole plays, all right. If not, go home, and good luck to you." They went. But they didn't go home, because as a company they had no home, so they went to bigger cities, including Warsaw, where they played first in a cabaret and then at the Nowósci and did very well.

Another *kleynkunst* company, perhaps the freshest and gayest of them all, was named Ararat, after the mountain on which Noah's ark grounded. It began in Lodz but toured elsewhere, including the Nowósci in 1934. The soul of Ararat was the prolific writer Moyshe Broderson, and their programs danced with his puns and quips, his charmingly silly songs and dazzlingly witty sketches. One number, for example—"Hodl, Ich fli!" ("Hodl, I'm Flying!")—was a take off on that new craze the flying machine. Broderson did his best writing in bed at night with the lights off, using a red fountain pen. One

A musical number presented by the *kleynkunst* or satirical "miniature" theater company Ararat, under Moyshe Broderson, in Lodz, Poland, around 1927.

morning he was horrified to discover only blank sheets of paper heaped up by the bed; the pen had run out of ink.

Broderson was tall and handsome and wore his monocle with an air. He was a wonderful talker, or gabber—in Yiddish, a *shmueser*—and like an inspired *badkhen,* he could at will spend an evening talking in graceful rhymes. He held court every afternoon at his own special table at an outdoor café, and when he finally had to leave for the theater he took all his party with him, talking and laughing in a straggling bunch that blocked the sidewalk. Broderson had his own circle of *patriótn,* just like a star. When he grew sideburns, so did one particularly devoted *patriót,* who sometimes followed him down the street. When Broderson got tired of his sideburns and shaved them off, however, the *patriót* did not. The quip went around literary Lodz: "You see what it is to be successful? Broderson even has a man to walk after him carrying his sideburns."

Broderson recruited a group of talented people. The designers and managers were mostly professionals, and so were the writers. The performers, however, especially in the early years, were mostly youngsters and were paid little or nothing. Broderson found Shimen Dzigan entertaining friends at a party for amateur athletes. "Young man," he said, "your place is in the theater." He discovered Yisroel Shumakher when he was still a high school student. Dzigan and Shumakher were to develop *kleynkunst* humor to perfection in Poland, then in Russia, and finally in Israel, where Dzigan continues to satirize the absurdities of politics and manners in the Jewish state. Mina Bern was a plump-cheeked, blond, blue-eyed schoolgirl who was visiting cousins in Lodz over vacation; she joined the group just for fun. She was to become a charming chanteuse, and she, too, continued her career as a refugee in Russia, then in Tel Aviv, and now in New York.

In miniature theater, the stage, sets, house, and audience were miniature, but the budgets often were not. Some groups remained local and amateur, like that organized by an academic club in Grodno and dedicated to in jokes and local material, or the similar ones in Vilna, Cracow, or Bielsk. These rarely lasted long. More typically, groups that began as amateurs became increasingly professional or else, under union pressure, took in an increasing proportion of professional performers, which meant professional salaries. Gilarina, for example (literally "Joymerriment," two words which traditionally appear together on happy ceremonial occasions), was mostly supported by the Bialystok community, but after a few years it was essentially professional. Sambatyon (named for a river of Jewish legend) was a professional venture from the start. Ararat went broke when Broderson became misguidedly ambitious and hired David Herman to direct the company in Osip Dimov's drama *Bronx Express.* They dumped the play the very next evening to return to what their public expected, and barely stayed in business. Besides finances, the strain of touring and the inevitable bickering splintered *kleynkunst* groups.

Personnel of *kleynkunst* theaters that expired often drifted into new ones. Broderson founded the Balaganeyden, for example, a name puckishly created by combining *balagan* (confused mess) and *gan eyden* (Garden of Eden). And his protégés Dzigan and Shumakher set up on their own in Warsaw.

In the 1930s everybody knew that whatever had happened in the world that day would turn up in the Dzigan-Shumakher show at night. Dzigan's monologues acted out the helplessness of ordinary Jews in the face of the conditions around them. It became enough for him just to pull his big red handkerchief out of his back pocket and flourish it despondently or fretfully, and already everybody was giggling. He reacted to anti-Semitic propaganda and they giggled. When food was short, he said he'd gone to a wedding party at a rich relative's house and been so confused by the quantities of food and the fanciness of the choice that by mistake he ended up eating a chrysanthemum. They giggled.

Dzigan made fun of Jewish butts, too: assimilation, snobbery, and fads. In his memoirs he recalls a monologue he created when Warsaw was swept by a fad for the little Japanese toy called a ya-ya: a small rubber ball attached to a paddle by a rubber string. (Note that *yaye* is also the Polish word for egg.)

Still from the film *Al-Kheyt (I Have Sinned)*, produced in Warsaw in 1937 by S. Goskind. The actors are Dzigan, Shumacher, and Rokhl Holzer.

When I appeared on the stage, a Jew with a little beard, dressed in a long black traditional coat, with a little round skull cap, the red scarf tucked into my vest, and started bouncing the ya-ya ball up and down, I already didn't have to say a thing, for the audience was already rolling with laughter. Then I told the audience that I put on *tfilin* [phylacteries] with ya-ya and showed them my left hand, where a ya-ya ball was bound on with a black rubber string like a phylactery strap. I wanted to see what time it was and pulled out of my vest pocket a ya-ya hanging on a golden chain. My wife, I said, cooks *tsholnt* [a Sabbath stew] with ya-yas instead of potatoes. My daughter gave birth to twins: two ya-yas. And one of my brothers-in-law can't have children, because there's something wrong with his ya-yas. . . .

Shumakher brings a baby carriage onstage and talks to the baby about the political situation. Anti-Semites have been attacking children in the park and at school, so the carriage is protected like an army tank. In another monologue Shumakher announces that he's leaving Poland. He catches a fly and addresses his farewells to it as it listens invisibly inside his cupped hands; lucky fly, he says, free to enjoy the streets of Warsaw.

Dzigan and Shumakher together performed zany skits. As members of two different political parties, they build a traditional holiday *sukka* (arbor), sit down to enjoy it together, but fight over politics till it falls down on their heads. The moral is clear. Another time they're building a balloon, to fly away and start a new nation in the sky. Or they're bears, surveying the world from the zoo and commenting on what they see.

The pair continued in various small theaters around Warsaw, sometimes playing the Nowósci, right up till the bombs began to fall. Their partnership lasted amicably till 1960, when they split to go their separate ways.

One special sort of miniature theater used the same kind of material as the others and in the same spirit, but with actors who were themselves miniature: marionettes. In 1926 Broderson, together with the painter Yitskhok Broyner and the composer Henekh Kon, took a tiny stage in a café in Lodz. Broyner made and moved the dolls, Broderson wrote the dialogue, Kon arranged the music and spoke the lines. They made a cartoon out of well-known figures, especially local personalities, and they called their theater Had Gadye (The Only Kid) after the traditional Passover song. In 1934 Broyner made a new set of marionettes for a theater that became the rage for a while at the Warsaw writers' club. And there were also some more local marionette theaters, especially the Vilna Maydim, whose splendid posters, so people said, were bigger than the tiny stage. Around this time, too, the Modikot marionette theater came from America and toured Yiddish Poland with great success.

Children's theater in Yiddish was already an established genre. Vilna, for example, had had a regular theater by and for children for years, connected with schools and coordinated with curricula. One of its main directors was A. Azro, a founder of the Vilna Troupe.

In 1938 Warsaw acquired a Young People's Theater directed by the darkly glamorous Clara Segalovitch. The shows for children became so successful that the company added evening performances for adults. They began with Itsik Manger's adaptation of Goldfadn's *Koldunye*. Manager frisked with the play, trying such tricks as letting a woman play the witch, which had been a man's role since Mogulesko created it, and imagining three peddler Hotsmakhs instead of one. This version was such an extravagant departure from the original that Manger published it under his own title: *Hotsmakh*, as "inspired by" Goldfadn. (Manger also wrote works about Goldfadn himself; about the prankish *badkhen* Hershele Ostropolyer; about the Broder singers Berl Broder and Eliakum Zunser, and especially Velvl Zbarzher and his troubadour's romance.)

Yiddish opera, though nowhere near as popular as operetta, did exist. Several cities intermittently had companies singing in Yiddish. Vilna presented operas in Yiddish translations as well as several original works composed with Yiddish texts. Warsaw enjoyed the premiere of *David and Bathsheba,* composed by Henekh Kon with libretto by Moyshe Broderson. Committees in London drew up ambitious plans for a combined Yiddish opera house and theater, to be directed by Jacob Ben-Ami; but the plans did not work out.

Popular Theater

In the years between the two world wars, the best money making propositions in the Polish Yiddish theater were still glamorous stars on tour, especially the welcome "guests from America." Many American actors toured Europe, South America, and South Africa. They usually came alone or with only a nuclear cast, but they always came with their own vehicles. They brought a trunkful of scripts, most of which were not whole scripts but rather individual roles, and they brought their own scenery. Sometimes they arranged to rent a theater before they arrived; sometimes they saw to that on the spot. They hired a new cast in every city, rehearsed briefly, put on the show, and moved on.

Sometimes these scripts were "literary"; Maurice Schwartz, for example, brought *Yoshe Kalb.* More often the guest stars brought lighter entertainment. In the 1930s the Nowósci was host to Jack Rechtzeit in *The Dancing Girl from Odessa, The Little Bandit, The Happy Gypsy,* and *Illegitimate Children.* Misha and Lucy German visited with *Mamma and Mother-in-Law.* Hymie Jacobson, Miriam Kressyn, and Ludwig Satz brought entire repertories.

Boris Thomashefsky visited Warsaw soon after the First World War. He brought one of his old-fashioned thundering melodramas. The climax called for him to smash a dish. On opening night he threw himself into the role and smashed six dishes. The next day the intellectual critic Dovid Frischman wrote dryly that Thomashefsky had come all the way to Warsaw to make a pogrom.

Two of the women stars who most delighted Yiddish audiences visited Warsaw in the 1920s. Clara Young was no great star at home in America, but in the early 1920s European Yiddish audiences did not have many glamorous female stars of their own, and her grace and softly pretty femininity captivated even stern anti-*shund*ists. Some of the same critics who denounced her flimsy plays hung around her chair at parties, smiling foolishly. Clara Young was the first to bring American glitter, froth, and lace to the relatively shabby Eastern European Yiddish operetta stage. She was to outlive her glamour, however, for she kept touring several decades more, especially in Russia, long after her friends were wisecracking that "she still was Clara, but she'd stopped being . . ." (Jacob Ben-Ami was in later years to dismiss her and all her charms with an aristocratic snort: "When she lifted her skirts to show her legs, her petticoats were a little cleaner than the others', that's all.")

Then there was Molly Picon. She entered Yiddish theater in Philadelphia as a child because her mother sewed costumes. She sang and danced in American vaudeville too. When she married Jacob Kalich, he recognized her special charm, wrote special plays and songs for her, and trained her to speak a rich, authentic Yiddish. Picon and Kalich went on tour to Europe. In Vienna Molly charmed cabaret audiences, who drove up in fancy carriages. In Warsaw the Jewish community split into two camps: Piconists and anti-Piconists. Even the latter were not so much proof against her personality as disapproving of her material. One play that showed her off to special advantage was *Mamele*, or *Little Mother*, later made into a movie. Molly, who was (and still is) tiny and peppy, with big round eyes in a little round face, played a young girl whose mother dies, leaving her the responsibility of making a home for her older brothers and sisters. She becomes not only housekeeper but also worrier, comforter, advice-giver. In this role Molly's grown-up gravity and devotion, imposed on her still childlike frisky spirits, made an adorable combination. Another of her roles, written for her by her husband, was that of a merry prankish *yeshive* boy named Yankl. In an old European tradition, Yiddish audiences found a woman dressed as a boy a piquant sight, and in this case the comedy was delicious. At the same period she starred in a Polish Yiddish film about a girl who dresses up as a boy, becomes a wandering fiddler, and, naturally, falls in love and complicates her life. *Yidl mitn Fidl (The Little Jew with the Fiddle)*, with songs by Abraham Ellstein and Itsik Manger, is still being screened and is charming entertainment.

Jacob Kalich entered Yiddish theater in a particularly dramatic way. As a young man, from an Orthodox Polish family, he helped some wandering actors borrow kaftans to wear onstage. When the actors left town with the kaftans, he felt responsible and ran after them. By the time he caught up with them, it seemed too late to go home, so he accepted their invitation and kept on traveling.

In 1934 Mikhel Mikhalesko came from America to the Nowósci with a repertory of operettas, distinguished by the New York style and panache with which he presented them. Mikhalesko presented *The Last Dance* and *The Prince of Love.* He also performed *If I Were Rich,* an unusual sort of operetta that aimed to be realistic and serious instead of frivolous and escapist. It was about workers rather than princes or gypsies. It even included a strike. Naturally, the censor took out whole hunks of the dialogue and even cut the score, in which fragments of the Internationale echoed as a motif.

Films

In 1935, despite the millions of Yiddish-speaking Jews in Europe, there were no Yiddish-language films for them to see. When Joseph Green came from America bringing a copy of *Joseph in Egypt,* which he had made by imposing Yiddish words on an Italian silent film, the two producing partners he screened it for recognized in it a goldmine. They stationed themselves at the two exit doors of their Warsaw theater and told Green they wouldn't let him leave the house till he signed a contract letting them show the film.

Green went on to produce and direct his best films on location in Poland, because technical expenses were much lower there than in New York or Hollywood. Two of his films are still shown occasionally in America, at universities or Jewish centers. One of them is *Yidl mitn Fidl* (1935). For the glorious wedding party scene during which the musicians help the bride to escape from the rich old groom she doesn't love, the dancing was directed by the choreographer of the Warsaw Polish opera company, and Green ordered all the food and decorations for an authentic, traditionally lavish Jewish wedding from the best kosher caterer in Warsaw. *A Brivele der Mamen (A Little Letter to the Mother)* (1937) stars Lucy and Misha German and the sensitive comic Max Bozyk in a tear-jerker of high quality. The son goes off to America to join his father; the mother embraces him at the Warsaw train station and goes home to wait for letters; many years pass, World War I and innumerable hardships separate them, but she manages to get to America and finds him at last. Green also made *Mamele (Little Mother)* (1937), starring Molly Picon, and *Der Purimshpiler* (1938), starring Zygmund Turkow, Hymie Jacobson, and Miriam Kressyn.

Probably the best-known Yiddish film was made in Poland in 1938: Anski's *The Dybbuk,* directed by Michael Waszynsky. Lili Liliana and Leon Liebgold play the exquisite young couple (and in real life later married); Max Bozyk plays a comic servant. The characters move singing through the lovely Polish countryside; shadows and startling angles intensify the approaching doom.

Other films made in Eastern Europe in the 1930s include *On a Heym (Without a Home)* from the Jacob Gordin play; *Al Kheyt (I Have Sinned);* and *Tkhies-Kaf (The Vow). Laughter Through Tears,* based on Sholom Aleichem stories, was shot in Russia in 1933. Ida Kaminska and even Ester Rokhl Kaminska also appeared in films. Jonas Turkow directed *In Polish Woods,* made from Joseph Opatoshu's novels. Zygmund Turkow, Dzigan, and Shu-

Molly Picon, as a girl masquerading as a boy violinist, drinks in a Polish
inn with her old father and two other traveling musicians. Eventually
she will fall in love with the young musician sitting opposite her, reveal
herself as a girl, and live happily ever after. The film is *Yidl mitn Fidl
(Little Jew with the Fiddle)*, produced by Joseph Green in Poland in
1937, with music by Itsik Manger.

Molly Picon, Bessie Thomashefsky, Clara Young, and other clever
soubrettes played boy roles, especially impudent *yeshive* students.

Zygmund Turkow and Miriam Kressyn appear in this scene from the
film *Purimshpiler (Purim Players)* made by Joseph Green in Warsaw
in 1937.

makher starred in *Freylikhe Kaptsonim (Happy Paupers)* by Moyshe Broderson.

War Approaches

Although the Scala Theater in Warsaw in 1939 put on a comedy called *The Crazy World,* in which Hitler himself figured as a character, the characteristic repertory of the times was not about current events. Partly the reason was censorship. People practically brawled over tickets for the opening nights of Dzigan-Shumakher programs because by the second week the censors were sure to have chopped out the juiciest satire. Indeed, the pair sometimes took dangerous chances. In their skit "The Last Jew in Poland," recalls Dzigan, the

> anti-Semites' wish to make Poland *Juden-rein* [in German, "purified of Jews"] has come true. But then the Poles look around them, and things aren't good. Commerce stops, the economy is ruined. Culture and entertainment are dead. The anti-Semitic student clubs go around with nobody to beat up. Where the lively Café Zhemiansky used to stand, now there's a funeral parlor. What can be done?
>
> But one Jew is found, who was late leaving Poland and is only now getting ready for his departure. Government delegations come to him to beg him not to leave. The students organize a campaign to prevent the last Jew from emigrating. They make him a banquet and play Yiddish songs for him. The Jew sets a condition: he wants a piece of gefilte fish and some *tsholnt.* The Polish radio appeals to its listeners for any one in the nation who knows how to cook those foods to present himself. They promise the Jew all possible benefits, and finally the Polish government awards him the medal "Polonia Restitutsia." The Jew accepts the medal and fastens it to "the place below the spine," and when he turns his back to the audience they can see that there's a medal hanging there already: the Cross for Service to Poland. The spotlight falls on both medals and all the cast onstage sings to the Jew the Polish song "May You Live a Hundred Years."

Dzigan and Shumakher were called in to the police the morning after they presented this sketch and were very nearly arrested. Clearly, the only safe way to talk about the frightening situation of the Jewish community was to do it obliquely—to present a play like Goldfadn's *Shulamis,* which is set in Jewish history, and let the audience infer the connection. Besides, the very use of the Yiddish language was a reference and a gesture. But perhaps the dangers of Eastern Europe in 1938 and 1939 were just too overwhelming to deal with in a play. One of the plays that appear most often in the repertories of serious companies in this period is Sholom Aleichem's *The Big Win,* which deals with

Avrom Morevsky as Prospero in Shakespeare's *The Tempest,* a production of the Youth and Folk Theater, directed by Leon Schiller at the Nowósci Theater in Warsaw in 1939.

romance and with the oppression of the working classes, but not with the Nazis. Audiences craved reassurance and escape.

The list of tenants at a Warsaw theater like the Nowósci reveals something of the Jewish situation and offers clues—perhaps more conclusive in hindsight —of how Eastern European Jewry was crumbling. In 1938, for example, Ida Kaminska's company gave a farewell benefit performance for one of their leading actresses, Rachel Holzer; she was emigrating to Australia. Warsaw received increasing numbers of Rumanian actors, for the Sidy Thal company could no longer tour Rumania and the Jewish Theater Studio in Bucharest had been closed. Palestine, a primary hope for refuge, figured on the Nowósci stage. A company called the National Stage, led by two German Jewish actors who had recently fled Berlin, played at the Nowósci in 1937–38 a repertory intended as deliberate propaganda for emigration to Palestine. Their plays were all Yiddish translations from stirring modern Hebrew originals, including *Battle for the Soil* and *Jacob and Esau.* A *kleynkunst* revue called *Tel Aviv* was performed by Polish Yiddish actors in imitation of its recent production in Palestine. The Hebrew theater Habima, which had moved from Moscow to Tel Aviv, visited in 1938 with assurances that in Palestine European Jews would find not a desert but a fully developed culture; they performed *The Dybbuk, Uriel Acosta,* Pinski's *The Eternal Jew,* Leivick's *Chains,* and even a play by the seventeenth-century classic Spanish dramatist Calderón.

Books and articles published since the war call the 1939 season of Yiddish theater in Poland and the rest of Europe a swan song. However, the Yiddish actors and their audiences could not fully know that the end was approaching. During the years 1938 and 1939 they were busy making plans which never reached fruition. In 1938, for example, the Polish Yiddish actors' union published their agenda for the next annual meeting, with photos of the executive officers, promising an extra edition of their newsletter in the near future. (The newsletter never appeared again.) A committee of Paris *kultur-tuers* in 1938 devised elaborate plans for adding a special archive of Yiddish theater in France to the Yiddish Theater Museum in Vilna. (Soon the museum itself would be destroyed.) The following year Gimpel's Garden Theater in Lemberg—the oldest Yiddish theater in Galicia, established by Gimpel himself in 1888 and owned by his family ever since—proudly erected a fancy new building. (No Yiddish actor ever used it.) Art theaters and intellectuals in Warsaw and elsewhere kept on publishing manifestoes, trying as always to reform Yiddish theater as if the only enemy that threatened it were *shund.*

The last season at the Nowósci, 1938–39, was a brilliant finale. Ida Kaminska's company was succeeded by Clara Segalovitch's Youth and Folk Theater in a stunningly ambitious presentation of Shakespeare's *The Tempest,* directed by the Polish Leon Schiller; some people remember this as the best Yiddish production they ever saw. Zygmund Turkow's version of Goldfadn's *Shulamis* closed the season.

Turkow had recently returned from an engagement in Paris. He revived the VYKT and issued a manifesto of the sort that invariably accompanied such ventures:

> The Yiddish community has never been so in need of a serious Yiddish theater as now.
>
> In a time of general depression and despondency, when we live with a sorrowful today and a clouded tomorrow, it is the holy duty of every conscious thinking man to encourage the Yiddish *gas* ["street," or community at large] and to nourish it with the spiritual food which the Yiddish masses need so badly in their battle for existence.
>
> Now more than ever we must take up the battle against *shund,* which has rooted itself deeply in all areas of our culture and especially in theater. *Shund* has found its own customer in the petty bourgeois and the bourgeois intellectual, on whom it works like a narcotic, atrophying both their taste and their spiritual powers of resistance.
>
> Theater must give him joy, optimism, elevation, and faith in tomorrow. . . .
>
> The theater must come out with a word which will strengthen the national consciousness, cement the social groupings in a cooperative power, which will be able to stand against the beast which lowers at our existence. . . . We now

have to come out with models from the positive side of Jewish life, of Jewish creativity and Jewish history.

We must show with examples from our distant past that we are a people who, long before the birth of Christ, celebrated love for humanity, love for labor, and dedication to the soil from which, through the ages, we were cast out and alienated and to which we are entitled, no less than are those who accuse us of being a people of parasites and usurers.

The new VYKT prepared productions of *Shulamis* and *Bar Kokhba*, the two Goldfadn plays that GOSET had recently presented in Moscow with similar hopes and similar results. VYKT also prepared *Uncle Moses, The Bellringer of Rotterdam, Vagabond Stars,* and a play about the Broder singers. They toured Lemberg, where the *kehile* scraped together a small subsidy for them. In Cracow, they played to crowds of refugees from Germany. In 1939 they opened *Shulamis* at the Nowósci. Turkow recalls the moment:

> . . . And then comes the mobilization. We keep playing. The city is a boiling pot. Yesterday's civilians appear in military uniform. . . . We play. Thousands of people look for ways and means to escape the country. The trains are overcrowded. But the line in front of the theater to buy tickets to our *Shulamis* is longer than ever.
>
> We are already the only and the last theater playing in Warsaw. The others are closed. Every day chorus members disappear, and actors. But we go on playing.
>
> Till the play is interrupted. One of the first German bombs over Warsaw falls on our theater. It is transformed into a ruin.

12 IN THE GHETTOS AND CAMPS

VOLUME V OF ZALMEN ZYLBERCWEIG'S *Lexicon of Yiddish Theater* is devoted to capsule biographies of actors, writers, and other Yiddish theater people who died in Europe between 1939 and 1945. In those years, most European Yiddish actors and their audiences disappeared permanently.

However, there was some Yiddish theater during the holocaust, even in the ghettos and concentration camps.

Throughout Europe there had always been many Jewish actors in non-Yiddish theater. Many of them had long since lost touch with Yiddish tradition; some didn't even know they had Jewish ancestors. In Western and Central Europe, most of them did not know the Yiddish language. Then, beginning in 1933, German Jewish actors and musicians were forbidden to perform the works of Goethe, Beethoven, and other Aryans and to perform for non-Jewish audiences. Similar bans were issued in Rumania in 1940, in Holland in 1941, and so on.

In Germany, the actors and musicians thus uprooted organized themselves in a *Kulturbund* for performance before Jewish audiences. Exiled from the artistic scene to which they had devoted their lives, they struggled to define for themselves a new identity as Jewish practitioners of a Jewish art in the German language. Their audiences, who had been evicted from German theaters and concert halls, were equally unequipped with a specifically Jewish tradition in art. Their experiment in Jewish German theater, beginning in Berlin in 1933 with a production of Lessing's *Nathan the Wise*, ended only with mass deportation.

In Rumania, Jewish actors pushed out of Rumanian theater had the option of turning to Yiddish theater. Rumanian Jewish actors got together to perform in Yiddish and Rumanian at a Bucharest theater called the Barasheum. They presented Rumanian translations of Yiddish light musicals, such as *Khantshe in America,* as well as new revues that had some satirical relationship with their current situation, such as *What Are You Doing Tonight?; Spring in Do Major; From One Joke to the Next; Different Money, Different Entertainment;* and *Hello, Barasheum.*

Rumanian policy was day by day forbidding one activity after another, but even when the Yiddish language became outlawed onstage, Rumanian Yiddish actors found a way. The practice of the Jewish religion was still allowed, so Yiddish theater continued in synagogues. Yiddish performers gave fragments of plays and readings of poetry. Since assembly was permitted only on religious or semireligious occasions, holidays that previously had been observed only nominally suddenly became full-fledged events and sometimes occurred several times a year. Actors even fabricated holidays. Peretz, Mendele, and other writers had birthday anniversaries (which qualified as "semireligious") every few months. Since it wasn't supposed to be theater, and therefore the audience didn't dare applaud, they yelled the toast *"Lekhayim"* at the end of every number.

Mass deportation ended Yiddish theater in Rumania until after the war.

In the Ghettos

In the ghettos imposed by fascist governments, Yiddish theater activities varied from country to country, and in Poland even from ghetto to ghetto. Starvation, disease, terror, and decimation were the general situation. But in the midst of the horror, different sorts of theatrical activity managed to hold on: the extent of the events depended on such variables as whether or not the Yiddish language was permitted, and whether the ghetto was controlled rigidly by one governor (as in Lodz) or by unsynchronized committees (as in Warsaw). All over, even in the temporary collection centers for deportation in Belgium, where there never had been much Yiddish theater, groups snatched brief evenings of songs and recitations. These rudimentary sessions nourished the audiences both with escapist entertainment and with an assertion of tradition.

The Warsaw ghetto was the largest in Poland, just as Warsaw had been the largest Yiddish cultural center of Poland. By 1942, 400,000 to 500,000 Jews lived imprisoned within the ghetto walls. Of these, 139 were members of the actors' union, including Isaac Samberg (the irrepressible "czar of Yiddish actors"), Jonas Turkow, and Diana Blumenfeld. They had no work. There was less and less food in the ghetto, fewer and fewer jobs, and more and more difficulty getting permits to go outside to work. The actors spent their days sitting on the dusty floor of the old union headquarters of 2 Leszno Street, which was inside the ghetto boundaries, and talking politics in whispers. They and their families were among the many paupers for whom the Joint Distribution Committee arranged to provide one bowl of soup apiece a day.

People couldn't go out on the ghetto streets after five o'clock in the afternoon. (Later the hour was seven or nine.) Jews caught after curfew were beaten or taken away. So they started to creep into each other's apartments to chat, play cards, and sometimes sing. In 1940 a man heard the well-known entertainer Simkhe Postel singing in a friend's apartment. He invited Postel to come visit him and sing, for pay, for his guests. Eventually a regular show business developed from this in the apartments of those ghetto residents who were still managing to live relatively well from savings or through black-market dealings. There were even impresarios. Entertainers and guests always had to stay the night after the shows, because of the curfew.

Since there was more excitement and prestige to having a darling of Polish café society or an opera star in one's living room than a Yiddish actor, the run of Yiddish actors lost the competition. Shows were sometimes poetic recitations, folk songs, arias, but more often they were loud, fast, and funny comedy routines or sentimental love songs, music hall songs, or comic recitations. Often they were in Polish or a mixture of Polish and Yiddish, for though it was illegal for Jews to speak Polish in the Warsaw ghetto, for many of them Polish came more naturally than Yiddish and the prohibition was largely broken in the ghetto's streets and homes.

A popular variety of home entertainment involved children. In his memoirs, Jonas Turkow describes groups of children taught to pipe out lewd lines and gestures which presumably they did not fully understand. The ugly pressures of the times led to decadent entertainments. Turkow describes a group of such children performing for a party of tipsy adults late at night, jigging wearily up and down, their eyes fastened on the buffet table where their payment waited.

Meanwhile a new profession surfaced in the ghetto streets, which were already squirming with desperate people clawing for a few kopecks for bread. These were the street entertainers, who were really glorified beggars. You might look out your window at a famous violinist from the Warsaw Philharmonic fiddling for kopecks. For these professional musicians there was a special hazard. Police who came upon them found sport in carting them away out of the ghetto to more fashionable parts of Warsaw to play Yiddish tunes in the street and be mocked. One such group was forced to play "Hatikva,"

Israel's national anthem, and liturgical melodies to accompany the sad labor
of a squad of Jews passing books in an assembly line out of the splendid Jewish
library into waiting German trucks.

You might also see out your window a ragtag bunch of orphaned children,
singing, dancing, and playing instruments, some simulating instruments by
humming or clapping their hands. In two years, with the increasing overcrowd-
ing in the ghetto and the growing pauperism, the streets became

> full up—literally impossible to pass through the beggars, who had taken to
> singing and playing. Here lies a family, barefoot and naked, swollen from hunger
> and cold, and makes noise: "Have mercy, Jews, we're dying of hunger," "save
> us," and so on. A few steps further—a corpse covered with paper. Then—a
> fiddler who with a shaking hand and extinguished eyes pushes the bow over the
> fiddle. A little further—a woman with a little child in its cradle, singing operatic
> arias to the accompaniment of the child's cries. Next to them—a cantor with
> a child in his arms sings cantorial melodies.
>
> This particular hell went on twenty-four hours a day, despite the curfew.

During the first year of the Warsaw ghetto, with growing momentum,
theater of two sorts appeared, filling obvious needs. The first was café theater.
A German woman, Magda Fogt, got several concessions to open cafés inside
the ghetto. After hers came many others, till Leszno Street was a sort of
Broadway, with a café, restaurant, or cabaret theater in almost every other
house. Music could be heard all along the street.

Here is a description by a girl named Mary Berg of one of the most popular
and expensive of the early cafés, which ironically had taken over as a new
tenant in a familiar address.

> At number 2 Leszno Street, there is now a cabaret called Sztuka [Art]. . . .
> In the ghetto, light was permitted until a certain hour. After that we had to
> sit around the house by the light of candles or kerosene lamps. When we
> reached the nightclub the street was dark. My escort suddenly said to me,
> "Be careful not to step on a dead man." When I opened the door the light
> blinded me. Gas lamps were burning in every corner of the crowded caba-
> ret. Every table was covered by a white tablecloth. Fat characters sat at
> them eating chicken, duck, or fowl. All of these foods would be drowned in
> wine and liquor. The orchestra, in the middle of the nightclub, sat on a
> small podium. Next to it a singer performed. These were people who once
> played before Polish crowds. Now they were reminded of their Jewish heri-
> tage. When I came in, M.Z., the renowned Polish actor, played the role of
> a comic character, eliciting lots of laughter. Afterwards a singer, U.G., sang
> old Polish hits and romantic songs. The audience crowding the tables was
> made up of the aristocracy of the ghetto—big-time smugglers, high Polish
> officers, and all sorts of big shots. Germans who had business dealings with
> Jews also came here, dressed in civilian clothes. Within the walls of the cab-

aret one could not sense the tragedy taking place a few yards away. The audience ate, drank, and laughed as if it had no worries.

Sometimes police descended, broke a few heads, made a few arrests, grabbed some liquor. But the presence of non-Jews was some safeguard, and anyway, compared to the smugglers' regular daredevil trips in and out past the ghetto walls, it was a minor danger. The entertainers regularly grew hoarse yelling over the noise of the merrymaking. As fewer and fewer Jews had money left for evenings at such cafés, the quality of the entertainment grew more desperately vulgar, summoning stores of raucous energy to drown out reality.

But even in the ghetto there was recreated the old dichotomy between professional *shund* and amateur educational idealism. The buildings were mostly apartment houses, occupied by increasing numbers of people. Because of the curfews, entertainment was confined within each building, and house committees took it upon themselves to organize and sponsor home entertainments. In this way they raised money to look after the starving residents in the building and to help settle the new arrivals.

Mary Berg and some of her friends organized a drama club to raise relief funds.

August 16, 1940
Our little group is having a lively time and finds preparations for the show absorbing. But one look outside the window is enough to awaken us to reality.
. . . We always have to leave our meetings one by one. The girls go out first and make sure that no Nazis are around. If everything is quiet they call the boys. . . .

September 11, 1940
Our first performance took place early this month. . . . Our success surpassed all expectations and the receipts were considerable. We were immediately asked to give other performances, all of which were very successful. . . . Our Lodz group [many of these youngsters came originally from Lodz] is proud of making such a hit in Warsaw. Some of us are now quite famous. . . . We call ourselves the "Lodz Artistic Group" or, as it is abbreviated in Polish, the LZA. This is curiously symbolic; the world *lza* in Polish means "tear.". . . [Of the proud young LZA, Mary was the only one to outlive the ghetto.]

December 25, 1940
Our theatrical group has received several invitations to give performances in cafés. We also have our own hall, and intend to give regular shows two or three times a week in the afternoon. We have rented Weisman's dancing school on Lanska Street. . . . Now we have our own public. . . .

January 2, 1941
Our New Year's shows unexpectedly drew an enormous audience. Because December 31 happened to coincide with the last day of Hanukka, we have

improvised a scene depicting the heroic fight of the Maccabees, which contained many timely hints. We lit eight candles on the stage. The audience applauded enthusiastically, and there was hardly a dry eye in the house. . . .All our matinees are a great success. Half of the receipts go to the refugee committee, for there is still an enormous flood of homeless refugees.

Naturally, one of the main concerns of the house committees was the children. They tried to have one relatively warm and cheerful area in each building where children could spend the day, and because classes were forbidden in the ghetto, they turned to theatricals as a kind of education. Theatricals would entertain the children, teach them some skills as well as some cultural and social lessons. Furthermore, money raised at children's performances could go into the common fund.

> In our kitchen [wrote one child] we are producing a very lovely play which our teacher wrote for us. I play the role of a Jewish mother who tries to steal a piece of bread for her children from a passer-by on the street. After that we danced the "famine dance." But the sun shines for us: the Germans are kicked out and we Jewish children live to see a good life and a new eera. This is how our play ends. When I am performing, I forget that I am hungry and I no longer remember that the evil Germans are still roaming about. In the morning I quickly run to the kitchen and I wish the day would never end, because when it is dark out we are forced to disband and go back to our homes.

For a while a group of children even gave marionette shows using puppets, costumes, and décor they made themselves.

At one performance in Vilna, a heroic young teacher, Mirele, led hundreds of children in singing, dancing, and choral declamation. Poems by Bialik and Peretz were recited, including one by Peretz that begins: "Don't think that the world is a tavern/ Without judgment and without a judge." After that recitation, the children sang the "Blue Danube" waltz. For them it was simply a pretty tune, but for the audience of grownups, the song's associations with a happier time suddenly destroyed their self-control. First one began to sob and then, in another part of the room, someone else, until the piping voices were drowned out by the sound of weeping.

At the end of 1940, a more ambitious amateur drama group was formed by a teacher and a hairdresser, who aimed specifically to subsidize the children's corners. They put on *kleynkunst* revues with material by Sholom Aleichem, Peretz, Broderson, Manger, and other dramatists and poets. They also presented complete plays by Gordin and Goldfadn and even Ida Kaminska's adaptation of a Lateiner play. They performed three times every weekend and advertised their shows through little fliers, handbills, and posters. When they were invited to perform by various house committees, they carried their scenery with them, and residents brought in their own stools and benches.

Then the company stayed the night till it was safe to go home.

This company had about fifty members, mostly young. It included six musicians, plus a separate little band of five harmonica players. There were painters and carpenters to make sets, tailors to make costumes. Professional actors such as Isaac Samberg sometimes appeared with them too. Often one or two of the members just didn't show up; he'd been arrested, or he had succumbed to the typhoid epidemic—but understudies were always ready. Only after a full year had most of the group disappeared, and even then the teacher and the hairdresser continued to give occasional concerts alone.

Among the children's performances, competition grew between the participating adults as to whose group was most talented, had the nicest costumes and best scenery. This led to a waste of precious funds for frills and also to a trend away from educational presentations. But a reforming committee, headed by Jonas Turkow, set itself to try to guard against this tendency.

As amateur theatricals spread and a number of buildings had their own adult or children's shows every weekend, poverty led to ingenuity and improvisation. One building set up a makeshift stage in a little locksmith's shop on the ground floor. Another group of tenants entered their theater area through bombed-out ruins, and had not only a stage level on the former shop floor but also balcony seating on the floor of the bombed-out apartment above, where children sat with their feet dangling down. In the Warsaw winter the people, crowded together on benches, accompanied the actors by constantly blowing on their frozen hands and stamping their feet. In the little town of Vlatzlavek, much too small for an official ghetto, the Jews met for theatricals in the little ritual house of the Jewish cemetery.

There were fewer and fewer materials. One ghetto production of *Shulamis* made costumes out of tablecloths, sheets, and towels. In Vilna, musicians buried their instruments before they were herded away to the ghetto. Later they sneaked out of the ghetto through a canal and smuggled the instruments back inside with them. A work gang that happened to include former musicians, taken regularly out of the Vilna ghetto for day labor, discovered a piano in an abandoned Jewish apartment. They disassembled it and every evening brought a few of the pieces into the ghetto, where they were finally able to put it together again. If they had been caught with the pieces they would have been punished, as smugglers, with death.

In these early years, though some amateur groups played operettas like *Shulamis,* more did revues or popular melodramas, such as *Money, Love, and Shame* or Thomashefsky's *The Essential Spark of Jewishness.* Turkow and his group wanted to establish a better kind of theater. They wanted it to be on a larger scale too, with professional Yiddish actors. But whereas the authorities allowed cafés and frivolous home entertainments (apparently as part of a campaign to demoralize or corrupt the ghetto morale), policy forbade anything more serious. The Judenrat, too, preferred to keep to musical entertainments, so as to be safer from displeasing the authorities by an unwise word. Besides, audiences were afraid to come together in groups large enough to fill a theater.

But with time, just as the ghetto had more concerts and art shows, so, too, it had finer theater. One step in that direction came when Turkow managed, by maneuvering of red tape, to shift the self-help committees from the Gestapo's to the propaganda chief's jurisdiction. The ghetto was then allowed to establish a network of soup kitchens, which could, like cafés, offer entertainment. Now it was possible to employ some professional actors and allow them to do worthwhile literary material. These soup kitchens, plus a crop of newly formed professional theaters, brought real theater to the ghetto.

In December of 1940, the second year of the ghetto, a Jewish woman got a concession for a commercial Yiddish theater. Rumor explained that she was a very good friend of the military commander of Warsaw. Meanwhile some people used the last of their capital to fix up one of the theaters inside the walls and named it the Eldorado. The first show was a revue, directed by Isaac Samberg, and the next few were old-fashioned operettas: *The Village Girl, The Cabaret Girl, A Home for a Mamma, Little Rivke the Rabbi's Daughter.* Turkow said that the style was so vulgar that at the opening he and others in the audience were positively embarrassed. Crowds continued to enjoy it, vulgarity and all, but Samberg and a few of the other actors quit—a noble gesture, considering how rare it was to find a steady job in the ghetto.

After 1941, when the Warsaw ghetto was sealed off, the situation was in some sense stable enough to allow for the institutional development of theater. The Warsaw ghetto had six professional theaters. There was the Melody Palace, and there was an art theater named the New Azazel after the *kleynkunst* band that had delighted Warsaw less than ten years before. At first people were afraid to go to the New Azazel, which happened to be near the main watchtower of the ghetto. But they accustomed themselves to that trip as to other dangers. Professional actors also hired halls for an evening. By 1942 there were some 3,500 to 4,000 theater seats in the Warsaw ghetto. Figuring performances six evenings a week at five-thirty, with two performances on Sunday, some 30,000 out of the half million in the ghetto could attend the theater weekly.

Included in those statistics were several theaters in the Polish language. One of the most ambitious was the Femina. Its actors were mostly Jews from Polish theater at first, but it also drew the more serious of the Yiddish actors, including Miriam Orleska, who had been one of the earnest youngsters who founded the Vilna Troupe on a cold, dirty stage in 1916. The program that Mary Berg saw at the Femina was not literary, but it was definitely creative.

April 20, 1941
The Femina Theater on Leszno Street is very successful. There one can see . . . many . . . celebrities of whom no one knew before the war that they were Jewish. The Femina has a mixed repertory: revues and operettas. Recently it staged *Baron Kimmel* and a revue in which prominent place was given to skits and songs about the Judenrat. There were biting satirical remarks directed against the ghetto "government" and its "ministers." These included many apt references to certain bureaucratic gentlemen of the community administration. . . .

October 29, 1941
Today I went to the opening of a play at the Femina Theater. It was a musical comedy dealing with present-day life in the ghetto, entitled *Love Looks for an Apartment.* A young couple is shown looking for a place to live. After a long search and much traveling about . . . they succeed in finding a tiny room in the house of a wily landlady who has divided a large room into two parts in order to be able to rent it to two couples. She manages to find a second couple for the other half of the room, and then the excitement begins.

It so happens that neither of the two couples is very well adjusted. As a result, two illicit love affairs develop, at first secretly, but, because of the overcrowded living conditions of the people involved, they soon become known. The two husbands switch rooms, and for a while everyone is happy, but then the husbands begin to quarrel with their former wives.

At night, when the two men come home exhausted from looking for jobs, they find their wives flirting with the president of the house committee, who sings a funny little song about the various taxes he has to collect for the community.

The end of the two love affairs is a sad one: all four young people are evicted for nonpayment of rent. The play concludes with a mass scene in a trolley car in which the travelers tell facetious stories about life in the ghetto, especially the various committees and commissions, whose number is constantly growing.

The audience laughed heartily and spent a few pleasant hours in the comfortable theater, completely forgetting the dangers that lurk outside.

Later, Mary commented on this entertainment and others:

Even these sad conditions give rise to various bits of gossip and jokes among us, and serve as material for songs and skits that are sung and played in cafés and theaters.

Every day at the Art Café on Leszno Street one can hear songs and satires on the police, the ambulance service, the rikshas, and even the Gestapo, in a veiled fashion. The typhus epidemic itself is the subject of jokes. It is laughter through tears, but it is laughter. . . .

These programs are tremendously successful. I used to be indignant at the jokes which took as their butt the most tragic events in ghetto life, but I have gradually come to realize that there is no other remedy for our ills. Marionettes have been made to represent our community leaders and the presidents of the various welfare institutions.

Perhaps in these years of ghetto life, people had learned to live on the volcano and could spare some spiritual energy for artistic experience. Or perhaps they turned to serious art as support against their misery. At the New Azazel, managed by Diana Blumenfeld, Isaac Samberg directed Molière's *The Miser,* in which he had starred in New York just a few years before. Instead of Molière, the fliers listed the name of the man who had translated the play from French, because Jews were forbidden to do plays by non-Jewish authors, just as they were forbidden to play music by non-Jewish composers. Samberg went on to direct Leivick's *Rags,* Mendele's *The Nag,* and other dramas. The New Kameri Theater presented an analogous repertory in Polish (though the Polish language was officially forbidden), including the modern comedy *Freud's Interpretation of Dreams.* Even the Eldorado Theater moved from *The Merry In-Laws* and *The Greenhorn Bride* to an experimental interpretation of Kobrin's *Yankl Boyle.*

There were theaters outside Warsaw too. Although very few actors were left in the Lodz ghetto, some performances did go on there in people's homes or wherever space could be found. In the fall of 1940, a program of bits from prewar revues was so popular in Lodz that it played three shows daily. In 1941 a group of amateurs got permission to open a little theater in the ghetto's Culture House, with the stipulation that they were to avoid all political or "serious" material. But they were shut down in the middle of a performance, probably because of one *kuplét* called "Things Will Get Better." When the Lodz ghetto became a labor camp, there were improvisations at the workers' regular exits, though such snatched moments were extremely dangerous for performers and spectators. Eventually the exits were sealed and the performances stopped. In 1943 there was briefly a children's theater by and for the ghetto's children, all of whom worked all day in factories. However, the Lodz ghetto was liquidated in 1943 and the children died in Auschwitz.

Even some smaller ghettos, such as Radom and Czestochowa, had theaters.

In Vilna, where the cultural atmosphere was traditionally elevated, there had never been the desperate frivolity of the cabarets and home entertainments of Warsaw's ghetto. Rather, the Jews in the Vilna ghetto sustained themselves more soberly, as testified by the ceremony in December 1942, marking the fact that the ghetto library had made 100,000 book loans in the fourteen months of its existence. Thus when, in the same year, a group of Vilna actors proposed forming a theater, there was a lot of community opposition. This intensified when people learned that the ghetto (Jewish) police were supporting the play, evidently for the sake of morale.

On the day of the first performance, fliers appeared on the ghetto streets and walls, bordered in black:

> In every ghetto you can find entertainment. And cultural activities are of course a *mitsve* [good deed]. But here in the sad case of the Vilna ghetto . . . where of 75,000 Jews only 15,000 remain, it is at this moment a scandal and an offense to our feelings. . . . YOU DON'T PLAY THEATER IN A CEMETERY. The organized Jewish workers have therefore decided to answer the invitation with a boycott. No one will attend the concert.

Nevertheless, supporters argued that a portion of the ticket money was to go to charity, and in the end the Vilna ghetto did accept and then embrace theater. Between January 1942 and June 1943 there were 119 performances for 35,000 spectators. These statistics cover only theater and not the symphony orchestra, the chamber orchestra, the jazz band, and the mandolin ensemble.

There were recitations of Hebrew and Yiddish poetry and the Biblical prophets. There were performances of sections of plays such as Leivick's *The Golem*, Sholom Aleichem's *The Big Win*, and Goldfadn's *Bar Kokhba*. Hirschbein's *Green Fields*, Pinsky's *The Treasure*, and *Man Under the Bridge*, a new comedy by A. Indik, were all given in their entirety; the last was performed forty-six times. The poet Avrom Sutzkever, a member of Young Vilna who survived to testify at Nuremberg, wrote a prologue especially for the ghetto performance of *Shlomo Molkho*, Aaron Glanz-Leyeles's poetic drama about the Marranos of Portugal.

A *kleynkunst* company named Diogenes offered the Vilna ghetto "remedy for its ills" in seven satirical revues, such as *Poor Corn and Wheat Dough, The Chase in the Barrel, Maybe There'll Be a Miracle,* and *Moyshe, Hold On.* The last took its title from one of its original songs by Kasriel Broyde, the final chorus of which asserts that armies are coming to the rescue and ends:

> Moyshe, hold out!
> Remember, we're going to get out!

Broyde, who wrote for the same show a prologue and epilogue based on Goldfadn's "Raisins and Almonds," was arrested during rehearsals and sent to a camp in Estonia, where he died.

A theater studio got together to perform Pinski's *The Eternal Jew* in Hebrew. Their leader wrote an original Hebrew play about ghetto life, which was given a reading by the Vilna League of writers and actors.

Theater in the Vilna ghetto ended with mass deportation in 1943. Two actors from Vilna were later rescued by the Red Army from a concentration camp; the rest were killed.

Two actors survived from Lodz.

The last play to be seen in the Warsaw ghetto was *Yankl Boyle* at the Eldorado. The ghetto was then liquidated. Few of the performers or spectators survived.

In the Camps

In the concentration camps, especially in early days, theater activity of a rudimentary sort did keep flickering. In the later years, sheer physical and emotional exhaustion extinguished it. But we do read of singing and recitation in bunkers.

In Auschwitz the actor Moshe Potashinsky, a Vilna Troupe veteran, stood on a bench in Bunker No. 3 to recite fragments from *Tevye the Dairyman* and modern Yiddish poetry. He survived, and in his memoirs he writes that the prisoners stood and listened, "some with tears in their eyes, moved. . . . One of the prisoners called out, 'If we have survived to sing in the camp, we will survive to see the Messiah!' "

In Women's Bunker No. 10, a few people recognized the actress Mila Weislitz and begged her to perform "something serious." The women in the bunker came from all over Europe and many of them didn't understand Yiddish, but they were rapt as she spoke and sang. For stage lighting she had the flames of the crematorium just outside the bunker window.

In another camp a young man from Lodz went from bunker to bunker to sing Yiddish theater and folk songs. In Ponyatov, many of the Yiddish actors from the Warsaw ghetto, including Simkhe Postel and Isaac Samberg, did slave labor during the day and managed to perform from time to time in the evenings. In 1943 most of them were taken to Camp Maidanek and shot.

Occasionally the theater was more organized. In Tzchenstochov, a camp that labored for the German war machine, the commander allowed a whole drama club to organize and even arranged for them to work only in the daytime so that they could rehearse at night. He let them set up a small bunker with a stage at one end, a curtain, and some stage lights. They were even allowed to make costumes. They opened with Goldfadn's *The Two Kuni-Lemls* and repeated it four times so everyone had a chance to see it. Performing weekends, they went on to present Goldfadn's *Kaptsnzon et Hungerman*, Lateiner's *Sara Shayndel from Yehupets*, a work called *I Am Innocent*, and a revolutionary play from the 1930s called *Cry China!* Then the S.S. took over the camp and all theater stopped.

In the Transnisteria, which was run by Rumanian officers, it was occasionally possible to organize whole performances in secret or by bribing officials. The rationale was that it was a prayer meeting. A group of young Yiddish writers, most of them Rumanian, put on amateur productions of Anski's *Day and Night* and other plays. They presented evenings of folk songs and poetry recitations, both classics and their own works. They also put on a playlet, *The Exodus from Egypt,* with obvious symbolic reference to their own situation.

In some cases the authorities themselves enjoyed being entertained by their prisoners. Former members of the light-hearted *kleynkunst* company Ararat climbed up on a table and sang revue theater numbers and folk songs for their commandants. They were rewarded with occasional cigarettes. In Auschwitz a young man who had been active in amateur theatricals in his small hometown of Bendin sang and recited, and got in return sometimes an extra bowl of soup, sometimes a piece of bread, once some clothing.

For a while in Teresienstadt there were performances of all sorts, from serious to frivolous and from singing to lectures. A chorus of 150 voices plus four experienced soloists, and—by special permission—a small orchestra, rehearsed for a long time for a grand performance of Verdi's *Requiem,* conducted by Rafael Shekhter. The artists included many who were famous in European concert halls and opera houses. After they performed for the prisoners, they performed for the Nazi officers, including a guest of honor, Adolf Eichmann. The commander of the camp had promised Shekhter not to separate the group before the performance, and though singers and musicians had occasionally disappeared during the rehearsal period, still on the whole he had kept his promise. The day after the concert, everyone who had participated went to the gas chambers.

In Kaiserwald-Riga were thousands of women prisoners who were rented out daily as laborers for an electrical company. In the early years of the camp, on Sunday evenings after work, they often organized concert programs for themselves, singing and reciting and even composing songs and poems. The camp commander was good to the women, and out of gratitude they decided to celebrate the commander's birthday with a marionette show. Flora Rom, a young woman from Vilna, together with some friends, worked hard on the project. Having no material to make the dolls, they cut pieces from their own dresses. Having no thread for sewing, they drew threads out of their own head kerchiefs. They got hold of a single needle on the black market. They made a stage from benches and a curtain from blankets. The program consisted of songs and playlets about their life, and it was a great success. In time, however, the women had no more strength to sing. Later, they died.

Among the theater people listed in the *Lexicon*, Volume V, were Isaac Samberg, ebulliant "czar of Yiddish actors"; Dr. Yitskhok Sziper, author of *History of Yiddish Theater Art and Drama from the Beginning to 1750*, the first scholarly investigation of Yiddish theater; Simkhe Postel, first of the Warsaw ghetto vaudevillians; Alter Kacyzne, author of the plays *Prometheus*, *Herod*, and *Der Dukes*; sultry Clara Segalovitch, whose Youth and Folk Theater presented *The Tempest* at the Nowósci in 1939; Adolph and Emil Gimpel and Malvina Yoles-Gimpel, sons and daughter-in-law of Yankev Ber Gimpel and heirs to the theater he founded in Lemberg in 1888; Yisroel Kompaneyetz of the Kompaneyetz family troupe, son of the founders and himself the father of child actors; Regine Zuker, whom Jonas Turkow called the queen of *shund*, meaning that she raised the popular operetta to what was, in its way, an art; and Miriam Orleska, who as a girl left a Polish drama academy to work for art theater in the Yiddish community—first with the Peretz Hirschbein Troupe, later with the Vilna Troupe, where she created the role of the bride Leah in *The Dybbuk*, and finally with the Femina in the Warsaw ghetto. Between 1943 and 1945, they were all killed.

13 YIDDISH THEATER SINCE THE WAR

THE NAZIS WIPED OUT MOST of the Yiddish theater in Europe, artists together with their audiences. However, as soon as the war was over, the survivors reasserted their need for theater. In the thirty years since, the need itself has become a survivor that keeps on defying extinction.

To the displaced persons confined in DP camps because they had nowhere to go, American Jews sent food, medicine, and actors.

In 1947, for example, Herman Yablokoff went to tour DP camps and hospitals. His company was a pianist and a German chauffeur named Hans; his bus was an ambulance and he was lucky to get it. On one occasion they visited a DP camp a few hours' drive from Munich. When they arrived, at about five in the afternoon:

> The whole camp already knew that there was going to be a concert that evening, but nevertheless Hans put up a few posters on the barracks walls, so it would be like the way things are done out in the free world. The posters which we brought along were printed in Latin letters on colored paper with a big photograph of me in the middle. They said: "The Joint Distribution Committee in the American Zone has the honor to present the first representative of the Yiddish Artists' Union in America, the famous theater artist and radio singer Herman Yablokoff, known over the world as 'The Clown.' The program will include Yiddish dramatic and musical theatrical creations and songs of Yiddish folklore. At the piano will be Professor Solomon Arzhevsky. The performance will take place at . . . o'clock. Entrance free." . . .
>
> The concert was announced for seven o'clock, but as soon as we arrived in the camp in the ambulance, the crowds ran to the "concert barracks," grabbed places on the long wooden benches, and waited.
>
> The German women who worked in UNRRA pressed my costume for the

"stage." That cost me all of one cigarette. Hans and Arzhevsky helped me carry the things into the "theater." The people who could not squeeze themselves into the barracks helped us drag the piano out of the ambulance and haul it up onto the platform. That way they got into a place where there was already no room to turn around. People were pushing and fighting. I requested that they open the broad side doors because there was no air in the barracks. I was frightened for the little children, they shouldn't, God forbid, be crushed. The Jews who were left outside made a rush for the open doors to grab a look and maybe hear a little something too.

"The piano is out of tune," Arzhevsky complained. "How am I going to play the 'Warsaw Concerto'?" He was as nervous as if he were going to play in the Salle Pleyel in Paris.

"You'll play," I encouraged him. "An artist manages somehow."

There was no light in the barracks. . . . Hans rigged up two big lamps to light my face at least. Someone "organized" for me a few candles so I could see to make myself up in a corner of the platform, behind the few quilts which hid me from the audience. . . .

While I was changing costume and make-up, Arzhevsky played the piano. I noticed that a few women left their seats and went out. At first I couldn't understand; the audience was applauding so hard, why should they leave? Weren't they enjoying themselves? When I went back onto the platform, it became clear to me: they had gone out to gather flowers to present to me after the concert, which lasted three full hours. Afterwards I had to start to answer their questions:

"What's going to happen to us? What will be the end?"

Yablokoff was not the only Yiddish entertainer to rush to Europe. When I visited Molly Picon and Jacob Kalich at their comfortable estate in the hills of upstate New York, a quarter century later, Kalich took me proudly through the grounds, ending at the garage. Its inner walls were gaily papered with souvenirs of their career together: overlapping theater posters in many colors and many languages. But one poster was hardly a poster at all, for it was only handwritten on a piece of plain paper. Unlike the others, it was protected by a sheet of clear plastic. It announced a performance in Germany in 1947. Kalich told me its story.

When American soldiers opened the gates to concentration camps and sent back pictures of the survivors, he and Molly were eager to give all they had to give, which was "a Yiddish word." But there was still no regular commercial transportation across the Atlantic. They pulled every string they could, and finally appealed to President Truman himself, who told them that if they could manage to find a berth on a ship, he would do his part by keeping quiet about priorities. In the end they found space on a freighter. In France and Germany, they traveled in open trucks from camp to orphanage to hospital.

The emblem of the DP theater at Bergen-Belsen, lettered in Yiddish, Hebrew, and English.

The DP theater at Bergen-Belsen around 1946.

Before they left America, it had occurred to them that the DPs were starved not only for food but also for possessions, nice things, the amenities of ordinary life. So they bought thousands of trinkets and wrapped each little package in colorful paper. After every performance they gave these presents out in handfuls.

They found out later what that gesture had meant to people. When playing in Miami, the Catskills, Las Vegas, or wherever, Molly was many times approached by women who, under their mink stoles, still wore the shiny little piece of inexpensive costume jewelry they had been given in the camps.

The DPs didn't just depend on guests. They made theater of their own too, obeying an impulse that was instinctive and imperative. Just as the camps immediately boiled with little magazines mimeographed on scraps of paper, so, too, camp inmates, few of whom had any professional theater experience, struggled to their feet and stepped out onto whatever stage they could find.

At least sixty such amateur groups appeared in DP camps between 1945 and 1949. They played for their own camps, to spectators still wearing striped prison shirts, and even toured to other camps and cities. Though many of them presented songs and dances without much thought or polish, some were more ambitious, presenting *kleynkunst* revue programs modeled on memories of Ararat and Azazel: folk and partisan songs, recitations of poems, original skits and songs about DP camp life. A program from Amkho, the first such group in Germany, shows a montage of scenes, including one of Hitler and Goebbels as woebegone organ grinders. Amkho even did acts from *The Dybbuk* and other classics and an original play by a camp inmate. Under the auspices of the Joint Distribution Committee, the American military, and administrators of the Jewish community, Amkho toured for several years. It marked its first birthday as a company with a special performance, a banquet, speeches, and a printed album of programs, pictures, and articles.

Often the names these amateur groups took for themselves tell the story of a DP's experiences: On the Road, The Wanderers, Bar Kokhba, In the Wilderness. Oyfboy (Building Up) appeared in a camp in southern Italy, where some of its members had been imprisoned a full six years. In 1946 Oyfboy put on Leivick's *The Golem,* Sholom Aleichem's *The Big Win,* and other plays, and even a program that they created out of original poetry, sketches, and songs. They had nothing. Lacking scripts, they reconstructed the plays from memory. When they needed a cigarette as a prop, they had to send a member out to beg it. Oyfboy and the rest dissolved as the members were resettled for new lives elsewhere, and their alumni ended up—usually not as actors—in New York and Los Angeles, Paris, Melbourne, and Tel Aviv.

A group at the DP camp at Bergen-Belsen, in the British sector, is one

Katsetnikes (Concentration Camp Inmates), presented by amateur actors in Brussels, March 1945.

of the few to have left a physical trace of its existence. About thirty-one inmates, mostly amateurs, some of whom didn't even know Yiddish, prepared a program of ghetto and partisan songs. On opening night, September 1945, they had managed only to get some colored chalk by way of make-up, and they looked, recalls their director, Sammy Feder, like children in a Purim play. Then, just minutes before the curtain, the chief rabbi of the British military in Germany and the head of the Joint Distribution Committee rushed backstage to the nervous actors, carrying

> in their hands a gigantic box full of . . . grease paints . . . and beards. There was enough to supply half the inhabitants of Bergen-Belsen. Many of the actors . . . were already made up and it was time to draw open the curtain. Therefore I instructed them to appear in the primitive make-up for the first act. (That became a tradition from then on, and in the following performances—in the camp and outside—we continued to appear in that make-up, in a spirit of "That ye shall remember," even though we already had plenty of grease paints.)
>
> The actors in the later sections of that first performance had the luck of using the make-up in the chest.

Yiddish actors in London sent the group more cosmetics as well as wigs, beards, and ear locks. The group toured European cities for a while. When they split to go their separate ways, Feder gave some of their costumes to a museum in Paris and some to YIVO in New York. But the original "gigantic box" Feder carried lovingly for another fifteen years of wandering till he settled in Israel. There, with a real emotional wrench, he donated it to the Theater Museum and Archive in Tel Aviv.

The professional European Yiddish actors in and out of camps pulled themselves together and remembered that they were professionals. By 1946, for example, MYKT (Musical Yiddish Kleynkunst Collective) was touring the many towns and villages in Poland where Jews had already resettled. They decided to move on westward.

> In order to leave Poland illegally (you couldn't leave legally), MYKT ensemble visited the Zionist Youth organizations of all persuasions.
>
> For performing at their collective settlements we received no money. But the leaders of the settlements repaid us by—giving us our freedom.
>
> They smuggled us over . . . past Polish, German, and Russian watchmen, in a tank in which they transport kerosene, together with our décors, equipment, musical instruments, and modest personal belongings, through the Russian-occupied zone of Berlin into the French zone. From there we could travel to the American sector like free men.
>
> In order not to suffocate in the airless tank, our friends made little holes in the ceiling and sides which served as scanty air holes.
>
> In the American zone of Berlin, we were met by representatives of the Army and members of the DP committee: those who were saved from the slave camps, who survived ghettos, and who were restored to life from the Aryan side—our sisters and brothers.
>
> "Is there going to be theater?"
>
> "Sure!" We unpacked the tools of our trade and, in a long barracks which served as center for cultural projects, we played our performances.

MYKT became the first of a number of professional European groups that played for camps in Germany and Austria even before the Americans got there. On MYKT's first opening night in a camp, in Lower Silesia, the spectators wished each other *"Mazel tov"* with tears of joy, as if they were all wedding guests.

Another group that was active between 1946 and 1949 was MYT (the Munich Yiddish Theater, or Representative Theater of DP Survivors). They played dramas and comedies by Pinski and Goldfadn, Glanz-Lyeles and Gordin, to some 400,000 spectators—including many who had entered the camp gates as children and never seen theater before. Joint gave them a bus to tour in, a truck for their sets, and an orchestra. They played in big theaters like the Prince Regent in Munich and in the clubrooms, garages, and dining halls of camps. They even sent their voices out over Hitler's favorite mouthpiece— Radio Munich.

Inevitably these professional actors wanted to organize. They wanted to

Scene from Victor Hugo's *Les
Misérables*, presented in Yiddish
at a DP camp in Germany in
1946.

DP theater group Ba-derekh (On
Our Way), in Berlin in 1946, acting out the experience of Jews
under the Nazis.

make clear the distinction between themselves and the amateurs who called themselves actors. They also wanted some sense of control over the quality of Yiddish theater; manifestoes denouncing *shund* were already abroad in the camps. So in Munich, in May of 1947, they founded the Organization of Artists. Yablokoff was there.

> The founding of the Artists' Organization in Munich occurred in an extremely impressive manner. About fifty Yiddish actors who had played theater before the war came together. They dragged themselves there from as far as Austria. How? —by foot. . . . The actresses behaved like stars and indeed managed a bit of chic. The actors brought folders and portfolios. Some had saved a few clippings of reviews from long ago; others, letters of praise from the committees of camps where they had already managed to perform for the survivors. Rarely did anyone bring along an extra shirt or a scrap of food.

The Jewish community gave them an office. Yablokoff gave them his type-writer. Armed with the dignity of their calling, the actors fanned out and looked for work.

The State Theaters of Eastern Europe

POLAND

In Poland, professional actors came out of camps or hideouts, drifted back from Russia and Asia, regrouped into ensembles, and returned to work. Already in November of 1944 Diana Blumenfeld, who survived the Warsaw ghetto, directed ex-soldiers and partisans in a program at the Peretz House in Lublin. As soon as a new area was taken back from the Germans, she and her husband Jonas Turkow and the actor Didye Epstein were there giving concerts of Yiddish songs. Two months after the war was officially over, Lodz had similar concerts. Bialystok soon had its own company of amateurs and professionals. Zygmund and Dora Turkow toured. Dzigan and Shumakher returned from Russia with their old gifts for satirical comedy unimpaired: in 1947 they took over a theater in Lodz with a revue entitled *Abi Men Zeyt Zikh (Just So Long as We Can See Each Other)*. At the time, many evenings of music, readings, and sketches had similar jaunty titles: *Hoopla! We're Alive!; A Gut Yor* (literally *A Good Year*, but also a polite response to a greeting); *Gevald, Vu Nemt Men a Minyan? (Help, Where Do We Find a Minyan?*—the ten-man quorum necessary for prayer services).

In all kinds of barracks and ruins, roles were being cast and rehearsals were in progress. In 1946 Warsaw saw a production of Sholom Aleichem's *Hard to Be a Jew.* A repertory theater formed in Lodz; its nucleus, under Moyshe Lipman, had spent the war years playing in Samarkand. Another group formed in Breslau under the direction of Yitskhok Turkow-Grudberg, Jacob Kurlender, and Sheftel Zak (who had just returned from Frunze). They produced plays by Sholom Aleichem and Gordin and also by Strindberg and other non-Jews. The Central Committee of Jews in Poland helped to support them.

These actors, too, immediately felt the old need to organize themselves, elect committees, and enunciate principles. They shared this perennial impulse with all the elements of the Yiddish community, perhaps as an inheritance from the highly structured *kehile.* Now the need became part of an instinctive effort to make the world solid once more. Perhaps it also echoed the Soviet system of networks of committees. In 1946 forty-some surviving members of the prewar Polish Yiddish actors' union met to reconsider the organization in the light of their new position as citizens of communist Poland. After much discussion, they officially dissolved the union and set it up again. Their first chairman was Moyshe Lipman; the next was Meir Melman, Ida Kaminska's husband, a soft-spoken man who was a lawyer in his youth and to this day retains a lawyer's calm, distinct, and orderly habits of mind. In 1949 the Yiddish actors merged with all the other performing artists in Poland.

One decade earlier Yiddish actors ran barely a step ahead of starvation. Now those actors who were still alive received the benefits that communist Poland gives to all its artists. A Yiddish State Theater was established. Its members became civil servants, ranked according to their importance to the company. They received a regular salary, a day off every week, and a month's vacation every summer. Ida Kaminska was appointed artistic director of the Yiddish State Theater and Meir Melman administrative director. A committee of company members was formed to keep an eye on the social consciousness of the theater's productions and attitudes.

In this new civil service era, the Yiddish State Theater was granted a fine new building in Warsaw. They took possession of it in 1955, in a ceremony commemorating the thirtieth anniversary of the death of Ester Rokhl Kaminska. Ester Rokhl had spent her whole life touring to earn her bread; Ida Kaminska, in turn, trudged Poland in the 1920s and 1930s and could barely pay her mother's hospital bills. Now they had a building, luxuriously equipped. But it wasn't always full. Significantly, the fancy equipment included headsets for simultaneous translation of Yiddish dialogue into Polish. For in 1955 there were only about 45,000 Jews in Poland (before the war there were about three million); some of the adults and most of the youngsters did not know Yiddish. The following year the situation grew worse, when a third of them emigrated —including half the actors in the Yiddish State Theater.

Three scenes showing the range of the Yiddish State Theater of Poland. *(Top)* Ida
Kaminska and Marion Melman in *Shots on Dluga Street*, by Anna Swirszczynska,
directed by Ida Kaminska in 1948. *(Bottom left)* Yitskhok Dogim and Ruth Kaminska
portray decadent Venetians in Ben Jonson's comedy *Volpone*, adapted and directed
by Yankev Rotboym in 1967. *(Bottom right)* Szymon Szurmiej as Willy Loman in
Arthur Miller's *Death of a Salesman*, which he also directed, in 1974.

State support liberated actors from the constant search for crowd-pleasers. The new era also drew a new repertory. Although they had special success with pieces drawn from folkloric tradition, the State Theater aimed to do plays of current interest, not specifically relevant to Jews. In 1954, for example, they presented *Julius and Ethel*, about the Rosenberg case; Turkow-Grudberg and Kaminska played the convicted couple. As of 1963 they had done twenty traditional Yiddish plays or plays built from traditional materials; three original Yiddish plays by Soviet Jews; five Polish plays in translation; four plays in translation from other socialist countries; and six in translation from Western countries. Sholom Aleichem remained a special favorite in all the communist countries, for his sympathies with the poor workingman made him seem a protosocialist.

Although the State Theater was not the only Yiddish theater in Poland, it was the most important one. In fact, it was a major institution in the Polish Jewish community. It was the arena for formal occasions, community "rites of passage." The Jewish ritual calendar had no place in postwar Poland, but at the State Theater, special dates were observed with festive performances. In 1947, for example, they celebrated the seventieth birthday of professional Yiddish theater with performances of Goldfadn's *Two Kuni-Lemls* and Gordin's *God, Man, and Devil.* They marked the twenty-fifth anniversary of Ester Rokhl Kaminska's death with a series of Gordin plays, which Ida Kaminska directed in her mother's style; in several cities, discussions and exhibitions were coordinated with the series. They celebrated Melman's fortieth year as an actor; he starred in *Di Aynzame Shif (The Lonesome Ship)* by Moyshe Dluzhnovsky. *Serkele*, by the doctor and *maskil* Shloyme Etinger, had its first performance around 1863, so in 1963 they presented the play and printed a special program, including a survey of the State Theater's achievements so far. In the same year they marked the twentieth anniversary of the uprising in the Warsaw ghetto with a play by Michael Mirsky called *Der Kheshbon (The Reckoning).* In 1964 they celebrated their own twentieth jubilee as a Polish Yiddish theater with a revival of one of their biggest successes, a dramatization of Eliza Orzeskowa's novel *Meir Ezofowicz.* Party dignitaries attended. As always, there were curtain speeches. Melman thanked the dignitaries formally for their support. Madame Kaminska spoke too. In her address she mentioned that only half the theater's regular audiences, which included non-Jews, knew Yiddish.

The acting style of the State Theater also expressed its institutional nature. Whether they did a modern drama or a play drawn from Yiddish tradition (like *A Mol iz Geveyn,* or *Once upon a Time,* directed by Avrom Morevsky), their approach was neither the broad declamation of the old-fashioned Yiddish theater, nor the expressionism that had been fashionable before the war, nor the varieties of avant-garde experimentation that interested Polish intellectuals in the 1960s, but rather a steady socialist picture-postcard realism with broad comic touches. In the late 1960s and early 1970s I saw Madame Kaminska in New York, playing the title roles in *Mirele Efros* and *Glikl Hameln Demands Justice.* Her acting, her direction, and her actors, some of whom had come with her from Poland, had dignity and attack, though their competence also had a muffled, static quality which was probably derived at least partly from their institutional status.

By 1967 Ida Kaminska had become an institution, with an energetic and authoritative presence radiating from her small body. That year she marked her golden anniversary in Yiddish theater as actress, organizer, playwright, director, traveler and sometime refugee, anxious mother (her daughter Ruth had been in a Soviet jail) and anxious grandmother. Naturally, there was a celebration at the State Theater, attended by celebrities of the Polish theater, political officials, and representatives of Jewish cultural organizations. But 1967 was a bad year for Jews because of the Six-Day War and the official USSR attitude toward Israel. Kaminska's tours, which had been arranged around Poland and other Communist countries, were abruptly canceled without explanation; the Silesian theaters where she was to play engagements suddenly wouldn't rent the space to her; the new Yiddish theater building that was to go up in Warsaw was abandoned; a film about Kaminska that had recently been made in Polish disappeared and has never been shown. The daily *Folkshtime* was reduced to a weekly. (The editor emigrated to Israel several years later, along with many other Jews who had considered themselves good Poles.) By 1968 Poland had only about 25,000 Jews, most of whom did not know Yiddish. Ida Kaminska, Meir Melman, and their immediate family left too.

In 1975 the Yiddish State Theater celebrated its twenty-fifth year as an official Polish State Theater with a handsome photo album and a production adapted from Peretz Hirschbein.

RUMANIA

Rumanian Jews are proverbial for their love of shows, especially the kind with gay music. In Israel the Rumanian actress Mary Soriano told me that performances to Rumanian audiences always last longer because they laugh more, applaud more, and demand more encores. Rumanians are proud that their country was the birthplace of professional Yiddish theater; the Rumanian consulate in New York continues to organize events commemorating Goldfadn's debut at Shimen Mark's Green Tree café in Jassy.

Poster for *The Dybbuk* by S. Anski, presented by the Bucharest Yiddish State Theater.

As soon as the war was over, little troupes began traveling through Rumania. In 1946, under the auspices of a multiplex committee (including representatives from the Joint Distribution Committee, the Yiddish Cultural Association [YKUF], the Zionist party, the People's party, an artists' organization, and incalculable others), Yankev Mansdorf and his troupe—recently returned to Bucharest—presented *I'm Alive* by Moyshe Pinchevski and then *Tevye the Dairyman* by Sholom Aleichem. There was a moving moment at the premiere of *Tevye*. As the curtain rose to reveal the sponsoring committee members standing in a row onstage, the audience gave them an ovation.

In the first year after the war, the company traveled around the country performing for the tiny knots of survivors who surfaced. In Jassy, shattered home of a lively Jewish community, they presented *The Witch* in the garden of what had been the Green Tree, in Goldfadn's honor. Once when the company was en route, they had to change trains at a hamlet called Dzibo.

Word got out that they were there. Jews crowded into the station and surrounded them, begging for theater. So the actors performed, without make-up, costumes, or tickets, on the railway platform, till their train came.

Soon two companies were getting support from the government and the Workers' party, one in Bucharest (1948) and another in Jassy (1949). In 1956 the government marked the eightieth anniversary of Goldfadn's debut by roofing over Green Tree garden and naming the resulting theater the Avrom Goldfadn. The Bucharest Theater was also fixed up and provided with simultaneous-translation equipment. On the occasion of its opening, a special book was printed, containing repertory lists, pictures of artists, dedications, and a history of Yiddish theater in Rumania, headed: "Now the Stars Aren't Vagabonds Anymore."

In 1958 the government founded a Yiddish State Theater in Bucharest, which would enjoy the same rights and support as the nation's theaters in other languages: Rumanian, German, and Hungarian. Members of the company have achieved ranks, titles, and service medals. A Rumanian-Hebrew-Yiddish fortnightly periodical is the only such Jewish publication in the Communist world.

RUSSIA

Yiddish theater was strangled in Russia. First the wartime refugees returned home from other countries. The state theaters of Kiev, Minsk, and other cities that had been evacuated were not allowed to return. In 1948 Mikhoels's body was found lying in the snow. In 1952 Zuskin, who succeeded him, was carried out of the hospital in a drugged sleep. The members of the Moscow Yiddish State Art Theater (GOSET) carried on for a while without a leader. But they stank of death, as did all Jewish institutions, and audiences were afraid to come near. At one production of *Koldunye* there were one hundred performers, including the musicians, for only twenty spectators. The actors sat day after day in the dormitory rooms allotted to them as Soviet artists. Their salaries had stopped. Those who could got jobs in other theaters, or other professions.

After Stalin died in 1953, conditions eased a bit. A literary monthly appeared in Yiddish: *Sovietish Heymland (Soviet Homeland)*. Under its auspices an ensemble of eight performers was organized, called the Moscow Dramatic Yiddish Concert Ensemble. They played wherever they were summoned to play, most often when American journalists or tourists were to be present. By 1966 the group comprised eighteen actors plus an orchestra.

Meanwhile, like stubborn weeds, other Yiddish actors appeared again. Meyer Broude recalls in his memoirs:

> After Stalin's death the atmosphere in the country became a little more free, so I went to the Secretary of the Central Committee of the Communist Party for Cultural Affairs, proposing to found a Yiddish state theater to serve the three Baltic republics: Lithuania, Latvia, and Estonia. In a few weeks I got an answer from the Administration for Artistic Affairs of the Cultural Ministry, that when they take up the question of creating new theaters, they will consider my proposal, too. They are considering it still to this very day, though a number of new theaters have in fact been created since.
>
> Little groups of Yiddish artists soon began to appear. They'd go on with Yiddish songs and readings. The first to come to Vilna was the actor Rakitin. He read the works of Sholom Aleichem, the first half in Russian and the second in Yiddish.

Broude met Nekhama Lifshits, a slight young woman with big eyes and a dramatic voice. She wanted to give concerts of Yiddish songs. Together they tried to organize a little company.

> It was not so easy to organize, or rather to legalize, such a group. . . . I went to Moscow and sat there seven months, selling everything I owned that could be sold, getting deep in debt, knocking on official doors. One could write a book about all the sorrows, all the sufferings, interventions, explanations, letters to high Soviet party and social figures. I went the whole long hard route to get permission to put on Yiddish concerts. . . . I wrote to Molotov three times. In those days he was a member of the praesidium of the Communist Party and Minister of State Control. In the last letter, I wrote to him in these words: "Is it forbidden in the Soviet Union to perform in the Yiddish language? If so, let them tell me so and I will stop trying."
>
> In Minsk . . . the official said we couldn't put up our posters, which contained a line in Yiddish. And we couldn't put on the posters, even in Russian, "Jewish songs and humor." We could only write "songs and humor," and then write down below in very small letters that the program will be given in the Yiddish language. And when we agreed to all that, he said that the matter still had to be taken up by the White Russian administration. "Since the problem of Yiddish culture has not yet been resolved in the higher circles of the Soviet Union, the Cultural Administration has decided to put off allowing your concerts."

Nekhama Lifshits left for Israel in the 1960s and eventually so did Broude. I met him in Tel Aviv in 1975, together with a whole ensemble of Yiddish actors newly arrived from Russia. He was distinguished from the others by his striking white hair and by something portly and prosperous in his bearing, though there is nothing prosperous about Yiddish actors in Israel—nor about new immigrants anywhere.

The ensemble calls itself Iditron, which is a combination of the Hebrew words *Idish* and *Teatron*. As I sat at one end of a long conference table in an otherwise empty meeting room, with the inevitable Israeli glass of tea before me, members of Iditron drifted in from rehearsal. I looked down two long rows of strained though cordial faces, none of them young.

People who have come out from behind the iron curtain shrug and smile when I, an American, ask questions. I imagine they must be expressing pity for my naïveté, or the impossibility of explaining all the intangible checks and frustrations, or they simply have the habit of caution. So when I asked what was the last Yiddish drama they'd seen or appeared in in Russia, the whole table was silent, smiled, and shrugged. Finally someone at the other end volunteered:

"So long ago, I can't remember."

I asked them about their own experiences. Some of them were professionals, like the director Aron Luria, who played under Mikhoels. Many had almost no professional experience, for where would they have got it?

The cities of Kishinev and Vilna have had semiprofessional groups of "young people" in their forties and fifties on and off since the 1950s. The Vilna group put on an amateur production of *Fiddler on the Roof* in 1972. Riga had a seventy-voice chorus, which was dissolved in 1965, and a drama club, which was dissolved in 1967. Nods and murmurs around the table as several told me the story of a performance that the Kishinev group was to give in Odessa. Three buses had been hired to bring them to Odessa, and the tickets had all been sold. At the last minute, the performers were told not to board the buses, for there had been a fire in the theater. The audiences in Odessa were told that the buses had broken down.

"So there was no fire," I say tentatively. They are too polite to answer. I persist.

"But did the Jews in Odessa ever find out what really happened?"

Shrugs. Smiles. "But they knew. Don't worry. Of course they knew."

Western Europe

Yiddish theater popped up wherever refugees had scattered. Mansdorf played *Othello* in Denmark, Sweden, and Switzerland. There were performances of Peretz in Antwerp and Brussels. After the postwar flurry of Yiddish theater in Western Europe, it gradually subsided into a combination of tours and amateurs.

FRANCE

In Paris, professional theater had always consisted basically of stars coming through on tour, from Maurice Schwartz and the Vilna Troupe to the dumbest operettas. The Parisian Yiddish public had long had a reputation for ignorance and vulgarity. For example, Jacob Ben-Ami acted there in *Samson and Delilah*. The play is about an actor and includes a scene at a rehearsal. Mr. Ben-Ami found the audience noisy and restless and later, on the street, overheard one spectator complaining to another that, "They should practice on their own time; that's not what I bought a ticket for."

In the 1930s the French community swelled with refugees, and the public demanding better drama enlarged. PIAT (Yiddish acronym for Paris Workers' Theater) and other amateur or semiprofessional groups played a literary and leftist repertory. PIAT toured France: Rouen, Nancy, Lyons, Reims, Strasbourg, and Metz. Two noteworthy dramatists were active in Paris: Chaim Sloves, who lives there still, and Moyshe Dluzhnovsky, who got to New York in 1941 and there wrote plays which were performed in Warsaw by the State Theater, and in New York at the Folksbiene and on radio.

Fighting had already begun when a song-and-dance comic named Sam

Brenendike Likht (Burning Lights) by Bella Chagall, presented at the puppet theater Hakol-Bakol under Simkhe Shvarts in Paris in 1948. The puppets and decor were created from sketches by Marc Chagall. The scene is a wedding.

Goldberg and his wife managed to slip into France from Poland. They had no money and worse, they had no papers. Goldberg parked his wife in a small hotel room with a few francs' worth of food. He waited till she closed the door behind him and locked it before he left, knowing that any contact could be a danger for a Polish Jewish woman with no papers. He wandered the streets of Paris until he found a kosher restaurant. At the restaurant he found *landslayt*, who put him on a train to Nancy, clutching a scrap of paper with a few French phrases and some names and addresses. That night Sam Goldberg sang and danced, piped his little harmonica and told jokes—and got on another train, to another town, with new names and addresses, where he did it again. When he had collected some money, he returned to his wife. Eventually the two got to England.

The first Yiddish performance after the Germans left Paris was Henry Vakhtel singing folk songs at a literary evening in 1944. By 1945 Paris had about twenty professional actors and two Yiddish theaters. One, which had essentially evolved from PIAT, was led by Yankev Mansdorf and Sheftel Zak. It played a rather literary repertory and called itself Yiddish Kunst (Art) Teater, or YKUT for short. The other was the Yiddish Folk Theater; included in its personnel were several members of the Kompaneyetz family, who had been in Yiddish theater in Eastern Europe since the previous century. In the next decade another company formed, the New Folksbine. There was also a

Hamans Mapole (Haman's Defeat), Chaim Sloves' post-war play using Purim play style and atmosphere, presented in Paris in 1946 by YKUT (Yiddish Art Theater). The street sign reads "Ahashuerus Boulevard."

marionette theater, which survived about two years; Marc Chagall participated in creating its décor.

Between 1949 and 1965 Chaim Sloves wrote *Nekome Nemer, Homons Mapole, Borukh of Amsterdam* (about Spinoza), and *Tsen Brider zaynen mir geveyn* (about the Warsaw ghetto). Theater activity in Paris now is intermittent and largely amateur.

Amsterdam has a cabaret with Yiddish entertainment.

Yiddish theater peaked in London in the 1880s, when Adler, Kessler, and Liptzin starred there. After that, London continued to have several theaters, but the principal one, in Whitechapel, was the Pavilion, which had served as an English theater for seventy-five years before Charles Nathanson bought it in 1898. Its company did the usual Yiddish repertory, plus a lot of adaptations of Shakespeare. Dina Stettin Feinman began in a London Yiddish chorus line and spent many years as star of the Pavilion; years after she died, Celia Adler thrilled the driver of a London taxi with the news that he was driving, in his own cab, his "Dinele" 's daughter. The Pavilion was finally declared unsafe in the 1930s, but it remained sentimentally important to the London Yiddish community. When it was blitzed, together with its archives, they mourned at its remains; four outer walls, covered with posters for *Lend Me Your Wife* and *Yidele's Bar Mitsva*, were all that remained standing.

Between the wars there were about a hundred professional actors, singers, and reciters based in London. There was also a public in Manchester, Leeds, Glasgow, and other northern British cities. Stars often came through, usually Americans on their way to Eastern Europe. They put together casts of local professionals and amateurs; sometimes youngsters taking piano lessons helped out as accompanists. The Vilna Troupe's visit in 1922 lasted two triumphant months at a fancy theater on London's West End. Dr. Paul Baratoff presented plays by Nordau and Toller as well as Yiddish repertory. Maurice Schwartz brought his Yiddish Art Theater to London four times between 1924 and 1939, once astonishing London with twelve plays, all well rehearsed and equipped with Schwartz's own sophisticated lights and décor.

London was the only European city with daily Yiddish theater throughout the war. Some days there were even morning, noon, and evening shows in various places. There were two regular theaters, on Commercial Road and on Adler Street. But during the blitz the liveliest theater was in the air raid shelters.

While the blitz raged all around, life went on underground. Clocks had no significance down there, and as the blitz continued, night life, at all hours, became less nervous and more friendly. Once the Russian Yiddish actor Mark Markov and his wife Etta Toffel went down into a shelter to give a spontaneous concert. They found an audience of about four hundred people, Jews and non-Jews. People rushed to help them set up, improvising costumes, hammering boards together for a platform, stringing up red curtains, and arranging rows of benches. When all was ready, someone played an accordion, there was applause, then silence, and the curtains opened to reveal Markov as a young *hasid* in a white silk robe with ear locks and skullcap. Etta Toffel wore braids. At the end of the show, the audience formed two rows and the actors walked through in state, after which their audience crowded around them and accompanied them up to the street. Most of the group were calling "Bravo." One elderly Englishman kept calling after them, "Good luck! Good luck! Good luck!" Other actors, and cantors too, gave performances in shelters.

As soon as the blitz ended, a small group met to help reopen Yiddish theater. They replaced furniture and sets that had been ruined. So many Yiddish actors had been evacuated to the country that Markov had to find new ones. He recruited some who had recently arrived in England as refugees, and others who knew Yiddish but had worked only in English theater. Some were amateurs. One of his new actors was a Jew who had owned his own German-speaking theater in Vienna until the Nazis. (At this period a number of sad little improvised cabaret theaters sprang up, playing in German for the 75,000 homesick German Jews in England.) Markov and Toffel also gave concerts in the Whitechapel Art Gallery, in other parts of London and the provinces, at army camps, and over the BBC,

In 1946 Adler Hall, which had been the principal wartime home of Yiddish theater, was taken over by a synagogue. The actors tried to transplant the theater from the old Yiddish neighborhood to North London, which was a new center of Jewish population. The venture, at the Alexandra Theater, didn't last. The English theater lapsed back into a way station for touring stars. In the 1950s there was a "Jewish Theatre" season in English at the Saville Theater, beginning with Israel Zangwill's *King of Beggars.* In 1962 the Yiddish Culture Organization, stimulated by a tour by Ida Kaminska, put out a retrospective pamphlet entitled "100 Years Yiddish Theatre."

England still has occasional vaudevilles gotten up by Sam Goldberg and other subterranean part-time entertainers, and occasional more refined programs of folk songs and art songs, readings and recitations. The fringe activities of the 1976 Edinburgh Festival included a production by a local Jewish community group: *Over the Grenits [Border] to Granton, A Satirical History of the Edinburgh Jewish Community.*

There is a saying in London which I have also heard applied to Yiddish theater and the Yiddish press in New York: "When, God forbid, an old Jew dies in London, they take another chair out of the theater. Why should it stand empty?"

Australia, Africa, and South America

AUSTRALIA

Just before the war, at the Nowósci Theater in Warsaw, there had been a gala benefit in honor of Rachel Holzer, a gifted young actress who was emigrating to Australia. Since early in the century, Jews in Melbourne had had a professional theater, largely supplied by touring artists. Typically, such artists played six to ten performances in Melbourne and then one in Sydney, with casts they made up from local actors, not all of whom had professional experience. That pattern has continued until today.

Since the 1950s, Australian audiences have seen a variety of "vagabond stars": direct from New York, Zygmund and Rosa Turkow; from Chicago, Dina Halperin, who directed and performed in Itsik Manger's adaptation of Goldfadn's *The Witch;* from Warsaw, Ida Kaminska, Meir Melman, and Yankev Rotboym; from Sweden, Khayele Grober; from Paris, Joseph Shein (formerly of the Moscow Yiddish State Art Theater); from Tel Aviv, Zvee Stolper and Leah Kenig. Many of these appearances were solo concert evenings of songs, recitations, and monologues, using no local talents.

A list drawn up in 1975 by P. Ringelblum, the honorary secretary of Kadimah, the Jewish Culture Centre and National Library, gives the names of professional Yiddish actors in Australia: "Jacob Weislitz [who played in the original Vilna Troupe production of *The Dybbuk*] (dec. 1966), Rachel Holzer (now semi-retired), Yacov Ginter, Nosn and Sarah Ginter, Yehuda Greenhaus (all dec.), Abraham Braizblat, Moshe Potashinsky, Mila Weislitz-Potashinsky, Ann Light . . ." The names show that this has been an interwoven little family.

Amateur activity continues. Between 1910 and 1925 Perth and Brisbane had attempts at amateur theater. Melbourne has had groups all along. Kadimah, which has existed there since 1911, sponsors the David Herman Theatre, which presents several performances almost every year. In 1933 the group offered a full season of four plays by Pinski, Dimov, Hirschbein, and Sholom Aleichem. In 1940 the Kadimah Yiddish Art Theatre gave two or three performances each of plays by Kobrin and Sholom Aleichem, Gogol and Ibsen, as well as a revue. In 1964, some 6,500 Australian Jews saw the David Herman Theatre in Sholom Aleichem's *Vagabond Stars*, Goldfadn's *The Two Kuni-Lemls*, and a comedy by the modern Israeli writer Ephraim Kishon. In honor of the twenty-fifth anniversary of Israel's independence, the David Herman Theatre presented *The Family Kahane*, and a Youth Theatre Group, also sponsored by Kadimah, offered a play in English, entitled *In Two Weeks at the Kinnereth;* both productions were directed by a visiting Israeli artist. Kadimah's groups have put on, in Yiddish, such American plays as Arthur Miller's *Death of a Salesman*, some one-acters by Arthur Kopit, and a comedy called *Lucky Strike.* Kadimah also sponsors literary evenings, concerts of Jewish music, and films in Yiddish and Hebrew.

In a letter to me, Mr. Ringelblum remarks that in the mid-1970s the Yiddish theater in Australia draws the twenty-year-olds and the fifty-year-olds; the generation in the middle, he says, is missing. But in 1974 a group of young people who grew up speaking English, led by a young actress named Fay Mokotov, organized themselves as the Melbourne Yiddish Youth Theatre. They gave four performances of *The Big Win* and drew twelve hundred spectators. They, and Kadimah, are planning more productions in the future.

SOUTH AFRICA

When Yankev Mansdorf and his wife Miriam traveled from Israel to Johannesburg, South Africa, in 1953, they found an audience waiting for them. For half a century Johannesburg, Capetown, Pretoria, Durbin, and Port Elizabeth depended primarily on tours that came for a month or a season from North America or Buenos Aires. Most often a star put together a company from local amateurs. David Kessler brought *The Dybbuk* and other plays in 1923. Stars since then, many of whom were brought by Sara Sylvia, have included the Burstein family, Maurice Schwartz, Miriam Kressyn and Hymie Jacobson, Joseph Buloff, Mark Markov and Etta Toffel, Max Perlman, Meyer Tselniker, Ben-Tsion Vitler, Henry Gerro and Rosita Landner, and Jacob Weislitz.

Since the start of the century, South Africa has also had amateur groups, such as the Zionist Dramatic Society and the Sociables. Johannesburg even had an English-language Drama and Opera Society, which performed an original comedy about an immigrant girl in South Africa and other plays of Jewish interest, as well as Gilbert and Sullivan operettas. Port Elizabeth— where, wrote one man, he "lived on drops of culture like a camel in the African desert"—imported a guest almost every year to direct the drama circle of the local literary club. In the 1930s Max Angorn formed an amateur group to play the smaller cities, where it didn't pay the professionals to visit, to bring such communities finer drama and give the profits to charity.

And there were other community enterprises as well. In 1951 the South African Yiddish Cultural Federation and the Yiddish African Theatre, together with African Consolidated Theatres, Ltd., presented *The Witch*, adapted to include a *badkhen* character who summarized the history of the Yiddish theater; he also explained the plot as it went along for the benefit of spectators who didn't understand Yiddish.

So when Yankev and Miriam Mansdorf arrived in 1953, the South African Yiddish Cultural Federation greeted them with a formal reception. Mansdorf soon set to work directing the Johannesburg Folk Theater, which had been founded in 1949 by Niuse Gold. He toured South Africa with the group. He also toured with "word concerts" excerpted from Mendele Moykher Sforim, Chekhov, and Shakespeare's Shylock. It so happened that Mansdorf's thirtieth jubilee as an actor fell while he was in Johannesburg, and the community organized an enormous banquet in his honor. Over eight hundred guests crowded in; a special album was printed, commemorating his career and the state of Yiddish theater in South Africa. After-dinner speech followed after-dinner speech, as representatives of one local Jewish organization after another explained why Mansdorf ought to stay on with them. Mansdorf was tickled at the idea of celebrating his jubilee at a side of the globe far from where he had spent his life, for it seemed to him to be especially appropriate to the life of a "vagabond star."

Despite all the pleading by the community for Mansdorf to stay, he had no regular status or livelihood there. There were plans to make him a secretary of the Cultural Federation, but they didn't work out, and besides, his visa was expiring. So he went on to Bulawayo in Rhodesia, where for several decades eight hundred families had maintained a Yiddish cultural organization, including literary and drama clubs. Mansdorf died there as he was making plans for subsequent seasons in South Africa.

Some Yiddish theater still goes on in South Africa. Max Angorn, who acted with fifty traveling troupes or more, now acts in English and also presents occasional concerts of recitations, readings, and songs. Paul Breitman, one of the early professionals, has been a cantor in Capetown for over thirty years. In the last few years, actors and singers appear occasionally on tour.

SOUTH AMERICA

The government of Argentina reduced immigration sharply before the war, so very few new Yiddish-speakers trickled in as refugees. However, the

Yiddish community was still lively, and so were the theaters, which kept mass audiences happy with musical comedies and melodramas, locally nicknamed "*tsholnt* plays." (*Tsholnt* is a dish of potatoes, grains, and meat; by no means elegant, but filling and traditional.) There were Yiddish radio programs and Yiddish records, many of them tangos.

The South American actors' union, founded in 1932, maintained its head-quarters in a neat little house in Buenos Aires. There the actors had parties, staged rehearsals, held funerals for their colleagues, and maintained a library. The union had funds for actors who became sick, old, or unemployed. It even had a farm in the country at which members could vacation.

The local talents had trouble supporting themselves, however, because in order to attract audiences they had to import big stars from North America and elsewhere. To import big stars they had to offer big salaries. The inevitable result was that most of the profits from Latin American Yiddish theater left Latin America in the possession of touring stars.

Many of these stars on tour played musical comedies, but some brought more literary vehicles. Jacob Ben-Ami came a number of times with Bertha Gersten and Jacob Mestel. In 1936, in honor of the author's visit to Buenos Aires, representing the Yiddish P.E.N. club at the international P.E.N. convention, Ben-Ami presented Leivick's *The Poet Went Blind* at the Nuevo Theater, to a crowd of four thousand spectators. Maurice Schwartz, Celia Adler, Herman Yablokoff, Zygmund Turkow, Ida Kaminska, Mina Bern, Dzigan, Max Perlman, the Burstein family, Jan Peerce, and Joseph Buloff were some of the stars who toured Latin America. Some evenings when Buloff was performing, the police had to divert traffic from the crowded streets around the theater.

Such "vagabond stars" are the mainstay of South American Yiddish theater now, not only in Buenos Aires but in Montevideo, Bogotá, Santiago, and Mexico City. Celia Adler played in towns that were scarcely more than clearings in the jungle, where the theater—a shed with a tin roof, so that falling rain was louder than the actors' voices—was the meeting place for Jews who lived hours and days of travel away. In 1963 Herman Yablokoff played in Lima, where audiences had long since stopped bothering to attend the pathetic little troupes that sometimes straggled through. He was a sensation, leading a correspondent to write wistfully to the New York *Daily Forward* that if President Kennedy could support the Alliance for Progress in aid of culture in South America, couldn't American Jews help support Yiddish theater in Peru?

In Argentina, from as early as 1902, with the founding of the Yiddish Society of Amateur Actors, there have been amateur groups in Buenos Aires

Posters for two productions presented by "vagabond stars" in Buenos Aires in 1932. *(Top)* Molly Picon plays her famous role of the mischievous *yeshive* boy Yankele, or Jacobito; Bessie Thomashefsky and Clara Young were two other stars whose publics enjoyed seeing them in boys' clothes. *(Bottom)* Joseph Buloff and Luba Kadison in the comedy *The Kibitzer.*

and in smaller cities, such as Rosario, La Plata, and Mosesville. In still smaller
settlements, elderly Argentinian Jews explained to Herman Yablokoff when he
was on tour there

> that the first visit by a troupe awoke in the young people a desire to play theater
> themselves. Often amateur groups soon sprang up. In the smaller colonies which
> didn't have libraries, a hue and cry went up: How can it be? It isn't right! A
> Jewish settlement without a library? So they created a library. They tried to
> acquire as many plays as possible. It was thanks to the drama circles that such
> libraries could exist.

Young Argentina, founded in Buenos Aires in 1926, gave rise a year later
to a drama school taught by Jacob Botoshanski and other writers and artists;
its studio performed serious Yiddish and European repertory. Other such clubs
in the 1920s included the Mendele Club, the Avantgarde, and the club of the
landsmanshaft from Galicia. A club named Idramst put out its own journal,
New Theater. From an acting school founded by the actors' union developed
the most important, most intense, and longest-lasting of these groups, the
Argentinian Yiddish Folk Theater (IFT). A Latin counterpart to Yung Teater
in Warsaw and Artef in New York, IFT associated itself with high standards
and leftist politics.

After the war, amateur activity continued. IFT also continued for some
time, under the direction of David Licht. There was theater for children, acted
by children. In 1960 the semiprofessional National Yiddish Folk Theater
formed at the Sholom Aleichem School, and for two years it played a repertory
ranging from Leivick's somber *Chains* to the Israeli farce *The Wedding
Certificate* by Ephraim Kishon. Teachers from the Jewish teachers' college
made an ambitious stab at Peretz's *The Golden Chain,* Etinger's *Serkele,* and
other classics. A group of young people presented revue programs in Hebrew,
Yiddish, and Spanish.

However, Yiddish theater in Latin America has shrunk to a minimum.
Buenos Aires had five regular professional theaters in 1939, two in 1949, and
only one, the Mitre, in 1960. Yiddish neighborhoods are dispersing. When
Jacob Mestel visited Buenos Aires in 1941, he noticed that children who had
chattered to him in Yiddish on his previous tour, five years before, now spoke
only Spanish. The Mitre began by playing six months in Buenos Aires and
touring six months; by the late 1960s it played only weekends and only part
of the year, though productions continued to draw eight or nine thousand
spectators. Literary evenings and concerts persist, and Argentina continues,
with Mexico City, the United States, and Israel, to be a center for the
publishing of Yiddish books.

Israel

Yiddish theater did not find a homeland in Israel. Yiddish, the language of the diaspora, remained in diaspora even when Yiddish actors reached Israel. They brought the diaspora with them.

In 1894 a group of amateurs presented Goldfadn's *Shulamis* in Jerusalem, as well as a play about the return to Zion, called *Zerubavel*. In 1905 another group formed in Jaffa, calling themselves Lovers of the Hebrew Stage. They began in Yiddish, but after the first few productions, some members of the group insisted that they switch to the Hebrew language. In the "war of the languages," as it is still known, Hebrew was already winning.

In conferences, learned journals, and the daily press, the debate seethed: What was the language for a Jewish state? Some thinkers imagined a nation in which two languages, or even three (with Arabic or French or German), wove a cultural scene like a colorful tapestry, expressing the gathering in of the scattered Jewish people. Between 1926 and 1930 Haifa did have a circle of Yiddish amateurs called Unzer Vinkl (Our Corner). And there were a few other such ventures in Jerusalem, Tel Aviv, Rishon Le-Tsion, and Zikhron Yakov. But meanwhile kiosks were set on fire for selling Yiddish newspapers, and on the street passers-by felt free to say, sharply, to strangers speaking Yiddish, "You're in Palestine now. Speak Hebrew!" In 1931, when a wealthy American Jew offered to subsidize a department of Yiddish literature at the Hebrew University in Jerusalem, the university refused to have Yiddish in their curriculum. As late as 1942 another amateur attempt at drama was interrupted by stones.

Ideologically Yiddish was always controversial in Palestine (after 1948, Israel). On the one hand, it was the first language of many Israelis and culturally important to many more. It was a bond between these Israelis and the many Ashkenazic Jews in America and other countries. It was the language of a fine literature and other cultural achievements.

On the other hand, Yiddish traditionally had less social prestige in Jewish society than Hebrew, an attitude reinforced by the Western *haskole*. Yiddish had developed entirely in the diaspora and was part of that experience, whereas many (though not all) of the Zionist groups in nineteenth- and twentieth-century Europe explicitly identified their goals with a rejuvenated Hebrew language, studied it, and struggled to speak it; many such groups put on plays in Hebrew. To these Zionist groups, Yiddish seemed the antithesis of Israel's modern goals. It was associated with the social order that the early socialist pioneers rejected when they dedicated themselves to working the Palestinian soil. It was associated with pieties which they rejected when they hammered their loyalties into a strictly secular or nationalist Jewishness. Yiddish was also associated with an image of cringing impotence which the settlers officially rejected when they declared themselves an independent nation.

Israelis who are native-born have always rejected Yiddish with all the other old ways of their immigrant parents, and many of the parents have fully sympathized with their attitude. Although as the language of most of the six million Jews killed by the Nazis it had special claim to respect from the survivors, the Israelis who had established an image of themselves as sunburned and muscular found even the association with the massacres of the holocaust threatening.

Sephardic and Oriental Jews do not share these complicated emotional attitudes. To them Yiddish culture is simply alien, and because Ashkenazic Jews have tended to be the best educated, most prosperous, and most powerful group in Israel, the Sephardim have felt and continue to feel some hostility to it.

As the war decade ended, the fury of hostility eased a bit. In 1949, soon after the establishment of the state of Israel, a literary periodical called *Di Goldene Keyt (The Golden Chain,* the title of a play by Peretz) began to appear, edited by Avrom Sutzkever. It continues to be the most important Yiddish literary periodical in the world. In the same year, David Pinski moved to Haifa, where his home on Mount Carmel, overlooking the blue sea, became a salon and nursery for young writers in Yiddish and Hebrew. Whereas there is on record only one performance of a Yiddish play in 1945, in 1950 there were forty-three performances of ten different plays. Refugees streamed in. Inevitably among them were Yiddish readers and writers, audiences and actors.

Like magnets, the actors found each other. Several got together and made a theater; they named it the Avrom Goldfadn because the father of Yiddish theater had started from scratch and they were doing the same. Among their earliest productions were his *Shulamis* and *Bar Kokhba.*

The Goldfadn Theater had no money. So they wrote to their colleagues in America, and the Hebrew Actors Union in New York organized a committee—some of whose members were refugees themselves, like Sheftel Zak—to send them supplies. In Israel there were not enough theater buildings to go around, and for Yiddish theater the shortage was worse because private landlords were reluctant to rent. So they improvised platforms out of doors laid over garbage cans. Once they built a stage out of egg crates, but it suddenly gave way under an actor's feet and he fell through to the ground. They traveled from town to town on the back of a truck. Their main home was a courtyard in Jaffa, where they sometimes seated their audiences on trunks and gasoline cans. For they did have audiences.

But Israel was driving to make itself a unified nation, fast, and the national language was to be Hebrew. In a survey called *Theater in Israel,* published in 1963, Yiddish theater appears at the end of the "Foreign Language Theatres" chapter, after English, French, and Arabic. The actors felt as if they were living in that standard melodramatic situation in which members of a family fail—or refuse—to recognize each other. Now that they had got to Israel, Yiddish was still a stepdaughter, as Mendele had called it half a century earlier, and Yiddish theater still subject to harassment. The bewildered actors were constantly denied permits, fined, saddled with inconvenient rules and restrictions. Once they were actually interrupted during a performance and brought into the police station. A court case allowed them to continue their existence, and they kept on organizing, trouping, and making big plans. But they also continued to pay not only a standard city tax but also the extra tax levied on "foreign language" theaters that visit Israel.

In 1952 the Goldfadn Theater planned a gala summer season to celebrate Yitskhok Leyb Peretz's birthday. They staged ambitious productions and piled up ambitious debts. Through fragrant Jaffa evenings they played Peretz's *Three Golden Rings* (dramatized by David Licht), Goldfadn's *The Two Kuni-Lemls,* Gordin's *Mirele Efros* and *The Kreutzer Sonata,* Sholom Aleichem's *Hard to Be a Jew,* Kobrin's *Yankl Boyle,* Hirschbein's *Green Fields,* a new play one of whose authors was a member of the old Kompaneyetz acting family, and several more. But they did not make enough money to break even.

Soon after they collapsed, they received from New York great chests full of gifts from the union there: scripts, musical scores, costumes, make-up, lights.

During the next decade, the official strangle hold on Yiddish theater loosened somewhat. At the same time, the membership of the Yiddish writers' organization tripled, rising to just over one hundred fifty; Yiddish books and periodicals appeared; and the Hebrew University established a department of Yiddish studies. Modern Israeli history is largely a history of immigrations, and the last three waves of immigrants from Eastern Europe were significant for Yiddish theater. In 1961 Rumanians began pouring in, with their old thirst for (in the formula of Mary Soriano) the worth of a ten-pound ticket: two pounds' worth of singing, two of dancing, two of laughing, two of crying, and two of décor. It was partly in response to this new population that the government lowered the tax that Yiddish theater paid over and above Hebrew theater. By 1965 the number of Yiddish performances on record rose to almost six hundred, in almost thirty plays. In 1967 came Polish Jews, who were used to having a stable professional theater. In the 1970s the influx has been from Russia, and the government has been trying especially hard to accommodate them.

Touring stars visit Israel, some bringing dramas of high quality in their valises. In this category, Avrom Morevsky and Ida Kaminska have visited from Poland, the latter several times. Golda Meir greeted Kaminska both as the prime minister and as a fan, and expressed herself in both capacities by coming backstage and giving Kaminska a hug. Maurice Schwartz played in Israel several times; in fact, he died in Israel in 1960, in the midst of elaborate though unpromising plans to establish a permanent theater there. Joseph Buloff has brought repertories ranging from *Death of a Salesman* and Chekhov one-acters to *The Diary of Anne Frank, Tevye the Dairyman,* and, in 1974, an evening of readings from Peretz. Jacob Ben-Ami acted and directed there.

A few artists based in Israel are on the same high level. In 1974–75, Eliahu Goldenburg presented a program of Sholom Aleichem selections arranged for three readers. Reading aloud is a special art which has largely lapsed among English actors, but Yiddish actors continue it in "word concerts," and this particular program was a gem. Herz Grossbard continues to give readings in Yiddish, pursuing a career began in prewar Europe. Also in this category are Dzigan's evenings of political satire mixed with music and other sorts of revue entertainment. When Dzigan celebrated his jubilee in 1972, Israeli dignitaries were there to applaud him. Although it is harder every year for him to find clever writers in Yiddish, he continues to issue records of his own clever monologues and to get away with his old impudence, as when he appeared dressed as Golda to poke fun at government policies.

For these more intellectual artists there are respectful audiences, even including some Israelis for whom Yiddish is either a shaky memory or a totally foreign language. Their performances are sometimes, though not always, mentioned in the Hebrew press. Kibbutzniks come to see these artists and invite them to perform at their local community centers. However, the total sum of all ticket-buyers is not enough to support any of the artists. Moreover, the Yiddish public tends to be the same people who buy tickets to the finer Hebrew theaters, and how many tickets can they afford in one year? Professional art theaters do not exist long anywhere without a subsidy, and whereas the Hebrew Habima and Kameri and several others receive such subsidies from the government, Yiddish theater—until very recently—had none. It still pays extra "foreign language" taxes, besides.

Thus it is inevitable that in Israel as everywhere else outside Poland and Rumania, the only professional Yiddish theater companies that last long are

Gelt, Libe, un Shande (Money, Love, and Shame), a melodrama about the underworld. This poster appeared on walls, kiosks, and billboards in Tel Aviv in the winter of 1975. Its message is in Yiddish and Hebrew, in Russian for new immigrants to Israel, and in a Roman-letter transliteration for those who cannot read Hebrew-Yiddish lettering. Among the actors pictured below are Hanna Ribber and Yosef Shakrub.

those that attract the masses with musical comedies or melodramas. Some titles of 1974 sum this up: *My Son the Doctor* (translated from a recent Hebrew hit); *Money, Love, and Shame; Sha, Sha, Here Comes the Groom; The Drunken Woman.* Usually well acted, these productions are wholly unsophisticated in texts and staging, though in *Money, Love, and Shame,* for example, there was an interesting scene in which criminals in a tavern put a thief on trial for stealing a pimp's woman, in a parody of a solemn rabbinical court. And inevitably such plays reinforce the common Israeli conception of the sum of Yiddish culture as vulgar and sentimental *shund*—a hapless, perpetual cycle which is common elsewhere as well.

Intellectuals who remember the Vilna Troupe and Yung Teater, the more educated Yiddish-speaking Israelis, and those more assimilated into Israeli life are eager to dissociate themselves from Yiddish theater. There are a few exceptions: the witty poet and broadcaster Nakhman Rapp, or the innovative folklorist Professor Dov Noy, who took his Israeli children to see *A Rumanian Wedding* and reported that they all laughed a lot. But more typical is the distinguished Professor Chone Shmeruk, who has written extensively about

Peretz and the history of Yiddish drama, but who rapped out firmly the minute I asked: "I haven't gone in fifteen years."

Yet clearly somebody goes. Mostly immigrants. Most of the people waiting outside the Ester movie theater in the port city of Ashdod the night *My Son the Doctor* played there (instead of the usual movie) spoke Russian. They looked like immigrants too; they had gold teeth, or gaps, and they had the dumpy flesh that looks like years of living on potatoes. When the doors opened, over an hour late, they filled all the downstairs seats, and from the balcony I watched them laughing so hard that their heads and upper bodies swayed constantly, like a field of grain in a high wind. Evidently, as long as there are Eastern European Yiddish-speaking Jews arriving in Israel, there will be Yiddish theater.

According to Natan Gilboa, one of the five or so impresarios who handle Yiddish theater, some one hundred families support themselves through popular Yiddish theater. Several actors manage to do so with glory. Mary Soriano, for example, young and good-looking, with a healthy crop of brown Israeli curls, is so popular that people ask at the box office for "two tickets to Mary." One woman who loved her as *The Drunken Woman* made her a huge jar of pickles and rode the bus for hours, with the jar on her lap, to bring them to the stage door. Mary has a calm eye for her position. She and her young Belgian husband, Michel Greenstein her director, and their regular company give the public what they want. Indeed, she recently toured to South Africa and South America. Other stars whose names come instantly to their public's mind include Max Perlman, Eni Litan, and Gita Galina.

Most of the other Yiddish actors in Israel get along with less fanfare. In 1975, when I was amusing and bemusing my Israeli acquaintances by asking around about Yiddish theater, the lead I was most often given was the Café Nitza on lively Allenby Street in Tel Aviv. Actors' union? Café Nitza. Actors' club? Café Nitza. Actors' addresses? (Many Israelis don't have telephones.) Actors' archives? Producers' offices? Café Nitza.

The Café Nitza is so ordinary a place that I walked past it twice, checking street numbers, and didn't even notice it. A typical little Tel Aviv coffeehouse, it has small square tables with flat red metal ashtrays, daily newspapers lying around for the reading, and a big machine for frothing up cups of expresso. It is the Yiddish actors' unofficial headquarters, and the waitresses accept messages for them pleasantly enough. But clearly they see no glamour at all in the middle-aged men and women who chat soberly around the little tables. A few feet away, beyond a pillar for privacy, the star of *My Son the Doctor* hunches intently over a forgotten glass of tea; he and a friend are doing the salaries-rent-investment arithmetic for next season's comedy.

These actors are used to traveling by bus or car three or four days a week, to movie houses or auditoriums in cities as far as three hours from Tel Aviv, and returning home late at night. They are used to all sorts of places to put on their costumes: sometimes they have a proper dressing room in a large Tel Aviv theater, but just as often it's a big space with concrete walls—the basement of the Ester Theater, for example, has a high partition to separate men and women, a plain counter running below the mirrors, and cigarette butts on the floor left from the Greek-language Israeli troupe that played there two weeks before.

They don't get much publicity. Most shows are advertised by posters tacked onto walls and kiosks, and reviewed in the Yiddish weekly *Letste Nayes (Latest News)*. Some also appear in the English *Jerusalem Post*. Evenings of recitations and music, or readings of an author's work on the occasion of his birthday or the anniversary of his death, are noted in *Letste Nayes*. For some performances you have to ask around, or check on the bulletin board of the Workmen's Circle or one of the few other Yiddishist organizations. Although the Workmen's Circle has an amateur group who in 1975 were preparing Bimko's *Oaks*, I learned of them only through a veteran member, the Yiddish broadcaster Mikhl (Vaynapel) Ben-Avram. They have put on a play every winter for the last eighteen years, generally playing ten to twenty performances a year, but I never came across a soul who admitted to having seen them. In fact, the statistics for Yiddish theater are generally suspect, for more plays may be going on than researchers find, in Israel and in other countries as well.

But as the threat of Yiddish dims into the past, Yiddish is becoming more legitimate and attractive, even romantic, as symbolized by Golda Meir's instituting the annual Prime Minister's Prize for Yiddish literature. Thus in the last few years there has been more public Yiddish theater than ever before. An annual festival of Yiddish songs has become a popular event. A band of handsome young Israeli singers in turtleneck sweaters and guitars put on an entertaining program of Yiddish *hasidic* songs and folk materials (in Hebrew translation). The Burstein family has been staging the charming *Megile of Itsik Manger*, the poet's reworking of the Purim story as if it were a Purim play presented by a bunch of tailors' apprentices in a *shtetl*. They used Hebrew and Yiddish in Israel, added Spanish in Argentina, English in America, and it ran for years. A big revue program honoring the hundredth year of professional Yiddish theater was given in Tel Aviv in 1975 and advertised in the Hebrew press. In 1974 the magazine section of a major Israeli daily, *Ha-aretz*, printed a glowing feature on Yiddish theater. The journalist, although clearly not a Yiddishist, praised the "deep bond between performers and public" (who applaud the minute a performer steps onstage, just "to let him know he's at home, among friends") and the excellent acting, but deplored that Yiddish theater was treated like a "stepchild" in Israel.

A major factor in the new attitude since 1973 is the Russian immigrants, whom the Israeli government is trying to integrate. They have been complaining that they heard more Yiddish radio before they emigrated, for Israeli radio (which is under government control) beams a Yiddish hour directly to Russia but only a half hour for home consumption. Their wish for Yiddish theater, especially for theater of a refined sort, is having its effect. The government, which subsidizes all kinds of ventures by new immigrants trying to establish themselves, has been giving support to two Russian Yiddish ensembles. One, which calls itself We Are Here, has already brought its pleasant program of singing and dancing on tour to New York. The other is Iditron.

When I was talking to members of Iditron around the long table, Zilia Elman took me aside to tell me that she had left her family behind in Russia because—one hand pressed over her heart, the other clutching mine, her eyes bright with emotion—she longed to play Yiddish theater. Another member, who knew no Yiddish at all, refused to talk about the old country. "Enough about Russia," he said. He was in jail fourteen years there, but "Never mind, not important. Enough about the past. Let us tell you about our future."

In 1974 Iditron performed the musical revue *Freylakhs*, reconstructed by its director, Aron Luria, from his memories of Mikhoels's production. Some twenty thousand theatergoers enjoyed the production, and the mayor of Tel Aviv came to a special benefit to show his respect for the whole undertaking. In 1975 they were preparing Goldfadn's *The Tenth Commandment.* But the government, which after all must help many new immigrants get started, could not go on indefinitely considering them new; eventually they would have to support themselves by selling tickets, a necessity which seems harsh and bewildering to people who have spent their lives in communist countries.

In the spring of 1975, the Israeli government established a Yiddish Art Theater, handsomely budgeted by the National Office of Education and Culture and the ministry responsible for the absorption of new immigrants. Under the direction of Shmuel Bunim and Binyomin Zemakh, a group of young actors and veterans turned from the Hebrew theater to the Yiddish, presenting Sholom Aleichem's *The Big Win* on a grand scale in Tel Aviv and on tour around Israel. Next, in conjunction with the Yiddish Art Theater, Ida Kaminska, who had just returned with Meir Melman from New York, starred in the play *Glikl Hameln Demands Justice.* The new group planned to present an entire season, perhaps including Itsik Manger's *Hotsmakh*, adapted from Goldfadn's *Koldunye*. But the early productions suited neither the intellectuals nor the masses sufficiently for them to support the company. The following year, Israel Becker was put in charge of a fresh attempt to establish a Yiddish Art Theater in Israel.

With or without a Yiddish Art Theater, the years 1975 and 1976 did offer Israelis several alternatives to the most popular level of Yiddish theater. After *Glikl Hameln*, Madame Kaminska turned to celebrating the hundredth anniversary of the birth of her mother, and toured Israel for about a month in Ester Rokhl's role as Mirele Efros, Gordin's "Yiddish Queen Lear." In the same year, Motl (Mike) Burstein played the title role in Asch's *Motke Ganef.* The commercial producer Natan Gilboa imported the Folksbiene from New York with Gordin's *God, Man, and Devil.* And other companies were rehearsing Anski's *The Dybbuk* and Singer's *Yoshe Kalb.*

In August of 1976, some five hundred delegates from sixteen countries met at the Hebrew University campus in Jerusalem for a World Conference of Yiddish Culture. After debates about such traditional subjects as the relationship between Yiddish and Hebrew and the nature of the community's responsibilities for Yiddish, they adopted a resolution asking the Israeli government and Jewish world institutions to help preserve the Yiddish language and culture.

14 YIDDISH THEATER IN AMERICA SINCE THE WAR

In the United States, as elsewhere in the world, Yiddish has been disappearing from daily use. Except in certain ultra-Orthodox communities (which do not support theater), most Yiddish-speakers are getting old, and the influx of Rumanian and Polish immigrants in the 1960s was too small to make much difference. Nevertheless, the United States remains, as Joshua Fishman wrote a decade ago in "Yiddish in America," the "quantitative and qualitative capital" of the world's Yiddish-speaking Jews. Although the scale is reduced, Yiddish theater in the United States and especially in New York still offers a wide range of experiences; I have seen in New York in the last five years almost every genre Yiddish theater ever offered, even including a *badkhen* and a *Purimshpil*. Moreover, the various feelings that Yiddish theater has always evoked within the Yiddish community continue to operate in all their complexity.

The Hebrew Actors Union headquarters on New York's Lower East Side is surrounded by tenements, bars, a few shops, and a Ukrainian church. By the end of the 1960s, the junkies and hippies who had disoriented the neighborhood mostly disappeared, though a face framed by long hair still sometimes peers curiously in through the window of the union's ground-floor office. The passer-by sees some middle-aged men, a desk, a telephone, a shabby sofa, a linoleum floor. He doesn't know he's seeing the heart of Yiddish theater in America.

In that office, slapping that desk with the flat of his hand, gesturing into that telephone, Herman Yablokoff and the other officers of the union argue through the deals, the financial backing, the contracts, and the casting. They are short men. Their cheeks are creased, their hair recedes. They resemble their cousins the Yiddish journalists and the Yiddish candy store owners, except that their features are larger and more forceful—suitable to glossy photos on easels in theater lobbies.

They remember in their bones the seven encores in Johannesburg, the private trains in Warsaw, the baskets of flowers in Newark. By contrast, an interview with me is small potatoes, and while some are courteous, even charming about it, others say, offhand and lordly, "I'm busy this month; try me next month," or "Maybe a week from Monday, but you'd better phone the night before to make sure"—and when I phone, they renege. They have long pasts; they know their role and are sure that they have illustrious futures yet to come. Just as, in Fishman's observation, a renascence of Yiddish literary activity among "the growing Jewish-American college population . . . would not surprise the older generation of lovers of Yiddish in the very least," so, too, the actors get from one production to the next, confident that the future will take care of itself. Indeed, in 1976 Leon Liebgold, Mr. Yablokoff's successor as union president, told a *Forward* interviewer that the actors are planning a National Yiddish Theater, to usher in the second century since Goldfadn's debut. Their certainty is manic, maddening, absurd, grotesque, but totally impressive.

Upstairs at the union is the social center for actors, as well as for those in related professions, such as ushers and composers. The Yiddish Theatrical Alliance, a fraternal and burial society, has its headquarters there, and so does the Yiddish Artists and Friends, a social group which visits the sick, telephones the elderly, and so on. The new committees getting ready to observe the centenary of Goldfadn's debut at the Green Tree Café meet there. The Hebrew Actors Club holds parties in this room; there are concerts and lectures, a few songs, a raffle, a card game; the women, in bright colors, serve refreshments on paper plates.

They've all known each other a long time. Except, maybe, on the subject of a contract that fell through, they limit their gossip and bad-mouthing to a shrug or a snicker. On the other hand, they rarely speak highly of each other. They stand to offer their chairs when the real old-timers come slowly in, especially the two who are associated with "literature": Celia Adler, appealingly small, flushed, and cozy, with an unexpectedly sonorous voice; and Jacob Ben-Ami, pale and scrupulously erect, his cigarette tilted Russian style between thumb and forefinger, acknowledging with a gentle nod and an occasional mischievous flash the people who visit his table to pay their respects.

The upstairs room also serves as a place for ceremonial occasions. For example, when Zalmen Zylbercweig died in Los Angeles in 1972, leaving Volume VII of his *Lexicon of Yiddish Theater* still unpublished, together with a garageful of related books and papers, the union held a memorial service for him. Israel Bercovici, the cultivated dramaturge of the Bucharest Yiddish State Theater, who happened to be visiting in New York, was only one of the speakers.

In this room candidates for membership used to have their grueling "auditions." No more. Now everyone who plays professional Yiddish theater in North America must join the union, and that includes actors who pass through on tour or who live primarily from American theater. Today the union welcomes young members; in the last five years membership has grown from one hundred fifty members to one hundred ninety, and all the newcomers are under thirty. But though the union's executive committees have recently included such younger members as Ruth Vool, Bruce Adler, Stan Porter, and David Carey, the members whom a visitor is most aware of are on social security pensions or close to it, and they prefer to leave meetings in time to get home before dark. Born in Chicago or Buenos Aires or Minsk or Tel Aviv, they frequently have belonged to other Yiddish actors' unions as well as to this one. Membership in the Hebrew Actors Union makes them automatic members of the American Actors Equity and the AFL-CIO.

In the open area of the union's ground floor I once saw Jacob Jacobs rehearsing a number for a new show. He was over eighty, and the two women following behind him were in their forties or fifties. They imitated his steps, humming the tune: one-and, two-and, cross over the feet, and turn and back. They repeated the simple sequence several times and they were done, ready to go out onstage. Certainly this is not standard in the New York Yiddish theater; most productions rehearse seriously for weeks and some even longer. However, in this case it wasn't the rehearsal that had trained them, but rather years of having to learn fast and make up as you go along. (I saw that very number about a month later, in the auditorium of a high school in Brooklyn, at a matinee in which the microphones weren't working; I couldn't hear the young romantic leads, but the comic song-and-dance, the *kuplét*, by Jacobs came belting out loud and clear.)

The union is one of the last outposts of *Yiddishkayt* on the Lower East Side. The National and the Second Avenue theaters were demolished in 1959; the Anderson Theater became a home for rock bands, with the smell of marijuana trickling out through its lobby onto Second Avenue; the *Jewish Daily Forward* moved its presses to midtown, selling the old premises to a Chinese institution. Many of the Jewish restaurants of earlier times now serve beans and rice or pizza. The elderly Jews who still live in the area are too frightened of street muggings, or too feeble, for the old leisurely stroll to a theater and then on to a café. Many more Jews have moved away, and find

(Top) Lillian Lux and David Carey in *The Rebitsn* (Rabbi's Wife) *from Israel*, a typical domestic situation comedy with songs, played at the Mayfair Theater, on Broadway. *(Bottom)* In the last act, the *rebitsn's* pious son becomes an up-to-date American.

the neighborhood unpleasant and inconvenient to get to. The Yiddish shows of the last few years are increasingly in Broadway theaters, in the Young Men's–Young Women's Hebrew Association on Ninety-second Street, in auditoriums of colleges and high schools, and in synagogues around the city and in the suburbs.

But enough contracts and combinations do keep going across the president's desk to provide for some sort of Yiddish show, somewhere in the New York area, on an average of once a week all year round. You find out about the major ones in the *Daily Forward* or the *Freiheit.* (The third New York Yiddish daily, the *Day-Morning Journal,* disappeared in 1972; in 1976, six Yiddish dailies in all, as well as thirty-two periodicals appearing less frequently, serve readers in North America, France, South Africa, and Australia.) You can also discover Yiddish theater events in the weekly *Allgemeine Journal,* or even in the *New York Times.* The rest you learn about on radio station WEVD, on bulletin boards of fraternal organizations or Jewish centers, and by asking around. In fact, despite the inexorable aging of the Yiddish-speaking population, competition from television, and the fear of city streets (which has hurt business at English theaters too), there have been more Yiddish plays in New York in the last few years than there had been for the past decade.

At work, the Yiddish actors' stage personalities are different from most actors'. They aren't slick or glossy; they provide some pleasurable friction, real human contact. Yiddish actors nowadays are rarely handsome or pretty or slim. The best ones are rarely young. Their clothes are never elegant. But they are always *there,* with gusto and dignity, with real facial features. They are too old to be lithe, yet there is something emphatic and graceful about the way they stand up and something crisp and authoritative about the way they turn. They refuse to be patronized. They animate the stage and make most other actors look plastic by comparison.

Most of the recent plays have been musical comedies, as their titles testify: *The Rebitsn from Israel* and *My Mamma the General,* starring Pesach Burstein and Lillian Lux (the former was the longest-running Yiddish show of the last quarter century); *The President's Daughter* and *Try It, You'll Like It* (a catch phrase from a television commercial), starring Jacob Jacobs; *Here Comes the Groom,* starring Leo Fuchs. Each play is superficially new, with its references to the Yom Kippur War or hippies. But essentially they remain like popular plays of half a century ago. They all have little stories of misunderstandings and romance, a young pair to sing love duets and an older couple to sing *kupléts.* They usually take place in a living room in the Bronx, or New Jersey, or Miami Beach, though *My Mamma the General* takes place in an

Israeli army bunker in the Sinai Desert. Many of them are directed by the stars, who also have a hand in the texts and songs. They all mean to give the audience a simple good time. Most of the time they still do business.

In the last quarter century, as the community's situation has changed, the majority of plots have become lighter. A widower comes to his senses at the last minute, for example, and instead of the peroxide divorcee he met in Miami, marries his housekeeper, a refugee—a nice woman, who loves him and will be good to his motherless children. Jacob Jacobs, perhaps, plays the marriage broker, who carries a herring, a bottle of schnapps, and two glasses in his pocket at all times, just in case of a sudden celebration. His daughter, Thelma Mintz, perhaps wears sparkly toreador pants, too much make-up, and a sneer, as the Other Woman; a fishwife, she stands with one hand on her hip and insults people. Or a young heiress from New York comes to a hotel near Tel Aviv for a blind date with an actor who is really only a fortune hunter. However, the actor gets the impression that an elderly woman terrifyingly decked out in false eyelashes and bangle bracelets is the heiress and marries her, thus outsmarting himself, while his simple young brother truly loves the heiress and wins her heart. Melodramas are rare now; I saw one in Tel Aviv about love and murder in the underworld , but none have been presented in New York in the last five years or more.

Kupléts are still the heart of the musical comedy. Jacob Jacobs, an octogenarian, sings a song that has nothing to do with the story line of the play. Its chorus repeats, in English, "I like it, I don't know why, I just like it." One verse is about a boarder who sleeps with his landlady. When her unsuspecting husband asks him why he stays on instead of moving to an apartment closer to his new job, the answer is, of course, "I like it." In another verse, Jacobs asks the audience, "Why, my friends, at my age, do I come out every night to dance and sing for you?" Everyone applauds and joins in the answer. Meanwhile, as the orchestra vamps between chorus and verse, Jacobs tilts his hat forward à la Maurice Chevalier, hunches up his shoulders like a spry old bird, and soft-shoe-struts, stiff-legged, along the edge of the stage.

Pesach Burstein, of the same generation as Jacobs, whistles between verses. Jack Rechtzeit, who is much younger, squats to dance a strenuous Russian kazatske. Nellie Casman, one of the rare female *kupletísts*, tiny and round and well over seventy, belts out a song with a chorus that means "It's all the same thing." ("You men out there, I know you're thinking I'm old and you'd rather have a young chippy, but believe me, when you turn out the lights . . .") And while the orchestra repeats the catchy refrain, faster and faster, she plants her two little feet in little red shoes firmly on the stage and starts to shake her bosom, which makes one cozy curve from shoulder to waist. She vibrates all over, till even the absurd red flower sticking up on top of her head jiggles, too, and she looks down at her own chest with such childlike surprise and satisfaction that the audience roars with delight.

America still has Yiddish vaudeville as well as musical comedy. In fact, until 1975 America had the one regular continuous Yiddish vaudeville house left in the world. Leon Schachter and Gittel Stern ran the Cinema Theater in Miami Beach, which offered a daily mixture of films and stage shows. For the benefit of the many old Jews living on social security in Miami Beach, there was a reduced rate: one dollar if you entered before three o'clock. There were long lines well before noon. The Cinema Theater closed when Schachter died, but now Mimi and Danny Sloan have reopened it. Miami has two other variety theaters during the winter season, too.

New York has vaudeville less regularly, with and without films. Off and on in the last few years, for example, at the Forty-sixth Street Theater at New Utrecht Avenue in Brooklyn, a classically cavernous Loews palace decorated with Greek-type friezes and undraped statuary, you can catch an endless procession of acts, several weekends a month, Saturday night and twice on Sunday. About half of the entertainment here is in English, despite occasional yells of *"Redt Yiddish!"* ("Speak Yiddish!") from the back of the hall.

I saw a typical line-up. A young man sang "The Impossible Dream" from

In Sholom Aleichem's *The Big Win* (sometimes called *200,-000*), two tailors, played by Stan Porter *(left)* and Bruce Adler, draw lots for the love of Diane Cypkin. Directed by David Opatoshu at the Eden Theatre in 1974.

Man of La Mancha, a song that has been adopted by the circuit and is understood to refer in this context to the founding of the state of Israel. A cantor imitated three cantors of various persuasions, all applying for the same position, by chanting the same liturgical passage in three different ways. (A sixteenth-century proto-Purim play contains a version of this very routine.) The cantor's children, boy sopranos, sang "The Impossible Dream" in harmony, plus another song or two. The ubiquitous Burstein family were the headliners. The parents sang a lively waltz called "Tel Aviv" in Hebrew and English; Lillian Lux, the mother, did musical impressions of a *shtetl* girlhood, in Yiddish; the father, Pesach (or Pesachke, as his fans affectionately call him), told jokes in Yiddish and English and whistled fancy harmonies; the son, Mike, who looks like Eddie Fisher, crooned in Hebrew. Later, a group of wholesome young people danced a pantomime of an old country wedding, from matchmaker to canopy.

The lively singing was accompanied by a four-piece band. The piano was played by the experienced musician Renée Solomon, a small, determined-looking woman standing solidly forward on her feet and conducting very competently with her head. The audience recognized her and most of the performers, and greeted them at once; they are regulars, many of whom tour continuously in this country and in Israel. Besides, they are often broadcast by WEVD disk jockey Art Raymond. (It is interesting to note that on other nights the Forty-sixth Street Theater houses equivalent programs in Italian and Greek.)

Similar programs sometimes take over a midtown New York theater for a night or two, as when Mimi Sloan presented a revue called *Some Like It Yiddish* at Carnegie Hall in 1972. Nightclub entertainers at resort hotels in Miami and the Catskill Mountains continue to include a Yiddish song or two in their repertory, a Yiddish word in their punch lines. The record industry still turns out an occasional album of Yiddish theater songs, *hasidic* songs, or vulgar monologues in Yiddish and English mixed.

Films are sometimes part of a vaudeville program, sometimes screened on their own at a synagogue or other Jewish institution. Many of the Yiddish films have been rented out in the last years from an agency which let them deteriorate. Every year another one shredded on the projector or turned to powder in its can. But recently there have been plans to rescue a number of the films by having fresh copies made.

An ambitious enterprise emerged in 1972, when Harry Rothpearl, a businessman who in his youth played the violin in a Maurice Schwartz production, established Jewish Nostalgic Productions, Inc. The community rejoiced at his

David Levinsky (Jack Rechtzeit), grown old and hard defends his business against the advice of his employees, played by *(from left)* Sandy Levitt, Zvee Scooler, and Morris Adler. This production of *The Rise of David Levinsky* was presented by the Folksbiene Ensemble in 1977.

plans and bombarded him with commentary and advice. He rented Schwartz's old theater at Twelfth Street and Second Avenue, which retains its glamorous associations despite its more recent tenants: burlesque and *Oh, Calcutta!* He started with Schwartz's biggest hit, *Yoshe Kalb,* in a dramatization by the director David Licht. The big cast included Jacob Ben-Ami, David Opatoshu, Miriam Kressyn, Jack Rechtzeit, Reizl Bozyk, Ruth Vool, Shifra Lerer, Helen Blay, Elia Patron, and David Ellin, who had played the title role for Schwartz himself.

In 1973 Jewish Nostalgic Productions offered *Hard to Be a Jew,* with Joseph Buloff dramatizing, directing, and starring. In 1974 it was Sholom Aleichem's *The Big Win,* directed by David Opatoshu, with new songs by Wolf Younin. In 1975 Buloff starred in a comedy about Jewish clothing manufacturers, *The Fifth Season,* which played originally in English on Broadway.

A group called the Yiddish Theatre Ensemble, consisting of skilled veteran actors, formed in 1975 and presented a musical comedy which they called *Sholom Aleichem, Columbus!* Composed by Yitskhok Dogim from material by Sholom Aleichem, the show honored America's bicentennial by portraying a family's emigration from Eastern Europe and adjustment to the new land. *Sholom Aleichem, Columbus!* played by invitation at halls, synagogues, and

Jewish centers all over the New York area.

For years the literary Yiddish theater was chiefly represented in New York by the semiprofessional Folksbiene. In 1971 Jacob Ben-Ami appeared in David Licht's production of Isaac Bashevis Singer's *In My Father's Court.* He enacted an old-country rabbi to whom people came for advice. Bertha Gersten played a woman tormented by remorse because in her youth she abandoned her illegitimate child; queenly, corseted in a period costume, she delivered a long monologue, almost a spoken aria, in the grand old-fashioned style. Joseph Buloff directed and starred at the Folksbiene in an intelligent production of I. J. Singer's *The Brothers Ashkenazi* (1970–71) and a charming version of Dimov's *Yoshke the Musician* (1972–73), with an expressionist denouement. The amateurs playing their twentieth—or fiftieth—roles at the Folksbiene evoked galleries of vivid characters.

Though the printed program always provides the English plot synopsis that is obligatory at all Yiddish theaters, most people at the Folksbiene seem to understand anyway what's going on. Upstairs in the old *Daily Forward* building, above the printing presses, crowded into the tiny lobby hung with pictures of Yiddish authors, they were voluble but seemed a rather more sober crowd than at musicals or at the Jewish Nostalgia Productions. Many women wore the "interesting" angular silver jewelry that they bought in Greenwich Village, or Jerusalem, in the 1930s.

The Folksbiene theater in the *Daily Forward* building was dark, long, and narrow, so you felt you were looking down a tunnel at the little stage, which seemed all the brighter by contrast. In 1973, in time to celebrate their sixtieth birthday, the Folksbiene left the Lower East Side for the discreet plush of the Central Synagogue on East Fifty-fifth Street. Lately there have been more young adults there than is usual for Yiddish theater.

In 1976 the Folksbiene chose Gordin's dark *God, Man, and Devil,* in honor of the hundredth birthday of the Yiddish theater. Under the direction of the Israeli director Israel Becker, they achieved an interpretation that was essentially simple, allowing the audience to sense through the confrontation of Hershele (David Ellin) and the devil (Leon Liebgold) the rhythms of the old theatrical tradition. Just before the company left for an unprecedented month's tour in Israel, the *Jewish Daily Forward* ran an article about their farewell performance headed: "Come Say Good-bye to the Folksbiene." By then the actors were already discussing the 1977 production, Abe Cahan's *The Rise of David Levinsky,* translated into Yiddish and adapted as a musical by Zvee Scooler and Isaiah Sheffer.

It is no accident that the Folksbiene is sponsored by the Workmen's Circle

(Arbeter Ring). This is the closest thing Yiddish theater has to a source of major community subsidy in New York. A secular fraternal organization, oriented to the labor movement, the Workmen's Circle remains in its educational and cultural activities the practical heir to the Bund and other Yiddishist socialist organizations of fifty years ago. The Workmen's Circle (Y. L. Peretz schools), the Farband (Labor Zionist Alliance), and the Sholom Aleichem Schools sponsor the only secular Yiddish school systems in the United States. In 1976 the Arbeter Ring sponsored a lecture series entitled "Perspectives on Yiddish Theater," a talk by Herman Yablokoff at the Y. L. Peretz Writers Club on the subject "One Hundred Years of Yiddish Theater," and other related activities.

The Workmen's Circle and Farband also sponsor tours by Ben Bonus and Mina Bern, the most refined and literary of the Yiddish entertainers. Mina Bern is blond and blue-eyed, and she smiles at her audiences as if they were welcome guests in her house. She began touring as an adolescent with the Ararat *kleynkunst* theater in Lodz; the war sent her trouping through Russia; she was a popular entertainer in Israel; in 1949 she married Ben Bonus and has since been based in New York. Ben Bonus has a matinee idol's mane of gray hair and a mobile face. He founded a Folksbiene Theater in Hollywood in 1943, the Yiddish Mobile Theater, which toured the country, several years later, and the Farband Players after that. And in the 1950s he was the first to bring *kleynkunst* to Broadway. In a review in the *Forward* in November of 1976, Yitskhok Perlov said that since Bonus's boyhood he "has been eating theater-bread"—which the critic likens to the wholesome, satisfying, grainy rye bread of the old country.

Their repertory is less show business than a graceful mix of art songs, folk songs, poetry recitations, monologues, and humorous sketches, in the tradition of *kleynkunst* and back as far as the Broder singers. Sometimes they perform with another few actors or a little chorus. They have had several productions running in large theaters in New York in the last few years: *Let's Sing Yiddish*, which filled the Brooks Atkinson Theater 110 times, and *Light, Lively, and Yiddish* (both with original material by the poet Wolf Younin), and for a while they had a refined version of vaudeville plus films on Second Avenue. In 1976 their title—*Long Live Columbus!*—paid tribute to the American bicentennial. They are especially popular with Jewish educational institutions around the country, from Duluth to Tallahassee, for they draw their material from the source where literature and folk culture converge. Ben Bonus and Mina Bern are idealists. They are proud that they use a pure Yiddish, untainted by Americanisms, and since they draw young people to their concerts, they think of themselves as pioneers and recruiters as well as artists.

Poster for a *kleynkunst* musical, brought to Broadway in 1966 by Ben Bonus and Mina Bern. The title and the sketches of dancers in Israeli costume demonstrate the integration of Zionism into the cultural awareness of American Jewish audiences. Notice that although the show is entirely in Yiddish, the title is advertised in English.

Yiddish Community and Yiddish Theater

The Yiddish community at large, as represented by institutions of various types and sizes, is still connected with Yiddish theater and still, in a sense, helps support it. For example, Miriam Kressyn and Seymour Rexite may travel to the Bronx to give a polished two-hour medley of favorite theater songs at a Golden Age Club. Leon Liebgold and Lili Liliana (who played the exquisite young lovers in the original movie of *The Dybbuk*) may entertain at a Workmen's Circle chapter meeting in Brooklyn. The Workmen's Circle sponsors free Yiddish Song and Drama Festivals on summer evenings in New York City and Long Island parks; sometimes up to twenty-five thousand people turn out to sit on the grass with blankets and picnics. In July of 1976 the festival, dedicated to celebrating the hundredth birthday of Yiddish theater, was sponsored jointly by the Workmen's Circle, the Hebrew Actors Union, the Parks

Poster for a typical small-town theater program consisting of drama, music, and recitation, professional and non-professional performers, celebrating events of interest to the local Jewish community and to the larger Yiddish cultural world.

Department, and the city's Bicentennial Corporation. The Jewish Culture Congress presented the Israeli Yiddish actress Hadassah Kestin at the midtown New York Hotel Piccadilly (March 1976) in a "word concert" which an article in the *Daily Forward* recommended to "the New York Yiddish intelligentsia and lovers of Yiddish theater and literature." In Miami Beach in the same month, people turned out to hear the cantor of their synagogue perform with monologist Hershel Gendler and singer Manya Gendler. In a sense, too, when Jewish organizations buy blocks of tickets to shows, that is a way of supporting the theater (though many organizations follow the old practice of fund-raising through benefits, but it is at American theater, not Yiddish).

Yiddish theater continues to be part of the community's conscious sense of history. Yiddish actors participate in observing authors' birthdays. At the Queens College auditorium an annual Sholom Aleichem Festival offers a program of songs and recitations, during which awards are given out for Jewish scholarship and community service. Special performances commemorate the anniversaries of the Warsaw Ghetto uprising and the founding of the state of Israel. The Workmen's Circle celebrated its seventy-fifth anniversary "diamond jubilee" in 1976 with an afternoon program of "Yiddish Musical Comedy Theatre" at Lincoln High School in Brooklyn. Of the recent books of Yiddish memoirs and memorial albums, a percentage are still by actors. The actors' union itself, which every year fills Avery Fisher Hall in Lincoln Center for its annual benefit, celebrated its eightieth birthday with a show, speeches, and sentimental ovations.

In 1976, as we have seen, the centennial of Goldfadn's creation of professional Yiddish theater coincided with the bicentennial of the United States. Yiddish theater history and American history were recurrent motifs, as in *Quickly Turn the Wheels,* under the auspices of the Joint Arts Council of Queens, in which David Ellin, Shifra Lerer, Reizl Bozyk, and others evoked the "sufferings and joys" of the immigrants at the turn of the century. *From Brod to Broadway,* a musical recapitulation of the history of Yiddish theater since the Broder singers, which had toured American cities in 1972, was revived in 1976.

Purim 1976 brought traditional folk theater to the American Jewish community. Members of the Y. L. Peretz chapter of the Workmen's Circle in Cleveland, Ohio, got together to eat *homontashn* and drink coffee, to choose their own Queen Esther, and to enjoy a showing of the Molly Picon film *Yidl mitn Fidl.* In New York, the West Side Minyan, a congenial young congregation whose prayers are traditional in form and experimental in style, pooled contributions of snacks and kosher wine. The entertainment at their party, half rehearsed and half impromptu high spirits, was essentially traditional. After they played a game called "mad libs" with the *megile,* reducing the story to nonsense by substituting an arbitrary list of verbs for the scripture, a young man in a Persian turban sang a comic ode which he had composed about the group, and everyone joined in for the chorus. Among the skits was a playlet in which Esther competed with Lilith and other famous women for King Ahashuerus's favor—a zany combination of Bible story and up-to-date feminism.

Even the Yiddish serious amateur movement still goes on in America. In Albuquerque, New Mexico, a club of twelve active members and some twenty "interested persons" put on Sholom Aleichem's *The Divorce* in 1966. In a town of less than seven hundred Jewish families, their four performances were sold out. The next year they took on *Tevye the Dairyman* and were again a success. In Montreal a group connected with the Yiddish Folk School formed in 1956 under the charismatic guidance of Dora Wasserman, a former member of the Moscow Yiddish State Art Theater. Within fifteen years they grew to over forty members, playing twenty times or more a season to big theater audiences in Montreal and other Canadian cities. In Milwaukee the Perhift group celebrated its fiftieth birthday in 1971 with an Israeli play in Yiddish directed by David Licht and a big banquet complete with artistic program. They still tour Wisconsin and all the way to Chicago. At Brandeis University in 1969, a student, Dina Roskies, conceived and organized a Yiddish performance called *Shalekh-Mones* (the gifts of cakes and fruit traditionally given on Purim). Two years later she directed a successful production by and for children: *Di Papirosn-Hendler (The Cigarette Peddlers),* about children in Warsaw hiding their Jewish identity from the Nazis. The story was dramatized by her husband, David Roskies. The Brandeis Hillel organization helped support both projects, and some other local institutions contributed toward the second one. In 1973 New York University students rented Town Hall in New York City for an evening of songs, a Sholom Aleichem one-acter, and some other light entertainment. The program called them the New Yiddish Youth Theater.

Thus, though the number of people actively speaking Yiddish has been drastically reduced, the spectrum of types of Yiddish theater persists—if on a reduced scale—and so do the ways in which theater participates in the life of the Jewish community. In fact, the very mention of Yiddish theater is still a catalyst; people can't help reacting, and through their reaction, revealing their relationship to Yiddish culture as a whole.

A recent scene illustrates a common attitude among American Jews. Facing a faculty committee at Bronx Community College of the City University of New York, I had to list my accomplishments, and I said that I was writing a book about Yiddish theater. The committee members sat doodling or taking notes; the atmosphere was formal but friendly. One professor said he had a question: "What's a nice girl like you doing writing about Yiddish theater?" The laughter lasted for minutes. The questioner and half the committee were Jewish.

The fact is that if they had been gentile, or young, they would not have laughed.

Younger Jews would smile. But they would be less likely to feel that they'd seen something intimate exposed, or that they had shared an in joke; as for all the associations that make Yiddish laughable to their parents and grandparents—of those they are simply ignorant. They don't know that to the "enlightened," Yiddish was a grotesque parody of German. They don't know that a century ago Yiddish was only a workaday "scullery maid" to Hebrew. On the contrary, I heard one college girl in jeans explain that she was studying Yiddish because her parents had always sent her to Hebrew school; ironically, Hebrew now seems prosaically sanitary, since it is the everyday language spoken by Israelis, while Yiddish is by contrast unsanctioned and appealing. For young Jews, primitive muddy *shtetl* streets and even Lower East Side tenements and embarrassing greenhorn accents are far enough away to be romantic.

Moreover, there is the current ethnic revival, which has led young Irish Americans to repudiate "Mother Machree" for an authentic Gaelic they never heard. Young blacks study their own history and proclaim that black is beautiful. A New York City neighborhood newspaper *(Wisdom's Child)* in February of 1976 listed forty-two ethnic theaters, most of them new or at least newly revived and reorganized. Besides Jewish theater groups in Yiddish, Hebrew, and English, and the relatively predictable black and Hispanic theaters, the list included Chinese, Irish, Latvian, Armenian, Philippine, Italian, Greek, Ukrainian, and Arabic.

Still another phenomenon stimulating interest in Yiddish culture is the fashionable nostalgia for the era of mass immigrations. For example, the movie *Hester Street,* delicately adapted from a story by Abe Cahan, and Irving Howe's rich book *World of Our Fathers,* are only two of the many explorations of the turn-of-the-century Lower East Side to win praise in 1976. And finally there is the brute fact of the holocaust, which made Yiddish into a language of martyrs.

Yiddish is a livelier participant in academic life than it was ten years ago. The girl in jeans I spoke to, for example, was a student at the Uriel Weinreich summer program run by YIVO and Columbia University—a program that grew from eleven students in 1968 to sixty in 1975. Other colleges and Jewish centers are teaching Yiddish these days, or at least Yiddish literature in translation. Since the war over 35,000 students have bought copies of *College Yiddish,* the primer by Uriel Weinreich. Graduate students are writing dissertations on Yiddish culture. In 1973 alone I met two young women who had come to New York specifically to research dissertations on Yiddish theater: one from France and one from Wales. At Queens College, where the enrollment in Yiddish and Yiddish culture courses has risen from fifty to five hundred since 1971, David Ellin teaches English-speaking drama students to act scenes in Yiddish. At the University of Southern Illinois, Professor Herbert Marshall is compiling an encyclopedia of Jewish theater. The American Jewish Historical Society in Waltham, Massachusetts, maintains a collection of Yiddish theater posters. An English-language quarterly on Yiddish culture, *Yiddish,* edited by Dr. Joseph C. Landis, is published at Queens College. In San Francisco, Joshua Fishman observed college students sporting buttons that said "Redt mit mir Yidish" ("Speak Yiddish with me"). It is also true, however, that in 1976 Yiddish began to suffer badly from widespread academic budget cuts.

The same shifts have made it possible for the American community at large to pay more respectful attention to Yiddish theater lately, as it has to

Yiddish literature in general. The Drama Desk saluted Yiddish theater at the Lambs Club in 1974. The Charles MacArthur Center of American Theatre at Florida State University held a three-day seminar on Yiddish theater in April of 1975, with serious panels and speakers. One month later, the Museum of the City of New York devoted one of its membership events to Yiddish theater in New York. Mayor Abraham D. Beame proclaimed December 5, 1976, as Yiddish Theater Day in New York City.

In the last five years, not only could Americans see *The Dybbuk* performed in Yiddish by the visiting Bucharest State Theater; they could also see it in English-language adaptations at the La Mama Theater Club off-off-Broadway and at the Mark Taper Forum in Los Angeles. It was the subject of a dramatic ballet by Pearl Lang. Dr. Mark Slobin conceived and produced a marvelously frisky translation-adaptation of Lateiner's operetta *David's Fiddle,* directed by Leonard Hellmers, at Wesleyan University. At the Henry Street Settlement, the American Jewish Theatre Ensemble under Stanley Breckner presented Peretz material, adapted into English by Isaiah Sheffer, imagined in the context of a performance in a concentration camp. An off-off-Broadway group calling itself the Jewish Repertory Company presented Asch's *God of Vengeance,* also in English. Diane Cypkin, who plays romantic heroines on the professional Yiddish stage, directed *Green Fields* in the round as culmination of her master's degree studies at Brooklyn College. A group of Princeton students banded together as the Brighton Lights Jewish Theater company, and performed *Green Fields* in English at a synagogue in Brooklyn. Small theater groups without any specific Jewish identification at all dramatized stories by Peretz and, on Broadway, I. B. Singer's short story *Yentl* was a big hit. And of course, one of the most successful Broadway musicals ever was *Fiddler on the Roof,* based on Sholom Aleichem's beloved *Tevye the Dairyman; Fiddler* was enormously popular not only on the American stage and in a Hollywood movie, but even in Europe and Japan.

Within the Yiddish-speaking community, the old complex of attitudes toward Yiddish theater still exists, almost undiluted. The passionate convictions of Jacob Gordin's disciples, for example, are still part of the ideological baggage of the Yiddish intelligentsia. I found this out several years ago, sitting in the office of an editor of a widely circulating national Jewish magazine— a very pleasant man whom I had just met. In my innocence I happened to mention that I liked Yiddish theater; it was so, uh, theatrical. Someone, I added, should write a book about it. Suddenly he was enraged.

"Don't patronize Yiddish theater! It's not folksy. It's not that *shund,* that garbage, those little songs, dirty jokes, stupid stories. Yiddish theater is real theater, it's art, it's drama, it's just as good as American theater!" And so on.

That's when I first discovered the raw nerve.

Later, I poked it deliberately when I praised Nellie Casman's singing to Artef veteran Hershel Rosen.

"Sure, she's vulgar," I said, "with her shaking and her suggestive lyrics, but she's a funny old lady; that's why audiences love her."

Though thirty-five years have passed since Hershel joined Artef, he still has the cocky walk of an old-time union brother and he still believes you can teach people social values, so he instructed me gently:

"Some things you laugh at when a stranger does them, but you would hate it to be your own mother. I can't be detached from Yiddish theater. I am personally humiliated by that old woman standing up there in public shaking herself. That's not what Yiddish theater should be."

Around 1970, when Madame Kaminska was trying to establish a stable Yiddish art theater in New York City, an organization called the Friends of Ida Kaminska put out a brochure that declared, in part:

> The foundation was formed by a group of dedicated Jewish communal leaders, writers, artists, teachers, theatre personalities and businessmen who had long felt the need for a Yiddish theatre of fine artistic standards, true to its highest traditions, attuned to artistic achievement rather than box office, and concerned with the future of Jewish culture. . . .
>
> An artistic advisory board of leading Jewish writers and theatre personalities will determine together with Mme. Kaminska, the repertory of plays which will help make this Yiddish Art Theatre a glittering showcase of Jewish culture.
>
> To establish the theatre on a firm and durable basis, in an adequate theatrical facility, the Foundation will raise funds from individuals, organizations, foundations, etc., who have an interest in preserving the cultural heritage of the Jewish people.

The brochure ended with "JOIN US" and a coupon to fill out: "Enclosed is my check for . . ."

A contributor to *Yugntruf (Call to Youth)* commented on the project: "Ida Kaminska has a principle: Yiddish theater must be pure, which means a literary repertoire and a clean Yiddish culture-language. . . ."

The enterprise never did prosper. There were not enough contributors and not even enough audiences. The theaters were unsuitable or inconvenient. Finally in 1974 Ida Kaminska and Meir Melman left their New York apartment and accepted an invitation from Israel. On that occasion she challenged the interviewer from the *New York Times* with a wry smile. "Would you visit me if I was not going away?"

In the same April 1971 issue, *Yugntruf* printed an article by Dina Roskies

Leo Fuchs in a comedy which demonstrates the participation of Yiddish theater in the cultural currents which surround it: in this case, the television program *Dragnet*.

entitled "Creating a Yiddish Theater." Dina was born after Hitler had already destroyed most of Europe's Yiddish-speaking communities; she is a product of an Albuquerque high school, Brandeis and Harvard universities, not a Russian gymnasium; but she is a gentle younger sister to Jacob Gordin's comrades the intellectual women of the revolution. In her article she rejects austerely such sentimental vulgarities as "television spectacles about Sholom Aleichem and the 'oy-vey-vaudeville' leftovers from a Second Avenue which our generation does not remember." She continues:

> One of the goals of the new Yiddish theater is to mend the torn thread of our cultural heritage. . . . Obviously, the Yiddish theater has more aesthetic goals —to become the very most sensitive and artistic expression of our people. But one must remember that the principle of art for art's sake has never prevailed in our theater. . . .

Through all these voices speak the familiar passions of the modern Yiddish intelligentsia. They assume that the community is polarized between intellectuals and the masses, and that their mission includes elevating theater for them all, for, among Jews at least, "low" theater should not exist. For them, art and taste are inseparable from morality and indeed from the worth of the community as a whole. They as individuals feel implicated in the corruption of a community that maintains "low" cultural institutions.

Their attitude toward Yiddish theater remains directly connected with their feelings about their language and literature. They are still publishing poems and articles. The measure of the theater is for them its texts and how they are treated. They feel responsible for the theater as they do for the language.

Aesthetics have ideological implications. Since the *haskole*, intellectuals have tried, in various spirits and out of various motives, to make their culture a modern Western culture, judgeable by the same criteria as all the others. People who saw Yung Teater or the *The Tempest* in Warsaw or GOSET in Moscow, for example, usually express their high quality by saying that they were the only "real" theaters there ever were in Yiddish, meaning not only the finest but also the only ones really "European" or really non-Yiddish. Similarly, Yiddish directors in New York and Tel Aviv have repeatedly told me that there is no difference between their work and that of a director in any other language, except insofar as an actor may happen to be portraying an old-time Jewish character. Nowadays it has become impossible to disprove that assertion; in the five years that I have gone often to Yiddish theater in New York (as well as in Miami and Tel Aviv), I have never yet had a chance to see a serious Yiddish drama that was not set among Jews in Eastern Europe

At a local theater in Brooklyn, another example of the Yiddish theater's free use of the culture of its environment. *The Farblondjet Honeymoon* also played in Montreal and Miami Beach in 1955. Jacob Jacobs stands in the back row in a white hat.

half a century ago or more. Yet I have the impression that most of these directors are mistaken; their productions are not like the modern Western theaters I am used to. The actors move and gesture more broadly, the minor characters are close to caricatures, and the roles are very often "types" of a specifically Yiddish sort. This is not necessarily a weakness; perhaps, rather, it is an integral convention. I thought *Yoshke the Musician* at the Folksbiene certainly as good as most plays on Broadway in the same year. But I think that it was probably as much specifically "Yiddish theater" as it was "theater," and for a Yiddish intellectual that is a genuine ideological problem.

The plays that art theaters have chosen to produce since the war reflect another problem. Whereas the finer Yiddish theater once prided itself on its association with writing and writers, very few serious modern plays have been produced since the war. "Literary" theaters gradually decreased their productions of Ibsen and other non-Yiddish writers in translation. In the postwar decade the Polish Yiddish State Theater, the Moscow Yiddish State Art Theater, theaters in New York and Paris did present some new plays by Markish, Bergelson, Sloves, Mirski, Pinchevsky, Dluzhnovsky, and a few other writers, and a high proportion of these plays dealt with Jewish experiences during the war and even later. These new plays were exceptions, however. "Literary" repertory consisted primarily of revivals, and with time the revivals have become almost entirely revivals (or adaptations, or montages) of the same few plays about traditional *shtetl* life. Intellectuals still want drama to educate. But whereas in the past they aimed to teach Jews to be modern Europeans or Americans, now their thrust is inward; they want plays to educate Jews toward Yiddish culture rather than toward the outside world, toward preservation of tradition rather than toward *haskole*. For them, only positive supportive views of Jewish life are acceptable now, and only classic authors.

Critics of Yiddish theater have problems that other drama critics do not face. How much, for example, are their responses softened by the sweet sound of serious dialogue in the Yiddish language, or by the emotional effects of seeing onstage a Jewish world that is gone? They can be as susceptible as "Moyshe" is to what Peretz Hirschbein scornfully called the "homey theatrical bathhouse" where everyone feels sentimental and close. And such feelings do creep into the most literary of productions—not only on the stage but in the audience, the more so since they are, in objective fact, a small group, and they are not young. These critics' true responsibility is unclear, for the majority of Yiddish theater, even among the more ambitious efforts, has about it something primitive, and Yiddish artists must be spurred to strive to highest standards; yet on the other hand, Yiddishists must stand beside the artists to support their intentions, and the public must not be discouraged from buying tickets.

Often, nowadays, there is almost no adverse criticism in print at all, for the critic clearly feels that to be too strict with a Yiddish play would be to annihilate it. Though in private conversation many intellectuals and artists do tear productions apart with as much savage relish as their non-Yiddish counterparts expend on their own theater, they often will add: "But of course you wouldn't say such a thing in your book for everyone to see." All these conflicts must bother not only the critics for the *Daily Forward* and the *Freiheit*, but also those for the literary *Zukunft (Future)* and the other periodicals, both the Yiddish ones and the English ones of Jewish interest, and even reviewers in the *New York Times* and the *Village Voice*. In fact, they bother every serious Yiddish theatergoer.

My purposes are historical, not critical, but when I evaluate my own impressions of the Yiddish literary theater I am struck by how they resemble the comments of Yiddish critics who have been dead fifty years: the acting and music often seem strong to me, the directing usually much less so, and the texts adapted at will by the directors tend to be weak.

On the other hand, it remains as true as ever that while the intellectuals *dreyn zikh a kop* ("turn their heads around," or worry) about such matters, most people are unconcerned. They have rarely gone to the literary productions and they are unlikely to do so now. If they go to Yiddish theater, they go to enjoy themselves. The children of the people who loved *Dos Pintele Yid (The Essential Spark of Jewishness)* by Boris Thomashefsky loved *Here Comes the Groom*.

Since I began to carry Yiddish books and magazines around New York City, I have had dozens of encounters, which follow a set pattern. The woman sitting beside me on a subway, the man on the next stool at Chock full o'Nuts, Irving who owns the Atlas-Paris Cleaners—they see a book I am carrying. First they try to spell out the title, and sometimes they succeed. They try to remember how long it's been since they tried to read Yiddish; then they try to recall the last time they saw anybody reading Yiddish who didn't have a long white beard. Whereas the intellectual Yiddishists are delighted but not really surprised that young people would read Yiddish, these people are more amazed than anything else. And then their faces soften, they beam, and they start reeling off the names of the stars they saw at the Second Avenue Theater or at the McKinley Theater in the Bronx or wherever. The plays they dismiss with an indulgent shrug; they don't remember any titles or authors, and they know the plots were silly. What they want to talk about is "what it was like": long hot afternoons squeezed in beside their mothers in the balcony, how she cried or laughed or gave them a smack for fidgeting, and all the food—oy vey —all the food she brought along. They shake their heads, smiling. "There's nothing like that now."

Those who still do go to the musical comedies worry no more than the actors do over whether the Yiddish is corrupted by English. They prefer real Yiddish tunes, but they don't mind if an American hit parade tune sneaks into the score. They certainly appreciate virtuosity in their performers. But they don't worry whether the play is universal art, or whether it is art at all. On the contrary, they sense that the art the intellectuals talk about has nothing to do with the values they derive from Yiddish theater.

The masses have always felt that intellectually ambitious Yiddish theater was *goyish*. Both Mogulesko and "Professor" Hurwitz actually called Jacob Gordin anti-Semitic. At the start, the avowed intention of such theater was to educate Jews to be European or American rather than traditional and parochial. Even when the dramatists' message changed to become the preservation of Jewishness—and certainly nowadays any manifestation of Yiddish culture must be construed as that—its very style is elitist, alien as opposed to *heymish* (homey).

Two scenes from the short film *Dos Mazl (Luck)*, a folk tale produced by Josh Waletzky, a young American film maker and song writer, in 1974. *(Top)* A festive group gathers to watch a *Purimshpil*. *(Bottom)* While the poor man sleeps, his young son and daughter are out finding their Luck, who will grant them a fortune.

Popular audiences feel, as their parents did, that their theatergoing experience is the essence of *Yiddishkat.* They feel it all the more strongly as they grow away from most of the customs and institutions of Yiddish culture. Beyond the usual pleasures offered by popular entertainments—romance, music, belly laughs—popular Yiddish comedies revert to the functions of the Purim play: release among insiders, affirmation of values and of the community's identity. Unlike the uncomfortable English-language Jewish-American types, such as the "Jewish mothers," "princesses," and "Portnoys," these comedies use Jewishness cheerfully and straightforwardly, stereotyped characters and all. They press button after button: Yiddish references to history or religion, Yiddish jokes, Yiddish curses. The Yiddish language itself becomes less a language than a code, an exchange of passwords between stage and audience. For this public, even when they go occasionally to Yiddish concerts or more serious plays, there is the drama onstage, and beyond that there is the drama of their ongoing relationship with it.

The difference between the masses who love the popular comedies and the intellectuals who despise them is a difference in definitions of *Yiddishkayt* itself. Since Mendele Moykher Sforim and the other *maskilim* consciously made Yiddish a modern literary language, intellectual Yiddishists have committed themselves to a fine, even a quixotic ideal. Because the institution of Yiddish theater somehow collects to itself feelings about the culture as a whole, that idealistic commitment embraces theater intensely. For example, the *Forward,* urging readers (in November 1976) to buy tickets to the benefit whose proceeds would go toward founding a new theater, proclaimed, "Remember! A people without a theater is not fully a people . . . and your name [if you buy a ticket] will be immortalized in the history of the Yiddish National Theater in America." Thus it is because the musical comedy and melodrama, the *shund,* express *Yiddishkayt* to the masses that the very existence of such low entertainment pains the intellectuals, for it seems to them to be a betrayal by Jews of Jewishness itself.

In terms of intensity, the intellectuals remain the most loyal audiences.

Often my little conversations with the musical-comedy fans, on the subway or at the Chock full o'Nuts counter, end when I say, "There are some good shows on this year," and they say, "Oh, yeah? Gee, I didn't know that. Well, I must go sometime, but you know how it is. . . ."

They respond emotionally to the theater, as they do to the language, but they feel no responsibility for either one. A lot of Jews must still go to popular Yiddish theater, for it survives, but what Joshua Fishman writes about the Yiddish language is equally true of the theater:

[Yiddish] was once the language of vociferous masses. Today, the masses are merely passive guardians of this language, whereas professors, poets and pietists are now its major strength. The masses, for whom Yiddish intellectuals were always so solicitous, never fully recognized the love that was lavished on them in the name of Yiddish. . . . In old age the language's select admirers have replaced the multitudes that failed to treasure its virtuosity. . . .

In his conclusion, Dr. Fishman writes that

there is a tremendous urge to live, a veritable elan-vital in the world of Yiddish. This urge is a striking one to behold, for it is as though a complete symbiotic relationship existed between the language and its devotees. They derive their driving force from their commitment to the language and the language continues to produce works of great beauty and to occupy positions of prestige and recognition as a result of the efforts that its tireless adherents constantly make on its behalf. If Yiddish were the language of a group less skilled in the arts of self-preservation, if it were the language of a group less conscious of language as an aspect of cutural survival, if it were the language of a group less blessed with intellectual powers, if it were the language of a group that could not reinforce ethnicity with religion and religion with ethnicity, then—if all these "ifs" were to come to pass—Yiddish might be in a sad, sad state indeed. Its imminent demise has been predicted repeatedly for well over a century—by advocates of "enlightenment" who considered it a deterrent to Westernization; by Hebraists and Zionists who considered it a deterrent to Hebrew and to the "ingathering of exiles"; by cosmopolitan socialists who considered it a deterrent to the unity of the proletariat; for scholars and sinners alike—Yiddish was always fair game. And yet it survives—although it is hard to say how and why.

If for "the language and its devotees" the reader substitutes "the theater and its devotees," both artists and public, the observation is equally valid. The Yiddish actors—jesters, Purim players, vagabond stars, darlings of the masses —keep trouping. Their plays and monologues live because they are alive to act in them. They still draw old "Moyshe" away from his *I Love Lucy* into the theater, and there they perform for him what was probably the function of the actors of prehistoric times: they invoke, ritually, the magical essence of the tribe.

GLOSSARY

badkhen (pl. **badkhonim**)	wedding bard, jester
Daytshmerish	form of Yiddish language with German words added and Germanic elements emphasized or overemphasized; originally associated with *haskole*, refinement, and intellectualism
dybbuk	in legend, soul of a dead person which has entered a living person's body
hasid (pl. **hasidim**)	adherent of *hasidism*. (Note: These are the familiar spellings; more accurate, phonetically, would be *khosed* and *khsidim*.)
hasidism	Jewish religious movement, beginning in the eighteenth century, committed to piety, ecstasy, and the guidance of wonder rabbis
haskole	Enlightenment movement, committed to modernizing the Jewish religion and community, which flourished in eighteenth- and nineteenth-century Europe. (Note: in Hebrew, *haskala*.)
heymish	homey, warmly familiar
jargón	familiar, disparaging term for the Yiddish language

kehile	organized Jewish community
kleynkunst	"miniature" theater, usually revue consisting of music, dance, and satirical sketches
kultur-tuer	one who actively supports the cultural activities of his community
kunst	art
kuplét	comic patter song, as in the French *couplet*
kupletíst	entertainer whose specialty is to deliver *kuplét*
landsman (pl. **landsmen** or **landslayt**)	person from the same town or region in the old country
landsmanshaft (pl. **landsmanshaftn**)	fraternal organization of *landslayt*
lets	clown, buffoon
magid	itinerant folk preacher
mame-loshn	affectionate term for the Yiddish language; literally "mother tongue"
marshelik	jester, master of ceremonies
maskil (pl. **maskilim**)	adherent of the Enlightenment movement
megile	Book of Esther, read on Purim
meshoyrer (pl. **meshoyrerim**)	synagogue choir singer
nar	fool, clown
oylem	public, audience
Pale of Settlement	in czarist Russia, the area within which Jews were allowed to live. The Pale comprised about 362,000 square miles of western Russia, extending from close to the Baltic Sea on the north to the Black Sea on the south, and including Lithuania, part of the Ukraine, and part of what is now Poland; its Jewish population at the end of the nineteenth century was about 5.5 million.

patriót (pl. **patriótn**)	fan of particular actor or company
payats	clown
Purim	festive holiday in early spring
Purimshpil	Purim folk play
Purimshpiler	performer in *Purimshpil,* usually amateur
shalekh-mones	gifts exchanged between households on Purim, especially sweet cakes, fruits, and wine
shtetl (pl. **shtetlekh**)	small town, village
shund	trashy art, especially theater
tsholnt	heavy stew which is allowed to continue cooking throughout the Sabbath day
Yiddish	Jewish; Yiddish language, developed from the eleventh century, and spoken by Ashkenazic Jews living principally from France eastward through Russia, as well as in those areas of America, Africa, and Australia where Ashkenazic Jews have settled. Its primary roots are Germanic, Hebrew, Slavic, and Romance. (Note: Sephardic Jews of Spain, Portugal, and Africa, and their descendants, speak not Yiddish but Ladino, whose primary roots are Spanish and Hebrew.)
Yiddishkayt	Jewishness; cultural "Yiddishness"
yold	sucker

SELECTED BIBLIOGRAPHY

The following acronyms are used:

YIVO: Yidisher Visnshaftlekher Institut [YIVO Institute for Jewish Research]
YKUF: Yidisher Kultur Farband [Yiddish Cultural Association]

1. Historical Accounts of the Development of Yiddish Theater
(These two lists include most of what are considered the major works in the field, as well as some other useful references.)

A. In Yiddish

Akhtsik yor yidish teater in Rumenia 1876–1956 [Eighty Years of Yiddish Theater in Rumania 1876–1956]. Bucharest, 1956. Note: text in Yiddish and Rumanian.

Bialin, A. H. *Maurice Schwartz un der Yidisher Kunst Teater* [Maurice Schwartz and the Yiddish Art Theater]. New York, Farlag Biderman, 1934.

Bukhvald, Nathaniel. *Teater* [Theater]. New York, Farlag-Komitet Teater, 1943.

Fertsik yor Folksbiene [Forty Years of Folksbiene]. New York, 1955.

Goldberg, A. *Unzer dramaturgie* [Our Dramaturgy]. New York, YKUF and Yekhiel Levenstein Buch-Komitet, 1961. Note: contains selections from plays as well as explanatory biographical notes.

Goren, B. *Di geshikhte fun yidishn teater* [The History of Yiddish Theater]. 2 vols. New York, Max N. Mayzel, 1923.

Horowitz, Norbert. *"Yidish teater fun der sharis-haplita"* [Yiddish Theater Among the Survivors]. In *Fun Novntn Over* [The Recent Past]. New York, Congress for Jewish Culture, 1955.

Litvakov, M. *Finf yor Melukhisher Yidisher Kunst-Teater, 1921–1924* [Five Years of the Yiddish State Art Theater, 1921–1924]. Moscow, 1924.

Mestel, Yakov. *Unzer teater* [Our Theater]. New York, YKUF, 1943.

Mestel, Yakov. *70 yor teater repertuar* [Seventy Years of Theater Repertory]. New York, YKUF, 1954.

Mukdoyni, Dr. A. *Yitskhok Leybush Peretz un dos yidish teater* [Yitskhok Leybush Peretz and the Yiddish Theater]. New York, YKUF, 1949.

Perlmutter, Sholem. Mestel, Yakov, ed. *Yidishe dramaturgn un kompositors* [Yiddish Dramatists and Composers]. New York, YKUF, 1952.

Rollansky, Samuel. *Dos yidishe gedrukte vort un teater in Argentine* [The Yiddish Printed Word and Theater in Argentina]. Buenos Aires, 1941.

Shatsky, Dr. Yakov. *Arkhiv far der geshikhte fun yidishn teater un drame* [Archives for the History of Yiddish Theater and Drama]. New York, YIVO Ester Rokhl Kaminska Teater-musey, 1930.

Shatsky, Dr. Yakov, ed. *Hunderd yor Goldfadn* [Goldfadn—100 Years]. New York, YIVO, 1940.

Shayn, Yosef. *Arum Moskver Yidishn Teater* [Around the Moscow Yiddish Theater]. Paris, Commission du Plan d'Action Culturelle, 1964.

Shmeruk, Khone. *Peretzes Yeush-Vizie: Interpretatsie fun Y. L. Peretzes* Bay Nakht oyfn Altn Mark *un kritishe oysgabe fun der drame* [Peretz's Vision of Despair: Interpretation of *Night in the Old Marketplace*, and critical edition of the drama]. New York, YIVO, 1971. Note: Professor Shmeruk's edition of Yiddish plays up to 1750 is now in preparation.

Tsen yor Artef [Ten Years of Artef]. New York, Tsenyorikn yuviley, 1937. Note: text in Yiddish and English.

Turkow-Grudberg, Yitskhok. *Yidish teater in Poylen* [Yiddish Theater in Poland]. Warsaw, Farlag Yidish-bukh, 1951.

Yidisher teater in Eyrope tvishn beyde velt milkhomes [Yiddish Theater in Europe Between the Two World Wars]. 2 vols. New York, Alveltlikhn yidishn kultur-kongres, 1971.

Zylbercweig, Zalmen. *Hantbukh fun yidishn teater* [Handbook of Yiddish Theater]. Mexico City, Z. Z. Jubilee Committee at YIVO in Los Angeles, 1970. Note: this is an annotated bibliography.

Zylbercweig, Zalmen. *Lexikon fun yidishn teater, Vols. 1–5* [Lexicon of Yiddish Theater, Vols. 1–5]. Vols. 1 and 2: New York, assisted by Yakov Mestel, Hebrew Actors Union of America, 1931. Vol. 3: New York, assisted by Yakov Mestel, Hebrew Actors Union of America, Farlag Elisheva, 1959. Vol. 4: New York, Hebrew Actors Union of America, Farlag Elisheva, 1963. Vol. 5: Mexico City, Hebrew Actors Union of America, 1967.

Zylbercweig, Zalmen. *Di velt fun Ester Rokhl Kaminska* [The World of Ester Rokhl Kaminska]. Mexico, 1969.

B. In Other Languages

Beck, Evelyn. *Kafka and the Yiddish Theater.* Madison, University of Wisconsin Press, 1971.

Epstein, Shifra. Documentary film and script of a Purimshpil in a contemporary hasidic community (NEA grant in progress, at YIVO).

Erens, Patricia. "Mentshlekhkayt Conquers All: Yiddish Cinema in America" in *Film Comment,* January-February 1976, pp. 48–53.

Fass, Moshe. "Theatrical Activities in the Polish Ghettos During the Years 1939–1942" in *Jewish Social Studies,* vol. 38, no. 1, Winter 1976, pp. 54–72.

Hartmann, Karl. "Das Judische Theater in Polen nach dem Zweiten Weltkrieg" [Yiddish Theater in Poland After the Second World War]. In *Länder un Völker in Östlichen* in *Mitteleurope,* vol. IV, no. 17, 1968. In German.

Le Théâtre Juif dans le monde [The Jewish Theater All Over the World]. Paris, Nouvelle Revue Juive, 1931. In French.

Levine, Dov. "Sipuro shel Argaz Ipur" [The Story of the Make-up Box]. In *Bamah,* no. 57–58, Spring/Summer 1973. In Hebrew.

Lifson, David S. *The Yiddish Theater in America.* Cranbury, N.J., A. S. Barnes, 1965.

Miller, James. *The Detroit Yiddish Theater, 1920 to 1937.* Detroit, Wayne State University Press, 1967.

Picon-Vallin, Béatrice. *Le Théâtre Juif Soviétique pendant les Années Vingt* [The Soviet Jewish Theater in the 1920s]. Lausanne, La Cité—L'Age d'Homme, 1973. In French.

Seiger, Marvin Leon. *A History of the Yiddish Theatre in New York City to 1892.* DA XXI, doctoral dissertation presented to the faculty of the Graduate School, Indiana University, August 1960.

Young, Stark. "Two Theatres" in *The Flower in Drama and Glamour.* New York, Scribners, 1955.

2. A Sampling of Yiddish Theatrical Memoirs

Adler, Tsili, with Yakov Tikman. *Tsili Adler Dertseylt* [Celia Adler Recounts]. 2 vols. New York, Tsili Adler Foundation un Buch-Komitet, 1959.

Bernardi, Jack. *My Father, the Actor.* New York, Norton, 1971.

Broude, Meyer. *Kulisen un Hinter Kulisen* [In the Wings and Behind the Scenes]. Tel Aviv, Hamenora, 1974.

Cahan, Abraham. *The Education of Abraham Cahan.* Translated by Abraham Conan, Lynn Davison, and Leon Stein. 2 vols. Philadelphia, Jewish Publication Society, 1969.

Dvorzhetsky, Dr. M., ed., with Reuven Rubinshtayn and M. Tsanin. *Yakov Mansdorf in Zayn Dor* [Yakov Mansdorf in His Generation]. Tel Aviv, cooperation of Culture Federation and Hebrew Histadrut in Johannesburg and the Jacob Mansdorf Fund in Rhodesia, N.D.

Dzigan, Shimen. *Dzigan-Der Koakh fun Yidishn Humor* [The Power of Yiddish Humor]. Tel Aviv, Committee to Celebrate Dzigan's Forty Years on the Yiddish Stage, 1974.

Kaminska, Ida. *My Life, My Theater*. Edited and translated by Curt Leviant. New York, Macmillan, 1973.

Kobrin, Leon. *Erinerungen fun a Yidishn Dramaturg: A Fertl Yarhundert Yidish Teater in Amerika* [Reminiscences of a Yiddish Dramatist: A Quarter Century of Yiddish Theater in America]. 2 vols. New York, Committee for Kobrin's Writings, 1925.

Perlmutter, H. *An Aktor in Auschwitz* [An Actor in Auschwitz]. Tel Aviv, Hamenora, 1972.

Perlmutter, H. *Bine-Maskes Bay Katsetlekh* [Playacting in the D.P. Camps]. Tel Aviv, Hamenorah, 1974.

Rumshinsky, Yosef. *Klangen fun mayn Lebn* [Notes from My Life]. New York, Society fun Yidishe Kompozitorn, Farlag A. Y. Biderman, 1944.

Thomashefsky, Bessie. *Mayn Lebens-Geshikhte* [The Story of My Life]. New York, Varhahayt Publishing, 1916.

Thomashefsky, Boris. *Mayn Lebens-Geshikhte* [The Story of My Life]. New York, Trio Press, 1937.

Turkow, Jonas. *Farloshene Shtern* [Extinguished Stars]. Buenos Aires, Tsentral-Farband fun Poylishe Yidn in Argentine, 1953.

Turkow, Zigmund. *Fragmentn fun Mayn Lebn* [Fragments of My Life]. Buenos Aires, Tsentral-Farband fun Poylishe Yidn in Argentine, 1951.

Turkow, Zigmund. *Teater Zikhroynes fun a Shturmisher Tsayt* [Theater Memories of a Stormy Era]. Buenos Aires, Tsentral-Farband fun Poylishe Yidn in Argentine, 1956.

Turkow-Grudberg, Yitskhok. *Yidish Teater in Poylen* [Yiddish Theater in Poland]. Warsaw, Farlag Yidish-bukh, 1951.

Weikhert, Mikhel. *Zikhroynes—Warshe 1918–1939* [Memories—Warsaw 1918–1939]. Tel Aviv, Hamenora, 1961.

Yablokoff, Herman. *Arum der Velt mit Yidish Teater* [Around the World with Yiddish Theater]. 2 vols. New York, Book Committee sponsored by Hebrew Actors Union, Yiddish Theatrical Alliance, Yiddish Actors' Club, and Yiddish Artists and Friends, 1969.

Young, Boez. *Mayn Lebn in Teater* [My Life in the Theater]. New York, YKUF, 1950.

3. Some Historical and Literary Background

Berg, Mary. *Warsaw Ghetto, A Diary*. Edited by S. L. Shneiderman. New York, L. B. Fischer, 1945.

Cahan, Abraham. *The Rise of David Levinsky*. Gloucester, Mass., Peter Smith, 1969. (First published in 1917 by Harper & Bros.)

Dawidowicz, Lucy S. *The Golden Tradition*. Boston, Beacon Press, 1967.

Fishman, Joshua. *Yiddish in America*. Bloomington, Indiana University Press, 1965.

Fishman, Joshua A., and Fishman, David E. "Yiddish in Israel: A Case-Study of Efforts to Revise a Monocentric Language Policy." Monograph in Advances in the Study of Societal Multilingualism. The Hague, Mouton & Co., 1974.

Goldsmith, Emanuel S. *Architects of Yiddishism at the Beginning of the Twentieth Century: A Study in Jewish Cultural History*. Rutherford, N.J., Fairleigh Dickinson University Press, 1976.

Hapgood, Hutchins. *The Spirit of the Ghetto*. New York, Schocken Books, 1972.

Howe, Irving. *World of Our Fathers*. New York, Harcourt Brace Jovanovich, 1976.

Linetski, Isaac Joel. *The Polish Lad*. Translated by Moshe Spiegel. Philadelphia, Jewish Publication Society of America, 1975.

Lipsky, Louis. *Tales of the Yiddish Rialto*. Cranbury, N.J., A. S. Barnes, 1962.

Liptzin, Sol. *The Flowering of Yiddish Literature*. Cranbury, N.J., A. S. Barnes, 1963.

Liptzin, Sol. *A History of Yiddish Literature*. Middle Village, N.Y., Jonathan David Publishers, 1972.

Liptzin, Sol. *The Maturing of Yiddish Literature*. Middle Village, N.Y., Jonathan David Publishers, 1970.

Madison, Charles A. *Yiddish Literature*. New York, Schocken Books, 1971.

Miron, Dan. *A Traveler Disguised*. New York, Schocken Books, 1971.

Rabinowicz, Harry M. *The Legacy of Polish Jewry: A History of Polish Jews in the Inter-War Years, 1919–1939*. Cranbury, N.J., A. S. Barnes, 1965.

(Rabinovitsh) Sholom Aleichem. *Wandering Stars*. Translated (from *Blondzhende Shtern*, here translated as 'Vagabond Stars') by Frances Butwin. New York, Crown, 1952.

Rischin, Moses. *The Promised City*. Cambridge, Mass., Harvard University Press, 1962.

Rosenthal, Maurice M. *Guidelines for a Yiddish Club*. Albuquerque, N.M., 1968.

Roskies, Diane K., and Roskies, David G. *The Shtetl Book*. New York, Ktav Publishing, 1975.

Sachar, Howard Morley. *The Course of Modern Jewish History*. New York, Dell, 1958.

Sanders, Ronald. *The Downtown Jews*. New York, Harper & Row, 1969.

Schwarz, Solomon M. *The Jews in the Soviet Union*. Syracuse, N.Y., Syracuse University Press, 1951.

Shakow, Zara. *The Theatre in Israel*. New York, Herzl Press, 1963.

Shmeruk, Khone. "Di Moyshe Rabeynu bashraybing" [The Moshe Rabeynu Tale]. In *Di Goldene Keyt*, no. 50, 1964, pp. 296–320. In Yiddish.

Slobin, Mark. "A Survey of Early Jewish-American Sheet Music (1898–1921)," #17 in the series *Working Papers in Yiddish and East European Jewish Studies*. New York, N.Y., Max Weinreich Center for Advanced Jewish Studies of the YIVO Institute for Jewish Research, 1976.

Warembud, Norman H., ed. *Great Songs of the Yiddish Theater*. New York, Quadrangle, 1975.

4. Published English Translations of Yiddish Plays

Asch, Sholom. *God of Vengeance*. Translated by Isaac Goldberg. Boston, Stratford Co., 1918.

Asch, Sholom, *Night*. Translated by Jack Robbins. In C. M. Martin, ed., *Fifty One-Act Plays*. London, 1934.

Asch, Sholom. *Sabbatai Zevi*. Translated by F. Whyte and G. R. Noyes. Philadelphia, Jewish Publication Society of America, 1930.

Asch, Sholom. *With the Current* Translated by Jack Robbins. New York 1933.

Block, Etta, trans. *One-Act Plays from the Yiddish*. New York, Bloch Publishing Co., 1929. Contents: Bimko, *"Liars!"*; Hirschbein, *Bebele* and *Lone Worlds*; Reisen, *Brothers*; Peretz, *After the Funeral, Early Morning,* and *Sisters*.

Goldberg, Isaac, ed. and trans. *Six Plays of the Yiddish Theater*. Boston, J. W. Luce and Co., 1916. Contents: Pinski, *Abigail, Forgotten Souls;* Rabinovitsh (Sholom Aleichem), *She Must Marry a Doctor;* Asch, *The Sinner, Winter;* Hirschbein, *In the Dark*.

Goldberg, Isaac, ed. and trans. *Six Plays of the Yiddish Theater*, 2nd series. Boston, J. W. Luce and Co., 1918. Contents: Pinski, *Little Heros, The Stranger;* Hirschbein, *On the Threshold;* Kobrin, *The Black Sheep, The Secret of Life;* Z. Libin, Poetry and Prose.

Gordin, Jacob. *The Kreutzer Sonata*. Adapted by Langdon Mitchell. New York, H. G. Fiske, 1907.

Landis, Joseph C., ed. and trans. *The Great Jewish Plays*. New York, Avon Books, 1972. Contents: Anski, *The Dybbuk;* Asch, *God of Vengeance;* Hirschbein, *Green Fields;* Pinski, *King David and His Wives;* Leivick, *The Golem*.

Lifson, David S., ed. and trans. *Epic and Folk Plays of the Yiddish Theatre*. Rutherford, N.J., Fairleigh Dickinson University Press, 1975. Contents: Aksenfeld, *Recruit;* Hirschbein, *A Secluded Nook;* Kobrin, *Yankl Boyle;* Leivick, *Hirsh Lekert;* Sloves, *Haman's Downfall*.

Pinski, David. *Cripples*, A Comedy in One Act. Translated by Isaac Goldberg. New York, Samuel French, 1920.

Pinski, David. *A Dollar*, A Comedy in One Act. Translated by Isaac Goldberg. New York, Samuel French, 1920.

Pinski, David. *Forgotten Souls*, A Drama in One Act. Translated by Isaac Goldberg. New York, Samuel French, 1916.

Pinski, David, *Laid Off*, A Tragedy in One Act. Translated by Anna K. Pinski. In *One-Act Plays for Stage and Study*, 7th series. New York, Samuel French, 1932.

Pinski, David. *Ten Plays*. Translated by Isaac Goldberg. New York, B. W. Huebsch, 1920. Contents: *The Beautiful Nun; Cripples; Diplomacy; A Dollar; The Inventor and the King's Daughter; Little Heroes; The Phonograph; Poland—1919; The Stranger*.

Pinski, David. *Three Plays*. Translated by Isaac Goldberg. New York, B. W. Huebsch, 1918. Contents: *Isaac Sheftel; The Last Jew; The Dumb Messiah*.

Pinski, David. *The Treasure.* Translated by Ludwig Lewisohn. New York, B. W. Huebsch, 1915.
White, Bessie F., trans. *Nine One-Act Plays from the Yiddish.* Boston, J. W. Luce and Co., 1932.
  Contents: I. D. Berkowitz, *Landslayt;* Daixel, *After Midnight;* Gordin, *Captain Dreyfus;*
  Levin, *The Doctor's First Operation;* Libin, *Colleagues;* Peretz, *The Sewing of the Wedding
  Gown* (also known as *The Seamstresses*); Pinski, *Sorrows;* Sholom Aleichem, *Gymnasium*
  (also known as *High School*); also the first two scenes of Leivick, *The Golem.*

For Yiddish plays published in the nineteenth and early twentieth centuries in Yiddish, it does
not seem worth giving editions, since many volumes are marked poorly or not at all; many lack
publishers' names, dates, places, and indications of the number of volumes in the series, and most
lack tables of contents. Besides, a large number of the minor Yiddish plays are now available only
handwritten, either bound or in notebooks. The best way to find a play in a library or bookstore
is by author or title.

The biggest collection of books related to Yiddish theater, as well as of scripts, photographs, sheet
music, records, and memorabilia is at YIVO. Other libraries with useful material include the New
York Public Library (Library and Museum of the Performing Arts at Lincoln Center and the
Jewish Division at 42nd Street), the Jewish Theological Seminary of America, Harvard University,
Brown University (the Harris collection), the University of Tel Aviv, and the Hebrew University
in Jerusalem. The Museum of the City of New York has posters, photographs, and memorabilia,
including costumes; the American Jewish Historical Society in Waltham, Mass., has posters.

The two bookstores where you are most likely to find books in Yiddish of Yiddish plays or theater
history are both in New York City: the CYCO book store in Atran House, 25 East 78th Street,
and Bernard Morgenstern, 150 East Broadway. Clearwater Publishing Company, New York, is
currently considering reproducing a substantial collection of Yiddish plays in microfiche form.

YIVO is developing an archive of Yiddish films. The Rutenberg and Everett Yiddish Film Library
rehabilitates and rents films under the auspices of the American Jewish Historical Society and
the Jewish Media Service in Waltham, Mass. Audio Brandon, in Mount Vernon, N.Y., also rents
some Yiddish films. The William E. Wiener Oral History Library of the American Jewish
Committee, 165 East 56th Street, New York, N.Y. 10022, has tapes of interviews with Yiddish
theater artists.

5. General Theater History: A Short List of Suggested Readings

Brandon, James R. *Theatre in Southeast Asia.* Cambridge, Mass., Harvard University Press, 1967.
Brockett, Oscar G. *The Theatre.* New York, Holt, Rinehart & Winston, 1964.
Chambers, E. K. *The English Folk Play.* New York, Russell & Russell, 1964.
Freeden, Herbert. *Jüdisches Theater in Nazideutschland* [Jewish Theater in Nazi Germany].
  Tubingen, J. C. B. Mohr (Paul Siebeck), 1964. In German.
Halbert, Herbert, and Story, eds. *Christmas Mumming in Newfoundland.* Toronto, University
  of Toronto Press, 1969.
McLean, Albert F., Jr. *American Vaudeville as Ritual.* Lexington, University of Kentucky Press,
  1965.
Nicoll, Allardyce. *The Development of the Theatre.* New York, Harcourt Brace Jovanovich, 1967.
Nicoll, Allardyce. *Masks, Mimes and Miracles.* New York, Cooper Square Publishers, 1963.
Slonim, Marc. *Russian Theater.* Cleveland, Ohio, World Publishing, 1961.
Williams, Jay. *Stage Left.* New York, Scribners, 1974.
Wilson, Garff B. *Three Hundred Years of American Drama and Theatre.* Englewood Cliffs, N.J.,
  Prentice-Hall, 1973.

INDEX

Page numbers in **bold face** indicate illustrations.

420